ALBAN BERG AND HIS WORLD

ALBAN BERG
AND HIS WORLD

Edited by
Christopher Hailey

PRINCETON UNIVERSITY PRESS
PRINCETON AND OXFORD

Copyright © 2010 by Princeton University Press

Published by Princeton University Press, 41 William Street,
Princeton, New Jersey 08540
In the United Kingdom: Princeton University Press,
6 Oxford Street, Woodstock, Oxfordshire OX20 1TW
press.princeton.edu

All Rights Reserved

For permissions information, see pages xv-xvi

Library of Congress Control Number 2010925390

ISBN: 978-0-691-14855-7 (cloth)
ISBN: 978-0-691-14856-4

British Library Cataloging-in-Publication Data is available

This publication has been produced by the Bard College Publications Office:
Ginger Shore, Consultant
Christina Clugston, Cover design
Natalie Kelly, Design
Text edited by Paul De Angelis and Erin Clermont
Music typeset by Don Giller

This publication has been underwritten in part by a grant
from Furthermore: a program of the J. M. Kaplan Fund.

1 3 5 7 9 10 8 6 4 2

Dedicated to the memory of George Perle

Contents

Preface and Acknowledgments	xi
Permissions and Credits	xv
Berg's Worlds CHRISTOPHER HAILEY	3
Hermann Watznauer's Biography of Alban Berg TRANSLATED AND ANNOTATED BY NICK CHADWICK	33
A Descriptive Overview of Berg's *Night/Nocturne* INTRODUCTION BY REGINA BUSCH TRANSLATED, EDITED, AND WITH COMMENTARY BY CHRISTOPHER HAILEY	91
Berg and the Orchestra ANTONY BEAUMONT	133
"... deinen Wuchs wie Musik": Portraits, Identities, and the Dynamics of Seeing in Berg's Operatic Sphere SHERRY D. LEE	163
"Remembrance of things that are to come": Some Reflections on Berg's Palindromes DOUGLAS JARMAN	195
1934, Alban Berg, and the Shadow of Politics: Documents of a Troubled Year INTRODUCTION, TRANSLATIONS, AND COMMENTARY BY MARGARET NOTLEY	223
Alban Berg zum Gedenken: The Berg Memorial Issue of *23: A Viennese Music Journal* TRANSLATED AND ANNOTATED BY MARK DEVOTO	269
Alban Berg and the Memory of Modernism LEON BOTSTEIN	299
Index	345
Notes on the Contributors	359

Preface and Acknowledgments

Alban Berg has never fit comfortably into the narrative of the "Second Viennese School." His expressive Romanticism with its nostalgic references to tonality, his attachment to the preoccupations of fin-de-siècle Vienna, and the sheer sensual appeal of his music have always made him suspect to doctrinaire modernists. Part of the problem, of course, lies in his devotion to Arnold Schoenberg, a figure who created a teleology of musical progress so compelling and domineering that in the searing intensity of its glare even Schoenberg's own works—contradictory and multi-faceted—have been bleached of their historical contingency. As for Schoenberg's students and followers, who among them is not first and foremost a disciple, even when a renegade? All except Alban Berg—so gracious and accommodating, loyal and devoted, and so very passive in his resistance. He maintains a special place in that narrative because even in its glare he managed to seek and find the shadows.

History is texture and texture loves a glancing light. This volume of essays, a companion to the 2010 Bard Music Festival, is an attempt to nudge Berg still further from the flattening perspective of Schoenberg's radiance by shining just such an angled light upon his music, his character, and his relationship to some of the broader issues of Viennese and European musical culture. If this carries with it more than a whiff of revisionism, it is a revisionism whose larger purpose is not to overthrow established figures but to reconnect them to their times.

To regard Viennese musical modernism as a saga of harmonic evolution from late-Romantic chromaticism through atonality to serialism is to dismiss nine-tenths of all that this rich musical culture produced. For decades research has been driven by a preoccupation with the consequences of the atonal and serial revolutions, a narrative that excluded, by definition, all composers who pursued other paths. This preoccupation encouraged a general cultural bias that also banished them from the concert and recorded repertory, published music histories, classroom syllabi, and academic research. In the 1960s and '70s, a postwar generation of composers, theorists, and historians was growing ever more conscious of the ruptures caused by totalitarian ideologies, the Holocaust, and the Cold War. It was a generation suspicious of dogma and teleology and eager to poke around in the rubble in search of overgrown paths and distant sounds. For them the question of musical syntax was but one of many contested legacies. Their interest in reviving forgotten figures and obscured connections also reflected a gradual transformation of the compositional landscape in which minimalism, neotonality, and stylistic pluralism were only the most prominent signs of the collapse of the familiar modernist narrative. This pluralistic approach led in turn to a more expansive view of modernism itself, including the cultural sphere—turn-of-the-century Vienna—that had nourished Schoenberg and his circle. It is in this context that the Mahler revival began in earnest and Alban Berg slipped out the backdoor of the Second Viennese School to take his place among the truants milling around the schoolyard.

One telling example of this transformation is the way a renewed interest in opera and music theater has revolutionized our understanding of twentieth-century music history. Berg's commitment to opera (a genre entirely absent in Webern's oeuvre and approached by Schoenberg with evident reserve) places him squarely in the midst of a remarkable resurgence of dramatic musical forms in early twentieth-century Austria, with direct links to two of its most significant practitioners, Franz Schreker and Alexander Zemlinsky. Zemlinsky and Schreker are two of dozens of Austrian composers, including Erich Wolfgang Korngold, Franz Schmidt, Julius Bittner, Egon Wellesz, and Ernst Krenek, who made the stage a crucial locus of musical and intellectual discourse. In a history with opera as its focus, harmonic language takes its place as one of many elements in a far wider field of cultural and aesthetic inquiry. If this serves to relativize Schoenberg or Webern's historical significance, their works, like those of Berg, are only enriched by an enhanced depth of field.

This volume is dedicated to the memory of the composer, musicologist, theorist, and teacher George Perle, who in many ways paved the way for this transformed cultural landscape. Perle got to know Berg's music in 1937, when he chanced upon a score of the *Lyric Suite*. He was immediately struck by certain features that suggested a highly idiosyncratic application of the serial method. It was an encounter that led to a lifelong fascination with Berg's music, as well as to a series of theoretical ruminations that had profound consequences for his own music, a remarkable body of work with little apparent debt to Berg's style but greatly influenced by his example.

The parameters of Perle's initial Berg publications were largely defined by issues that interested him as a composer, issues concerning musical language and creating tonal coherence within an atonal context: what he came to call twelve-tone tonality. In the 1970s and '80s Perle led a phalanx of Anglo-American Berg scholars who virtually redefined Berg's significance within the so-called Second Viennese School. It was, in a sense, a rescue operation because although Perle himself was no doctrinaire purist, his argument was driven by the conviction that Berg's credentials as a modernist were to be found in the layered complexity of his music—in those intricate stratagems of design by which Berg himself seemed determined to dodge the epithet *Romantic*.

Perle's Berg studies led him ever deeper into Berg's biography, a line of inquiry that culminated in the discovery (shared with Douglass M.

Green) of the secret program for the *Lyric Suite*. This work took Perle to the borders of a world beyond row forms and structural symmetries. Still, aside from some cursory attention to Alexander Zemlinsky, the official dedicatee of the *Lyric Suite*, most other Viennese contemporaries outside the Schoenberg orbit, including Schreker, are entirely absent from his writing. This was not for lack of interest or curiosity; in fact I first met George Perle at a lecture on Schreker in the late 1970s. But at the time Perle began his research these figures were still consigned to the oblivion of historical amnesia and it would be another two decades before the necessary sources would become generally available. What Perle did, however, was to take the first decisive steps in unyoking Berg from Schoenberg. His now classic books on *Wozzeck* and *Lulu* established the centrality of opera for Berg's compositional individuality, and by focusing on the specific contours of that individuality, he identified numerous areas that in fact brought Berg closer to his marginalized contemporaries. Perle's research not only broke new ground, it set a standard for quality and integrity to which all subsequent scholars must be deeply indebted.

This volume, compiled under newly imposed space constraints for this series, cannot aspire to a comprehensive reassessment of Berg or his era. Such a project is in any event a long-range and ongoing process that will involve countless specialized studies on individual topics, composers, and works. Still, in conceiving this collection I sought out authors who combined expertise on Berg and his music with a willingness to examine their broader contexts. In my own work on editions of the Berg/Schoenberg correspondence and Berg's early songs I have been privileged to engage with a number of distinguished Berg scholars, four of whom are represented in this book. Douglas Jarman, second perhaps only to Perle as an authority on Berg's music, and Mark DeVoto, for years one of the pillars of the International Alban Berg Society, have each edited volumes of the complete critical edition of Berg's works being published in Vienna under the day-to-day guidance of Regina Busch, herself a scholar of wide-ranging accomplishments. Nick Chadwick, long a mainstay of the music division of the British Library, likewise has significant credentials as a Berg specialist as well as an encyclopedic knowledge of the period and its sources. Together these scholars represent a brain trust of extraordinary distinction whose authoratative research interests have extended far beyond Berg to such topics as Kurt Weill, Claude Debussy, and Anton Webern, as well as Adorno and jazz. Complementing these dedicated Berg specialists are Antony Beaumont, whose authoritative biographical studies and editions of scores and writings of Busoni, Zemlinsky, and Alma Mahler give his work particular depth, and Margaret Notley and Sherry Lee, who approach Berg against a background of expertise in cultural history and critical theory. As always in this series, Leon Botstein's contribution draws upon an enviable wealth of erudition and sweeping cultural perspectives, refreshingly grounded in the practical experiences of a musician. I am most grateful to each of the contributors, whose labors spring from that idealism for which material recompense is always inadequate. Their professionalism and dedication to this project have accounted in large measure for its timely, largely crisis-free completion.

As in past Bard volumes, *Alban Berg and His World* combines historical research and musical analysis with annotated documents, which in this instance have been included among the essays rather than forming a separate section, as has been more usual. The volume's topics are arranged chronologically, framed by two essays, my own and that of Botstein, which address questions regarding Berg's relationship to Vienna and its legacies. Two issues of editorial practice deserve special mention. Berg and his contemporaries made extensive and sometimes eccentric use of punctuation as a means of expressive emphasis, particularly in their handwritten correspondence. These idiosyncrasies, especially an addiction to endless series of dashes and dots, are reproduced as accurately as possible on the printed page, though for practical reasons underlining is represented by italics. For clarity's sake, all editorial ellipses are given within square brackets — [. . .] — to distinguish them from dots and ellipses found in the original sources. The second issue concerns the spelling of the name Schönberg/Schoenberg. With his emigration from Germany, Schönberg changed the spelling of his name to Schoenberg and it is in this form that it appears throughout the volume, save in source citations and translations of documents that contain the original spelling. Retaining evidence of this small but noticeable inconsistency is a useful reminder of the rupture that overtook European musical life after 1933.

* * *

All acknowledgments must begin with Leon Botstein, whose vision created both the Bard Music Festival as well as this series of companion volumes. Under his guidance these books and festivals have created a forum for engaging with issues of musical and intellectual history at the very highest level. It is of particular significance that this two-pronged Bard project has sought to balance the needs and interests of specialists and the informed general public, for it is at the intersection of these spheres that one finds the most meaningful cultural dialogue. Being involved with this festival has been a stimulating, challenging, and genuinely rewarding experience and my gratitude for the opportunity is an inadequate expression for the larger debt that is owed Leon Botstein for his manifold contributions to contemporary musical culture.

The Bard Festival is made possible by a remarkable team that includes Leon Botstein's co-Artistic Directors Christopher H. Gibbs and Robert

Martin, Executive Director Irene Zedlacher, Associate Director Raissa St. Pierre, as well as Susana Meyer, Associate Director of the Fisher Center, and Program Committee member Richard Wilson. It has been a pleasure to work with them all, but particular thanks must go to Irene Zedlacher, whose attention to detail—from spotting missing punctuation to tracking down elusive sources—is matched by a level-headed grasp of the larger picture, and to Christopher Gibbs, a trusted colleague whose advice and judgment have been vital in navigating the shoals of unfamiliar waters.

I also owe warm thanks to Regina Busch for sound advice and stimulating exchanges regarding the intricacies of Berg and his world. My thanks are also extended to the Alban Berg Stiftung and to the Music Division of the Austrian National Library and its director Dr. Thomas Leibniz, and most particularly to Dr. Andrea Harrandt who oversees the Berg Fonds. In addition, thanks go to the Music and Autograph divisions of the Wien Bibliothek and to my colleagues at the Arnold Schönberg Center and the director of its archive, Therese Muxeneder.

The volume would not be possible without the dedicated group of collaborators involved most directly with its production beginning with Ginger Shore of the Bard College Publications Office and Fred Appel of Princeton University Press, who guided the publication of the book and its path into the world. Thanks, too, to Don Giller, who set the musical examples, Erin Clermont for her careful proofreading, and Ruth Elwell for preparing the volume's index, and most especially to Natalie Kelly, the volume's skilled compositor. The lion's share of my thanks must go to Paul De Angelis, the all-seeing, all-knowing production editor, whose patience, care, and wise counsel, from elements of style to fundamental issues of organization, are largely responsible for the polished consistency of the finished project. I am particularly indebted for his excellent suggestions in helping shape the reading edition of Berg's *Night (Nocturne)*. When the science of cloning has been perfected to include book editors, Paul De Angelis would be a good place to begin.

Finally, I owe a special note of heartfelt gratitude to my wife, Esther da Costa Meyer, whom I met under auspicious circumstances at an earlier Bard Music Festival. Her sage advice, support, and encouragement in all things large and small have been invaluable.

Christopher Hailey

Permissions and Credits

The following copyright holders have graciously granted permission to reprint or reproduce the following copyrighted material:

Estate of Erich Alban Berg for: Figure 2 in "Berg's Worlds" by Christopher Hailey; Figures 1, 2, and 3 in "Hermann Watznauer's Biography of Alban Berg"; Figure 1 in Mark DeVoto's introduction to "Alban Berg zum Gedenken."

Wienbibliothek in Rathaus, Vienna, Austria, for Figure 1 in "Berg's Worlds" by Christopher Hailey; and for Figure 3, autograph of mm. 356–60 of Alban Berg's Chamber Concerto, in Douglas Jarman, "Remembrance of things that are to come" (Alban Berg, Kammerkonzert, Music Collection, MH 14306/c).

The Berg Fonds at the Austrian National Library, Vienna, Austria, for Figures 3, 4, and 5 in "Berg's Worlds" by Christopher Hailey; Figure 1 in "A Descriptive Overview of Berg's *Night/Nocturne*"; Figure 2, autograph of mm. 137–45 of *Der Wein* by Alban Berg (ÖNB, F21 Berg 25/I, fol. 17.); and Figure 1 in "Alban Berg and the Memory of Modernism" by Leon Botstein.

The Alban Berg Stiftung for Figures 2 and 3 in "A Descriptive Overview of Berg's *Night/Nocturne*"; and, for Figure 1, facsimile of opening measure of the short score of *Wozzeck*, in "Berg and the Orchestra" by Antony Beaumont. Thanks to Patricia Hall of the University of California, Santa Barbara for providing the image.

Boosey & Hawkes Music Publishers Ltd. for Musical Example 9, Richard Strauss, *Die Frau ohne Schatten*, Op. 65 in "Berg and the Orchestra" by Antony Beaumont. (Copyright © 1919 by Adolph Fürstner. U.S. Copyright renewed. Copyright assigned 1943 to Boosey & Son (London) Ltd. (A Boosey & Hawkes Company) for the world excluding Germany, Italy, Portugal and the former territories of the U.S.S.R. (excluding Estonia, Latvia, and Lithuania).

Universal Edition and European American Music Distributors, LLC, for Musical Examples 11, 12, and 13, excerpts from Alexander Zemlinsky, String Quartet no. 2, op. 15, in "Berg and the Orchestra" by Antony Beaumont (Copyright ©1916 by Universal Edition AG, Vienna); for Musical Example 2, excerpt from Franz Schreker, *Die Gezeichneten* (Copyright ©1936, 1996 by Universal Edition AG, Vienna) in ". . . deinen Wuchs wie Musik" by Sherry D. Lee; and for Figure 1, Alban Berg, *Lulu*, Act 2, mm. 685–90 (Film Music Interlude) in Douglas Jarman, "Remembrance of things that are to come."

PERMISSIONS AND CREDITS

B. Schott Söhne and European American Music Distributor, LLC, for Musical Example 1, Erich W. Korngold, *Die tote Stadt*, Act I scene 5, Marietta's "Lautenlied" (Copyright ©1920 by Schott Music, Mainz, Germany © Renewed 1948), in " . . . deinen Wuchs wie Musik" by Sherry D. Lee.

Artists Rights Society (ARS), New York / VBK, Vienna. Wien Museum Karlsplatz, Vienna Austria, for Figure 1a, Arnold Schoenberg (1874–1951), Portrait of Alban Berg. © 2010 Artists Rights Society (Photo: Erich Lessing / Art Resource, NY, in " . . . deinen Wuchs wie Musik" by Sherry D. Lee.

Hulton Archive/Getty Images, for Figure 1, Alma Mahler, nee Schindler, Photography, 1909, in "Alban Berg and the Memory of Modernism" by Leon Botstein.

The Bildarchiv at the Austrian National Library, Vienna, Austria, for Figure 4 (ÖNB, Pf 829:C[2]), in "Alban Berg and the Memory of Modernism" by Leon Botstein.

And, for documents appearing in "1934, Alban Berg, and the Shadow of Politics" by Margaret Notley, the following copyright holders: Caroline Piazolo-Reich for the letters from Willi Reich to Alban Berg and to Theodor Wiesengrund-Adorno; the heirs of Erich Kleiber for the letters from Erich Kleiber to Alban Berg; Universal Edition for the letters from Hans Heinsheimer and Erwin Stein to Alban Berg; Gladys N. Krenek for an excerpt from "Ravag's Message and Austria's Message" by Ernst Krenek, from *23*, 25 October 1934.

ALBAN BERG AND HIS WORLD

Berg's Worlds

CHRISTOPHER HAILEY

Vienna is not the product of successive ages but a layered composite of its *accumulated* pasts. Geography has made this place a natural crossroads, a point of cultural convergence for an array of political, economic, religious, and ethnic tributaries. By the mid-nineteenth century the city's physical appearance and cultural characteristics, its customs and conventions, its art, architecture, and literature presented a collage of disparate historical elements. Gothic fervor and Renaissance pomp sternly held their ground against flights of rococo whimsy, and the hedonistic theatricality of the Catholic Baroque took the pious folk culture from Austria's alpine provinces in worldly embrace. Legends of twice-repelled Ottoman invasion, dreams of Holy Roman glories, scars of ravaging pestilence and religious persecution, and the echoes of a glittering congress that gave birth to the post-Napoleonic age lingered on amid the smug comforts of Biedermeier domesticity. The city's medieval walls had given way to a broad, tree-lined boulevard, the Ringstrasse, whose eclectic gallery of historical styles was not so much a product of nineteenth-century historicist fantasy as the stylized expression of Vienna's multiple temporalities.

To be sure, the regulation of the Danube in the 1870s had channeled and accelerated its flow and introduced an element of human agency, just as the economic boom of the *Gründerzeit* had introduced opportunities and perspectives that instilled in Vienna's citizens a new sense of physical and social mobility. But on the whole, the Vienna that emerged from the nineteenth century lacked the sense of open-ended promise that characterized the civic identities of midwestern American cities like Chicago or St. Louis, or European upstarts like Berlin. This was certainly true in a physical sense because to the east, north, and west Vienna's growth was checked by wetlands and alpine foothills. But the containment was temporal as well. It was as if Vienna were approaching a kind of saturation point in which density, not sprawl, would be the strategy for accommodating modernity.

The City

Vienna's inner city, the *Innenstadt*, was all that had once been contained within the walls and fortifications that, in another age, had meant the difference between survival and destruction. Now this cluttered warren of shops and churches, apartments and palaces, here the traces of periwigged elegance, there the vestiges of an ancient Jewish ghetto, was suddenly free to look out upon the world past the open spaces and hulking monuments of the Ringstrasse, past its rows of trees and manicured parks toward the surrounding districts of the *Vorstadt*. The *Innenstadt* was Vienna's core, the site of its vast bureaucracy from the imperial court to the myriad ministries that managed the immense, multinational Austro-Hungarian Empire. Within or arrayed along the Ringstrasse were also the institutions of the city's cultural memory, its libraries, archives, museums, and theaters, its schools, academies, university, and conservatory—in short, all that embodied the attainments of ages past. But what brought it all to life were those narrower apertures of the moment, often shoehorned into narrow streets, a cramped courtyard, or along its bustling streets: the editorial offices of its newspapers, the frayed headquarters of its clubs and political organizations, the huddled confabulations of the *Fiaker* stand, and, above all, the edgy *Gemütlichkeit* of the coffeehouse. These were the organs of Vienna's self-reflection, its purchase upon the present.

Berg was born in the very heart of Vienna's central first district. By economic class, religious upbringing, and educational background, he enjoyed a degree of material comfort, social integration, and professional entitlement that set him apart from many of his colleagues within the Schoenberg circle, and most especially from Arnold Schoenberg himself. Though Berg was an indifferent student who had to repeat two grades and had no ambition toward achieving a university degree, he was an obsessive reader. In her Berg "Dokumentation" prepared late in life, Helene Berg is at pains to frame her husband's early aspirations within the bourgeois cult of *Bildung*, or self-betterment through cultural edification:

> Since his family had an excellent library young Alban grew up in a world filled with "wonders," that is, immortal works by our great musicians and thinkers! From these he also absorbed those lasting life *values* that deeply influenced his spiritual and intellectual development. Thus, barely 16 years old, he had a thorough knowledge of all classical music and was exceptionally well read. There are 11 volumes [. . .] filled with the most profound and beautiful maxims from the Bible, our great poets, philosophers, and musicians, which

Figure 1. Berg reading in the family residence, Breitegasse, c. 1900.

Alban copied out between the ages of 15 and 20 in order to be able to read and ponder them always.¹

In Berg's "Von der Selbsterkenntnis" (Of Self-Knowledge), each quotation is assigned a category such as "Beauty" or "Longing" and all are carefully, even pedantically cataloged and cross-referenced. Berg's love of methodical detail is a reflection of his own, sometimes ponderous habits of mind. These habits were cultivated amid bourgeois comforts and pleasures that Berg could not do without, though they might be husbanded when reduced means dictated ascetic privation. But there is pleasure, too, in the savored indulgence, and this was much in keeping with Berg's love of minutiae. His life rocked gently in the wake of *Gründerzeit* opulence. He, too, had a book-lined study—as we see in his *Night (Nocturne)*, introduced in this volume by Regina Busch—and his devotion to his library bespeaks a deeper longing for guidance and the confirmation conferred by authority. In this Berg was a child of an age in which home libraries, the clutter of treasured possessions, and the admonitory gaze of hallowed figures peering down from walls or bookcases reflected a world of interdependent, overlapping social, cultural, and historical sureties. Berg's social psyche was predicated upon the pervasive imbrications of this collective order; his moral compass was set by figures who challenged its authenticity.

From an early age, perhaps exacerbated by the loss of his father in 1900, Berg was drawn to forceful personalities, to writers like Gerhart Hauptmann, Henrik Ibsen, and August Strindberg. Central, however, were four men Soma Morgenstern described as Berg's *Hausgötter*—Gustav Mahler, Karl Kraus, Adolf Loos, and Schoenberg—all of whom exercised a powerful influence in shaping his intellectual and aesthetic universe.² They offered orientation, prescription, points of affiliation, and the articulation of deeply held experience. But there was something more, for these were outsiders (three of the four were Jews) who had forced their way into the inner sanctums of Viennese culture and proceeded to castigate the moneylenders in the temples at which they all worshipped. These were scourges of society, Berg's society, who provided conduits for his self-righteous anger. It was an anger that bordered at times on self-loathing.

Berg chose these *Hausgötter* not out of elective affinity but from a pronounced obsession with self-discovery. Consider by contrast Schoenberg, Mahler, Kraus, or Loos. These were men of conquest who erected defiant bastions on terrain they won and held. They found allies and engendered fierce loyalties, but they also made and cultivated enemies. Berg, on the other hand, held no ground, was forever pulling back, lacking the talent for making enemies. Not that he shrank from engaging in polemical battles— as in his public attack on Hans Pfitzner or his debates with the music critic

Julius Korngold—but he staked his terrain in others' names, never his own. In other issues, such as politics, he was considerably more circumspect, so very unlike his chosen mentors.

In their presence Berg could be diffident to the point of obsequiousness. He himself was not a scintillating conversationalist, but was content to sit listening in the background, a tendency exacerbated by his physical self-consciousness. His height was an embarrassment in a world of short men. Moreover, vain as he was, he spent a lifetime cultivating a sensitive, sensuous mouth, whose half-closed lips concealed an awkward and silly gap between his front teeth that undermined his studied likeness to Oscar Wilde. To the acute awareness of his size and appearance were added a perception of internal frailty: he had chronic bouts with asthma and was firm in his belief that his heart was weak and undersized.

To Berg's pantheon of *Hausgötter* Morgenstern adds a fifth name: Peter Altenberg, the apostle of *Natürlichkeit*, a "character" at once provocative and intensely vulnerable, whose eccentricities bespoke a kind of naïve authenticity to which Berg may have aspired but could never emulate. It is through Altenberg that Berg indulged his own vulnerabilities and slipped most easily from Vienna's *Innenstadt* into other, more private environments.

The Suburb

In the organism that was Vienna, its outermost districts were like lungs, literally cleansing the air through a belt of green but also absorbing ideas flowing in and out of the inner city through the filtering membranes of civic memory. And that daily, rhythmic act of expansion and contraction, going down into the city—*hinunter in die Stadt*—and returning home again along the spokes and arteries radiating from the center and into the crooked weave of neighborhoods, was to slip back and forth in time. To look up from the Ringstrasse into that green haze on the hills that announced spring, or watch autumn disappear as limbs grew bare and the fields above turned brown, was to reconnect with nature's cycles. And to pass through the *Vorstadt* to the *Vororte*, to communities like Hietzing that bled into the countryside beyond, was an ever-present reminder of life outside Vienna—not of the larger world, not that "Draußen" beyond the borders of the land—but of that alpine *Hinterland* and the pastures along the Danube from which the city took its deepest breaths.

If the "memory" of Vienna's *Innenstadt* was the past on display, a feast for the eye and the imagination upon the fullness of time, there was in the *Vororte*, those districts beyond the outer perimeter, a different kind of memory, less public, less constructed, shot through with those little anachronisms from the living past that anchor recall in the particularities of place. Here everyday experience offered a refuge for memory under siege from those insistent abstractions and agendas of modernity. Here those barriers of class, culture, education, or generation so carefully cultivated in the *Innenstadt* melted away in daily interactions in shops and markets, on park benches or in trams, among neighbors, in social and family circles, through myriad religious, cultural, or civic affiliations. Compared to the outsized scale of the Ringstrasse, the outer districts represented a parallel universe from another age, still cut to human dimensions and flowing at a slower pace. It was the premodern world extolled by Ringstrasse critic Camillo Sitte, the theorist of urban planning who championed organic growth, the picturesque square and winding street against the tyranny of the apartment block and soulless boulevard.

For twenty-five years, from 1911 until his death, Berg lived in just such a time-forgotten world, in the quiet, leafy Viennese district of Hietzing in a parterre apartment located on what Heinrich Jalowetz described as "a hidden suburban lane that always seemed to conceal its approach from the visitor."[3] During his studies with Berg, Theodor Adorno made his way there twice a week:

> At the time I thought the street incomparably beautiful. With its plane trees it reminded me, in a way I would find difficult to explain today, of Cézanne; now that I am older it has not lost its magic for me. When I went to Vienna again after my return from emigration and looked for Trauttmansdorffgasse I got lost and retraced my steps to my starting point at the Hietzing church; then I simply took off without thinking, blindly as it were, relying on my subconscious memory, and found my way there in just a few minutes.[4]

For Berg, Hietzing was the world of habits and routine, family, friendships, entanglements—and secrets.

Berg's earlier life followed him here. He remained closely involved in family affairs, his own and, increasingly, those of his wife. And despite crises, feuds, even lawsuits, he accepted the responsibilities of a husband, son, brother, uncle, and in-law with the same dogged persistence that characterized his attention to detail in his music. He never lost touch with the schoolmates and acquaintances of his youth, including his fatherly mentor, Hermann Watznauer, whose interest in Berg was tinged with a homoeroticism that may have been reciprocated. Throughout his life Berg inspired devotion from friends and colleagues, and he cultivated close relationships with his students, several of whom he enlisted as couriers in his marital infidelities.

These romantic entanglements, only intermittently physical, were largely relegated to correspondence where he could indulge in adolescent fantasies at a safe remove. His capacity for hopeless infatuation is as evident in his courtship of Helene Nahowski as it is in his relationship with Hanna Fuchs-Robettin. Helene Berg was wise enough to look the other way when her husband went in search of stimulus for his flagging creative potency. He made no intellectual demands upon the objects of his affection or indeed upon those with whom he socialized. He was quite content to sit in on a good round of gossip with his wife and her friends, and though he could be blunt in his assessment of Alma Mahler's flawed character, he adored her company. Their friendship had a central significance for Berg's creative life, which Leon Botstein explores in his provocative discussion of *Lulu*.

Like so many of his Viennese contemporaries, Berg was obsessed with the issue of social morality. He had absorbed the sexual theories of Kraus, Freud, and Otto Weininger, and had read the works of Altenberg and Arthur Schnitzler in which sexual hypocrisy and complex gender relationships are constant preoccupations. It is a world that Berg knew well, having fathered an illegitimate child with a servant girl at the age of eighteen. Moreover, his sister was an outspoken lesbian and his mother-in-law was once the emperor's mistress. Berg loved the role of confidant at the center of these *liaisons dangereuses*.

Berg's capacity for excusing human foibles, his own and those of others, reflects the moral largesse of an avowed sensualist. This is readily apparent in his attention to his appearance and dress, as well as his tastes in food and drink, art and literature. In his youth his favorite painting was Correggio's highly charged *Jupiter and Juno* and throughout his life he retained an aesthete's tactile delight in handicrafts and graphic design, for which he himself showed a decided flair. This is not to say he did not love technology and modern gadgets. He went regularly to the cinema, was inordinately pleased with his first typewriter, listened with delight to the radio and the phonograph, and took childlike glee in owning his own automobile. But he was devoted to the refined sensibilities of another age, to the aesthetic pleasure and meticulous pride one takes in slow, careful craftsmanship.

Tucked away in the folds of the rational, technological world that Berg craved were currents of mysticism and the occult, matters of earnest inquiry in Berg's Vienna and reliable topics of titillation around *Kaffee und Kuchen*. Berg also studied the psycho-biological works of Wilhelm Fliess, consumed the nature writings of Strindberg and Maeterlinck, finding all about him, in the world he observed, confirmation for their theories. He himself was a firm believer in numerology and astrology, and, like Schoenberg and Webern, was stirred by the mystical reveries of Honoré de Balzac's *Séraphita*. He was therefore not at all surprised when, in September 1929,

Figure 2. Berg's study in his Trauttmansdorffgasse apartment in Hietzing.

he received a letter from one Günter Marstrand informing him of his suspicion that "the composer of *Wozzeck* and none other" was the reincarnation of the Habsburg emperor Charles the Fifth. From the correspondence that followed over the next two months it would appear that Berg took a supportive interest in the project, in the course of which it emerged he was indeed the reincarnation of Charles V, that members of the emperor's court had been reborn into the Schoenberg circle, and that Schoenberg himself was the latest iteration of the emperor's mother, the mad Queen Juana.[5] Berg declined Marstrand's subsequent offer to collaborate on a reincarnation opera, whose libretto involved Brutus, Charles the Bold, Robert Schumann, and the Arctic explorer Robert Falcon Scott, but one could argue that both *Wozzeck* and *Lulu* imply a kind of eternal cycle of return. What intrigued Berg was the interrelationship between human destiny and a higher natural order as revealed in astrological movements, numerological relationships, and cyclic patterns that fed his own obsessions for order and meaning, obsessions buried deep in the technical procedures and structure of his works, as Douglas Jarman shows in this volume in his discussion of Berg's fascination with retrograde forms.

Berg's scores can be dauntingly complex, the product of intricate, even mind-numbing calculation. But he is also a Romantic, whose warmth and expressiveness betray his attachment to the past and a commitment to an audience he shaped in his own image. These two sides of Berg stand in productive tension with each other and reflect a personal synthesis of the central dichotomy of Viennese music that veers between the sensuousness of its native musical traditions and the rigor of its classical inheritance, between instinct and reflection.

All this was possible because Hietzing was just outside the *Innenstadt* orbit. Here Berg could insulate himself from the city, quite literally so when, after the success of *Wozzeck*, he re-glazed his apartment windows. "You might say," he told an interviewer, "that the fact that I had frosted glass installed in my windows is not without deeper significance; they prevent people from looking in on me, but they also spare me from having to see what's going on in our beloved Vienna."[6]

The Countryside

Vienna's social and cultural season, the world of the *Innenstadt* concerts and performances, balls, boardroom meetings, political rallies, parliamentary sessions, and the cozy companionship of the café, extended from October to April. September and May were months for drifting in and drifting out of the city, but June, July, and August were devoted—for those who could afford it—to the pleasures of *Sommerfrische*, that enchanted state of being in the countryside, on a lake, in the mountains, whose routine generally involved a productive morning, a leisurely lunch, afternoons in nature, and evenings of conversation, culture, and companionship.

Where one spent one's summer vacation, like the district in which one lived, was a marker of station or at least aspiration. Some were bound by family ties to a particular region or owned property that served as their regular summer retreat. Berg's family had a country estate, Berghof, in Carinthia at the Ossiacher See, and it was here that Berg spent the summers of his youth and adolescence. Watznauer's biographical study of Berg, presented in this volume by Nicholas Chadwick, contains an evocative account of his visits there. This graceful landscape was deeply ingrained in Berg's psyche and the sale of Berghof in 1921 was the cause of much agonizing and heartache. Though he returned as a paying guest in later years, he never recaptured the magic of those early summers, whose echo resonates in the Violin Concerto.

No less dear to him was the small Styrian mountain village of Trahütten, where Helene Berg's parents owned a rustic chalet. In her "Dokumentation," she recalled their life there during the composition of *Wozzeck*:

> There was always uninterrupted quiet in the house [. . .] out of respect for his work. From the early morning until noon at the piano, in the afternoon walks with his notebook through the magnificent ancient forests which were extraordinarily useful for his creativity. (His profound love of nature is so clearly evident in the music of *Wozzeck*!) Above all he loved the mountains and next to that the water (lakes, springs)—the great thickets, blue gentian, the mushrooms in the forest clearings, which he liked to hunt, and, in the fall, the clatter of typical Styrian windmills, which sounded so wonderful coming up from the valley. [. . .] In Trahütten he had no social life since he lived only for his work. In the evening a wonderful book until falling asleep.[7]

These were probably Berg's most productive summers and it was in hopes of replicating this undisturbed working environment, as well as recreating something of the magic of the Carinthian vacations of his youth, that he and his wife, having sold Trahütten, acquired an isolated lodge on the southern shore of the Wörther See in 1932. In this "Waldhaus"—out of season, withdrawn from time—he worked on *Lulu* and wrote the requiem that was his Violin Concerto. With heavy, tasteless irony, he called it his "concentration camp."[8]

Berg, like so many others, did most of his composing during his summer vacations, and uninterrupted concentration was certainly a principal

Figure 3. View of Berghof on the Ossiacher See.

appeal. But these were also places in which, freed from social constraints, in an atmosphere of significantly relaxed routine, and surrounded by a natural world that took human concerns into benevolent, if indifferent embrace, one unfettered one's mind to dream and speculate. Here innocence could flirt with terror, nostalgia with the great unknown, and the purity of a snowy landscape suggest blackest tragedy. In the midst of the First World War, writing from the wintry solitude of Carinthia, where he had gone to tend to family business, he wrote to Schoenberg of the horrors of the battles raging to the east:

> I heard of a "successful"—I don't know whether it was German or Austrian—military ruse: in order to entice the Russians out of their trenches, a large bell, which on the previous night had been fastened to a tree close to the Russian trenches, was rung by a rope. The curious Russian heads that appeared—there were 25—presented excellent targets for the fatal bullets. It *may* have been curiosity—but *if* for one or the other it was forgetfulness of the situation at the sound of a bell reminding him of a past time and a beloved place—then what is here considered "successful" is *beyond all measure horrible*. [. . .] *suddenly* occurred to me that only a short time earlier I faced the possibility of having to take aim at people, real people— —and

that—had I been declared fit at the examination—my spirit would surely have broken under this necessity of killing people.[9]

There is no doubt that Berg's own subsequent military experience, its outrages and indignities, flowed directly into *Wozzeck* and that his opera's protagonist carries traces of the composer's self-portrait. But far more important is the evidence this opera provides for Berg's capacity for empathy, for reaching across the chasms of circumstance toward those common bonds of humanity. Schoenberg was skeptical of Büchner's play as a suitable subject for an opera. Wozzeck is certainly no traditional hero, just as Lulu is no conventional heroine. In this regard Berg has much more in common with Alexander Zemlinsky and Franz Schreker, whose operas are likewise peopled with outsiders, dreamers, and figures on the margins of society. Marie and Lulu are unthinkable without Grete—or for that matter Schigolch without Dr. Vigelius—protagonists in Schreker's *Der ferne Klang*, for which Berg prepared the piano vocal score.

In his earliest, pre-Schoenberg compositions—mostly songs written during summer months for performance within the family circle—one can already detect the basic contours of Berg's musical physiognomy, including a pervasive, drooping melancholy that flows directly into Marie's music in the Bible scene in *Wozzeck*. Indeed, the principal idea for this scene derives from an early sonata fragment in F minor that seems to grow seamlessly out of the snug world of a Schumann character piece. The gravitational pull of such music reflects a weariness that could never rouse itself to the kind of breakthrough one finds in the finale of a Mahler symphony, a weariness that has never known the bristling, jittery energy of a Schoenberg quartet. Mahler and Schoenberg likewise knew states of weariness—in *Das Lied von der Erde* or *Gurrelieder*, for instance—but it is the weariness born of a long, hard journey. These are composers whose music is of a piece with their restless worldly wanderings across cultures and continents. Berg, however, was no seeker of adventure, but a creature of habit who preferred a settled life. One is struck by the contrast between the serenity of Berg's Trahütten idyll and the raw emotion of his opera, but in this country environment Berg held both worlds, the vistas and the abyss, within himself.

Abroad

Even before he began his studies with Schoenberg, Berg was an eager foot soldier in the cause of new music. Richard Strauss, Hans Pfitzner, Mahler, and, of course, Wagner were early passions. After entering Schoenberg's orbit he became involved with progressive cultural organizations, including the Verein für Kunst und Literatur, the Tonkünstlerverein, Schreker's Philharmonic Chorus, and Schoenberg's own short-lived Chorverein. After Schoenberg moved to Berlin in 1911, Berg became his point man in Vienna, overseeing donations for the Schoenberg fund, making rehearsal and concert arrangements, and acting as a one-man clipping service. In his work for the music publisher Universal Edition Berg prepared the index for his teacher's *Harmonielehre*, thematic guides, arrangements and piano vocal scores of his works, and even led one or two choral rehearsals for *Gurrelieder*, one of the few instances in which Berg engaged in professional musical activity. These all-consuming tasks were no doubt performed at the expense of his own compositional activity and slowed the dissemination of his works.

Ironically, it was the war, during which Berg was spared from frontline service, as well as a lengthy estrangement from Schoenberg and other members of his inner circle, that gave Berg the freedom to pursue his own projects, most especially *Wozzeck*. The emotional strain of that period is clearly reflected in his play fragment, *Night (Nocturne)*, and displaced, again, in *Wozzeck*.

At war's end in 1918 Berg was thirty-three years old and still relatively unknown in or outside Vienna. He was once again enlisted in Schoenberg's cause, but now, through his writing, he began to establish an independent profile. His principal activity centered around Schoenberg's Verein für musikalische Privataufführungen, for which he wrote a brochure that set the society's agenda: repeated performances removed from the trappings of public concerts; banishment of critics and all signs of approval or disapproval from the audience, unlimited rehearsals in the interests of clarity. What is most significant, however, is that this was not a society for new music but for a new music *audience*, an audience formed on a secessionist model that had a distinguished pedigree in Vienna. As we read in Berg's own words, it was to be an audience of catholic tastes: "No school shall receive preference and only the worthless shall be excluded; for the rest, all modern music—from that of Mahler and Strauss to the newest, which is practically never, or at most rarely heard—will be performed."[10]

The first year's programs included Germans and Austrians well known to Berg's circle, including Mahler, Reger, Zemlinsky, Bittner, Schreker, Weigl, Korngold, Webern, and Berg himself, though not yet Schoenberg. More significant was the number of foreign names, which would eventually range from Bartók, Debussy, Ravel, and Satie to Busoni, Cyril Scott, Scriabin, Stravinsky, and Szymanowski. The society's model was replicated, with variations, across Europe, but it was in Germany that new music found its most intensive cultivation. By 1921, the year the Schoenberg Verein was dissolved, there were new music organizations in over two-dozen cities, half a dozen in Berlin alone. As with the Verein, these organizations served to overcome the cultural isolation that had resulted from four long years of war and the political and economic turmoil of its immediate aftermath. New music concerts afforded audiences the opportunity to take stock of the enormous multiplicity of styles that had emerged since 1910 and gauge the difference between what was merely "contemporary"—by virtue of chronology—and what was qualitatively "new." The "now" of the modern was in flux and hotly contested, and the phenomenon known today as the *Gleichzeitigkeit des Ungleichzeitigen* (roughly, the "non-contemporaneousness of the contemporaneous") was a testament to the accelerated tempo of modern times. For composers and publishers, most especially Universal Edition in Vienna and B. Schott Söhne in Mainz, this meant that a burgeoning new music industry offered lucrative opportunities, particularly for stage works and large-scale concert genres.

One particular manifestation of this sense of temporal urgency lay in the rise of the international new music festival, for which the Amsterdam Mahler Festival of 1920 served as a kind of spiritual progenitor. In Germany the annual festivals of the Allgemeine Deutsche Musikverein (ADMV), founded in 1859, had long served as a sounding board for composers associated with the New German School of Wagner and Liszt, but in the 1920s the organization came to embrace a much broader and all-inclusive agenda. More influential still were the Donaueschingen Chamber Music Festival, begun in 1921, and the festivals of the International Society for Contemporary Music (ISCM), founded a year later in Salzburg.

These festivals made the notion of regional schools that had once clustered around such figures as Schoenberg, Schreker, Thuille, or Reger much more difficult to sustain. The "now-ness" of new music meant that styles and aesthetic currents, such as linearity, neoclassicism, *Gebrauchs*- and *Gemeinschaftsmusik*, jazz, or mechanical music leaped across regions to become generational markers, undermining allegiances to individual personalities. It was a culture of slogans fostered by dedicated new-music periodicals such as *Anbruch* and *Melos*, the journalistic organs of Universal Edition and Schott, respectively. This, in turn, encouraged a kind of lateral awareness by critics and audiences in which points of descriptive comparison were more readily drawn from the present than from the past.

It was in this transformed environment that Berg became more widely known, most particularly through his Piano Sonata, op. 1, and his String Quartet, op. 3. But in 1921, when the sonata was performed at the first Donaueschingen festival, it was not a success. "Music of the day before yesterday of the immediate past" opined Hugo Holle of the *Allgemeine Musik-Zeitung*, and it was a typical response. Berg's post-*Tristan* chromaticism—Adolf Weissmann called it "decadent," "flabby," and "mollusk-like"

—fared badly in the company of Hindemith's energetic String Quartet, op. 16, which, virtually overnight, established its composer as the dominant figure of his generation.[11]

Only Berg's orchestral works—the Praeludium and Reigen from the Three Pieces for Orchestra, performed at the Austrian Music Week in Berlin in 1923, and the premiere of the *Wozzeck* fragments in the 1924 ADMV festival in Frankfurt am Main—finally established him as a major figure in his own right. The link to Vienna, Mahler, and Schoenberg, was of course self-evident, but it was Berg's foray into opera that established quite different points of comparison, above all with Richard Strauss, Schreker, and even Pfitzner in a debate that still swirled around the viability of the post-Wagnerian opera. The essays in this volume by Sherry Lee and Antony Beaumont examine these and other relationships between Berg and his contemporaries.

The premiere of *Wozzeck* in Berlin at the end of 1925 was the event of the season. Nothing of similar length, coherence, or sheer emotional power had emerged from the post-tonal world of the Schoenberg circle. Still, given the musical preoccupations of the period, it was less Berg's harmonic language than his use of closed vocal and instrumental forms to shape his scenes and acts that caused the most immediate stir, provoking comparisons with such works as Busoni's *Doktor Faust* and Hindemith's *Cardillac*. And it is this aspect that Berg himself, for varied and complex reasons, would continue to emphasize—almost to the exclusion of all else—in his articles and lectures on the opera. It was in part a strategy to undercut his growing reputation as a "Romantic," just as his elaborately constructed serial relationships would later serve to offset his music's pervasive references to tonality.

After the success of *Wozzeck*, Berg's life changed dramatically. He was now an international celebrity, a rising star of a powerful publishing house. For the first time in his life he was earning a living from his own music, engaging on his own terms with a world outside Vienna. His travels to performances of his music took him to Germany, Switzerland, England, Belgium, Holland, France, Italy, Czechoslovakia, as well as the Soviet Union. He was in correspondence with leading figures in the arts and culture at home and abroad, and over time his circle of friends and acquaintances widened to include both conductors and composers such as Erich Kleiber, Karl Böhm, and Gian Francesco Malipiero, who were otherwise far removed from the sphere of the Second Viennese School. Berg's allegiance to Schoenberg himself remained firm and was manifest on multiple levels, not least in his adoption of his teacher's twelve-tone method. And yet he resisted physical proximity to Schoenberg, be it in Schoenberg's suggestions of a shared vacation or Schreker's repeated offers of an appointment at the Berlin Musikhochschule. Berg remained steadfast in his devotion to the environments that had nurtured him.

For all his travels and newfound contacts, Berg may have been most directly involved with contemporary musical life through his service on the juries of the festivals of the ADMV (in 1928, 1931, 1932, and 1933) and the ISCM (1928 and 1931).[12] The apparent ease with which he dealt with fellow jurors of all aesthetic stripes, including Alfredo Casella, Désiré Defauw, Gregor Fiteberg, Hans Gál, Joseph Haas, Philipp Jarnach, Emil Nikolaus von Reznicek, Ernst Toch, and the same Hugo Holle who once dismissed his piano sonata, attests both to his diplomatic skills and his commitment to the task at hand. Evaluating hundreds of scores, many in manuscript, was time-consuming and wearying work, but Berg was diligent and regularly met his deadlines. His notes and correspondence reveal his understandable efforts to win performances for members of the Schoenberg circle, but they are also evidence of a remarkable catholicity of tastes. One striking example involves the preparations for the 1929 ADMV festival in Duisburg, for which the local opera proposed its recent production of Szymanowski's *King Roger*, premiered in October 1928. The press had been nearly unanimous in its rejection of the work ("the most impotent opera to appear in years," wrote the critic of the *Kölnische Zeitung*), and the members of the festival's central committee were largely in agreement.[13] Things had reached an impasse when Berg wrote to ADMV president Hermann Bischoff, assuring his colleagues that though he found Szymanowski's work every bit as bad as they did, he nonetheless suggested that a performance might not be out of place.

> [It is,] after all, one of the styles in which operas today are written; I liken it to Schreker and Korngold, a category which is not otherwise represented in the Duisburg program, while all other styles, from the most conservative to the most modern, are. That is also why our program is so good. Atonal music is represented by Schönberg and Gropp; the last of the Wagner epigones by Kick-Schmidt; the genre of the successful master operas by one each by Strauss and Reznicek; the Pfitzner school by Braunfels; a dance work by Tiessen. Finally, with *Maschinist Hopkins*, the latest kind of up-to-the-minute topical opera with all the requisite elements like jazz, crime, and social-political issues. [. . .] So, as I say, why shouldn't there be an opera along the lines of Schreker or Korngold to complete the picture?[14]

Berg's reasoning leaves his real motives strangely veiled. He would have the jury believe he was simply inspired by a concern for a fair representation of existing compositional styles. This is certainly in keeping with

Figure 4. Berg with members of the ISCM Jury, Oxford, 1931.

what we know about his even-tempered deliberations in other juries. But it is just as possible that his advocacy for Szymanowski—and for that matter Schreker and Korngold—sprang from a genuine affection, even affinity, that he would have been reluctant to admit.

The central problem with *King Roger*, which in the end was not performed at the festival, had more do with the fact that Szymanowski was not a German or a German-speaking composer (Austrians and Swiss composers were regularly included in the ADMV festivals). By the later 1920s German chauvinism had reemerged as a force in cultural politics, and defining "German-ness" went far beyond questions of language and passports. Two of Berg's categorizations—the "atonal" and the "topical"—might well have described *Wozzeck*, and both attributes made his opera a target for conservative critics. For critics on the left, on the other hand, the opera's implied social criticism served to position it in the company of works far more politically engaged. In reviews, commentary, and program books it is apparent that the opera had begun to be read in ways that Berg could not have foreseen.

Berg was not necessarily displeased with this politicized reading of *Wozzeck*, a factor that contributed to its success when it was performed in Leningrad in 1927. He himself, however, avoided overt engagement with politics or issues of social justice. His sympathies with Red Vienna, the Socialist regime that governed the city during the 1920s and early 1930s, had more to do with personal loyalties and the largesse of its progressively minded cultural policies, of which he was a beneficiary.[15] Before 1918 he had been a monarchist, and following the brutal civil strife of 1934 he became a committed supporter of the Austrofascism of Dollfuss and Schuschnigg. However, as a disciple of Kraus he maintained his right to an oppositional stance—on principle—which was easy enough from the privacy of his study in Hietzing.

The belated discovery of Büchner's *Woyzeck* fragment had inspired numerous stagings and multiple treatments, including a second *Wozzeck* opera by Manfred Gurlitt. Berg found the appearance of this second *Wozzeck*, likewise published by Universal Edition and premiered just a few months after his own opera, particularly awkward. In a letter to Erich Kleiber he wrote, "I've already had a look at the piano vocal score of the Gurlitt *Wozzeck*. I am objective enough to be able to say that it's not bad or unoriginal—but I'm also objective enough to see that the broth in the kettle of this opera, that is, in the orchestra, is too watered down, even for 'poor folks' [*arme Leut*']."[16] Berg's perspective, still heavily indebted to Wagnerian notions of musical drama propelled by a cohesive symphonic argument, reveals both the strengths and limits of his own setting. Gurlitt's opera, with its lean, simplified textures and stylistic heterogeneity, is far less emotionally manipulative and much more in keeping with the aesthetic of the 1920s one hears in the music of such contemporaries as Hindemith or Kurt Weill. It better captures the fragmentary, dry-eyed objectivity of Büchner's play and, with its choral interpolations, addresses the wider social context more directly. Gurlitt in fact offers a powerful interpretation of the play that deserves a hearing.

In a sense, then, the topical relevance of Berg's opera was accidental. Under the influence of such thinkers as Weininger, Kraus, and Strindberg, Berg's reading of the play was not so much societal as characterological. A curious page, preserved in the Berg *Nachlass*, bears on this subject. It is the plan for a trilogy, in which *Wozzeck* was to have been the first of three operas—*Wozzeck, Vincent, Wolfgang*—representing three ascending degrees of the male persona: Servant (*Knecht*), Friend (*Freund*), Master (*Herr*). Wozzeck was of course the *Untermensch* or *Knecht*; Vincent (van Gogh) the *Freund* (of Gauguin); and Wolfgang (Amadeus Mozart) the *Herr*.[17] Little more is known of this project, which does not appear to have progressed beyond this initial sketch. Nonetheless, it would appear that Berg, like the doctor of Büchner's play, viewed Wozzeck as a specimen. He does not question the hierarchy—Servant, Friend, Master—but relativizes its significance by subsuming all difference in larger patterns of fate. This is given symbolic significance in the central Van Gogh opera in which the second half was to have been the mirror image of the first half, an idea that survives in miniature in the retrograde of the orchestral interlude at the very center of *Lulu*.

Only after 1925, when Berg began casting about for his next operatic project, did it became apparent how caught up he still was in prewar preoccupations. His first choice was Gerhart Hauptmann's *Glashüttenmärchen* (Glassworks fairy tale) of 1906, *Und Pippa tanzt!* (And Pippa dances!) a play that had once tempted both Schoenberg and Schreker but by the mid-1920s seemed rather dated.[18] Still, it is a beguiling work with many enticing musical allusions. Berg's decision to move on to Wedekind's *Earth Spirit* tragedies, which had more to do with questions of royalties than real preference, was, if anything, a step back toward fin-de-siècle obsessions with the femme fatale/femme fragile dichotomy. To be sure, Wedekind would provide material for G. W. Pabst's masterful Lulu film featuring the inimitable Louise Brooks (*Pandora's Box*, 1931), though an updated setting and Brooks' bobbed flapper look do much to disguise the passé plot. Berg's choice of *Lulu* seems odder still at a time in which composers were grappling with weighty societal issues in a remarkable series of *Bekenntnisopern* (confessional operas) that included Schoenberg's *Moses und Aron*, Hindemith's *Mathis der Maler*, Weill's *Bürgschaft*, Schreker's *Der Schmied von Gent*, and Krenek's *Karl V*.

By 1933 Berg realized he was caught in a bind. Like the great majority of Universal Edition's composers, his works would have ever fewer performances in Nazi Germany, with a substantial loss to his royalties. As his correspondence with his publisher and various conductors makes clear, he remained convinced that his works could overcome any objection purely on their aesthetic merits—their beauty and dramatic strength.[19] Universal Edition urged Berg to expunge all explicit text passages in his *Lulu* excerpts since a number of conductors, including Otto Klemperer, had already raised moral objections to the opera's subject matter. For Wilhelm Furtwängler the question was less one of morality than of politics. In a letter of 23 May 1934 he addressed the issue with remarkable frankness:

> You have no need to prove yourself a German composer to me. I have known you and your music for a long time and would have no qualms about accepting "Lulu" if it did not seem to me that this text, given the public sentiment in Germany *at this particular moment*, is completely impossible. This has nothing to do with the question of race—Wedekind was in fact "Aryan"—rather with the fact that these days one cannot imagine how a performance of this *Earth Spirit* tragedy would have the least prospect of success.[20]

Furtwängler's letter was written a year and a half into Hitler's regime, during which time events had moved with remarkable speed. By April of 1933 the infamous Law for the Reconstitution of the Civil Service had led to the dismissals of Schoenberg and Schreker from their teaching positions at the Prussian Academy of the Arts, an institution in which Berg was a member.[21] Berg had his own first taste of the new political order in correspondence with the central committee of the ADMV. On 9 May 1933, Joseph Haas wrote to Berg that "the music political situation in Germany has made immediate personnel changes in the music selection committee unavoidable," and that "you, dear Herr Berg, are the exponent of an artistic direction to which the German national movement is most vociferously opposed. The central committee respects your artistic beliefs but sees no way for you to continue to represent those convictions in the music selection committee. For that reason the central committee has concluded that the most forthright way to resolve this tricky question would be for those members of the music selection (including you), who are likely to become the focus of the debate, to offer their voluntary resignations now."[22] In a letter of 17 May 1933 Berg resigned with grace, but not without pointing out and offering proof that he did not have "a single drop of Jewish blood."[23]

Berg was fully aware of the racial policies of National Socialism. He had already seen its consequences for Schoenberg and Schreker and received heartrending letters from Jewish friends and colleagues such as Jalowetz, who faced summary dismissal from his conducting position in Cologne.[24] Yet at no time could he bring himself to take a public stand against anti-Semitism. Decades later, in a soul-bearing letter to Helene Berg, which he drafted but never sent, Soma Morgenstern recalled an incident from these very years in which Berg came to see him, saying:

"I have something unpleasant to show you. I've received these forms to fill out. The people from the *Reichsmusikkammer* [in Germany] have asked me to send proof of my 'Aryan' origins. I don't need to tell you how repugnant this is to me. But I have to do it." I could see how repugnant it was to him. But I didn't agree that he had to do it. "I wouldn't advise you *not* to do it," I said to him, "if I knew that it would be useful to you. Your music isn't 'Aryan,' and it's not going to seem any less 'degenerate' to Dr. Goebbels just because you have proof that you're 'Aryan.'" [. . .] "But what should I do with this rubbish [*Wisch*]?" —"Ernst Krenek also received this rubbish and he told me what he did with it." —"What did he do?" —"He threw it in the wastebasket—perhaps because he didn't want to plug up his toilet." —With a sigh Alban said: "Ernst Krenek isn't married to Helene."[25]

Morgenstern may well have imagined this anecdote a devastating indictment of Helene, but it is in reality more revealing of Berg, whose duplicity was only compounded by his willingness to shunt the blame upon his wife. In point of fact as early as 1925 Berg fired off a card to Wilhelm Wymetal protesting an article that had implied Berg was a Jew and offered generations of genealogical proof to support his assertion.[26] It was a gambit he repeated whenever such suspicions found their way into the press, as, for instance, in an article in the *Westdeutscher Beobachter* from 1931 or again at the end of 1933, when a program on the Bavarian Radio likewise implied that he and Webern were Jews.[27] In a detailed letter of protest of 20 December 1933 Berg not only included his family tree up to the generation of his great-great grandparents, but ridiculed the "absurd idea" of his Jewishness by stating that "everyone knows [. . .] I could not be a Jew or of Jewish extraction and still be a member of the Prussian Academy [of the Arts]." He demanded a retraction "in accordance with the German spirit and Aryan decency [*Redlichkeit*]."[28] Not long thereafter he could lament to his non-Jewish friends and acquaintances that in Germany he suffered from being *thought* a Jew, while in Vienna he suffered from *not being* one.[29] It is telling that at the end of 1934, as Margaret Notley shows in documents from this fateful year, when Berg wrongly assumed that Erich Kleiber was a member of the Nazi Party, his only concern was that this might dim Kleiber's prospects for a position in Austria, where the Nazi Party was outlawed.[30] It is anybody's guess how Berg might have responded to the events of 1938. He would never have lapsed into Webern's naïve patriotic jingoism, but it is highly unlikely that this deeply rooted *Lokalpatriot* would have chosen exile or resistance.

The Irretrievable Self

The three environments that shaped Berg's temporal and psychological universe—Vienna, Hietzing, and the mountains and lakes of Styria and Carinthia—represented, in turn, the authority of history and its collision with modernity, the pleasurable, plodding habits of routine, and the timeless amorality of nature. One is almost tempted to draw parallels to Freudian notions of superego, ego, and id, as a reading of Berg's dramatic fragment *Night (Nocturne)* might suggest. Here, voices from tomes on a looming bookshelf, followed by reveries on a divan, the comforts of alcohol close at hand, and, finally, an imaginary trek through a snowy mountain dreamscape, all suggest a journey of self-discovery through the archaeology of psychic environments.

It was only in the final decade of his life that Berg was lured out of his cocoon to travel widely, meet new friends and colleagues, and engage with music across a broad aesthetic spectrum. Berg's own success placed him at the crossfire of music and politics, and by the end of his life that crossfire had followed him back to Austria. Throughout this period of heady success and political, economic, and ideological turbulence Berg maintained his allegiance to the settled temporalities of city, suburb, and countryside that continued to nourish his work. He always returned to his womblike shelter, an artist at once fully contemporary and yet strangely out of time.

Berg himself, like his protagonist Lulu, was an enigma to those who knew him, or, rather, he was all things to all people. Morgenstern's defense of his friend echoes the almost universal affection Berg enjoyed in the reminiscences of his contemporaries, as the memorial issue of the journal *23*, translated by Mark DeVoto in this volume, attests. And, as in the Morgenstern letter quoted above and in much postwar scholarship, it is often as not Helene Berg whose reputation had to suffer in order to protect Berg's own, even when it was she who was betrayed. Helene was no doubt aware of Berg's desperate, feeble affairs, but through her eyes we see only the devoted husband, whose heavily edited letters chronicle a storybook romance from courtship to the fumbling intimacies of his final illness. If we are to believe Morgenstern, Berg even encouraged him to have an affair with Helene Berg, an anecdote that raises questions about Berg's own sexuality and points up the misogyny so characteristic of the period: "Alban had the nobility, the honesty, by his very nature, to say to me, loud and clear, that he was no jealous husband, and he gave us *plein pouvoir*. [. . .] I declined. Not because I was so timid. Not because I believed in 'outdated taboos.' Simply because I myself was not so pure and free of jealousy as Alban was."[31]

Helene Berg's own tone in writing of her husband is strangely detached, as if describing a much loved and admired stranger:

> Those of us closest to Alban all experienced him *most profoundly* and *loved* him! I was and always will be—indeed, more and more—deeply moved by the nobility of his soul and his great spirit!—and it is part of the magic of his being that, in addition to all else, he was a "high-spirited child" with a thousand pranks and jests.[32]

The metaphor of "high-spirited child" is emblematic because, like so much else, it serves to remove Berg from accountability. Part of the hagiographic tone of much of the writing about Berg springs from a desire to bask in the glow of the "magic of his being." He was no doubt gentle, kind, and caring, and countless letters and drafts bear witness to his solicitous sense of occasion for a birthday, an anniversary, a death. But there is always something *unverbindlich*, noncommittal, about his sincerely expressed concern, a politeness that is a form of self-protection, a surface geniality that bespeaks a profound reserve. Adorno said as much when he called Berg the "foreign minister of the land of his dreams."[33]

It is certainly curious that Berg, born to bourgeois comfort, should have chosen two of opera's grittiest subjects, but he was careful to select texts by authors fully sanctioned by the *Innenstadt* circles he looked to for guidance in matters of taste. Who knew that stories of abuse, tawdry passion, and gruesome murders could be set to music that is so deeply satisfying and appealing?

Berg prided himself for his ability to enlist our sympathies for his protagonists, but these protagonists, Wozzeck and Lulu, remain elusive. We know a great deal about their tormented lives, their victims, and their own ghastly ends. But their outbursts—"Wir arme Leut'" and Lulu's song—though heartfelt, are strangely oblique, as if their raw pain and passion were sublimated beneath the artist's compositional refinement. These are protagonists without an *Ich*, as they are passed from hand to hand, from one situation to another. It is significant that the other potential opera text to which Berg was drawn, Gerhart Hauptmann's *Und Pippa tanzt!* is likewise centered around an unknowable waif.

Berg was keen in his indictment of society's hypocrisy, which concerned him far more than its injustice, but the true object of his concern was himself. Hermann Gail, a music critic from Berlin and would-be Berg biographer, once observed about *Wozzeck*: "Berg's music is of such profound feeling and ethical depth that it leaves even the inspired play far behind."[34] In approaching these subjects of depravity and decay, Berg never abandons the vantage point of bourgeois moral privilege. Through careful dramaturgy and lavish compositional detail he invites his audience to view this world through the prism of high art. His is an empathy that at its deepest level bespeaks self-love and satisfaction with its own moral righteousness. This is why both operas, despite their subject matter, have entered so comfortably into the repertoire in a way that the far more radical works by Schreker have not. Schreker's music eschews the comforts of "high art" and keeps its bourgeois audience off balance in a manner that oddly adumbrates the distancing effects of Brecht and Weill.

Berg wrote music to be savored, music that serves up dramatic experience that is conscious of its place within a darkened auditorium. Adorno's story about the hours he spent trying to console Berg after the success of the Berlin premiere of *Wozzeck* rings hollow, an obligatory sop to the notion that modern art disdains its audience.[35] Berg, as a card-carrying modernist, may well have fretted about appearances—the implications of success for the quality of his music, but only in the eyes of his fellow modernists; he himself would have adored his newfound operatic public because it was a public from his world. He enlisted their empathy for his wretched protagonists, knowing full well that his success in doing so was a special plea for his own noble sentiments—and, by extension, their own.

By 1935 Berg was quite literally out of time. For some period he had begun to feel old beyond his years. In a March 1933 letter to one of his "lovers," Anny Askenase, the wife of his friend the pianist Stefan Askenase, his tone is apologetic, though tinged with the faint aroma of his narcissism: "When you see me again you'll be horribly disappointed because in your memory, given the year-long separation and flattering photos you have, you'll have a much more beautiful image in mind, younger, thinner, when in reality I've only grown much more repulsive [*schiech*]."[36] He may well have been haunted in this last year by the early deaths of both his father (at age fifty-four) and his brother (at age forty-nine); perhaps, too, with thoughts of Mahler, dead at fifty, whose *Kindertotenlieder* must have been much on his mind as he composed his requiem for Manon Gropius. The Violin Concerto is the only one of his mature works that he wrote, as it were, in real time. Shortly after its completion an insect bite led to a carbuncle in his lower back from which he suffered throughout the fall. It was Helene Berg's attempt to lance the abscess that inadvertently led to the blood poisoning from which Berg died on 24 December 1935.

In 1885, the year of Berg's birth, the physicist Ernst Mach published *Die Analyse der Empfindungen* (The analysis of sensations) in which he posited the individual as a passive record of sensory impulses and coined the phrase "Das Ich ist unrettbar" (The self is irretrievable) to describe the sense of self that is never the same, constantly in flux, at every instance unrepeatable and ultimately unknowable. This concept had a particular resonance for the writers of *Jungwien*, Austria's literary impressionists, including Schnitzler, Hugo von Hofmannsthal, and especially Hermann Bahr, who were entirely attuned to the notion of modernity that Baudelaire had described as early as 1863 as "the fleeting, the ephemeral, the contingent." It is the concept of a self that is wholly subject to time.

Everything in Berg revolted against this notion—his settled habits and sedentary life, his gravitation toward fixed compass points (though not of settled morality), his belief in overarching controlling forces, from numerological patterns to the alignment of the stars. He was a man of obsessive preoccupations with the hoarding instincts of a pack rat. Ironically, Berg read and set Baudelaire's texts in *Der Wein*, but in his understanding time was not so much "fleeting," "ephemeral," or "contingent" as viscous, tactile,

Figure 5. Berg in front of the Waldhaus in Auen on the Wörther See, summer 1935.

and even reversible. Adorno made much of Berg as the composer of music forever in transition but whose changes were incremental and might be reduced to a single, insignificant link, be it a gesture or a note from which all else flows. One might take this link to be the core, but it was something that Berg sought in vain to find within himself.

Contradiction and paradox are central ingredients of Berg's persona and of his music. He was a man of open amiability and of many secrets; a faithful friend and an eager consumer of malicious gossip; a composer of fierce modernism who courted popular appeal. The elusive qualities of his character make it easy to be sucked into a vortex of eternal regress and self-absorption. Berg, the man, we follow at our peril. Berg, the composer, however, transformed the spinning vortex of his unknowable self into extraordinary music that reaches beyond the self toward a common understanding of the human condition.

Berg's music is Viennese, heavy with memory and layered with associations. His capacity for accommodating the city's contradictions gives him a special place among its musical modernists. Through Schoenberg's instruction and example he was completely immersed in the precepts of Viennese Classicism, that line of development from Haydn and Mozart through Beethoven and Brahms that placed great emphasis on rigorous construction, motivic development, and structural coherence—in short, what one might call a syntax of organicism. Berg's music, however, also has a lyrical, expansive, even discursive quality that looks back to Schubert, and to aspects of Viennese popular music. These contrasting compositional and aesthetic impulses are by no means mutually exclusive, as we see in Mahler, but among composers of the so-called Second Viennese School Berg stands apart in making the tension between these worlds a productive component of his creative persona, as well as a tangible part of our experience of his music. It is precisely the sensual appeal of Berg's music, rather than the rigor of its construction, that has made him the most "popular" member of that famous trinity of "Schoenberg, Webern, and Berg"—a popularity that has made him suspect to more doctrinaire modernists.

This was precisely the quality that enticed so many musicians into his orbit, including a remarkable number of Americans. The composer Ruth Crawford spent an hour and a half visiting Berg in his home in May 1931 and wrote to thank him for the "inspiring conversation" about her own music and "modern music in general":

> May I too express again to you—(probably more intelligibly in English than I did in my very inadequate German)—that the experience of hearing *Wozzeck* last August in Aachen was one of the most memorable ones in my life? And, after this last season in Berlin, during which I heard many performances of new music, it stands far on the heights in comparison, unapproachable in beauty by any works I heard there. I am seldom so "convinced" by modern music as I was by *Wozzeck*.[37]

This is praise that returns over and over in Berg's correspondence, and it is not infrequently combined with criticism of Schoenberg. The Italian composer Malipiero, whom Berg got to know in 1931, wrote an earnest cri de coeur soon after they began using the intimate *Du* form of address in the autumn of 1934:

> I want to tell you quite honestly that I admire Arnold Schoenberg deeply but that his works do not affect me in a way that would justify calling them art. I find *Pierrot lunaire* very stimulating but the earlier works leave me cold and the others are alien to me. [. . .] In contrast you are the *only* Schoenberg "descendant" who has remained independent and whose relationship is only theoretical, *not* spiritual. When I hear *Wozzeck*, your *Lyric Suite*, *Der Wein*, I forget *where* it comes from. You remain yourself and the theoretical *disappears*.[38]

To Crawford and Malipiero, Berg's music suggested another, more expansive kind of musical modernism, one that even today can serve to break down those arbitrary distinctions that have hampered a fuller understanding of the aesthetic crosscurrents of early twentieth-century music. It is a curse that harmonic language—the evolution toward atonality and serialism—has become such an exclusive arbiter of musical "progress" and that this tonal/atonal divide has blinded—and deafened—audiences, critics, and historians to many more obvious shared relationships between Schoenberg's circle and other, still tonal (or differently "atonal") Viennese contemporaries, like Zemlinsky, Schmidt, Schreker, Hauer, Weigl, Marx, and Korngold. The epithet "Second Viennese School" has proven a remarkably inelastic and unproductive historical category that can no longer accommodate the multifaceted nature of Viennese musical modernism. Though Berg was himself committed to this historical construct, his music gives it the lie. Berg's works, with their Janus-faced forward and backward–looking aspect, straddle the divide in ways that redefine such terms as "new," "modern," and "progressive" within specifically Viennese parameters. This, together with the range of his concerns, the subject matter of his operas, and the expressive immediacy of his music, makes Berg, both as a historical figure and a musical personality, the true center of early twentieth-century Viennese music, perhaps the most thoroughly characteristic and all-embracing representative of this remarkable cultural environment.

NOTES

1. Helene Berg, "A. Berg Dokumentation," Berg Fonds, Music Collection, Austrian National Library, F21 Berg 434. This passage also exists in typewritten form, F21 Berg 3141/2–3.

2. Soma Morgenstern, "Im Trauerhaus," *23: Eine Wiener Musikzeitschrift* 24/25 (1 February 1936): 16. See Mark DeVoto's translation, "In the House of Mourning," part of "Alban Berg zum Gedenken," in this volume.

3. Heinrich Jalowetz, "Abschied von Alban Berg," *23: Eine Wiener Musikzeitschrift* 24/25 (1 February 1936): 12–15, 14. Translated by Mark DeVoto in "Alban Berg zum Gedenken," in this volume.

4. Theodor W. Adorno, *Alban Berg*, trans. Juliane Brand and Christopher Hailey (Cambridge: Cambridge University Press, 1991), 13.

5. Marstrand's initial letter is dated 9 September 1929 (F21 Berg 1068/1). He explores parallels between Schoenberg and Juana in a letter of 6 December 1929 (F21 Berg 1068/6). In letters of 18 July 1930 and 1 August 1931 (F21 Berg 1068/7–8) Marstrand describes his proposed reincarnation opera.

6. Carl Marilaun, "Beim Komponisten des *Wozzeck*: Ein Gespräch mit Alban Berg," *Neues Wiener Journal*, 20 January 1926.

7. Helene Berg's biographical sketch (F21 Berg 3141/5) is one of several catalogued with other miscellaneous biographical materials under "Diverses Persönliches I."

8. Berg to Schoenberg, letter of 6 December 1933.

9. Letter of 14 December 1914, *The Berg-Schoenberg Correspondence: Selected Letters*, ed. Juliane Brand, Christopher Hailey, Donald Harris (New York and London: W. W. Norton & Company, 1987), 222.

10. Alban Berg, "Society for Private Musical Performances in Vienna: A Statement of Aims," translation (modified) by Stephen Somervell, in *Music Since 1900*, ed. Nicolas Slonimsky (New York: Charles Scribner's Sons, 1971, 4th ed.), 1307–11, 1308.

11. The Holle and Weissmann reviews (the latter originally appeared in *B.Z. am Mittag*) are quoted from Josef Häusler, *Spiegel der neuen Musik: Donaueschingen* (Kassel and Weimar: Bärenreiter and J. B. Metzler, 1996), 29.

12. For further information concerning the activities of the ADMV and ISCM, see Martin Thrun, *Neue Musik im deutschen Musikleben bis 1933* (Bonn: Orpheus-Verlag, 1995); and Anton Haefeli, *Die Internationale Gesellschaft für Neue Musik (IGNM): Ihre Geschichte von 1922 bis zur Gegenwart* (Zurich: Atlantis Musikbuch-Verlag, 1982).

13. This is contained in a letter from Hermann Bischoff to the Music Committee of 5 November 1928 (F21 Berg 567/11a–b).

14. Berg's letter is quoted by Hermann Bischoff in a letter to Duisburg Opera director Saladin Schmitt of 20 November 1928 (F21 Berg 567/14b). Of the works to which Berg alludes only Schoenberg's *Die glückliche Hand*, Helmut Gropp's *George Dandin*, Paul Kick-Schmidt's *Tullia*, Max Brand's *Maschinist Hopkins*, and Heinz Tiessen's *Salambo* were performed at the 1929 festival. The other operas under consideration were Braunfels' *Galathea* and Reznicek's *Satuala*; a Strauss opera had not been specified.

15. From 1919 to 1934 the Social Democratic Party was the dominant force in Vienna's municipal government. Schoenberg's close friend, David Josef Bach, was a leading figure in Social Democratic cultural affairs and from 1919 to 1933 led the Social Democratic *Kunststelle* (art office) that organized artistic activities for workers. Berg received the city's art prize in 1924 (for *Wozzeck*) and served on its jury from 1929 to 1931.

16. Letter of 29 June 1926 (F21 Berg 480/184/1), published in *Alban Berg: Maschinschriftliche und handschriftliche Briefe, Briefentwürfe, Skizzen und Notizen*, Quellenkataloge zur Musikgeschichte vol. 34, ed. Herwig Knaus und Thomas Leipnitz (Wilhelmshaven: Florian Noetzel, 2005).

17. Berg's outline for the three operas is to be found in F21 Berg 70/2.

18. Schreker came closest to Hauptmann's work in his own opera, *Das Spielwerk und die Prinzessin* (1913), which Berg knew well.

19. See discussion of this point by Margaret Notley in "Berg's *Propaganda* Pieces: The 'Platonic Idea' of *Lulu*," *Journal of Musicology* 25/2 (Spring 2008): 95–142.

20. F21 Berg 755/2.

21. Berg was nominated for membership in the Academy by Schoenberg and Schreker at the beginning of 1929; he was appointed in January 1930.

22. F21 Berg 807/11.1.

23. F21 Berg 807/11.2. Significantly, Haas had never raised the issue of "race."

24. See especially Jalowetz's letter of 15 March 1933 (F21 Berg 892/22): "You know, of course, what's happening here. It is also likely that all Jewish artists will be dismissed. Although I still have a year left in my contract and my *Intendant* tells me he'll stand up for me, he fears, as he himself told me today, that my contract will be of no use. You can imagine what that means; if it comes to that all of Germany is closed for me. And what will I do then?"

25. Soma Morgenstern, *Alban Berg und seine Idole: Erinnerungen und Briefe*, ed. Ingolf Schulte (Lüneburg: Dietrich zu Klampen Verlag, 1995), 378. Translated (modified) by Mark DeVoto.

26. Correspondence concerning Wymetal's article, "Wiener Musikdämmerung," in the *Allgemeine Musikzeitung* 52/14 (1925) can be found in F21 Berg 132/II/49 and 480/70/1–3, published in *Alban Berg: Handschriftliche Briefe, Briefentwürfe und Notizen*, Quellenkataloge zur Musikgeschichte, vol. 29, ed. Herwig Knaus (Wilhelmshaven: Florian Noetzel, 2005).

27. Concerning Berg's correspondence with the *Westdeutsche Beobachter*, see F21 Berg 480/1, 2, 20; 480/195/1, 1a; 480/449; 480/450; 480/451; 480/545; and 1383/1–4, published in Knaus, Quellenkataloge, vols. 29 and 34. Correspondence regarding the Bayerische Rundfunk retraction can be found in F21 Berg 436/1–10; 480/347/1/2; 539; and 1133, partially published in Knaus, Quellenkataloge, vols. 29 and 34.

28. Letter of 20 December 1933 (F21 Berg 436/1).

29. Berg uses nearly identical formulations in letters to Casella and Malipiero on 17 July 1934 (F21 Berg 480/275/7 and 480/79/1). Both letters are published in Knaus, Quellenkataloge, vol. 34.

30. See the "October 1934 to February 1935" section of Margaret Notley's "1934, Alban Berg and the Shadow of Politics: Documents of a Troubled Year," in this volume.

31. Morgenstern, *Alban Berg und seine Idole*, 376, trans. Mark DeVoto.

32. Helene Berg, "A. Berg Dokumentation."

33. Adorno, *Alban Berg*, 33.

34. Hermann Gail, "Alban Berg. Skizzen zur Gegenwartsmusik (III)," *Mainzer Anzeiger* (30 January 1929).

35. Adorno, *Alban Berg*, 10.

36. Undated letter, end of March 1933 (F21 Berg 3442), published in *Altenberg bis Zuckerkandl: Briefe an Alban Berg, Liebesbriefe von Alban Berg*, ed. Herwig Knaus and Thomas Leibnitz (Vienna: Erhard Löcker, 2009): 222.

37. Letter of 3 August 1931 (F21 Berg 641/2).

38. Letter of 26 September 1934 (F21 Berg 1062/9), published in Knaus and Leibnitz, *Altenberg bis Zuckerkandl*, 44f.

Hermann Watznauer's Biography of Alban Berg

TRANSLATED AND ANNOTATED
BY NICK CHADWICK

The biography of Alban Berg by Hermann Watznauer (1875–1939) is a unique record of the young composer written by someone who was virtually a member of the Berg household during Alban's formative years. In particular, the first two parts capture with disarming, sometimes naïve, vividness a period of his life when he was still entirely unknown, living within the parameters of home, school, and summer holidays at the Berghof, the family estate on the Ossiacher See in Carinthia. Beginning with a portrait of the Berg household and an autobiographical sketch of the young Watznauer himself (who uses the pseudonym "Hermann Herrenried" throughout), Part I describes Watznauer's first meeting with Alban and ends with the request made to him in summer 1899 by Conrad Berg, Alban's father, to act as a father figure to his son in the event of his death. Part II chronicles Alban's somewhat fraught school career from 1899 through 1904, when he finally passes the Matura and is able to leave. During this period, the main relief from the grind of school work is afforded by the summer holidays, and Watznauer includes extended quotations from the lengthy letters that Alban sent him from the family's Carinthian retreat.[1]

It is not for nothing that Watznauer quotes a sentence in his introduction from Peter Altenberg's *Wie ich es sehe* (How I see it, 1896), which neatly summarizes his philosophy of his role as the young Berg's mentor. Together with the two sentences preceding Watznauer's quotation, the passage runs as follows: "We cannot form human beings according to our thinking but only according to theirs. Their ideal lies hidden within them, not within us! / One could almost say: Education means 'to eavesdrop on organic growth.'"[2] Watznauer, whose musical knowledge was limited, was careful not to impose his own ideas on his young charge, but to draw out what was within. His friendship with Berg, which satisfied a deep need within himself for "appreciation, esteem, friendship, and love," was the beginning of an interest in the "redemption" of the young that was to last throughout his life and led to the founding in 1918 of his youth organization, Deutsche Jugendkultur; this continued in existence until it was disbanded by the Nazis in April 1939, not long before Watznauer's death on 22 July.[3]

It is obvious from the tone of the biography that Watznauer was more than a little in love with the "lovable and handsome Alban." Throughout his life he usually had a protégé—some "lad" with whose cultural and spiritual development he was concerned. He took his young charges on hiking trips that inspired his books *Wolf und Walters Wanderfahrten* (Wolf and Walter's hiking excursions) and the three volumes of *Shatter: Fahrtenerlebnisse* (Shatter: Excursions and adventures), stories inspired by the German writer of boys' stories, Karl May.[4] Indeed, the first volume of *Shatter*, which Watznauer published privately, includes not only a fictitious character who "bore the unusual first name Alban" but also a character with the surname Herrenried, the fictitious name that Watznauer gives himself in this biography.

Watznauer's friendship with Berg continued to the end of Berg's life, although it was less intense from about 1906 onward. Part III of the biography, which starts in the autumn of 1904 with Berg's appointment as an unpaid trainee (*Rechnungspraktikant*) in the Lower Austrian Government Office and with his lessons with Schoenberg, continues the narrative up to 1906, when his family's improved financial circumstances enable him to give up his post and devote himself entirely to music. This part closes with Berg's complete letter to Watznauer of 18 October 1906, on the subject of Ibsen's *A Doll's House*. No better demonstration can be imagined of the breadth and depth of Berg's literary interests; there is no doubt he would have been more than adequately equipped for a career as a writer or critic had he decided on such a course. From 1907, Watznauer discontinues the narrative and restricts himself to entries from his diaries; his last entries are for 1929, though there is a closing entry by Berg himself for the American premiere of *Wozzeck* in Philadelphia on 19 March 1931. Given the abbreviated nature of this material, we have decided to omit it here.

The following translation uses as its principal source the autograph manuscript in the Manuscript Collection of the Wienbibliothek im Rathaus.[5] Where relevant, I have mentioned marginal comments in the endnotes. Some of these, particularly in Part III, are in Berg's hand.

It should be emphasized that what follows is not a translation of the version given in Erich Alban Berg, *Der unverbesserliche Romantiker: Alban Berg 1885–1935* (The incorrigible romantic: Alban Berg 1885–1935), which omits most of the material relating to Watznauer's early life as well as the greater part of Berg's letter of 18 October 1906.[6] Variants in that edition have been mentioned in the notes where appropriate. For the texts of the quotations from Berg's own letters, I have followed Watznauer's versions, which on the whole are faithful to the originals, which are now housed in the Mary Flagler Cary Collection in the Morgan Library, New York. Where differences from the originals affect the translation, they have been noted. Omissions indicated in Watznauer's text are shown thus ". . ."; those not indicated are shown thus "[. . .]."[7]

I have also taken into account the copy in the Music Collection of the Austrian National Library, which includes some important comments by Berg.[8] This is presumably the copy that Watznauer sent to Berg with his letter of 18 April 1929, in which he summarizes his activities between 1914 and 1928. He retired on health grounds at the end of 1926 and had been writing the biography since early 1927; he had also been much involved with Deutsche Jugendkultur. This letter, as he said, "is also meant as an excuse—why I've taken so long over *your* biography."[9] Berg was complimentary: "Your biographical sketch has given me *great pleasure* and tremendously interested me and Helene," Berg replied on 22 April; "I really mean 'interested,' for you won't believe how much of what you report I'd completely forgotten for ages. In any event, if there should ever be a need to write a biography about me, *your* records are the most complete, the most reliable, and second to none in the source material!"[10] They are still an invaluable source for biographers.

Alban Berg

PART I

Introduction

I have given myself the task of writing a part of the life story of Alban Berg, because I am of the view that the ten-year-long friendship that joined me to him in his formative years might give me the right to do so.

However, since I do not understand a lot about music and at best have as much feeling for music as that possessed by the more advanced members of the public, I shall confine myself to describing what I have experienced and seen for myself. I clothe the chronological events in the story of a friendship. Although at the outset the older friend may well come to the fore, he soon has the sense to make way for the younger, as he knows that his role as mentor mustn't be accorded too much importance. He has always striven to take to heart the words of Peter Altenberg: "To educate means to eavesdrop on organic growth." It may be the case that the value of his friendship is to be sought therein. No one can know for certain.

1. *Old Houses*

If one looks at the evolution of a city one will always find phases that show a conspicuous resemblance to the periods of development in young human beings—the years of puberty. Everything struggles to grow. Everything stretches out and expands. Much is new, a good deal is old, and everything is on the move.

Vienna, the old imperial city on the Danube, was experiencing such a phase in the eighties and nineties of the last century. The Ringstrasse had been completed, the ramparts dismantled, the Stadtbahn built and the old-fashioned horse-drawn tramway reconstructed as a modern electric system with a network extending far out into the country districts. The amount of building work was huge. Commerce, trade, and industry were enjoying a golden age. Vienna had turned into a large metropolis of the modern era.

In the Innere Stadt and other central districts, however, there were still quiet, dreamy spots where large old houses stood, with high, steep roofs and fantastic-looking chimneys, which slumbered on untroubled by building work and the din from the streets. Two such old houses play a significant role in the story of the friendship that I want to relate: the former Schönbrunnerhaus, which stood just where the house at 8 Tuchlauben stands today, and the Schwarzspanierhaus, in which, once upon a time, Beethoven died.

2. *The Berg Family*

The old Schönbrunnerhaus was a roomy structure, with a broad, three-branched stone staircase lit from above that afforded a comfortable and elegant ascent to the upper floors. In this building, at the beginning of 1899—we will keep a firm note of this date—a respected Viennese family were installed; their apartment occupied half of the spacious third floor.

It was said of this family that in spite of a modern outlook it retained "good old German" ways and customs. Home life was conditioned by a solid prosperity and a conscious simplicity, and a healthy sense of family life guaranteed the beneficial development of the children, who possessed a quite exceptional comeliness and amiability.

The family of which these things were said bore the name of Berg.

3. *The Father*

Conrad Berg, who in 1899 was in his fifty-third year, was head of a large export firm.[11] His pale face had uncommonly sharp and refined features. The eyes were deep-set, and eyelids that were unusually widely spaced terminated in a finely curved sweep under prominent, graying eyebrows. Tall and gaunt in appearance, he would not have struck anyone as a businessman. Rather, he might have been viewed as a senior civil servant, the representative of aristocratic officialdom, so thoroughly correct and refined was he in bearing and character. He spoke little, but one nevertheless had the feeling that he took a lively part in social intercourse. Each of his movements was deliberate, calm, and showed complete propriety. Beneath the proud and dignified bearing, however, hid a permanent weariness, a tiredness that could not be concealed.[12]

Death had already lodged itself in the chief organ of life. From time to time the heart refused its support; it was no longer willing to function properly. Conrad Berg, however, was not a man to accept defeat. He did not allow himself any sort of respite, continued to work unceasingly, behaved as if nothing was the matter and was prepared to take the risk – –

4. *The Mother*

The mother was quite different. In matters of health, Frau Johanna Berg, née Braun, was the exact opposite of her husband.

As well as running her extensive household, she worked with energy and efficiency here and there and managed a shop that sold devotional objects. One thing she could not understand was that it was possible to be ill. She had a command of English and French as well as German, was exceptionally well-read, and fond of music. She understood the artistic value of the pictures and objects of plastic art which were to be found in abundance and variety among the ecclesiastical devotional pieces. She had the happy temperament of the healthy, native, typical, true Viennese woman. Everything that she undertook prospered. Sentimentality and excessive displays of emotion were foreign to her, but under the robust exterior and matter-of-fact nature was concealed a sensitive, tactful, warm heart. Only those who had the key to it were able to unlock it—they were few and occasions to do so came rarely. In such moments she was bright and sunny and infinitely kind—just like Goethe's mother, Frau Aja.[13]

If, however, anyone happened to praise the good upbringing of her children, she became quite terse and matter-of-fact. She wouldn't stand for *that*. "My children are not brought up at all," she would answer in a defensive tone designed to make her opinion clear once and for all. She understood "upbringing" as something distorted and unnatural. And that she hated. In fact, none of her children was either distorted or unnatural.

5. *Hermann*

Anyone in the Bergs' circle of acquaintances who spoke of "the American" was referring to the first-born son, Hermann Berg. He had emigrated to America in his fourteenth year, started as a trainee in one of the largest import and export firms,[14] and very soon obtained a position that was respected and well paid. After he had acquired American citizenship he was in the habit of coming to Europe once or twice a year to do bulk purchasing for his firm, visit his parents, and have a good time. The American did not know the meaning of relaxation. He was in his twenty-fifth year.[15] His mother said that in his youth he had been the most beautiful of her children. One could have no conception of the enchanting beauty of this young person. And what a mother said, that can be believed.[16]

Hermann Berg had little interest in art, more in sport. He had turned completely into an American. Nevertheless his artistic sensibility was manifested in one respect: he was a master of amateur photography.

6. *Charly*

Karl Berg, who was seventeen years old at that time, was never called anything but Charly.[17] His name appeared this way even on his visiting cards. He was an amiable young man, good in company, of pleasing appearance, and full of rapturous enthusiasm for music and literature. As a boy he was possessed of an unusually beautiful, smooth alto voice.

He had a boundless admiration for Richard Wagner. Although he was nowhere near mastering vocal and keyboard technique, he used to play *Meistersinger*, the *Ring* and *Tristan und Isolde* from beginning to end and sang all the vocal parts, both male and female. The effect was not at all bad. His voice was flexible and immediately appealing and gave its all until nothing was left; then it was worn out and ceased to be of service.

Charly was also a talented poet. His verses were good and showed the spirited verve that went with youthful high spirits. In company his manner was compelling and vivid. His conversational ability was amazing. He was always like a new person: different every day, even every hour. The deep warmth and kindness that lay concealed in his personality had no chance to settle down or open out.

When Karl Kraus brought out the first number of *Die Fackel*, the young man was caught up in a frenzy of enthusiasm that knew no bounds.[18] From then on, *Die Fackel* was his gospel, his path to salvation; no one else was able to wrest so many good things and so much beauty from these bright red little volumes that looked so inviting. When he read aloud from them—and this was a very frequent occurrence—his temperament was fired by the lucidly chiseled words. A dazzling display of polished stylistic fireworks bubbled up and foamed and discharged itself over his willing audience. Charly Berg really knew how to tear at the heartstrings.

He idolized his younger brother Alban beyond all bounds. There can be scarcely any doubt that Alban had his elder brother's effusions of

Figure 1. Smaragda, Alban, Hermann, and Charly Berg with their mother Johanna Berg, c. 1900.

enthusiasm to thank for his first profound musical impressions. Charly filled the younger lad's childhood with torrents of grand harmonies. It must be confessed that the school education of this fiery young creature was entirely inconsistent with his mental capabilities. What he heard there was thoroughly dull and unpleasant, but at last, with the help of a so-called rapid results course the Matura was behind him,[19] and the path to a working life lay clear and open before him. Charly Berg followed in his father's footsteps and likewise devoted himself to the export business.[20]

7. *Alban*

And so we have now reached the main character of the present story.

Alban, the third of the brothers, had entered this world in the old Schönbrunnerhaus on 9 February 1885, and so at the beginning of 1899 was on the brink of completing his fourteenth year.

In Class 1 of the Realschule he had been a *Vorzugsschüler*, a star pupil.[21] Now that he was in the Fourth he was having to contend with difficulties. As for his physical constitution, in his childhood years he was, as the Viennese say, a *fester Kerl,* a sturdy chap, chubby-faced and almost a bit plump. At thirteen years old he started to shoot up. He became almost skinny, and the time of superabundant good health was over. But still he was a right young lad, with a roguish face from which two candid bright eyes peered mischievously into the world. The eyelids, which were unusually widely spaced, terminated toward the top in a finely curved, clearly defined sweep. Intellectually he was far superior to his schoolmates of the same age. It was not that he knew a lot (he was not a precocious child, let alone a prodigy), but rather that he showed discernment in appraising objects—physical objects. This feeling for weighing merits or demerits would have developed to advantage in the packing department of his father's export house and in his mother's warehouse. How varied, how diverse were the goods that went by the shipload in such large quantities to America! There were a thousand types of usable practical objects, arts and crafts productions, toys, trifles, trumpery, valuable artworks and trash of the cheapest sort, genuine jewelry and deceptive imitation substitutes. In his mother's shop as well were many things worth looking at: gaudily colored prints, artistic reproductions of famous images of the Madonna, gilded and silver-tinted prayer books bound in leather, fine wood-carvings and reliefs, articles to satisfy the tastes of the suburbs, the country people, and the shrewdest art connoisseur—in short, much for a child who kept his eyes open to look at. And Alban was such a child! Already his sureness in the appraisal of artistic value and his grasp of artistic matters were exceptionally well developed. In the musical field his

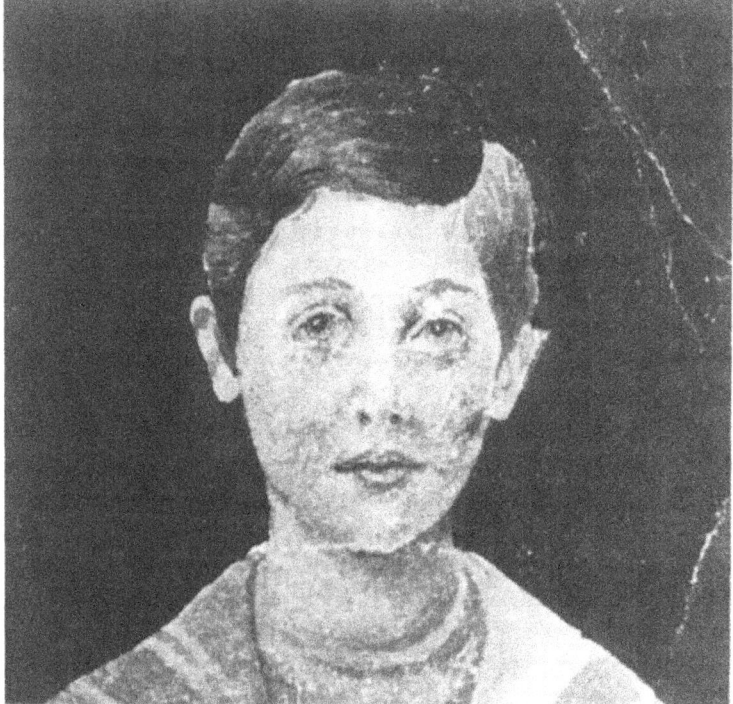
Figure 2. Hermann Watznauer, pencil portrait of Berg, February 1899.

achievements at that time were not at all out of the ordinary. He learned piano from his sister's governess and cultivated this generally popular accomplishment in the same way as all Viennese children of good family, but his talent was definitely not outstanding. Had someone approached and asked him whether he was fond of music, he would not even have been certain whether he could answer in the affirmative.

8. *Smaragda*

When a girl is twelve years old there is really nothing to be said about her, or only very little. Smaragda was known as Smara and called "Götzel" by the governess, which was quite pointless.[22] She was a lovely, healthy girl, with wonderful hair in long, thick plaits that were arranged in all manner of ways. She had two sides, the girlish and the tomboyish. To the outside world she was wholly girlish, but in her character there was much of the tomboy. She scarcely played with dolls. Her intellectual talents were quite unusual. Also, she played the piano incomparably better than her elder brother Alban, to whom she clung with effusive affection.

9. *Fräulein Götzlick*

The governess, who was also the children's piano teacher and acted as help to the lady of the house, was in appearance an ascetically thin, unmarried lady of indeterminate age—Fräulein Ernestine Götzlick.[23]

One could not imagine this singular person ever sleeping. She was unceasingly active, unfailingly attentive and helpful. She always had her hands full, so to speak, and her movements were swift. She was always in a hurry, never inactive even for a moment, and also proved herself exceedingly frugal. She seemed to live on air. The Berg family was often envied for this rare creature, useful in so many ways. "How lucky you are to have such a jewel in the house," people would say; "she is worth her weight in gold."

Fräulein Götzlick also had a very special talent that had nothing to do with her domestic and pedagogic duties but found warm acceptance in the right circumstance. On festive occasions such as birthday and name-day parties, on Christmas Eve and of course on New Year's Eve, she always came up with very special surprises. Tableaux and short scenic presentations with songs and music were her speciality. She organized them really magnificently. The children learned songs and arias and duets and poems. They were put into costumes, and something to serve as a stage was erected indoors or in the garden. Violin, piano, or lute were brought in to help out, and such a charming effect was produced that the parents and guests were presented with a delightful entertainment. True, the attractiveness of the children was a vital element in these presentations; however, their success would certainly not have been so great without the skillful direction of the production—which was entirely in the hands of Fräulein Götzlick.

However, the woman had one fault. She enjoyed playing the man-hater, which was quite unnecessary.[24]

10. *Baroness Salzgeber*

Above the Bergs' flat, on the fourth floor of the Schönbrunnerhaus, lived Baroness Marie von Salzgeber, the widow of a regional government official, with her two student sons.[25]

This woman was eternally young. Slim and tall in build, she had the look of a lady of high rank. She was always dressed in light cream colors and wore her copious blond hair in plaits wound round her head;[26] from a distance her appearance was reminiscent of that of Empress Elisabeth. She was extraordinarily frugal and needed almost nothing for herself. Because of her lively disposition and social good qualities she was a welcome guest everywhere. She was the best mother imaginable. In later years she knew how to inspire several well-to-do aristocrats to found a home for middle-class widows and orphans. The Kaiserin Elisabeth-Heim owes its origin to her.[27]

11. *The Schwarzspanierhaus*

Let us leave the Schönbrunnerhaus for a while and go by way of Am Hof and the Freyung, past the Schottenring and the Kolinplatz, into the old Schwarzspanierhaus in which Beethoven died; in 1899 we find it still as it used to be.

The large courtyard is still there, and, in the middle, the circular fountain, which in the silence of the night murmurs like a woodland spring and sings its dreamy songs. The tall, steep tiled roofs are overshadowed by the solid, massive chimneys, which have the appearance of pallid specters in the cold moonlit sky and cast shadows so eerie and vast that they make one's flesh creep. And Beethoven's apartment is also there still, with its broad, spacious rooms—a leftover from the good old days. It seems as if someone had forgotten them and left them there untouched. Until recently the Schwarzspanierhaus still maintained its good old tradition, which was firmly adhered to: anyone who wanted to obtain an apartment there had to be in the "good books" of the "Heiligenkreuzer" religious community.[28]

12. *Hermann Herrenried*

It is always an unfortunate business if a child is brought into the world on, of all days, a high national holiday or some other day of immoderate festivity. The parents' delight and particular excitement is swept along in the general tide of enthusiasm, and it can happen that there is an idea that there must be some kind of connection between the destiny of the tiny little mite and the event underlying the general air of festivity. It can happen that this creature who has scarcely entered the world is burdened with ideals and requirements that by no means accord with his nature, which he can never fulfill.

Hermann Herrenried was just such a hapless individual.[29]

He was born on 16 August 1875 in the Schwarzspanierhaus, in a wing that is still occupied. It was the very day on which the monument to Hermann the Cheruscan in the Teutoburger Wald was unveiled with colossal pomp and circumstance.[30] Since 1866 the happy father, a senior official, had been infected with hero worship and was fully convinced that Destiny had assigned him a hero as a son.[31] As a result the firstborn son, heir to the Herrenried line, was given the name Hermann.

The mother was descended from a great industrial family. They had a bright, spacious apartment and lived in comfortable circumstances.

Hermann's sister was two years older than he. His brother was born later, also after an interval of two years.³²

As a child Hermann was exceptionally delicate and sickly. He made no progress at the Gymnasium. He was put into the Realschule and, after failing there also, was sent at the age of fourteen to Reichenberg to study construction engineering at the technical secondary school there.³³ He was successful, and his health also started to improve. After taking the Matura he returned to Vienna. As he was good at his subject, he made swift progress as a technical employee in municipal undertakings.

13. *First Meeting*

To come to a correct assessment of a long-lasting friendship, of a so-called *close* friendship, of such a friendship as the twenty-four-year-old Hermann Herrenried showed toward the fourteen-year-old Alban Berg, one must above all realize that the disposition to such a friendship was already in existence long before. A special basis for it must be present—an ability, an urge, perhaps even a need that drives toward it. Destiny will then make her own contribution to promote, favor, and preserve this friendship. And indeed, in this case everything happened as if of its own accord.

Hermann Herrenried's youth was overshadowed by the brilliance of his elder sister. Helene was a child prodigy, and an uncommonly beautiful and spirited girl. Later on she was highly esteemed and admired as a pianist and singer. In her father's life she was the sun, in whose rays he willingly allowed himself to bask. Hermann, however—Hermann was a disappointment! He developed with indecent slowness, and this offended his father's vanity. Also, he was not in the least as obviously handsome as his brother and sister—simply a disappointment! In addition, the family's financial circumstances were not nearly as favorable as at the start of the Herrenried marriage. Stringent economies had to be made. His father's income fell year by year.

Thus there welled up in Hermann's consciousness a sensation that wore him down. He felt his inferiority; it seemed to him as if his life had been derailed. And now he was standing in the thick of the Sturm und Drang of adolescence, consumed with longing for appreciation, esteem, friendship, and love.

On top of this it happened that his parents, brother, and sister moved for a short time to Graz. He was alone in Vienna, fell among bad company, and it looked as if he would sink completely. Then his parents returned to Vienna. An invitation was received to a meal at Baroness Salzgeber's, and it was there (at the beginning of January 1899) that Hermann Herrenried met Alban Berg for the first time.³⁴

14. Herrenried's Change of Direction

It will be advisable to quote the words of an important authority on youth if we wish to get to the bottom of the psychological processes that at this time shattered Herrenried's being to its depths and that released into him such boundless enthusiasm when he met the Berg family, above all the father and his youngest son.[35]

"It is not unusual," this author writes, "to come across young people in an utterly desperate state, and when asked about it they cannot explain the real cause. They wander through the city streets, stop in front of any and every shop window, seemingly looking for girls to rid them of the burden that drives them on.

"But they find no girls (even though there exist not just a handful but a whole country full of them!) because they are always held back by something else that seems almost to ring in their ears like a sort of consciousness of something better, an unattained hero-love. . . . And if one inquires further and searches for the most secret motives for their wanderings—motives unknown even to themselves—bit by bit there come to light hidden, concealed indications that they are seeking a father. If their natural father has become for them an enemy, nothing remains to them but to take refuge elsewhere."

Hermann Herrenried, in spite of his twenty-four years, was a father-seeker of that sort. As he became aware of Conrad Berg's majestic appearance and shyly and anxiously attempted to conceal his unseemly curiosity, it became perfectly clear to him that this was the father he had for so long lacked, this was the ideal figure he had always imagined; this was, in truth, the man who reshaped and crucially determined his whole subsequent existence, though he spoke little and only occasionally to him. Simultaneously and with the same force, Hermann Herrenried felt drawn to the youngest son, the lovable and handsome Alban.

As a boy Herrenried had had to suffer bitterly from his parents' inconceivably unhappy marriage and from the pressure of school, which was at that time making more demands on him. The thirteen-year-old had inexplicably fallen into disfavor with a teacher who had too many children to cope with, and had become the scapegoat for his nervy, ironic tormenting. So it happened that the weak, good-natured, gentle lad considered the idea of killing the teacher and himself. It must have been a terrible need that caused the thought of such appalling deeds to mature; by chance he was deflected from his intention in time. A solution was found to prevent Hermann's failure. But in those terrible days a second disposition, that would blossom only later—that of *redeemer*—had taken shape in the boy. Whenever and wherever he saw a boy who might be approximately the same age as he was then, he was irresistibly seized with the thought that the lad must be just as unhappy as he was when he experienced his deepest affliction. The urge to "redeem" became active in him.[36]

Of course, it is impossible to claim that these perceptions had emerged plainly in his consciousness; nevertheless he now felt his desires doubly satisfied. He had found a father corresponding to his ideal and a boy he believed he could "redeem." True, Alban Berg did not at first give the impression of needing "redemption." Even so, the idea of making friends with the Berg family was exceedingly tempting for Herrenried. But then, as if in warning, his sense of inferiority intervened. Full of shame, Herrenried thought of his other highly questionable social life, of the dissolute low company in which he moved. He found himself unworthy, of too low a standing, and was about to escape from the family party. But his intention had been noticed, and it was Alban himself who hid his overcoat and hat to keep him from going away. So Herrenried had to stay. At the meal that followed soon afterward the party was divided up into "grown-ups" and "young people." Herrenried found himself sitting with the young people, next to Alban. All of a sudden he heard the word *Hessgasse*. That was decisive. Alban was attending the Realschule in the Hessgasse, the same school (indeed he had just completed the same class) in which Herrenried had so pitifully foundered ten years earlier. Now there was adequate material for conversation. Thus arose between the young man and the boy the great friendship that was to unite them for so many years.

For Herrenried this was a day of crucial significance. It gave his life a wholly new direction. He quickly decided to break off from his earlier social life, and all his thinking and striving was directed toward gaining a firm foothold in the Berg household.

The route to his office crossed Alban Berg's route to school and on the days that followed he made sure that he met his young friend on the way. He was invited into his parents' flat and thus actually was welcomed into the Berg family circle.

Soon after this a farewell party was held in Baroness Salzgeber's apartment. Then the tenant families had to move out. The old Schönbrunnerhaus had played its role—it was knocked down.

15. *8 Breitegasse*

The export business Conrad Berg was housed at 8 Breitegasse (now Carl Schweighofergasse), Vienna VII, and in February 1899 the family moved there, into a large, many-roomed flat on the second floor of the courtyard block.[37] From the windows one looked into the garden courtyards, and over the roofs of the Court Stables appeared the mass of houses of the

Inner City, the silhouette of which presented an unexpectedly beautiful sight on evenings or misty days.[38]

Scarcely had the Bergs settled in than Herrenried was invited as a guest. There now began an almost daily contact between the young man and the Berg household. He took genuine pains not to cause any offense and did everything he could to gain favor. Here he had found what he had sought in vain during the fearful time of his childhood: a well-ordered, comfortable family life.

It is hard to say what sort of feelings the younger friend, the boy, harbored for the older man. It could be that he was carrying within himself characteristics of that ideal father figure the lad had seen in his imagination. At that time Herrenried was still thoroughly immature. There were quite serious gaps in his knowledge. In the four years he had spent in the provincial town of Reichenberg he had become somewhat coarse;[39] no claims could be made that his manners were exemplary. Now, however, he set out in earnest to broaden his mind and to share with his young friend anything he found of value. When they talked about Herrenried, they did not use his full surname but an abbreviation with a condescending ring to it—Herndl—a name that implied that Herndl was a good chap, a dear fellow, in spite of all his shortcomings.[40] Charly, however, who always had a habit of hitting the nail on the head, added the attribute "of Nazareth" whenever he caught Herndl pontificating; and with the term *Herndl of Nazareth* you had said pretty well everything that could be said about Herrenried.

One day, a few weeks after the move from the Schönbrunnerhaus, he was summoned to Alban's father's office. In serious tones Conrad Berg indulged in reflections on the role that Herrenried was playing in his family, particularly in relation to the education of his youngest son, and on the responsible nature of this role. While sanctioning Herrenried's presence in his household, he urged the young man, who was visibly moved, to make a real effort to conduct himself in an exemplary fashion: if he did so, the father might cherish the hope that Herrenried's would be a good and successful influence on his youngest son. Herrenried was overjoyed, happy, and proud. Success at last!

In the spring Alban started to be unwell. He was having problems with his knee joints. A painful inflammation occurred; he was unable to walk and had to be carried about the apartment. He was having less success at school. When the summer holidays came, the lad was weak, thin, and thoroughly wretched. Then, however, the eight-week-long stay in the country beckoned, with its promise of recovery—at the Berghof, on the Ossiacher See![41]

16. *The Berghof*

There are places—Hallstatt, for example—that are situated amid splendid scenery and are picturesque in appearance but have nothing to offer those who choose to linger there. And there are other places and properties that appear to offer nothing when looked at from outside, but disclose to the eye of someone staying there a myriad of scenic attractions. The Berghof is like that. There is a knoll, a *Bühel* or *Bichel,* as the peasants say. Here stands the farmhouse with its plots of land, exactly halfway along the lake on the southern shore. Toward the west is a wide view over the lake to the Hotel Annenheim and toward the Dobratsch.[42] In the east lies the brilliantly white Ossiach, and the lake becomes so lost in the billowing hills that its end still seems a long way off. Over on the other long side of the lake, on the northern shore, is Sattendorf, at the foot of the Görlitzen, a broad, solid mountain ridge on whose summit snow can sometimes be seen, even at the height of summer.[43]

On the south side, where the Berghof is situated, the shore, or rather the level shore suitable for agricultural development and settlement, is very narrow; immediately one comes up against the mountains that climb, steep and densely forested, into the unknown. It is still pretty wild up there on the rocky heights, and there are small inky-black ponds there that hardly anyone has visited.

Conrad Berg had acquired the farm property on favorable terms.[44] The manor house had been brought to a comfortable state of repair; an American icehouse was constructed and a large chicken run erected in which pure-bred poultry were reared. Working quarters and stables were situated a little distance away. The most frequented area was the large covered veranda, open on three sides, which projected into the garden on the narrow side of the house. Here all meals were taken, visitors received, and on warm summer evenings people often used to sit together for a considerable time.

Descending the hill by the narrow gravel path toward the lake, one arrived at the boathouse, the bathhouse, and the landing stage for the steamboat. Afternoons in good weather things became very lively at the Berghof, as it was a refreshment stop for summer visitors on the Ossiacher See. However, it was no ordinary refreshment stop: not so much a business geared to making money as a diversion—if one may be permitted to use the expression.[45] Everything—both what one received and how it was served—was exquisite and the prices very modest.

These, then, would seem to be the most important things that might be said about the Berghof.

Herrenried, who had four weeks' holiday, was invited to stay there as a guest of the family. He and the governess, as well as the two children Alban and Smaragda, arrived at the Berghof at the beginning of July; the parents were to follow a fortnight later. So it happened that for the first time Herrenried had to play the role of mentor on his own. He felt himself very clumsy, and sensed a certain apprehension, a certain uneasiness. Further, an experience on the very first day made him recognize in just what a miserable state of health his young charge Alban was, a recognition not calculated to make his first steps into the pedagogic sphere any easier.

It was really only an insignificant matter—a small accident that occurred!

Herrenried had rowed with Alban across the lake. The two had then walked up a rocky glen (Herrenried had a passion for rocky glens). It was cool there, and very romantic. It happened that the boy, who was climbing on in front, tripped over a stone and ended up falling.[46] To be sure, he was immediately on his feet again—but in falling he must have sustained a small, quite insignificant wound on his arm. In short, a few drops of blood appeared, and the sight of them caused the sickly lad to have a dizzy turn, a slight faint. Herrenried caught the boy as he dropped. He was thoroughly alarmed, and, as a total novice in such matters, really did not know what he should do. A short rest lying on a grassy patch warmed by the sun very soon cured the malady, and it was possible to set off on the return, if very slowly.

Herrenried had imagined the role of mentor to be easier. He pondered and brooded over it. Then he resolved to read a book about first aid for accidents.

17. *The Bequest*

"Come with me, Herrenried, we'll go for a walk," Herr Conrad Berg, who had arrived at the Berghof the previous day, called to the young man. The recipient of this summons had just that moment been using a rake to put into well-nigh exemplary order the gravel in front of the manor house (a job undertaken on his own initiative, out of enthusiasm, so to speak). Quickly he put the implement to one side and, bounding forward a few paces, followed the old man, who strode on in front. They walked down the courtyard, which sloped toward the working quarters, went past the American icehouse and the stable wing, and turned into the carriageway that led toward Ossiach.

Herrenried was by no means delighted with this unexpected walk. Since it really should have made him happy, he felt this with intense shame: he should have felt honored and uplifted, but there was nothing of that. He was unprepared. Put in such a position, with no notice, he did not know how to manage to get a conversation going, and whether it was at all appropriate for him to begin it. In fact, he was not clear what he ought to say. Absolutely nothing occurred to him.

The morning into which they strode was bathed in sunshine. Everything was still asleep in the manor house, or people were on the point of getting up.

Deep furrows were carved in the carriageway along which they were walking. The wheel ruts of the wagons had produced two parallel depressions, and over long stretches tall islands of grassy tufts had sprung up between them.

Herrenried had the sensation that all around was complete silence, but that was only a self-induced illusion. The chickens and ducks made their customary morning racket, dogs barked without obvious cause, and over the meadows hung a humming and buzzing: frankly, it would have been absurd to describe that as "silence." Again and again the thought came to him that sometime soon he must say something. However, he was still as hesitant as ever. At last the uneasy silence was broken by the serious, pale man who walked beside him, and whom he admired so intensely.

"Well, Herrenried, and how do you like it with us at the Berghof?" he asked while continuing to move.

"Very much," the young man hastened to affirm in a voice that sounded exaggeratedly loud, giving the impression that the speaker had something significant to say at this point. "Very much, Herr Berg, it's beautiful here . . . and . . ." —but soon he faltered. He was perfectly aware that this precise moment was the most favorable opportunity for him to say a few words of thanks, a few words that would show how deeply he appreciated the hospitality that had been offered him. But however much he exerted himself to find the right words, it was all in vain.

They reached a bend in the road and passed by a wooden cross with a little roof sheltering an image of the dying Christ that was presumably intended to prompt pious reflection. Horrified, Herrenried noticed that the figure of the dying or already dead man nailed to the cross was smiling, indeed almost laughing. There was certainly no mistake about it. The corners of the mouth were definitely drawn up too high. And as for the anatomical knowledge of the artist, it must have been extremely inadequate, as the body hanging on the cross lacked the necessary number of ribs: two were missing on either side. Also, the inscription, "Jesus of Nazareth," looked a little shabby, and a few letters were so badly faded that one felt obliged to supply them from memory. Thus distracted, Herrenried's imagination was indulging in the most peculiar reflections. As a result, he was astonished all of a sudden to have reached a place far distant from the wooden cross. He became aware of the singular stillness and solitude of this spot only when the old man at his side relaxed his pace and finally came to a stop.

"I have something serious to tell you," the latter began in an almost solemn tone. "I am ill, seriously ill, young man. My condition is possibly worse than I myself suspect. It may be that my time will soon run out. Please, don't interrupt me, hear me out. To put it briefly, it concerns Alban. The others are already grown up and my daughter has her mother to hand. There is no one who could take a father's place. Not even you, Herrenried, you are too young for that. However, you have a strong influence on the boy. Please, consider that seriously. Perhaps you can scarcely judge what that means.

"Still, you are Alban's friend, and I approve of this friendship. Later—do you understand what I mean?—later you shall be the fatherly friend; that is what I must ask of you for my peace of mind. Do you promise me that?"

From Herrenried's lips came a scarcely audible, despondent "Yes." He scarcely knew how to conceal his agitation and grasped quite mechanically the hand that was offered to him.

"And now we'll go home," said the old man, preparing to turn back, "and, Herrenried, obviously you must keep quiet. It would be quite absurd to upset my family unnecessarily with my medical condition."

No further word was spoken on the way back. Herrenried was visibly depressed.

"Now I've been a total failure once again," he thought. "What will the good, noble man think of me? Anyone else in my position would have found a few sincere, significant words to say. And what did I do? I said 'Yes,' that's all. And that 'Yes' came out very feebly, it probably sounded ludicrous, utterly ludicrous! God! if only I were a bit more stable, if only I were capable of putting my thoughts precisely and clearly into words—! It really makes me ashamed, but on other occasions I fared just the same."

And all at once the anxieties were back—those numbing, oppressive anxieties that always came over him in school when he was given a German essay to write. As soon as he was confronted with a problem that required thought, he was lost. He began to ponder it and brood over it: you could tackle it this way or that, from all sides, in fact; you could say this thing or that, you could for example find an alluringly simple transition to another subject and treat *that* in general or in particular terms. Also, *one* example could be given—or indeed two—no! three, four, a huge number—it was really terrific how everything fit together, expanded, how it grew into something gigantic, into something marvelous! Now to start! But how? Like this—or like this? Or something else? This accursed opening! My God, half an hour already gone! Three-quarters of an hour! And the sheet of paper in front of you still completely blank! Quick, quick, just a few words, a few words at least! No good! The brain gave nothing away, it wouldn't be forced into anything, it remained inexorably locked up. It was useless! - - -

"Yes, it was always the same with me," said Herrenried to himself. "Nothing has changed, and I'm now a grown man – – –!"

Again they passed the wooden cross. The shadows of the trees were lying upon it. The inscription was becoming indistinct in the obscurity. The word *Jesus* in particular could not be read; perhaps it was no longer there. But another word appeared suddenly in its place. Herrenried could hardly believe his eyes! Was it a hallucination? Was he feverish? It was really quite absurd, but no, he saw it quite clearly: the word *Herndl* was written there—*Herndl of Nazareth*—and above it, the dying or already dead figure smiled—no, laughed.—

In the evening, Herrenried lay in his cheerful, bright, spotted pinewood bed that harmonized with the rest of the furniture and gave the room an almost rustic appearance; as he was on the point of going to sleep, he realized that a day lay behind him whose importance should by no means be underestimated. He thought about his morning walk and how full of significance it had been. It was really very creditable, the sick father's confidence in him. It was an honor, a recognition—Herrenried's influence must therefore have been valued – – –! How good that was—! "It really would be possible to take a little pride in this," Herrenried thought, "but who knows, perhaps nothing at all will come of it—perhaps Alban really doesn't need a fatherly friend – – – But if he should need one – – – then, *then* it will be me. – – –"

18. *Holiday's End*

A fortnight later Herrenried's holiday came to an end.[47] The night train he was using for the return journey to Vienna came off the rails a few kilometers beyond Klagenfurt. An S-bend had been taken too fast. The carriage in which Herrenried was sitting clattered for about two hundred meters over the railroad ties before coming to rest on a rising slope, and was left almost intact. Other carriages plunged down the embankment opposite, and many wounded and dead were pulled from under the wreckage. A few days later, in Vienna, Herrenried suffered the aftereffects of the railway accident in the form of a nervous shock that disturbed his sleep in the most tiresome manner. A hydropathic cure removed the problem. For Herrenried the whole accident might have had little significance except that, following on the hydropathic cure, the young man joined a swimming club. Again, this was not in itself a matter of importance, for one may conceal with a quiet mind Herrenried's sporting accomplishments—still, the fact that it happened cannot be denied.

PART II

1. *Transition*

In the following installment, for a certain period of time, the biographical description has been split up according to the school year, a chapter heading that has an excessively dry ring and will not find universal approval. However, it must be admitted that for young students (and we are dealing with one such student here) there exist only school years, semesters, and holidays. The calendar year has almost no importance at all; the school calendar has a quite different look, and the most important day of the year is not New Year's Day, when everything remains just as it was, but the day on which the school year comes to an end and the long summer holiday begins—a day that all young students experience with extremely mixed feelings.[48] Decisive changes often come with the conclusion of the academic year. For many city-dwelling children the start of the holidays means a departure from town, a stay in the country of several weeks, a change in surroundings, new experiences. In short, the last day of school in the year is the most important day; the first day has second place.

2. *The School Year 1899–1900*

By mid-September all members of the Berg family had arrived back in Vienna. The stay in the country by the Ossiacher See had worked wonders. Alban in particular could enjoy a thoroughly robust state of health. He was now entering the fifth class.

The new apartment in the Breitegasse offered many amenities. The running of the household was well regulated and appropriate to the family's increasing prosperity, and there was nothing to disturb, no occasion that affected the comfortable family existence in a disagreeable way. The anniversary of Conrad Berg's business again gave Fräulein Götzlick a welcome, supererogatory occasion, so to speak, for displaying her full artistic abilities, and there was an endless abundance of delightful presentations.

Alban had at his disposal a large, quietly situated study. He was in the habit of bringing together a few of his school chums for a meal now and then, and hardly a day passed on which he and his friend Herrenried did not spend a few hours together. As before, the younger friend's route to school crossed the older friend's way to his office, and even if they did not meet in the morning they definitely would do so during the long lunch break, which gave them ample time to exchange ideas and experiences, which they both did to the greatest extent imaginable. As witness to the length of these reciprocally thematic and problematic speaking sessions there exists only one witness, a willing audience for many years, but a silent one. This is the pedestal-like, cast-iron street hydrant that stands at the corner of the Breitegasse and the Siebensterngasse. There the friends could be seen standing and talking in the most stimulating manner every single day during lunch break. The schoolboy's satchel and civil servant's briefcase lay in quiet harmony on the broad-rimmed cover of the hydrant; the owners of these leather containers had so much to say to each other that it was often a full hour before they finally decided to part company.

On most days in the late afternoons, Herrenried appeared in the Berg home for a further brief chat, and on many evenings he then remained there as a guest for the evening meal. At that time the friends got to know each other better and better, and only now did it become clear that it was the love of music, present in both of them, that established so firmly and securely the foundations of their mutual friendship.

From his earliest youth, Herrenried had been an art enthusiast—an *aesthete,* as those in civil service circles liked pejoratively to describe him. Music in particular had made an impression on him! However, with regard to music he had no sort of attainment to offer, and only in the restricted art of singing did he have the ability to accomplish anything. Thus, since his aptitudes were not of the sort to bear fruit in the sphere of creative work, the awareness and discovery of these merits lacking in himself in the musical talent of his young friend gave him an especial pleasure. At first the indications appeared hesitantly, and at that time were noticeable particularly in the boy's piano playing. The manner of expression hinted at deep artistic sensibilities, at an inner sympathetic response to musical artworks, at a complete dedication to music.[49]

It was undoubtedly certain that a considerable talent lay dormant in this new follower of Art. His enthusiasm grew from day to day. Every free moment was given over to playing the piano, to music. The reader will find it almost funny when he learns that now all of a sudden the junior sought to fire the older friend with his enthusiasm for making music. At his friend's most pressing request, Herrenried had to make up his mind to learn the *prima* piano part of Mendelssohn's *Reformation* Symphony; he did not find the task at all easy, as his technical ability gave an awful impression. At long last he got far enough to be able to play the work together with his young friend. The boy was more than a little proud of this success as a teacher.

From time to time the two now attended concerts together. The younger lad's interest in music increased by leaps and bounds. His thirst for knowledge was boundless. His birthday drew near, the day on which he completed his fifteenth year—9 February 1900. On his table of presents Herrenried placed the *Golden Book of Music*—out of which, as the composer of *Wozzeck* himself would later say, the boy gathered his musical knowledge.[50]

Winter was over and spring was on the way. Then at the end of March there came a sudden setback, with snow and frost. Alban's father, Conrad Berg, whose state of health at that time could generally be described as satisfactory, suddenly suffered an alarming attack of convulsive heart problems. It is true that he recovered from the first seizure, but still nothing more could be done. After a few days' violent struggle the sick man was released from his sufferings, on 30 March 1900.[51]

With the father's death the family's financial circumstances changed at a stroke. The export business passed into other hands, and the financial returns contracted quite significantly. The family had an extremely modest income at its disposal, and it was necessary to partition off part of the large apartment and let it out. Several weeks later the "American," Hermann Berg, came to Vienna. There were deliberations about the state of affairs and what further steps should be taken. Once it had been established that the youngest son, Alban, was not showing particularly good progress at school, a plan emerged to send him to America, where his progress in the export and import business would certainly have the support of his eldest brother.[52] However, a wealthy aunt brought the plan to nought.[53] She committed herself to pay for Alban's studies, and thus he remained in Vienna.

Certainly it will not arouse too much interest to learn that Herrenried and Alban were keen cyclists, though in an extremely modest way. From time to time the two of them could be seen riding to the Lusthaus in the Prater on the cycle tracks, which at that time were so well maintained; on Easter Monday 1900 they undertook a cycle tour via Mödling and Heiligenkreuz to Kaltenleutgeben, where they paid a visit to "the American's" former boss in his magnificently situated miniature castle. Alban subsequently spent many a fine Saturday there. He had fallen in love with the "well-tempered" Bösendorfer piano that stood in the music room.

In the summer holidays the family made its way to the Berghof, as every year. It was not the same as before. The "American" brought with him too much that was alien; the dreamlike and tranquil aspect of life had to content itself with a very modest role.[54]

3. *The School Year 1900–1901*

A new school year again! Alban Berg is now entering the sixth class. He has become more quiet and turned in on himself. He loves seclusion and avoids mixing with his schoolmates; music is his only friend. Again and again we find him at the piano, alone or playing duets with his devoted sister, who practically idolizes him.

For a while Herrenried had buried himself away like a mole. He had taken a room in the studio building of the sculptor Pendl at the bottom of the Prater, almost out in the fields; there he studied intensively for his construction-engineering exams.[55] Then in mid-January 1901 he went and stood in line and received the diploma.[56] He celebrated the award in an extremely odd way—one might even call it "eccentric." One Sunday he picked up his young friend from the apartment in an elegant hired carriage. They repaired to the Zentralfriedhof, where Herrenried laid a bunch of violets on Conrad Berg's grave. Then they drove to the Pendl house, where they had a light meal, after which they made for the opera house, where they had very good seats for *Fidelio*.[57]

"You ought to try composing something yourself some day—a song, for example," Herrenried said one day, when his young friend had just come to the end of a critique of some musical works, delivered loftily with great enthusiasm.

"Yes, if only I knew how to start! The idea has already often occurred to me," the younger one agreed.

And Herrenried displayed his limited knowledge. He had heard something about a division between program music and absolute music. And it had not escaped him that in the accompaniment to Schubert's Müller songs a prominent role is given to the water and the mill wheels. He had been told a great deal about the sounds of nature, of the forest and meadows, and the translation of these into musical terms had been made out to be music's essential characteristic; thus in fact Herrenried had succumbed to a one-sided view that could hardly be said to be propitious for the furtherance of a musical talent.

A few days later, Alban placed on the piano some music he had written, and after a few introductory chords his sister began to sing. Herrenried listened: the first musical creation of his young friend! A small unassuming work maybe, which the mature composer denies has any compositional value, but a document of deep musical feeling, a sign that music had turned into a genuine experience. The boy remembers the summer holidays, the Berghof idylls, the shore by the lake, and his longing turns the lines of Franz Evers into sound: "Sommerträume ihr—purpurne Abende . . . Blühende Götter wandeln in seliger Jugend über die funkelnden Gefilde des Lichts ---" (You summer dreams—purple evenings . . . The gods, in their blessed youth, move in a glow across the gleaming realm of light---).[58]

That still sounds fairly joyful, almost imperious. However, as early as the second song,[59] which he produces soon after, the young composer chooses words that betray quite a mournful frame of mind: "Der Jugend Träume, sie sinken mählich in das Nichts zurück" (The dreams of youth, they sink gradually back into nothingness), he laments with Siegfried Fleischer; "die Welt durchschauert ein Grabeshauch" (a sepulchral breeze shudders through the world). Then again in Op. 1, no. 3 (as he labeled his third youthful work) he sings with Herr Walter von der Vogelweide and the sweet nightingale a merry "tandaradei." - - -[60]

The Berg household did not welcome premature enthusiasm or expressions of effusiveness, but still the songs found three willing interpreters: Charly, Smaragda, and Herrenried. Charly certainly got the most out of them.[61] The mother was proud of the first works of her youngest son— but she was too devoted to *practical* success. The songs gave her pleasure, but she was far from thinking about the development of any talent.

Thus the school year drew to a close. Alban's state of health had considerably deteriorated. For weeks on end he had to stay away from school and was no longer able to make up what he had missed. Before the end of the school year it was already agreed that he would have to repeat the Sixth voluntarily. The boy sought relaxation, and the dear old Berghof, which had always worked wonders before, again received him during the summer holidays.[62] Since the family was forced to take in paying guests, Alban found plenty of distraction, pleasant and unpleasant.

4. *The School Year 1901–1902*

In autumn 1901 we find our young hero in the Sixth for the second time. He was a voluntary Repeater. Now and then he missed school because of illness, but on the occasions when he was excluded from lessons two friends vied with each other to keep him up to date. One of them, Paul Hohenberg by name, was a young fellow of quite unusual intellect and ability. His knowledge of things to do with art, particularly in the field of painting, was amazing. His poetical talent, too, was of a praiseworthy standard, and the verses he sent his friend well deserved to be clothed by him in the mantle of music.[63] The second school friend, the unassuming and clever "star pupil" by the name of Fail, definitely deserves a mention.[64] His kindness and zeal in helping his friend in his studies made of the indefatigable fellow a Good Samaritan in the truest sense of the word.

Not much was heard from Herrenried at this time. Only a short, insignificant epistle, "Appreciation and Understanding of Art," which he sent to his friend in mid-October, was evidence of his continuing involvement with Alban's work and activity.[65]

In February 1902, a few days after Alban had completed his seventeenth year, an event occurred at school that caused a general sensation and gave the daily papers many opportunities to probe the tragedy from all angles in columns of reports and discussions to make it palatable to the readers. The "star pupil," the seventeen-year-old Egon Wieländer, a classmate who occupied the seat on the bench behind Alban, had shot himself in his room at night. On the last page of his diary to be written could be read in clear handwriting under the date 18 February the following entry: "Was at the Deutsche Volkstheater in the evening to see 'Alt Heidelberg,' enjoyed myself; then dined, at 11.30 shot myself." – – –

The impression on Alban did not last or have a direct influence. He was himself in the thick of the period of "up one moment, down the next"[66] and had enough to do coping with his own problems. Herrenried, on the other hand, still had a vivid memory of the humiliations that he had experienced in just this fateful school. He set to, and in the short space of just four weeks wrote the book *Sein Selbstmord* (His Suicide), a school-age version of *The Sorrows of the Young Werther*, which he gave as a reading in the Berg home.

In the spring Alban again reached for his music pen. He set "Spielleute" (Minstrels) by Ibsen, the poem "Wo der Goldregen steht" (Under the laburnum) by F. Lorenz, and the "Lied des Schiffermädels" (Song of the sailor's lass) by Bierbaum.[67] "Ein Spielmann, der muß reisen" (A minstrel who must journey), a short song that keeps to a folksong style, was written at the Berghof over the summer holidays.[68] During a storm in which an oak standing in front of the house was shattered by lightning, the idea came to him to put "Grenzen der Menschheit" into song form; in fact, we find the stormy atmosphere reproduced in the first part, which stands in marvelous contrast to the reverent, devotional character of the following section.[69] A love song follows, gushing forth from the heart of a pure youth: "Kniend im Staube lieg ich vor dir, bist mein Glaube und mein Brevier" (I kneel in the dust before you; you are my belief and my guide), and a song that he dedicated to his older friend: "Über meinen Nächten träumt ein leiser goldner Klang – – –" (Over me at nighttime a soft, golden sound dreams– – –)[70]

5. *The School Year 1902–1903*

In autumn 1902 we find our young friend again in Vienna. He has now reached the final grade of the Oberrealschule; he is entering the Seventh. Longing for a distant ideal of womanhood grips him. And so he takes up the verses of his friend Hohenberg, and the song "Hier in der öden Fremde—Ach so fern von dir" (Here in the bleak beyond—Oh! so far from thee) is written.[71] With two poems he comes under the spell of Heinrich Heine and longingly sings the words "Sommergrün, das ist dein Bildnis, vielgeliebte schöne Frau" (The green summer foliage is your likeness, you much loved, beautiful woman) and "Mir träumte traurig schaute der Mond und traurig schienen die Sterne" (I dreamed that sadly gazed the moon and sadly shone the stars)[72] – – – Two further compositions follow: the song "Sternenfall" (Starlight) to lines by Karl Wilhelm and the song "Sehnsucht" (Longing) to a poem by Paul Hohenberg.[73]

Figure 3. Berg and Hermann Watznauer, c. 1902.

Yet again, Alban's state of health at that time left a lot to be desired. How he was doing can be gathered from the following letter, which he sent to Herrenried on 20 November:[74]

"You left us on Thursday. As always with me, high spirits were followed by melancholy!! I was gripped with that old world-weariness that clings to me like an old inherited malady. I had something more to do.[75] Soon it was done. Then I felt drawn to the piano. I wanted to capture the first impression that Hofmannsthal's poem awoke in me: 'Hörtest Du denn nicht hinein, daß Musik das Haus durchdrang—' (Did you not hear within, how music was heard through the house—).[76] I got so far. Then it wouldn't go any further. Then I read 'Dichtung und Wahrheit,' but it gave me little pleasure.[77] At last it was evening. To my spiritual pain was now added a physical one. Yet it was of such a kind as seemed to me a beautiful pain. We had supper. Then again a little music: Grieg's glorious *Autumn* Overture— which just suited my mood—then a lot of beautiful stuff from *Dalibor*.

"We went to bed. I lay there with a heavy heart. I had that feeling when one anxiously touches one's heart and can only pray, 'O! let it go slower— quite softly and gently—stay still!' And so I fell asleep in the blissful belief, forever – –![78]

"When I awoke again after a while, I really believed that my last hour had come—there was such a terrible rumbling in my head. It seemed to me as if there was a half-congealed red-hot leaden mass inside my head, at every movement of which it beat against the top of my skull and tried to burst it open. [. . .]

"Soon I didn't dare to move anymore—other than a little, to stop the pain—and stared like a paralytic into the bleak darkness! The next day dawned no less bleakly—if it is possible to speak of the dawn—it was as if someone had slightly cleaned a dusty window. . . ."

So much for the letter that probably gives the clearest picture of the state of mind of our young friend.

The winter had not yet come to an end when for a second time, two weeks after Alban Berg's seventeenth birthday no less, an event occurred that shook the entire artistic world.[79] Hugo Wolf, the creator of the Mörike, Goethe, and Eichendorff songs, died in the Vienna Landesirrenanstalt after five years of mental derangement.[80]

Although at this time Alban was by no means in the best of health, Herrenried nonetheless let himself be induced by him to attend the funeral of the deceased composer. It was a sunny Shrove Tuesday. First of all they made their way to the mortuary of the Allgemeines Krankenhaus, where the corpse had been very meanly laid out on display. They continued past the medieval-looking circular building that was known colloquially as the Narrenturm and reached the Votivkirche at the same time as the funeral procession accompanying for the last time the mortal remains of Hugo Wolf.[81] The service of blessing[82] was short but solemn. The little group[83] of mourners was lost in the vast space of the great church. When Alban arrived back home he had a temperature, and he succumbed to a state of debility that lasted for a few days. His mother was angry. It was declared openly that Herrenried was to blame for the illness, which was not entirely wrong.

As for the young man's compositional activity during this period of time, it should be mentioned that there was absolutely no break in production. Two songs were composed: "Ich liebe dich" (I love thee) and "Ferne Lieder" (Distant songs).[84] Two duets followed: "Im Walde" (In the forest) and "Viel Träume" (Many dreams). Two more songs—"Ich will die Fluren meiden" (I will shun the meadows) and "Geliebte Schöne" (Fair beloved)—followed before the studies for the approaching Matura exam began.[85]

Quickly, all too quickly, the hours, days, weeks fled away – – quite suddenly, before anyone had taken in the fact, the date of the Matura was upon them.[86] The Seventh-former Alban Berg was wholly unprepared. Up to now he had composed around twenty songs, had read exceptionally widely, and had at his command an epistolary style hardly matched by any of his schoolmates. All of this, however, was disregarded in the examination: knowledge, not ability, was demanded! So it happened that as early as the written examination, which preceded the oral by about a month, he failed; his knowledge in "German Language" was marked as unsatisfactory and admission to the oral examination refused.[87] There was the prospect of a second year as a Repeater. The boy was thoroughly exasperated, and the blow was devastating.

"You call my school fiasco a jest of Fate – –" he wrote a month later to Herrenried, who wanted to comfort him— "I find so little that's funny in it that I could weep when I think about it – – it's a drama with the saddest of endings – – a tragedy – – more tragic than many tragedies – – – !!! . . . The 13th of June 1903 (the day of the written examination)[88] has taken away all my pleasure – – – I am a dreary fellow – – heavy guilt weighs me down – – which doesn't allow any joy – – – I'll bury myself in Ibsen – – – also a little in Grillparzer's autobiography."[89]

The letters that were sent at that time from Vienna to the Berghof and vice versa were of an astounding length and very remarkable in content. Their length varied between 24 and 64 pages. The schoolboy who was "unsatisfactory" at German was amazingly well-read. One letter—to choose just a single example—touched on Goethe's *Elective Affinities, Iphigenie, Tasso,* and *The Sorrows of Young Werther*; Schiller's *Wallenstein*, Ibsen's *Ghosts, The Master Builder,* and *Lady Inger of Östrât, Freund Hein* by Emil Strauss, Ibsen's *Rosmersholm*, Grillparzer's *Hero* and *The Jewess of Toledo*.[90] Obviously it would be taking things too far to give the letters here in full. However, one passage must be singled out that is so succinct that one receives a clear picture of the way the letter-writer thought and felt.

"You will have noticed," he wrote to his older friend on 16 July 1903, "that when the name of a work of art is uttered, whether of dramatic or visual art, music, or poetry, immediately a feeling arises in the heart or in the soul that is in tune with it, so to speak – – If I hear Segantini's 'Scholle' mentioned, immediately there arises in me the idea of the powerlessness of the person who can't tear himself away from the soil, who has to wrest everything from it and in the end is grateful to it for this[91] – – – – I only need to hear the name 'The Ninth' – – what a wonderful mixture of emotions stirs in my breast – – or the 'Last Quartets' – they feel like marble inside me – – – marble columns that tower into the heavens – – –"

Emerging from these moods was the song "Still ist's, wo die Gräber sind meiner Liebe" (Where the sepulchers of my love are, it is still), and two further songs, "Am Abend" (In the evening) and "Wenn Gespenster auferstehen" (When ghosts arise). – – –[92]

Kind, good friends with whom one could feel at ease were staying at the Berghof during these summer holidays; they brought a little sympathy or at least respect for the young aspiring artist.[93] There was balm for his wounds, and he willingly surrendered to its healing influence. It was a year since the first great passion that had almost destroyed the adolescent.[94] The storms had abated a little. Alban had found peace and rest as "childhood had slipped from his shoulders, this soft, dark cloak";[95] now he began to compose and to think.

"Yesterday evening," he wrote to Herrenried, "I was very pleased with the following beautiful remark of Frida's" (a friend of his sister's):[96]

"It was night. Smara was out strolling with Nora.[97] From the veranda, conversation drifted over to where we two, Frida and I, were sitting on the bench with the beautiful view of the gray lake and the black mountains. We spoke of the stars – – of the Great Longing – – of world-weariness – –. How was it so? She felt exalted by the view of the distant planets, I felt humbled, inconspicuous, small!

"'Since he who feels greatness, is himself great' – – – Isn't that beautifully said, beautifully felt, and beautifully appropriate?"

6. *The School Year 1903–1904*

A Repeater for the second time, this time in the Seventh! Can anyone guess what that means? Can anyone have any idea what it means when a boy who has matured far beyond school is senselessly and purposelessly held back for years, forced back in his spiritual development? Or when he has to sit like some degraded creature among thinking-machines, whereas he should have the right to be counted among the creators and doers?

Again he sits in this spiritual junk shop. The school subjects come and go, are numbered and carefully organized, and radiate such dullness that even someone with a reasonably clear-thinking head gets a feeling of dizziness. Thank goodness that at home our young friend has his piano, his art, his music. With ever greater power the untutored lad strikes the keys in a short yet piercing shriek—a mighty song pulls at the heartstrings and, full of longing and hope, pours forth from his wounded soul: "Das ist der großen Flamme letztes Glüh'n; —das müde Haupt Marien Magdalenens auf deinen Knie'n!" (This is the final glow of the mighty flame; —the weary head of Mary Magdalene resting on your knees!)– –[98]

The suicide of Otto Weininger, the young thinker who at that time was little known, passed Alban Berg by with scarcely a trace.[99] All that was reported at this juncture was that the tragedy occurred on 4 October 1903 in the Schwarzspanierhaus. Weininger had rented a room above the Herrenried apartment—just for one night, while he prepared to end his life.

Six weeks later, on 15 November, a ceremony took place in the great courtyard of the Schwarzspanierhaus on the occasion of the demolition of the old front wing, which contained Beethoven's dwelling. In the courtyard removed materials lay all around; in part the tiles had been taken off the roofs, and the huge chimneys stood ungainly and exposed in the tangle of roof timbers. Everything looked very pathetic and in a ruinous state.

Someone gave a speech. The Männergesangverein, the men's choral society, sang several choral pieces. From a window in Herrenried's parents' apartment Alban looked down into the courtyard upon the surging sea of black umbrellas beneath which the singers were hidden. The rain poured down. Afterward, when the ceremony was over, Herrenried led his young friend into Beethoven's apartment. Everything was still as in the old days. The latches had been removed and so the pair could walk into the rooms without being disturbed. In the room where Beethoven died, they deadened the sound of their footsteps and stood silently side by side, lost in contemplation. It was like a short devotion.—

Four songs were completed before the end of the year: "Vorüber" (Past!), "Scheidelied" (Song of parting),"Schlummerlose Nächte" (Sleepless nights), and "Nachtgesang" (Night song).[100] In early spring 1904 two further songs appeared: "Es wandelt was wir schauen" (All that we see, changes), to verses by Eichendorff, and "Liebe" (Love), to the poem by Rainer Maria Rilke.[101]

However, it was then necessary to think seriously about the forthcoming Matura exam; certainly with due study there should be no possibility of disaster.[102] "In the Seventh," Alban told his friend when asked about it twenty years later, "I learned absolutely nothing more, failed, had to repeat, whereupon I learned even less and knew much less than the previous year. It's still quite incomprehensible to me today that I nevertheless managed to pass the Matura at all." —In short, on this occasion our young friend was let off lightly by this most medieval institution, which today as much as ever is destined by the State to ruin the nerves of young men—this officially organized memory game of catch-me-if-you-can called Matura.[103] At long last his knowledge in German language satisfied the requirements, and Alban Berg was thus an Abiturient of the Oberrealschule. With such uplifting feelings in his heart he at once traveled to the Ossiacher See so that his overheated brain could cool down at the Berghof.

There he received from Vienna the news of the serious illness of his friend Herrenried. An appendicitis recognized too late was very seriously endangering the life of the sick man. The doctors were at their wits' end. All assistance appeared to be in vain. At the last moment there was a turn for the better and Herrenried lived. At the beginning of August he traveled to Kitzbühel in the Tirol to convalesce; a 32-page letter from his young friend reached him there.[104] Enclosed with the letter was a song titled "Grabschrift" (Epitaph), which was dedicated to the convalescent.[105] Two further compositions come within that period: "Wandert ihr Wolken" (Travel, ye clouds), and the song of a dying person, "Im Morgengrauen" (At daybreak).[106]

The liberation from school immediately started to have a beneficial and recuperative effect on Alban's disposition. Selected excerpts from a letter of 1 August 1904 bear eloquent witness to this:

"I sit alone in my room—before me in the corner is Papa's bust—further forward, my favorite picture of Beethoven, then the statue of Brahms – – left and right of them, pictures of Mahler and Ibsen, my living ideals. On my bedside table stands the statue of Beethoven and over that hangs my favorite picture: Correggio's *Jupiter and Io* (sadly only a reproduction!)— So those are my surroundings – – a small child of humanity among gods and heroes!

"—And when I look out of the window I see grass blowing wildly and the tops of trees bending, and the sound of a double chorus of rain showers and howling winds comes in my direction – – I [. . .] thank God that each hot day is followed by several hours of thunderstorm . . ."

The effects of the Matura had not yet quite faded away. The "American," Hermann Berg, stayed at the Berghof for a short time as in previous summers. He had been afflicted with a painful rheumatism; the youngest brother, Alban, who was responsible for nursing him, expressed himself in the following terms on the subject:

"I might add that I noticed how already I've half forgotten the days of nursing that seemed to me impossible to forget – – How every five minutes Hermann had fresh pains, how he cursed, complained, even wept about this and that – – Oh! it was awful! – – – and yet I got through it – – unlike the Matura, which I dream about over and over again and get fearfully worked up about at least two nights in every three."

The words preceding the end of the same letter strike quite a different note, as do the wishes at the end itself.

"My brother Hermann," wrote the young man, who was awakening to new life, "my brother Hermann had also bought a kite – – a plaything for which I have a certain weakness.— It's a splendid feeling when after a long effort one has got it into the sky and it floats above– – – – *"exciting"* is what I'd like to call it, with Hilde Wangel – –!"[107] And right at the end: "Please write to me very soon! And soon get well like your old friend Alban."

Previously the young man had always been weakly and pale. Now he was already beginning to brag about his health; it was true that he was building up his strength and toughening his body, so that it was a joy to read the letters in which he told of his vitality and his summer pleasures.

"You needn't envy me my crossing of the lake," he wrote on 20 August 1904 to Herrenried. "In my eyes the achievement has lost a lot of its overall value since Frida achieved the same thing, even though she took twice as long (70 minutes). Now I'm longing to swim to Annenheim . . ."[108]

He thus had quite bold activities of a sporting nature in view, and as for his general disposition, it was totally different from that of the period *before* the Matura. Of course, it can be assumed that since he knew his friend was still in pain he was trying hard to cheer him up with pleasant news at this time. Nevertheless he could hardly have managed to describe such amusing scenes if his attention had not been engaged a little, if he had not readily joined in himself. So we have the following that he wrote about the *Kaiserfest*:[109]

"Our boat was the most original ever seen on the Ossiacher See. Following Frida's plan, we bought in Villach the most tasteless, brightly colored, loudly checked fabrics—peasant scarves, material for making blouses, etc., etc. We draped our boat with this screamingly vulgar jumble of material. At both ends a 'fantasy' flag—enough to make you kill yourself with laughter! Over the seat in the middle, an arch, draped with a tea towel, and from one flag to the other a rope on which hung frightfully ridiculous little pennants. Our personal appearance fit the ensemble and was the pièce de résistance: Frida, Smara, and I were dressed as Negroes in the most vulgar costumes. I was in patent-leather boots, garish red socks, white trousers with big turn-ups, golden waistcoat, high collar, pink peasant-type neckerchief, huge shirt cuffs and black frock coat, straw hat . . ."[110]

So much for the high-spirited, lively Abiturient, who had been deemed satisfactory in German. – – – A few pages farther on in the letter is inserted a magnificent descriptive account that demonstrates so well the skill at depiction that to such a great extent marks out the mature artist:[111]

"There were eight of us sitting down to supper," he began. "—It was very dark around us, uncannily bright just here and there as, far from us, bright lightning flashed over the cloud-covered sky and bathed the lake in a dazzling blue – – The leaves rustled eerily around us—and our lights were like torches in the storm. Then lightning flashed again over the landscape like the brandishing of whips of fire. Thunder rolled in the distance, and soon a ruddy glow crept upward behind the mountains, and climbed—and spread right up to the clouds, which were dazzlingly lit up and whose purple glow was reflected in the lake – –; then more lightning flashed through the night—the red disappeared for a moment, overcome[112] by the flashes from the lightning. You could see brown-gray columns of smoke rising upward toward the heavens. – – Then it became red again—now weaker, now stronger—then ever darker. Now only a faint glow on the billowing clouds—deathly gray on the lake. . ."

"The following day the careful hostess telegraphed Vienna: 'Charly, don't forget the fire insurance!'"[113]

"One of the most magnificent storms I've ever experienced moved over the countryside a few days ago," he reported further.[114] "—It came so suddenly and with such terrifying force that it was quite horrific. The trees bent, apples dropped off in shoals, small trees were falling, either just snapped off or completely uprooted. Cloths, towels, kitchen utensils flew about in the house. The rain came in a horizontal spray against the house.

"'What will the lake look like now?' Frida and I were thinking. Battling against the storm, we hurried out into the open country. There stood the cohorts of *Hiefler*, poles with clover hay, bent by the wind. Here and there one plunged to the ground. The hay whirled up and raced against the storm. – – Then we looked at the water as it roared furiously up toward us. It was like a newly plowed white field.

"'How divine!' The words rose to our lips. We hurried just as we were, down to the bathhouse. As we made our way along the landing stage, we had to hold desperately on to each other, the wind blew at us so. With the full strength of our bodies we forced ourselves against the door—we were just able to slip inside as another terrible gust of wind got trapped in the door, which slid out of our hands and crashed shut, so that its planks and boards flew asunder with a crunching sound.— Now we were standing in the face of the storm, and at every breath we got soaked by a heavy wave. I forced a cabin door open and from here we watched the tremendous spectacle.

"As the storm began to abate, or that is to say, very slowly became calmer (if 'calm' is really the right word, since according to Frida it was 'as beautiful as the sea'), and since the waves and the rain were reaching the cabins as well, we tried to reach safer shelter. We were frozen through and through. The icy wind blew onto our wet clothes! . . . We went home full of enthusiasm for such splendor – – upstairs in the house everybody was having their midday nap. . ."[115]

And so now we shall leave the young man by the Ossiacher See, enthusing about his storms and savoring the pleasure of his new lease of life. A turning point is not far off! Crucial changes are in the offing. It is still not at all certain whether the young composer, the self-taught creator of thirty-two songs up till now will be able to "stick with music."[116] Destiny has an important say;[117] often it is stubborn and hesitates for a good long time before it decides to proffer the cornucopia of success. —

PART III

1. *Rechnungspraktikant*

At this point in the present biography we find ourselves in the autumn of 1904.

Alban Berg was nineteen and a half years old. As far as his fitness for military service was concerned, one could rest assured that there was no possible room for doubt: in spite of his noteworthy sporting exploits with regard to swimming, he was utterly unfit for it. According to the military standard he was adjudged far too slim and spare in relation to his height, which was above average. Nevertheless he had a good figure and was of pleasing build. His facial features and his manner frequently gave an impression of weariness and exhaustion. In the concert hall or at the opera, whenever he was listening to a musical work that was quite new to him, his mouth would remain slightly open, which created an unfortunate impression. He looked as though he was unable to take in what he was hearing. However, in private, in the all-too-rare periods of relaxation and rest, in the quiet small circle of his friends, he appeared quite different. The full compelling spiritual and intellectual spell of his youth[118] shone from his large clear eyes, whose eyelids were unusually widely spaced and terminated in a steep, clearly defined curve under prominent eyebrows; as for the precisely structured profile of his head, with its finely shaped nose, one was quite ready to describe this as beautiful—indeed, as strikingly beautiful.

As Alban the Abiturient declared no intention of any sort of starting technical studies, although he was now in the position to offer documentary proof he was qualified to do so, it was clear in the Berg household —particularly so far as his mother was concerned—that it was now necessary to take a job, if possible a steady and lucrative one with a pension at the end.

That the Regional Government Office offered tempting prospects at that particular time was incontestable. For this, of course, one needed patronage—a very superior recommendation, on the very highest level if possible—as one was dealing with a respected body, a regional authority, which had no need to take on just anyone. To cut a long story short: patronage was forthcoming, and Alban started work on 17 October 1904 as a Rechnungspraktikant—a trainee accountant—in the service of the above-named authority; he was unpaid, obviously, but there was the prospect of payment.[119]

So the youngster exchanged the school bench for the office chair. This seating accommodation was situated in front of a writing desk whose damaged paintwork revealed innumerable coats underneath, in a room that was as large, say, as a classroom. On the longer side the room had five windows, on the shorter side two, the need for which could not have been accounted for by anybody.

No light entered through these large openings and only at one window, the one in the corner, did a glimmer of brightness appear; this gave rise to the notion that on sunny spring days the office manager, who had stationed his writing desk there in the place nearest the window, could find himself in the enviable position of doing without artificial light. Over each of the writing desks and worktables burned an electric light bulb dangling from a bit of cord. The trainee accountant—in order to make his place a bit more like home—had felt called upon to affix a green shade over the lamp at his disposal; it created an impression that the beginner was destined for something better. At some time the walls of the room must have been covered in a painted design. However, they did not really reflect it anymore, and their dark gray color got lost in the gloom, so that the contours of the room, being quite obscured and, as it were, blotted out, vanished altogether. As for the air held prisoner in the room, apparently on purpose—to say it could have been cut with a knife would have been far too mild. Surely it would have been possible to *saw* it into pieces, for it was dense and compressed in form. The smell that clung to it reminded one of roast potatoes, of apples on the oven being made into the most delicious of stews, of fig coffee essence, of burnt milk, officials' cigars, cigarette stubs, and pipe tobacco.[120]

The opacity of the atmosphere was like a "hit in the face" (if one can say such a thing).[121]

In this place—right in the middle of it, to be precise—Alban Berg, the trainee accountant, sat and worked away in the most industrious manner and, to all appearances, with the utmost dedication, dazzled by the prospect of eventually becoming a real Regional Government Officer. The first piece of work entrusted to him was, so to speak, intended to reveal the level of his competence, and was not overdifficult. Nevertheless, it required a certain adroitness and brought home to him the reason he had passed the Matura, and in particular the reason he had not been let off the hook all that lightly with his German.[122] The piece of work of which we're speaking, then, dealt with that most important, useful, and vital subject: the import and export of pigs in and out of Austria. Alban, the trainee accountant, was drawing up tables that showed the exports and imports of swine.

2. Theory Pupil

It would be quite wrong to be tempted to think that the trainee accountant did not fulfill his obligations or gave other cause for complaint. Not at all. He showed himself to be willing and was always friendly and obliging toward his colleagues. One could genuinely have thought that the job suited him and satisfied his expectations.

That was certainly not the case. What made him appear so quietly contented and reconciled to his lot was something unconnected with his office work. Rather, it was something that happened outside office hours, in his free time: Alban Berg was taking theory lessons with Arnold Schönberg.

What that means, or rather meant at the time, can only be grasped by someone who has lived through and shared in the heated, bitter struggle for Schönberg and his theories. Schönberg was decried as a fool, and the paths he took were so new, so unknown, that it required great faith to follow this prophet through the desert into the newly discovered wonderland. However, Alban Berg was one of the few who possessed this faith—this great, profoundly religious belief in the master.

"What a person!" writes Rudolf Schulz-Dornburg about Schönberg on the occasion of his fiftieth birthday.[123] "To look him in the eyes is to have faith in his wonderful soundness—soundness that is the finest mark of the truly complete artist.[124] Sensing his presence in a place, one feels with force the unique nature of his personality already articulated in historical terms, beyond the four walls. For him and for us it is fine to see him now as from his heights he hears the ever-growing jubilation of the ascending masses who for long enough reviled and spat at him."

And Josef Polnauer, too, found fine words for the fiftieth birthday of the master:[125] "'Kunst kommt nicht von Können, sondern von Müssen (Art comes not from *can* but from *must*)' says Schönberg's article 'Problems in Teaching Art.'[126] For the pupil, then, it was sufficient that he 'was able to do' what his forebears had 'had to do.' But even this legacy will only be acquired by someone who truly owns it. One learns only what one has been able to experience, and one experiences only what one has talent for.

"Schönberg—for all his pupils the most profound phenomenon, stirring them to the depths of their being—leads them as teacher from experience to experience. A genius in this respect, he very soon recognizes the character and gifts of each; then he compels them to seek for themselves what it avails them to know. Often he allows them to err, now and again to discover as well; he to whom it is granted, and who deserves it, eventually also discovers himself. No one of good will goes from him unblessed. All, however, must strive, nothing is granted to them straightaway; they will always remain in a state of restlessness, of movement. But life is like that, and since they must live, they learn.

"In a similar way, in an earlier age it would have been possible to find a teacher and an apprenticeship, since craftsman and teacher—practice of art and teaching of art—were one and the same. . . .

"Now once again, after almost two hundred years, a very great man is here, at once craftsman and teacher.[127] He is a teacher from his innermost need to achieve clarity about the methods and the course of his art. [. . .] He has the drive and the disposition that forces him not only to scrutinize the traditional teachings about his art but also nothing less than to conceive them anew, to discover them anew—and he is capable of doing these things. It is to be hoped that in the foreseeable future we shall see, newly erected by him, the entire music-theoretical teaching edifice."

So much, then, for Arnold Schönberg.

In autumn 1904, at the same time he was beginning his career in the Regional Government Office, Alban Berg made his way to Arnold Schönberg with several recently completed compositions, the latest of which, titled "Traum" (Dream) and labeled Op. 14, no. 1, constituted his thirty-second setting as a self-taught composer.[128] On the strength of these works, Schönberg accepted him as a theory pupil.[129]

The happiness and overwhelming joy felt by the youngster are indescribable. If anyone saw him coming away from the home of the master, who was not at all famous and occupied an extremely modest flat in Liechtensteinstrasse—the gait, bearing, and look on the face of this disciple of art betrayed his deep inner contentment.[130] Alban Berg was a fellow to be envied!

There was at that time in the old imperial city on the Danube something else to give pleasure to music-loving, enthusiastic young people, something no other city in the world had to show: the Vienna Hofoper under the direction of Gustav Mahler! To be sure, Mahler also was being hotly debated at that time, but "unknown and still unimportant" like Schönberg he certainly was not.

The greatest musical event from this period was incontestably the first performance of Mahler's Third Symphony under his personal direction.[131] The composer was cheered from all sides and repeatedly recalled,[132] and at the end Alban, the most zealous of the art enthusiasts, took possession of the baton with which the composer had conducted the immortal work.[133] We will add that the object in question was one of those insignificant thin little sticks of the sort that at each performance one might keep several specimens at hand.[134]

Thus Alban's studies began under the most favorable auspices, within the golden age of the Vienna Hofoper and while the greatest master of the theory of harmony was active as a teacher. Before the end of the year 1904, which had turned out to be so momentous and significant for the young man, he brought to thirty-five the number of his compositions.[135] The songs "Furcht" (Fear), "Augenblicke" (Moments), and "Die Näherin" (The seamstress) date from this period.[136] It is to be assumed that these short pieces were submitted to Schönberg in the theory lessons, and discussed with him.

3. Winter and Spring 1905

If a biographical portrayal is to get properly close to reality it cannot always be exciting. Sometimes points of repose occur, pauses in which nothing special happens, when time passes smoothly and regularly and every day looks like every other. But often in just those tedious, unexciting periods events are in preparation that throw everything off its usual course and alter our destiny decisively.

In the winter of 1905 we find our young friend occupied as a dutiful civil servant in the Regional Government Office and working industriously as a theory student with Schönberg. At that time, whatever was available to the young musician in the way of relevant works, he knew how to obtain. He frequently used to play duets with his willing sister, and he certainly did not miss special concert and opera performances. True, he had to be satisfied with cheap seats, as the funds at his disposal were very modest. Two songs were composed: "Erster Verlust" (First loss), to a poem by Goethe, and "Süß sind mir die Schollen" (Sweet to me is the soil of the valley), to verses by K. E. Knodt.[137] Then, on 10 February (we can establish the exact date from Herrenried's diary), the three songs Op. 16 nos. 1, 2, and 3 were completed.

What was it about these three compositions—which, incidentally, were very short? Did they really bear the mark of artistic accomplishment, the characteristics of completed works—so soon and so suddenly? Might the ideas, the inspiration that sparked them have been particularly fortunate? All this must remain open, left to the investigations of interested music critics. For the present story it is simply a question of establishing that these three songs made an especially deep impression on the friends of the young composer. The easily singable songs and their ear-tickling melodies led to a further outcome: fired with eager enthusiasm, Hermann Herrenried, whose pleasant singing voice was hitherto untrained, went to a singing master for lessons.

The songs in question were settings of Arno Holz's cheerful, lively verses, "Kleine Blumen, wie auch[138] Glas, seh' ich gar zu gerne" (I love to see the little flowers, peeping out like glass), Carl Busse's gentle little poem "Ich und du" (I and you), and Gustav Falke's heartfelt evening prayer "Fromm" (Piety). Following these there was written a further song, "Ballade des äußeren Lebens" (Ballad of external life), to words by Hugo von Hofmannsthal.

If we now turn our attention for a little to Alban's sister Smaragda, we find that she had developed into a strikingly beautiful young lady. She had also devoted herself to art—to the art of singing—and her low, sensitive voice was bewitchingly beautiful. She made her debut on 12 April 1905 at a function in aid of the Kaiserin Elisabeth-Heim at which her brother Alban acted as her accompanist.

Once again there followed a trio of songs, Op. 18, which was completed on 29 April.[139]

Summer came. This time there were no long holidays; there was no comfortable, enjoyable relaxation, no possibility of getting lost in dreams and introspection by the shores of the Ossiacher See, at the Berghof. Alban had to remain in Vienna and be "on duty." However, in the mornings, before work started, the young man was able to enjoy with his friend a tiny compensation for the summer holiday he was missing. The pair used to sit in the Volksgarten in front of the town hall, where with a rush the cool, lofty fountain shoots its water into the sky and the fine, cool watery mist from the grass sprinkler rises into the air in a rainbow-colored half-circle. They would look at the wonderfully maintained, thickly planted flower beds, whose blaze of color caused them to forget all mundane things and to make their way to work in a state of inner exaltation and contentment.

4. *Frau Weidman*

In the summer of 1905 a new guest appeared at the Berghof: Frau Julie Weidman, the sister of Frau Johanna Berg and widow of the property owner Josef Weidman, who had died a year earlier.[140] Josef Weidman was a well-known personality throughout the city. He ran a first-class business in leather fashion accessories and represented the world-famous champagne firm of Moët & Chandon.[141] Opposite the west entrance to the park of the palace of Schönbrunn, at the beginning of the Hietzinger Hauptstrasse, he had an elegant family house that had been renovated and modernized. The finely composed street facade was crowned by an attic story, which a well-known Viennese artist had embellished with graceful cupids.[142] On the ground level were a spacious music room, a dining room, coach houses, stables, and servants' living quarters. On the first floor were to be found the reception rooms, living rooms and bedrooms, and in the attic story were servants' rooms. Among the guests at the Weidmans' were numbered many outstanding representatives of the arts, among them Charlotte Wolter and Katharina Schratt.[143] The Emperor Franz Joseph, too, spent many a convivial evening there.

Josef Weidman was a passionate sportsman. For several years he was continually seen driving four-in-hand. He undertook extensive travels and brought back from Egypt a good-looking Nubian boy, Mohamet by name, whom he provided with a high-quality education.[144] Weidman was regarded as extraordinarily wealthy and happily married. Only one care dimmed the couple's happiness: they had no offspring. So long as Herr Weidman remained in the land of the living, communication between the sisters was restricted to occasional short visits; now that Frau Weidman was widowed, however, relations again became closer, and in summer 1905 she stayed at the Berghof as the guest of her sister.

At first, exaggerations and mistakes that occasionally crept into the conversation of this lady—who was full of joie de vivre—attracted no particular attention. As the thoughtless remarks became more frequent and people became convinced that it was no longer a question of momentary absent-mindedness, a doctor was consulted who diagnosed the initial stages of an incurable mental illness. In the autumn the sick woman returned to Vienna, to her home in Hietzing.

Meanwhile Alban pursued his music studies with the utmost zeal. In the summer he wrote three new songs, Op. 19, and in the autumn and winter yet another three songs, Op. 20. They were settings of the poems "Am Strande" (On the shore) by Georg Scherer, "Im Zimmer" (Indoors) by Johannes Schlaf, "Reiselied" (Song of travel) by Hugo von Hofmannsthal, "Spuk" (Ghost) by Friedrich Hebbel, "Die Nachtigall" (The nightingale) by Franz Evers, and "Winter" by Johannes Schlaf.[145]

A rapidly advancing deterioration set in toward the end of 1905 in the condition of the ailing Frau Weidman. At the insistence of the patient's legal advisor and doctor, Johanna Berg was obliged to make the decision to take up residence in the villa of her sick sister, and so Frau Berg, with her children Alban and Smaragda, moved into 9 Hietzinger Hauptstrasse.[146] (Charly Berg, the elder brother, had married on 6 November 1904.)[147]

The Berg family's move meant that Hermann Herrenried, who was living at the end of Ausstellungsstrasse in the Prater, in the studio house of the sculptor Pendl, might well have disappeared from his young friend's mental horizon. At the same time, however, Herrenried moved to 17 Berggasse, Vienna IX, which was not far from where Schönberg lived and from where it was easy to reach Hietzing on the Stadtbahn.[148]

It hardly needs saying that even outside his hours of study Alban sought to extend his knowledge, through attendance at concerts and theater performances. We gather from Herrenried's diary that he was present at the lieder concert on 29 January 1905 at which Gustav Mahler's *Kindertotenlieder* and songs from *Des Knaben Wunderhorn* were performed.[149] He went to see *The Wild Duck* on 20 April 1905, *Rosmersholm* on 21 November, and heard Mahler's Fifth Symphony on 7 December 1905.[150] Herrenried had written a play in three acts called *Alban* at this time; on 10 November 1905 he gave a reading of it in the Berg family circle.

5. The Large Inheritance

The year 1906 had scarcely begun when an event occurred that at one stroke transformed the Berg family circumstances. Frau Weidman's illness had progressed with alarming speed, and a recovery was now quite out of the question. The lady, who was completely deranged, suffered an attack of pneumonia; a frightening struggle with death began, which lasted for days—then came release.[151] As the only relative of the deceased, Frau Berg was sole heir. At first everyone was fully convinced that a huge fortune was involved, one that would pass to the heiress. There was also a lot of real estate property—ten large apartment blocks.[152] However, these houses were heavily mortgaged, the death duties were large, and when the size of the inheritance was finally clear it was recognized that a huge fortune was certainly *not* at stake here. Even so, assets were involved, the interest from which ensured a good income for the Berg family.

Apart from his official duties, Alban was being exceptionally industrious, despite the troubled times at the Hietzing villa. The following works were composed: the three songs Op. 21—"Fraue, du Süße" (Lady, thou sweet one) to words by Finckh, "O wär' mein' Lieb' jen' Röslein rot" (O my Luve's like a red, red rose) by R. Burns, and "Verlassen" (Abandoned), a Bohemian folksong—and also the four songs Op. 22—"Regen" (Rain) by Johannes Schlaf; "Traurigkeit" (Melancholy), "Hoffnung" (Hope), and "Flötenspielerin" (Flute-playing girl), by Peter Altenberg.[153]

Among the guests frequenting the Berg house was a young man, Adolf Ritter von Eger, the son of the Director of the Southern Railway, who was known as "Pips" and was starting to take a fancy to Smaragda.

6. *Twenty-one*

On 9 February 1906 Alban Berg reached the age of twenty-one. The years of greatest anxiety were over. Family circumstances were good, and the young man could allow himself to hope that he could at last devote himself entirely to music. This dream, however, was not to be realized so quickly. Johanna Berg was a practically-minded woman, and as the young man had good prospects of soon becoming a genuine Regional Government Officer, she was far from thinking about his course as a musician. She ran with style the large household she now had at her command. The Weidmans' staff had in part been kept on, and she had at her disposal a servant, chambermaid, cook, and auxiliary staff.

In Ober St. Veit, close to the wall of the Lainzer Tiergarten, the family owned an idyllic country house with a flower and vegetable garden, where peaceful and enjoyable times were spent.[154] Just at that time, however, the young musician was immersing himself entirely in his studies. He was working day and night with a dedication and stamina that was almost unbelievable. So as not to be reminded of the time of day, he sealed the windows of his study by means of the shutters and worked by electric light—he did not want to see whether it was day or night. To overcome fatigue he resorted to stimulants. He started drinking exceptionally large amounts of strong tea, a passion that would not desert him for years.[155]

7. Salome *in Graz*

A new star had risen in the musical firmament: Richard Strauss. His short opera *Feuersnot* had been performed at the Hofoper, whose doors, however, remained closed to *Salome*. Then there came news from Graz that the first performance in Austria was in preparation there. Herrenried had some good, kind friends there, a distinguished, art-loving family called Hofmann, who extended an invitation to Alban and himself.[156] And so the two friends traveled to Graz. They arrived at lunch-time on 16 May and were given a very warm welcome and hospitality. After lunch there was music making by family and friends. Herrenried sang a selection of his friend's songs, and all looked forward with feverish impatience and boundless anticipation to the evening, when the performance of the opera was to take place.[157] The entire musical world seemed to be gripped by excitement. Gustav Mahler, Puccini, Arnold Schönberg, and Alexander Zemlinsky had sped to Graz. Unbelievable things were being said of the rehearsals. Alban and his friend were present in a box at the performance, as guests of the Hofmann family. The performance was like a gala performance. The success was tremendous. Dr. Ernst Decsey wrote at the time, "Not before now has the operatic stage experienced such satanic, such artistic power."[158]

A small group of musicians and enthusiasts gathered afterward in the Thalia Restaurant, and in the morning the friends returned to Vienna.

8. A "War of Liberation"

Scarcely were the two friends back in Vienna than there arose an open disagreement between Alban's mother and Herrenried.

The young Alban felt deeply unhappy as a local government trainee! The strenuous study he was engaged in outside his office work was by no means to the benefit of his health. He looked wretched and lost weight from day to day. To Herrenried the young man's condition appeared to give serious cause for concern. He arranged for his friend to be examined by his own doctor. When the latter confirmed that Alban did indeed have an illness, Herrenried started to consider a plan to release his friend from his office work. At that point he encountered vehement opposition on the part of Alban's mother. Notwithstanding the favorable circumstances in which the family was living, relinquishing the promising position in the Regional Government Office was something this practically-minded woman would not hear of. In the heat of the moment Herrenried, exasperated beyond endurance, spoke angry words; matters came to an open breach, and he was forbidden to enter the house. The banishment lasted a full four weeks. Alban's sister Smaragda tried to act as mediator. What at first seemed virtually impossible was achieved, and Herrenried was restored to favor. Alban was now diagnosed as sick by a different doctor and thus secured a period of sick leave while still retaining his post.[159] Breathing a sigh of relief, the young man began his leave on 23 June 1906 and spent it at the Berghof. On 1 August he received his decree of employment as Regional Government Officer with an annual interim payment of 1,600 crowns.[160]

If we trace Alban's composing activity at this time we find the following works: the song "Spaziergang" (A stroll) by Mombert, committed to paper at the Berghof; "Soldatenbraut" (The soldier's bride) by Mörike, composed on 17 September at the country house in Ober St. Veit; "Eure Weisheit" (Your wisdom) by J. S. Fischer, written on 18 September, likewise in Ober St. Veit; also, "Liebesode" (Lovers' ode) by Otto Erich Hartleben on 19 September and "So regnet es sich langsam ein" (The rain is slowly setting in) by Cäsar Flaischlen on 20 September, both composed in Hietzing.[161]

9. The Letter

In the meantime, Adolf von Eger had asked for the hand of Alban's sister Smaragda in marriage. They became engaged, and "Pips" (whose name we have mentioned earlier) spent most evenings in the family circle; Herrenried and Alban's brother Charly also joined in. To make these evenings more interesting, plays were read with the parts distributed. Ibsen was especially favored, and *Nora (A Doll's House)* aroused such enthusiasm that the intention was that the parts should be learned by heart and the play performed in the Berg household—a plan that of course never came to fruition. The intensive preoccupation with *A Doll's House* was the occasion for every sort of discussion. In particular, Herrenried and his young friend came into sharp disagreement about Nora's nature, which led to a written exchange of views that came to an end with Alban's letter of 18 October 1906. This letter is now reproduced virtually word for word, with full consideration for underlinings and dashes. A commentary on it is quite unnecessary, as the letter expresses itself with such clarity and eloquence that it produces a deeply moving effect on its own:

18 October 1906.[162]
[BORKMAN:] "So we have deceived each other. And perhaps ourselves, both of us?"
[FOLDAL:] "But then, isn't that what friendship is, after all, John Gabriel?"
[BORKMAN:] "Certainly—to deceive, that is friendship."[163]
That is Ibsen's conception of friendship – – and as in so much, he's correct! *Correct* in the "*traditional*" conception of friendship. <u>People in general</u> can't imagine that someone can be a friend who vigorously defends a different point of view, and they feel, with Ibsen, "that the most costly thing about friendship lies not in what one does on its behalf but in what one refrains from doing out of regard for it. Because of this"—so the letter to Brandes continues—"many seeds of spiritual growth are stunted in one go!"[164]

Yes! Ibsen is correct to say this in the *traditional* sense! But *my* view of friendship is essentially different from *Ibsen's*—and yours: I don't think it right that it should be necessary for "our ways to part," as you say, just because now and then we have disagreements. One of us would have to give in (unless he is convinced he is right)—in other words, as Ibsen says, deceive himself and the other party; and for the one who "gives in" this friendship might in fact turn out to be "costly"—he would end up a spiritual cripple. But since we obviously don't want this and I *believe* in friendship—in spite of Ibsen's *unbelief* in it—my own idea of it is quite different and, I hope, the only right one. – You can see that at its best in our dispute over Nature, which has lasted for years. Assuming that your view about my relationship to Nature was correct—it isn't entirely, since I adore Nature fanatically and regard her as my instructress in many things; with some exceptions, e.g. in music—assuming, then, that it was correct, I simply belong to the category of people who reach knowledge of Nature from the opposite direction. These people find an example in this:

that since painters paint clods of earth violet and the distant mountains blue, Nature is actually made thus. And so we are like two miners who work a seam from opposite sides and meet in the center (in the recognition of Nature).[165] But—as I've said before—I'm certainly no mere theorist –! If perhaps earlier I used not to be receptive to Nature, I fared only like the last of the Buddenbrooks: "He had [again] felt how painful beauty is, how she plunges deep into shame and desperate yearning and yet also devours the courage and fitness for ordinary life."[166] But I've long been equal to the appreciation of Nature's beauty, truth, and greatness.[167] She is the basis of my existence! The beauty of the solitary world of the mountains, or—I'm being more modest here—the noble form of my house palm, the unique sweep of the cheekbone of the skull of a dead person – – all this I worship from the bottom of my heart, and it offers me something more imperishable than all philosophical systems and mere theories, be they even Weininger's. On the other hand many of the books I have read have created in me—or rather, awakened in me—reverence for Nature; for this I am grateful to them and admire them—from Goethe down to Altenberg.— And all that follows on from Nature—the preference for what is natural in everything, the woman with no book learning, the judgment made without a statute book, hatred of "the press" (that importation most inimical to Nature)—all this and much else I owe mainly to my reading of Goethe, Ibsen, Wilde, Kraus and Weininger!!! — — But there are things that can't be measured by the yardstick of Nature – – things that have sprung *solely* from the human spirit, towering far above the material world—things that are *real* only in our *longing* for them, "when the sublime and beautiful things, the good and wise things, that we long for, turn into reality—not a reality that can be picked and put in the mouth or that can be counted and put in one's pocket!" (Otto Ernst).[168]

Music is like that – – – and quite a few literary works that are written from within a *longing*-filled heart! – – : – –

– I've now got to *A Doll's House*. To find a "Nora" in Nature is quite impossible—I mean the Nora of the last half-act. I know enough about "doll's houses," and I know about women who've run away—but I don't know a "Nora"! Ibsen doesn't know her either. The original story of Nora is one of dozens of cases that every mortal comes up against over the years: "A real doll's house—the wife makes fraudulent financial transactions—the husband gets wind of it, a divorce is considered; then the amount of the bill is met and the wife – – – – – is restored to favor."[169]

Your two examples of "doll's houses" are on the same level. Even in her second marriage Frau W . . . will not find the "miracle," which she will never have been expecting anyway.[170] And according to your description, your mother and her children were probably "dolls" of your father—but a "Nora" your mother has never become—thank goodness! – And the worst "doll" that I know, Frau B . . . . , who was *really pampered* by her husband but never knew that her husband had formerly declared himself bankrupt, was quite happy in this role and today still knows nothing of "miracles."[171]

And since Ibsen was certainly a great connoisseur of women, we can regard Nora not as *misrepresented* but as originating purely in her author's imagination. He wishes to show us how, seen in the most ideal light, the "doll" of the first two acts, and together with her all the "dolls" in the world, *ought* to change – – not how they do in reality. Then it is madness—as you yourself say—to speak of *growth*. – That would be like wanting to carve a marble statue from a wood block. – – It can only be viewed—and here "our ways must part"—as a death-defying leap from the Natural into the Supernatural, a step that even the female interpreter of the part must go along with, as far as possible.[172]

However, so that for you this view of mine won't seem unfounded, I'll try to demonstrate it. It's undoubtedly the case that the Nora of the last half-act is great and distinguished, that she is a "woman of Nature," a *true* woman, of a sort that doesn't exist in reality, however. *Before* this she is not like that. She's a completely different person; she's the *very* thing that you deny her to be, – a "normal woman" – – an average woman: elegant, cheerful, coquettish; she dallies, sings, has a sweet tooth, borrows and—lies and dissembles. –

She has a kind heart, motherly love, and is capable of self-sacrifice. Whether she does all this out of pretense I'll discuss later on; however, one need only think of her persistent and well-practiced lying to be able to maintain that she is no "woman of Nature." One can maintain this with certainty all the more when one considers that, in everything, "she would play-act even in front of her husband"—as you say. In *Wilhelm Meister* Goethe writes of a woman "that she is *no hypocrite*. I love her for that, indeed I am her friend, because for me she is such a pure representative of her kind. She is the *true Eve*, the *progenitrix* of the *female sex*"[173]—that is, the proper "woman of Nature." – – How utterly different Nora is from this woman! – – Ibsen, indeed, didn't really believe in the existence of the true woman, who exists *only* in the *thought* of each of the more profound thinkers (Nietzsche, Schopenhauer, Weininger)—; *poets* are not under consideration here

– – they write *poetry*, after all. But Ibsen is one of the few poets who distinguishes between Poetry and Truth.[174]—and if in Nora he has drawn a *true* woman, he himself then admits in *Borkman* that he has never found her, even if he "nevertheless has the feeling that out there, in the far distance, somewhere, he can find the true woman."[175]

In the first two acts, then, Nora is a normal woman. Now it might have been possible that she would just *play* at being that, and that fundamentally she was a "woman of Nature" (who, as is known, doesn't tell lies and nibble at sweets but presents herself as she is and rejects her own harmful tendencies). But Ibsen, that finest of delineators of character, would certainly not have omitted to show this. How easy it would have been. Helmer[176] is not onstage very much; people enter who are to be taken seriously as fine characters: Rank, Mrs. Linde. Does Nora—except when she's terrified—then drop her theatrical mask (unless she really is like that)?[177] How does she speak to Mrs. Linde, who would certainly be a worthy recipient to whom she could openly pour out her heart? To put it mildly: it's so childish, this talk about the old admirer who is leaving "all his money" to her—and on it goes! And Rank—this touchingly loyal figure—how does she talk to him? The episode with the stockings is true and unadulterated "normal woman" behavior.– How can she say in Act 3, "I have never felt happy, only gay," when in the company of Mrs. Linde in Act 1 she bubbles over with feelings of happiness and joy about her husband's appointment?[178] Yes! in these exchanges it's possible to show word for word how petty and insignificant she is in the first two acts. Or can you imagine that a superior woman (think of Frau Stein—or equally of Frau Hofmann)[179] would act and think as follows: to cry "Well, I'm damned!";[180] to reprove the servant by shouting: "The Bank Manager!';[181] to talk only about herself, and with such complacency, on her first meeting with Mrs. Linde; then the stockings episode; or the excessive craving for "more money, yes, more than we need!"?

Oh, no great, noble woman thinks and acts like that! And that little bit of feeling for nature! It's *no more* than our Milly possesses (Berg's servant—author's note)[182] when she talks about the sea or the Berchtesgaden mountains—without any claim to "greatness!" — How superior to Nora is Mrs. Linde! She recognizes the moral peril that the Helmer couple are in; <u>she</u> it is who first discovers the absolute necessity for the great transformation from a "doll's marriage" into a true one; <u>she</u> it is who is on the way to growing out of "normal womanhood"—on the way to becoming a priestess! —And Helmer himself is nothing other than a "normal man" who is admirably suited to his wife as long as she doesn't undergo the "miraculous" transformation. And that happens *only* in the last act. If Nora, *during her life*, really had been a *great* woman like that, she would have been awaiting with longing the moment when the "miracle" would be revealed. And she resists it with a fear bordering on hysteria. Certainly she says, "Now the miracle will happen –" but she quickly adds, "It must not happen at any price!" and sends Mrs. Linde to see Krogstad. And later, when Mrs. Linde returns with nothing achieved, she repeats, "After all, it's a great joy to expect a miracle," and tries the next moment to open the lock of the letterbox with hairpins when nobody is watching her. (This action too is devoid of any sense of "greatness"—especially when the clumsiness of its execution is taken into consideration!)— Right at the bitter end, when, after the return from the ball, Helmer goes into the next room, Nora once more hopes to be saved by Mrs. Linde and *whispers quickly and breathlessly*: "What now?!" (You can hear the anxiety and suspense.)[183] And *only* when Mrs. Linde says, "You must tell your husband!" does Nora know "what she has to do!" I can't recognize anything "great" from the woman's behavior here! *Up to this point* one has the feeling that, had Krogstad demanded his letter back, everything might have remained *as before*.[184] For she herself answers Mrs. Linde, "I'm saying nothing!" and it's easy to imagine her continuing thus: "As I have nothing to fear from Krogstad" (as Mrs. Linde assures her), "I'll forgo the miracle!"

But the author doesn't let it end there; on this realistic foundation, as in all his works, he now constructs his idealism. – – It is optimism for the future—when we dead awaken—that rests on the pessimistic present.[185] Perhaps one day women will act like Nora, perhaps one day the cry of longing will be fulfilled that has been unheeded up to now: "I hope that, when I go out into the great, wide world, I am approached by a noble, lovely young woman, who beckons to me, who shows me the path to glory!"

"But no! Young women approached me, but such a maiden was not among them" (Ibsen)[186]—up to now, only this holds true.

Dear Hermann,[187]

For me also "the matter is serious, as you will see from my even longer letter"[188] – – "But *I* don't fear" that through these differences of opinion a mutual estrangement will develop! Stick to your guns – – If it seems to you that I don't go along <u>with</u> you, at least believe that someday we'll meet in the middle of the mine, toward which we'll work through the *deaf rock* and *precious ore*, and that we will call out to each other a cheery "Good luck!" –

Alban

10. Freedom!

Several weeks after the long "Nora" letter came the most decisive turning point in Alban Berg's career. Since 23 June 1906 he had held a permanent appointment as a Regional Government Officer, and on 31 October he left the service of this high authority and now devoted himself wholly to the study of his beloved music.[189] Before the end of the year and reaching into 1907, two works were composed: "Der milde Herbst von anno 45" (The mild autumn of the year '45), op. 66, to words by Max Mell, and "Was zucken die braunen Geigen" (Why do the brown violins twitch), op. 67, to words by Delle Grazie.

NOTES

1. I am grateful to the Alban Berg Stiftung for allowing me to quote from Berg's letters.
2. The quotation occurs in the section "Die Primitive," part of the "Revolutionär" sequence. I am grateful to Professor Andrew Barker for help in tracing this.
3. The full title of the organization was Eltern-Vereinigung zur Förderung deutscher Jugendkultur in Wien (Parents' Organization for the Fostering of German Youth Culture in Vienna). For more information on Watznauer in general and on his relationship with Berg, see Nick Chadwick, "From *Freund Hein* to Hermann Hesse: Hermann Watznauer and His Friendship with Alban Berg," *Music & Letters* 79 (1998): 396–418. Parts of the current introduction and translation already appeared in this article.
4. *Wolf und Walters Wanderfahrten* was published under anonymous authorship, Vienna: Manz, 1920; *Shatter* was published from 1924 through 1930 by various publishers.
5. Formerly the Wiener Stadt- und Landesbibliothek. The manuscript in question bears the shelfmark H.I.N. 204582 (formerly I.b.179.610); I am grateful to the Wien Bibliothek for permission to use this source. Henceforth, Parts I, II, or III are indicated by WAB:I, WAB:II, or WAB:III, followed by page number(s).
6. Erich Alban Berg, *Der unverbesserliche Romantiker: Alban Berg 1885–1935* (Vienna: Österreichischer Bundesverlag, 1985), 9–106; henceforth *DuR*.
7. I am grateful to the Morgan Library for allowing me to use the letters in their possession.
8. Berg Fonds, Music Collection, Austrian National Library, F21 Berg 434; henceforth referred to by the shelfmark.
9. The full letter is quoted and discussed in Chadwick, "From *Freund Hein* to Hermann Hesse," 414–16.
10. Original in the Mary Flagler Cary Collection, Morgan Library, New York.
11. This firm traded under the name of Conrad Berg but was in fact a subsidiary of the New York export firm of Geo. Borgfeldt & Co., for which Conrad's eldest son Hermann worked in America. For more on Conrad Berg's business interests, see Rosemary Hilmar, *Alban Berg: Leben und Wirken in Wien bis zu seinen ersten Erfolgen als Komponist* (Vienna, Cologne & Graz: Böhlau, 1978), 15–16.
12. Watznauer originally wrote "a tiredness that could not be overcome."
13. Frau Aja was Goethe's nickname for his mother, Catharina Elisabetha Goethe (1731–1808).

Notes to WATZNAUER'S BIOGRAPHY OF ALBAN BERG

14. Geo. Borgfeldt & Co.
15. Since he was born on 16 September 1872 he was actually in his twenty-seventh year.
16. "Seine Mutter sagte, er wäre im Jünglingsalter das schönste ihrer Kinder gewesen. Man könnte sich von der bezaubernden Schönheit dieses jungen Menschen gar keinen Begriff machen. Und was die Mutter sagte, das konnte man glauben" (WAB:1, 7). In F21 Berg 434, the second and third sentences have been run together, with a comma after "machen."
17. WAB:I, 8. Charly was born on 5 May 1881 and was thus seventeen at the beginning of 1899, not eighteen as stated in *DuR*, 14.
18. This was in April 1899. A note to that effect has been added in the margin of WAB:I, 9.
19. "aber schließlich ward die Matura mit Hilfe eines sogennanten Schnellfinderkurses überstanden" (WAB:I,10). However, a marginal note in WAB says "Kein Matura [—] Einjähriger Kurs" (No Matura [or] Einjähriger course), which implies that Charly did *not* pass the Matura (the Austrian school final examination) and was therefore ineligible for Einjährig-Freiwilliger status in his war service (see also the note immediately below). *DuR*, 17, has merely "aber schließlich wurde alles überstanden" (but at last he had put it all behind him). Alban's marginal remark, "Einjährigen-Prüfung" (Einjähriger exam) in F21 Berg 434 appears to be incorrect.
20. Like his father, Charly was employed by Borgfeldt & Co. Erich Alban Berg added a note about his father Charly's war service in which he appears to explain that he did not gain the Matura and therefore was ineligible for the Einjährig-Freiwilliger status, which would have enabled him to become an officer in one year instead of the normal three years.
21. The school Alban attended was the Comunal-Oberrealschule on the Schottenbastei in the Innere Stadt.
22. Presumably a diminutive of *Götze*, meaning "idol"; thus "little idol," which could also be linked to the governess's own surname, Götzlick.
23. WAB calls her "Erneste"; some sources spell the surname Götzlik. The original subhead for this section reads *Die Götzlick* (WAB:I, 15). Erich Alban Berg has inserted her correct first name, Ernestine, before the surname.
24. This is possibly a hint that Ernestine Götzlick may have encouraged Smaragda Berg's lesbian tendencies.
25. "Widow of a regional government official": *Statthaltereiratswitwe* in original (WAB:I, 17), which also says that Marie von Salzgeber was a "Freiin," or baroness in her own right.
26. "Sie . . . trug das reiche Blondhaar in Gretchenfrisur" (WAB:I, 17).
27. The Kaiserin Elisabeth-Heim für Witwen und Waisen, Frauen und Mädchen des gebildeten Mittelstandes (Empress Elisabeth Home for Widows and Orphans, Women and Girls of the Educated Middle Classes) was founded in 1900.
28. Presumably a reference to the monks of the Cistercian abbey of Heiligenkreuz, near Mödling, southwest of Vienna.
29. In WAB Watznauer gives himself the pseudonym Herrenried and writes in the third person. In *DuR* this has been changed to the first person.
30. The Hermannsdenkmal, erected by Ernst von Bandel on the Teutoburger Wald near Detmold in northwestern central Germany, commemorated the defeat in 9 A.D. of the Romans under Varus by Arminius or Hermann of the Cherusci tribe. The Battle of the Teutoburger Wald is commonly regarded as the seminal event in German history.
31. In 1866 the Seven Weeks' War, in which Prussia defeated Austria, established the preeminence of the idea of a common "German" heritage.
32. Helene Watznauer (1873–1924); Leopold Watznauer (1877–1956).
33. Reichenberg is now Liberec in the Czech Republic.
34. Although the main text of WAB:I, 22, says "Anfang Jänner 1899," it seems that the correct date was November 1898, if a note in the margin, apparently not in Watznauer's hand, is to be believed. See also *DuR*, 22, which confirms the latter date.

35. The identity of the "important authority on youth" is unknown.
36. "Erlösertrieb" (WAB:I, 26).
37. The Breitegasse, in the Neubau district west of the Burgring, runs in a southeasterly direction from the Burggasse; the southern half, from the junction with the Siebenstern Gasse to the Mariahilferstrasse, is the present-day Karl Schweighofer-Gasse.
38. The Hofstallgebäude later became the Messepalast (exhibition hall) and is now the Museumsquartier (museum complex).
39. "Er war in den vier Jahren, die er in der Provinzstadt Reichenberg zugebracht hatte, ein wenig versummpert [sic]" (WAB:I, 30).
40. Although Herndl is here presented as an abbreviation of the fictitious surname Herrenried, it could also have been used as a short form of Hermann, the first name of both Watznauer and Berg's eldest brother; see, for example, the letter to Berg from his nephew Erich dated 13 August 1918, in H. Knaus and T. Leibnitz, eds., *Altenberg bis Zuckerkandl: Briefe an Alban Berg, Liebesbriefe von Alban Berg* (Vienna: Löcker, 2009), 205. In their correspondence, Watznauer often signed his letters to Berg "Waz," "Watz," or "Watzl"; Berg addressed him as "Herman" or "Hermann."
41. This sentence originally opened the first paragraph of Section 16, but as it clearly belongs here, I have followed *DuR*, 28, in moving it to its present position at the end of Section 15.
42. Dobratsch (7,107 ft.), mountain to the west of Villach.
43. Gerlitzen (6,263 ft.), mountain dominating the northern shore of the Ossiacher See.
44. *DuR*, 29, gives the date of this purchase as 1894.
45. "Es war . . . kein Betrieb, der aufs Verdienen eingerichtet war, eher ein Sport, wenn man es so ausdrücken darf" (WAB:I, 34).
46. The words "glatte Bäume" (slippery trees), possibly in Berg's hand, have been added in the margin, presumably as a correction to "einen Stein"; possibly Alban had stumbled over the slippery roots of trees.
47. The new heading at the beginning of this section is apparently a later interpolation.
48. The original German contrasts the school year to "Das gregorianische Jahr" (WAB:II, 1).
49. "auf die völlige Hingabe an die Musik" (WAB:II, 4). In F21 Berg 434 Berg has altered "an die Musik" to "an diese" (to these), which seems to refer back to "musical artworks" (*Tonkunstwerke*).
50. William Spemann, *Spemanns goldenes Buch der Musik: Eine Hauskunde für Jedermann* (Berlin & Stuttgart: Spemann, 1900, and many later editions). This was a compendium of every sort of musical knowledge and would have provided Alban with a sound, if somewhat academic, musical knowledge.
51. According to Berg's own annotations in F21 Berg 434, Conrad Berg's death was a more sudden affair; the first seizure happened "in the afternoon" and death occurred "after a few hours" of violent struggle in the night of 30 March 1900. Further annotations in WAB:II, 6, whether in Berg's hand or not is unclear, mention "angina pectoris— *Jahrelang*" (angina pectoris—lasting for years) and *"eine Nacht"* (one night), presumably referring to Conrad Berg's fatal heart attack.
52. Hermann Berg had been appointed Alban's guardian.
53. Alban's maternal great-aunt, Marie Bareis, Edle von Barnhelm.
54. "Das Traumhafte, Beschauliche mußte sich mit einer sehr bescheidenen Rolle begnügen" (WAB:II, 7). The sentence originally ran: "Das Traumhafte, Beschauliche ging beinahe verloren" (The dreamlike and tranquil aspect of life there was almost lost).
55. The sculptor in whose studio building Herrenried took a room was Emanuel Pendl (1845–1927), responsible for work in several buildings on the Ringstrasse.
56. "Mitte Jänner 1901 war er dann angetreten und hatte das Diplom erhalten" (WAB:II, 8).

57. Watznauer's memory appears to have been faulty here. In a pencil note in F21 Berg 434, Berg has added "3. Gallerie [sic] 1. Reihe Carmen" (in the first row of the 3rd Gallery, Carmen). There was a performance of *Carmen* on Sunday, 20 January 1901, which might be the performance attended by Watznauer and Berg. I am grateful to Christopher Hailey for this information.

58. This is the song "Heiliger Himmel" (The holy heavens), op. 1, no. 1.

59. "Herbstgefühl" (Feelings in autumn), op. 1, no. 2, published in *Alban Berg. Jugendlieder*, ed. Christopher Hailey, vol. 1 (Vienna: Universal Edition, 1985), 2–3.

60. Op. 1, no. 3 is titled "Unter der Linde" (Under the lime tree).

61. "Charly holte sicher am meisten hervor" (WAB:II, 11).

62. This is contradicted by a pencil note in Berg's hand in F21 Berg 434, which indicates that he had to stay "opposite, in an awful pension in Sattendorf." Sattendorf is on the opposite side of the Ossiacher See from the Berghof.

63. For more on Paul Hohenberg and his friendship with Berg see Joan Allen Smith, "The Berg–Hohenberg Correspondence," *Alban Berg Symposion Wien 1980: Tagungsbericht*, ed. Rudolf Klein (Vienna: Universal Edition, 1981), 189–97.

64. The name of the friend Fail was inserted at a later date in WAB:II, 13, and has been corrected by Berg to "Feyl" in F21 Berg 434.

65. This essay, "Kunstsinn und Kunstverständnis," which is dated 7 October 1901, is discussed in Chadwick, "From *Freund Hein* to Hermann Hesse," 408–9.

66. "himmelhoch jauchzend zu Tode betrübt" (literally: crying to the heavens, troubled to death), a quotation from Goethe's *Egmont*.

67. "Spielleute" is Ibsen's poem "Spillemænd" in the translation by Ludwig Passarge. The song is published in *Jugendlieder*, 1:4–6. "Wo der Goldregen steht" and "Lied des Schiffermädels" were published in ibid., 1:7–9 and 10–11 respectively.

68. "Abschied" (Parting), published in ibid., 1:14.

69. Published in ibid., 1:15–19. Watznauer misremembered the song or else was thinking of a different one: it is slow throughout, and at no point can its character be described as "stormy."

70. The title of the first of these two songs is "Liebeslied" (Love song).

71. "Sehnsucht I," published in *Jugendlieder*, 1:12–13.

72. The first of these songs is "Vielgeliebte schöne Frau," published in ibid.,1:20–21; the second is "Sehnsucht II," published in ibid., 1:22–23.

73. "Sternenfall," published in ibid., 1:24–25, and "Sehnsucht III," published in ibid., 1:26–27.

74. This letter was in fact written a year later, on 20 November 1903. The original is headed "Am Borgfeldts Sterbetag" (On the day Borgfeldt died). George Borgfeldt died on 20 November 1903; see Hilmar, *Alban Berg*, 24 n26.

75. In the German, "something" appears as "Einiges" (WAB:II, 18); the original letter has "ein weniges" (a little).

76. The musical setting for these lines is included in the original letter. The original Hofmannsthal text of the first stanza is as follows: "Hörtest du denn nicht hinein, / Daß Musik das Haus umschlich? / Nacht war schwer und ohne Schein, / Doch der sanft auf hartem Stein / Lag und spielte, das war ich."

77. Berg read *Dichtung und Wahrheit (Poetry and Truth)*, Goethe's account (1811–14) of his early life and the development of his ideas up to his arrival in Weimar in 1775.

78. The upper part of the exclamation mark is in the form of a cross.

79. In fact, 9 February 1903 was Berg's *eighteenth* birthday.

80. Wolf died on 22 February 1903 in the Lower Austrian (Niederösterreichische) Landesirrenanstalt, correctly so named in *DuR*, 41.

81. Narrenturm can be translated as "fools' tower."

82. "Die Einsegnung" (WAB:II, 20). The original reading was "Die Einsegnung unter

dem Chorgesange des Hugo Wolf Vereines," that is, "The service of blessing accompanied by the choral singing of the Hugo Wolf Verein."

83. A marginal note referring to this phrase says, "Alban fragen?" (Ask Alban?) (WAB:II, 21).

84. Published in *Jugendlieder*, 1:28–29 and 30–32 respectively.

85. Published in ibid., 1:33–34 and 35–37 respectively.

86. It was not the Matura examination that Berg took and failed, but the end-of-year exam that he needed to pass before taking the Matura itself. See Hilmar, *Alban Berg*, 23, 171.

87. He also failed to satisfy in mathematics.

88. The phrase in parentheses is Watznauer's.

89. The letter is dated 16 July 1903.

90. Grillparzer's *Hero* is "Hero and Leander," in other words, *Des Meeres und der Liebe Wellen*. The authors' names in this sentence were supplied by the translator.

91. Berg refers to Giovanni Segantini (1858–99), Italian divisionist painter active in Switzerland, who was particularly popular in Germany and Austria.

92. The first of these, "Schattenleben," was published in *Jugendlieder*, 1:38–39; "Am Abend" was published in ibid., 1:40–41.

93. The Berghof visitors' book (Wienbibliothek im Rathaus, Handschriftensammlung, H.I.N. 204583, formerly I.c. 179611) contains entries at this time for Frida Semler and Eleonora Kahle (see below), August and Ossi Goettel, and "Dr. Mandl Ob[er]stl[eutnan]t. (Otto Mandl)."

94. Presumably a reference to Alban's affair with Marie Scheuchl, a servant in the Berg household. See also Chadwick, "From *Freund Hein* to Hermann Hesse," 399–400.

95. "das Kindsein ihm von den Schultern gefallen war, dieses sanfte dunkle Kleid": a quotation from Rilke's novella *Die Weise von Liebe und Tod des Cornets Christoph Rilke* (The lay of the love and death of Cornet Christoph Rilke).

96. The phrase in parentheses was inserted by Watznauer at the foot of the page. Frida Semler, later Frida Semler Seabury (d. 1974), the daughter of George Semler, a business associate of Borgfeldt & Co. the parent firm of Berg's father's company. For more on this subject, see Donald Harris, "Berg and Miss Frida: Further Recollections of His Friendship with an American College Girl," *Alban Berg Symposion Wien 1980*, 198–208.

97. Eleonora Kahle, a friend of Frida's. See also D. Harris, "Berg and Miss Frida."

98. The song's title is "Vom Ende" (The end).

99. Otto Weininger (1880–1903), Austrian philosopher whose book *Geschlecht und Charakter* (*Sex and Character*), published earlier in 1903, became a sensation after the author's suicide.

100. The German differentiates between these four songs: "Zwei Lieder und zwei Gesänge" (WAB:II, 29). "Vorüber" and "Schlummerlose Nächte" are published in *Jugendlieder*, 1:42–43 and 44–5 respectively.

101. Published in ibid., 1:46–47 and 48–49 respectively.

102. "freilich mit dem Studieren wollte es niemals zu besonderem Draufgehen kommen" (WAB:II, 30).

103. "dieses behördlich organisierte, mnemotechnische Fangerlspiel" (WAB:II, 30).

104. The letter of 1 August 1904. For more on Watznauer's visit to Kitzbühel see Chadwick, "From *Freund Hein* to Hermann Hesse," 410–11.

105. Published in *Jugendlieder*, 1:52–53.

106. Published in ibid., 1:50–51.

107. Hilde Wangel, a character in Ibsen's play *The Master Builder*.

108. Frida Semler was again spending the summer at the Berghof.

109. The seventy-fourth birthday of the Austrian emperor Franz Joseph I was celebrated on 18 August. The event described in this excerpt took place the evening before.

110. More of Berg's account of the *Kaiserfest*, omitted by Watznauer at this point in WAB, is included in *DuR*, 49–50.

111. This section is dated 21 August in the original letter.
112. The original letter has "wie besiegt" (as if overcome).
113. The "careful hostess" is Johanna Berg.
114. This section is dated 22 August in the original letter.
115. The original letter has "Nachmittagsschläfchen" (afternoon nap). A further excerpt from this letter is included in *DuR*, 52.
116. "wird 'bei der Musik' bleiben können" (WAB:II, 40).
117. "Das Schicksal hat ein gewichtiges Wort dreinzureden" (WAB:II, 40).
118. "der ganze, bezwingende Zauber seiner durchgeistigten Jugend" (WAB:III, 2).
119. Berg's patronage came from Baroness Salzgeber, according to *DuR*, 53. 17 October was the date on which Berg received the decree of appointment; he started work the following day, 18 October. See Hilmar, *Alban Berg*, 28–30.
120. The original refers to "Feigenkaffeesud" (WAB:III, 5). *Feigenkaffee* can be either coffee substitute made from figs or ground coffee with fig essence added.
121. "Die Undurchsichtigkeit dieser Luft war, wenn man so sagen kann, in die Augen springend" (WAB:III, 5).
122. This and the following sentence are clearly intended to be heavily ironic in tone.
123. *Arnold Schönberg zum fünfzigsten Geburtstage, 13. September 1924*. *Musikblätter des Anbruch* 6 (August/September 1924) (special issue): 305. Quoted by permission of Universal Edition, Vienna.
124. In the original, "soundness" appears as "Zuverlässigkeit."
125. *Arnold Schönberg zum fünfzigsten Geburtstage*, 316–17. Josef Polnauer (1888–1969) was a pupil of Schoenberg and later of Berg. He was archivist of the Verein für musikalische Privataufführungen.
126. The wordplay in this quotation is impossible in English. Schoenberg's article "Probleme des Kunstunterrichts" was published in *Musikalisches Taschenbuch* (Vienna, 1911): 22–27. An English translation is in *Style and Idea: Selected Writings of Arnold Schoenberg*, ed. Leonard Stein (London: Faber & Faber, 1975), 365–69.
127. The period of two hundred years refers to J. S. Bach and possibly his son Carl Philipp Emanuel, who, in Polnauer's view, represented the last "Meisterlehrer" (master and teacher combined).
128. "Traum," to words by Frida Semler, was in fact his thirty-*third* song; it is published in *Alban Berg: Jugendlieder*, ed. Christopher Hailey, vol. 2 (Vienna: Universal Edition, 1987), 2–4.
129. In fact, it was Charly Berg who took some of Alban's songs to Schoenberg on the strength of an advertisement that Smaragda had noticed in the *Neue musikalische Presse*, 8 October 1904. As well as "Traum," some or all of the following songs were shown to Schoenberg: "Liebe," "Wandert ihr Wolken," "Im Morgengrauen," and "Grabschrift." See also Hilmar, *Alban Berg*, 32–33; *DuR*, 56. A facsimile of the ad can be found in Erich Alban Berg, ed., *Alban Berg: Leben und Werk in Daten und Bildern* (Frankfurt am Main: Insel Verlag, 1976; henceforth *Daten und Bilder*), 89.
130. Schoenberg's flat was at 68/70 Liechtensteinstrasse, in the 9th *Bezirk*, north of the Ringstrasse.
131. On 14 December 1904 by the Vienna Philharmonic in the Musikverein. This was the first performance in Vienna; the premiere had taken place in Krefeld on 9 June 1902.
132. "hervorgerufen" (WAB:III, 11); *DuR*, 56, has "vor den Vorhang gerufen" (called in front of the curtain), which seems to imply, erroneously, that the performance took place at the Hofoper.
133. According to Willi Reich, *The Life and Work of Alban Berg* (London: Thames and Hudson, 1965), 19, this incident occurred after the first Vienna performance of the Fourth Symphony on 12 January 1902.
134. For an illustration of the baton, see *Daten und Bilder*, 104.
135. The number of his compositions at this point was in fact thirty-six.

136. "Das Lied 'Furcht' und die Gesänge 'Augenblicke' und 'Die Näherin'" (WAB:III, 12). "Augenblicke" and "Die Näherin" are published in *Jugendlieder*, 2:5–6 and 7–8 respectively.

137. Published in *Jugendlieder*, 2:9–10 and 11–12 respectively.

138. Correctly "aus." This is the song "Er klagt, daß der Frühling so kortz blüht" (He laments that the spring blooms so briefly), which was Berg's most accomplished song up to that date. It is published in ibid., 2:13–15.

139. It has not been possible to identify which songs comprise Op. 18.

140. *Weidman* appears to be the correct spelling, not "Weidmann" as in WAB. For further information on the Weidmans see Hilmar, *Alban Berg*, 18–19. Josef Weidman had in fact died more recently, on 11 January 1905.

141. In F21 Berg 434 the words "u. Cognac" (and Cognac) have been added after "champagne" in red pencil, possibly by Berg.

142. The Villa Weidman, 6 Hietzinger Hauptstrasse, had been renovated in 1902 by the Slovene architect and designer Jože (Josef) Plečnik (1872–1957), one of Otto Wagner's pupils, who was to become famous for his work in Prague and Ljubljana (Laibach). He redesigned the attic story of the street frontage as well as overhauling the decor and furnishings of the interior. For illustrations see *Daten und Bilder*, 100–101; for further information, with illustrations, see Damjan Prelovšek, *Jože Plečnik, 1872–1957: Architectura Perennis*, trans. P. Crampton and E. Martin (New Haven and London: Yale University Press, 1997), 48–50, 64, 66.

143. Charlotte Wolter (1834–97), for over thirty years the most celebrated actress at the Burgtheater. According to *DuR*, 59, Weidman had a liaison with her. Katharina Schratt (1853–1940), popular actress at the Burgtheater from 1883 and close friend of Emperor Franz Joseph.

144. According to *DuR*, 59, his name was Mohammed Medlun.

145. "Die Nachtigall" is the song beginning "Die Nachtigallen schlafen," titled "Aus 'Pfingsten, ein Gedichtsreigen.'" "Am Strande" and "Winter" are published in *Jugendlieder*, 2:20–2 and 23 respectively; "Im Zimmer" was published as the fifth of the *Seven Early Songs*.

146. In fact, no. 6; it has been corrected in the margin (WAB:III, 20).

147. To Stefanie Leska.

148. Watznauer's new address was in the next apartment block to Sigmund Freud's home and doctor's office at 19 Berggasse.

149. This concert, in the Kleiner Musikvereinssaal and conducted by the composer, included the premieres of the *Kindertotenlieder*, the four Rückert songs for which Mahler wrote orchestral accompaniment, and four of the *Wunderhorn* songs including "Revelge" and "Der Tamboursg'sell."

150. This was the Viennese premiere, conducted by the composer in the Musikverein.

151. Her death occurred on 15 November 1905, not early in 1906.

152. This number has been changed in red pencil (by Berg?) to "7" in F21 Berg 434. However, Watznauer's information appears to have an element of truth: according to Hilmar, *Alban Berg*, 19–20, there were eight apartment blocks as well as the property in Hietzinger Hauptstrasse and a country property farther out, in Ober St. Veit; this makes ten houses in all.

153. "Fraue, du Süße" and "Verlassen" are published in *Jugendlieder*, 2:24–26 and 27–29 respectively. "Regen," "Traurigkeit," "Hoffnung," and "Flötenspielerin" are published in *Jugendlieder*, 2:30–34.

154. This was the property known as Stock im Weg, which was situated a couple of miles west of the Weidman villa. The vast Lainzer Tiergarten was the imperial hunting-ground. It is now a public park.

155. In F21 Berg 434, "jahrelang nicht" (not . . . for years) has been amended, possibly by Berg, to "nie" (never).

156. Watznauer had gotten to know Frau Hofmann, the widow of a wealthy Graz candle manufacturer, and her son Hans when recuperating from appendicitis at Kitzbühel in the summer of 1904. See Chadwick, "From *Freund Hein* to Hermann Hesse," 410–11.

157. The performance was conducted by Strauss himself.

158. *Grazer Tagespost*, 17 May 1906; reference in Alex Ross, *The Rest Is Noise* (London: Fourth Estate, 2008), 547.

159. "und so erwirkte man im Amte einen Krankenurlaub" (WAB:III, 28).

160. On 1 August Berg received his "Anstellungsdekret" (WAB:III, 28). As for the payment, Watznauer apparently misread Berg's annotation in his biographical questionnaire (Staatsbibliothek zu Berlin—Preußischer Kulturbesitz, N.Mus.ep.17) as "jährl. Adjutum 1.600 K" instead of "jährl. Adjutum v. 600 K" (annual interim payment of 600 crowns). A facsimile of the questionnaire appears in *DuR*, 152–53; the annotation in question is on p. 153. That 600 crowns is the correct sum is proved by the official letter of 11 October accepting Berg's resignation, which states that the annual *Adjutum* of 600 crowns will cease from 31 October and thus implies that his trainee status was unchanged. See Hilmar, *Alban Berg*, 31.

161. "Spaziergang," "Eure Weisheit," and "So regnet es sich langsam ein" are published in *Jugendlieder*, 2:35–40; "Liebesode" was published as the sixth of the *Seven Early Songs*.

162. The date is in Watznauer's hand in the original letter.

163. Henrik Ibsen, *John Gabriel Borkman*, Act 2.

164. Georg Brandes (1842–1927), Danish critic.

165. In Watznauer's text (WAB:III, 33), though not in the original letter, the passage from "two miners" to the end of the sentence is enclosed in quotation marks. In F21 Berg 434 the quotation marks enclose the whole sentence and are in red pencil.

166. "The last of the Buddenbrooks" refers to Hanno Buddenbrook. "Again" appears in square brackets in WAB and in the original letter. Quoted from Thomas Mann, *Buddenbrooks*, part 11, chap. 2 (my translation).

167. "Aber schon lang bin ich der Naturschönheit, der Naturwahrheit—und—Größe gewachsen" (WAB:III, 33). The inexplicable dash between "Naturwahrheit" and "und" is not in the original letter.

168. A quotation from *Meersymphonie*, a novella by the North German writer Otto Ernst (1862–1926). The original is as follows: "In der Kunst ist all das Erhabene und Schöne, das Gute und Weise, das ihr ersehnt, zur Wirklichkeit geworden. Nicht zu einer Wirklichkeit, die ihr abpflücken und in den Mund stecken, die ihr zählen und in die Tasche stecken könnt." In the original letter the name of the author was inserted later, probably by Watznauer.

169. In the German, "the original story of Nora" appears as "Die Urgeschichte der Nora" (WAB:III, 35). The original letter speaks of "the amount of the bill" as "der Betrag des Wechsels"; WAB:III, 36, says merely "der Wechsel" (the bill).

170. "Frau Wolf," rather than "Frau W . . ." appears in the original letter. At several points in Ibsen's play, Nora mentions a "miracle" that she expects to happen.

171. "Frau Borgfeldt," rather than "Frau B . . ." appears in the original letter.

172. "A death-defying leap" appears in the German as "ein Salto mortale" (WAB:III, 37).

173. *Wilhelms Meisters Lehrjahre*, book 2, chap. 4: "daß sie keine Heuchlerin ist. Ich liebe sie deswegen, ja ich bin ihr Freund, weil sie mir das Geschlecht so rein darstellt, [das ich zu hassen so viel Ursache habe]. Sie ist [mir] die wahre Eva, die Stammutter des weiblichen Geschlechts." The words within square brackets are omitted by both Berg and Watznauer without comment.

174. "few poets": in German, "Dichter" can mean either a poet or a writer of prose literature. "Poet" is retained here in order to maintain the comparison with "thinkers," even though Ibsen's most famous plays are in prose. "Poetry and Truth" is presumably a reference to Goethe's *Dichtung und Wahrheit*.

175. Foldal in *John Gabriel Borkman*, Act 2.

Notes to WATZNAUER'S BIOGRAPHY OF ALBAN BERG

176. Nora's husband, Torvald Helmer.

177. "Wenn es nicht ihre echte ist" (WAB:III, 39), literally, "if it isn't her real one."

178. Nora says this in Act 3 to her husband.

179. Charlotte von Stein (1742–1827) was chiefly known for her friendship with Goethe. Frau Hofmann was the widow Watznauer became acquainted with at Kitzbühel.

180. Nora expresses to Mrs. Linde a desire to utter an expletive in front of her husband, but cannot bring herself to do so.

181. Nora pulls rank on the servant by reminding her of Helmer's new title.

182. Not in the original letter.

183. *"Whispers quickly and breathlessly"* is Ibsen's stage direction (translator's italics).

184. The letter to Helmer in which he exposes Nora's fraud.

185. "When we dead awaken" is a reference to the title of Ibsen's last play.

186. This and the previous passage are from *Lady Inger of Östrât*, Act 3.

187. "Herman" in the original letter.

188. Presumably a quotation from a Watznauer letter, now lost, to which this is a reply.

189. According to Watznauer's earlier statement, Berg's appointment occurred on 1 August; 23 June is the date on which Alban started his sick leave.

A Descriptive Overview of Berg's *Night* (*Nocturne*)

INTRODUCTION BY REGINA BUSCH
TRANSLATED, EDITED, AND WITH COMMENTARY
BY CHRISTOPHER HAILEY

In 2001 a trove of hitherto unknown manuscripts came to light during renovations of the Viennese apartment house at Trauttmansdorffgasse 27 in which Alban Berg had lived. Tucked away among similarly bound scores of older printed music in Berg's study was a folder labeled "Liszt Piano Works" containing a file with manuscripts and printed scores by Berg and Schoenberg. These included drafts and sketches to Berg's piano vocal scores for Schoenberg's Gurrelieder, Pelleas und Melisande, op. 5, and Chamber Symphony, op. 9; *material relating to Berg's opera* Wozzeck, *Act 2, scene 2; a printed score of Schoenberg's Chamber Symphony, op. 9, heavily annotated by Berg; and, finally, the fragment of a play by Berg titled* Night (Nocturne).

In 2009 Berg's manuscript was published in color facsimile, with a full transcription, annotations, and an introduction by Regina Busch.[1] That introduction has been adapted and translated in consultation with the author. The principal changes involve combining three sections of the original article dealing with sources and dating into a single abridged section, "Sources and Dating," re-working the concluding discussion of musical references and sources, and shortening many of the endnotes (endnote abbreviations are indicated as such).

REGINA BUSCH

Alban Berg's Play *Night* (*Nocturne*)

When in October 1912 Arnold Schönberg asked Berg about his compositional projects, he had unusually specific suggestions: "Have you ever thought of writing something for the theater? I sometimes think you would be good at that! In any case it could be very stimulating for you. Just see that you don't take the *Dream Plays* away from me, for I'm considering them myself. But some other Strindberg work! I consider that very feasible!"[2] Berg was not entirely unprepared for the question and answered that after finishing the *Altenberg Lieder* he hoped to move right on to a stage project, "if only I had a suitable text." "I was already considering Strindberg's Chamber Plays," he continued, "and now that you suggest Strindberg that of course seems all the more compelling."[3]

Berg's response was more than a student's polite reply. Strindberg had long played a central role for the composers of Schönberg's circle. In his book *Das Grab in Wien*, Paul Stefan recounted an episode in which Mahler, at a restaurant with Schönberg and his pupils, spoke in glowing terms about Dostoevsky:

> But it was apparent that he was not really being understood because only a few knew Dostoevsky's books in any detail. And so he said: "You must change that, Schönberg! Have these people read Dostoevsky. That is more important than counterpoint!" Silence. Then someone said: "We have Strindberg." Laughing, we had to concede.[4]

In 1912 this enthusiasm for Strindberg had, if anything, intensified, though another preoccupation was Balzac.[5] Both authors were on Berg's mind when, several months before his exchange with Schönberg, he wrote to Webern on 29 July 1912 about future projects: "And then in Vienna something grand, to which I feel a great urge."[6] In this same letter Berg was brimming with enthusiasm about Strindberg's affinity for music, which stimulated him on many levels, as well as Schönberg's plan for setting Balzac's *Seraphita*:

> Your letter [. . .] moved me very deeply: specifically the news of Schönberg's work on a theater piece based on *Seraphita*. That is fantastic! Surely with music?! God! What we can all expect from that!! Just thinking about this plot gives me goose pimples. Not to mention with music by Schönberg—in three evenings!!! – – –
> Schönberg also told me —about 1½ years ago —that is, spring, 1911, about his idea of somehow making *musical* use of "Jakob ringt" (*Jacob*

Wrestles). Back then he wanted to write Strindberg at length, even had the idea of asking Strindberg for a "text." It would have been wonderful, if Schönberg had written—and Strindberg had answered. You once said that Strindberg would certainly have loved Mahler's music. Anyway, he had such an affinity for music. I just read 2 dramas: "Vor höherer Instanz" (*At a Higher Court*) (around 1900) I. Advent (which has now been incorporated into the Jahresfestspiele with *Easter* and *Midsummer*) and II. Rausch (Intoxication), that Müller has just published in a single volume together with *Totentanz* (*Dance of Death*). Naturally, these are incredible works, the first one has an especially supernatural grandeur.

Now, in both plays there are 2 places that call for music. At the reconciliatory conclusion of Advent (in a gorge surrounded by high mountains): "The scene is full of shadows, that all look up toward the mountains in the background."[7]

Singing in the background with 2 sopranos and an alto, accompanied only by string instruments and a harp.

Then Latin text
After which chorus of soprano, alto, tenor and bass
Again text
Then the appearance of Christ in the manger, adored by 3 kings and shepherds, and again chorus, trio of 2 sopranos and an alto.

Gloria in excelsis Deo
Et in terra pax Hominibus bonae voluntatis

Isn't that fabulous: 2 sopranos and an alto, string instruments and harp!

But in the 2nd play! It is in a scene at the beginning of an adulterous relationship between the protagonist of the play (who left his lover and child) with the lover of his friend.

"During this reply someone in the next room begins to play the finale of Beethoven's D-minor sonata (op. 31, no. 2). The Allegretto at first *piano*, then ever louder, passionate, excited, finally wild. — — —

Throughout the entire (long) scene the pianist in the next room has been practicing the D-minor sonata, sometimes *pp*, sometimes *ff*; now and then there is silence; sometimes one only hears bars 96–107 in the finale."

I can't remember the finale, dear friend, don't have it here; perhaps you'd be so kind and write out the melody of the first bar and what is happening in bar 96. I am keenly interested in Strindberg's relationship to Beethoven's music!

> But to return to Balzac! I'll read *Seraphita* here once again, I brought it along. Just think: this winter I wanted to write a long symphonic movement toward the end of which I wanted to include a boy soprano singing (from above) words from—*Seraphita*. Naturally—as so often with me—it never got beyond the planning stage. But now I'm all the more happy—thrilled with Schönberg's undertaking.

Although Berg never set any Strindberg to music, he left us the fragment of a stage work of his own, titled *Night (Nocturne)*, for which he intended also to compose music. He gathered together his notes for this work, arranged them according to a preliminary plan, and brought them into typewritten form. Inserted in this typescript are a few small handwritten notebook pages with scattered ideas that he was unable or chose not to develop. Autograph entries on the typescript show that Berg submitted the text to at least one more revision before laying it to rest.

The folder for *Night (Nocturne)* contains a sheet, one side of which has a Preliminary Plan with notes for a Prologue, four parts (or acts?) numbered I to IV, and an Epilogue. On the other side of the sheet are Notes for the Monodrama that pertain to Parts I to III, including some detailed descriptions of musical situations (with musical examples). Finally, there are 24 pages containing the actual text of the work, written out in the form of a libretto.

The text of Part I extends to page 11. Since Part II begins with page 50, Part III with 100, and Part IV with 150, one can assume that Berg anticipated a far larger work than is suggested by the existing text. Indeed, even Part I with its 11 written pages is still not complete. Parts II, III, and IV have respectively six, four, and two numbered pages, and even here several of the verso sides are blank.

At the end of the folder there is one further unnumbered page with the heading *Diverses* (Various), containing notes regarding the musical setting of two text passages: "All the strings are out of tune within me" and "A string has snapped within me."

Inserted into the typescript are pages torn out of a small notebook of the kind Berg had been using since around 1911 for jotting down lists, letter drafts, and various ideas.

Sources and Dating

Night (Nocturne) can be dated between the end of 1915 and the middle of 1917. The typewritten page labeled Preliminary Plan (recto) and Notes for the Monodrama (verso) are dated by hand "Winter 1915/16," but the

Figure 1. Berg in uniform, 1915.

main body of the play, which is written on stationery with a typewriter from Berg's office in the Austrian Ministry of War, is no doubt later. Berg joined the Ministry of War only on 15 May 1916 and there are references in the play to works Karl Kraus first published in November 1916 and January 1917. Moreover, there are notes relating to the play in two partial notebooks housed in the Berg Fonds of the Music Collection of the Austrian National Library and these notebooks—F21 Berg 479/23 and F21 Berg 479/11—can be dated between January and May 1917. Indeed, it is likely the notebook pages found inserted in the typescript were torn out of one of these two notebooks.[8] Finally, Berg drew central ideas and quotations from Dostoevsky's novel, *Der Jüngling* (*A Raw Youth* or *The Adolescent*), a loaned copy of which he was reading in November 1916. Shortly thereafter he received "several Dostoevskys I did not have" as a Christmas present from his wife.[9] It is possible *Der Jüngling* was among them. In any event, there is a copy in Berg's library in which the passages cited and quoted in *Night (Nocturne)* are carefully marked or underlined.[10]

Arrangement, Structure and Nature of the Text

In many respects the play *Night (Nocturne)* remains incomplete. We have a rough formal outline that governed Berg's notes and remained unchanged over the course of his work, but we know little about the individual parts. It is clear he planned a prologue and epilogue, but whether the Parts I through IV, which make up the core of the actual drama, were intended as scenes (with transitions), acts, individual movements, or connected sections of a continuous dramatic work can only be determined through more detailed study. In his sketches Berg occasionally writes of "Scene 1" and "the next scene (in the lane?)," but this sounds more like a scene change within a section.[11]

The keywords in the Preliminary Plan and the Notes for the Monodrama characterize situations and moods, describe stage props and scenic details, background noises, and lighting changes. These are scattered, still undeveloped notions, ideas, and themes. They are linked to the content of each of the four individual sections, but their relationship to the work as a whole remains entirely unclear. There are also references to characters, described as HE and THE OTHER, usually written in uppercase. A few especially important concepts are likewise emphasized through capital letters, for example, DREAM or MOUNTAIN TREK. In the course of the play it becomes evident that these concepts apply to entire sections, central scenes, or important situations and themes. Among these CRY (also Dream-CRY) plays a special role; it returns repeatedly as CRY of the Night and seems to be a central reference point for the events of the play; at one point there is even an Address to the Cry of the Night (Typescript page 3).

Berg articulates his text using underlining, uppercase, spaced-out, and red lettering, as well as indentation, varied spacing between lines and blocks of text, graphic symbols, and a few carefully written annotations. The unnumbered pages of the Preliminary Plan and Notes for the Monodrama do not look like the pages comprising the main body of the work, which look more like a libretto in which the individual roles are typed in red in the left margin and the text and stage directions, written in black, are indented on the right.[12] However, this changes over the course of the play. On the left one occasionally finds THE OTHER or "Voices from the Library" written in red, but most of the text is probably assigned to the figure described as HE, though he is never named as a character. Instead, from the very beginning of the drama, there are concepts in the left margin such as BEGINNING, PEACE, Sacrifice, or ARROGANCE, GOD, One's own Peace!, Inhibition, as well as indications regarding the ordering of the text, like Earlier? which are not used with any consistency, either within a particular scene or the work as a whole. Rather, it appears that every new section of text represents a change of perspective and that these concepts apparently serve as keywords for reference and reflection. Perhaps these are *inner* voices added to the external impulses that come from the Voices from the Library, the "Voices from the Books that gaze down on me" (Typescript page 3).

There are about four pages in which only HE and THE OTHER speak (or sing?). Their texts are probably by Berg himself, or—since it may not be possible to distinguish clearly between internal and external voices—reflect the voices of other authors that Berg puts into his own words. For instance, in one of the undeveloped passages involving a dialogue between HE and THE OTHER Berg writes: "Thoughts similar to those Kraus explores in the poem 'Mythology'" (Typescript page 2).[13]

The first real voice from the library is "Dostoevsky: *Der Jüngling*, volume 2, page 32" (Typescript page 5); there then follow Lichtenberg, Rosegger, Strindberg, and Karl Kraus. Berg writes the utterances of these (and other) voices into the text in the form of text incipits, abbreviated titles, or sources and page references. In many instances the entire quotation is inserted into the text and treated as a part of the monologue or dialogue. In the course of Part I the passages formulated by Berg become increasingly less frequent, giving the impression that the text was to have become a series of quotations. But this could be a mistaken assumption. Many pages and parts of pages are left blank, which, together with the layout of the drama, suggests that the "Voices from the Books" were to have been equal interlocutors with Berg's own thoughts.

Parts II and III contain little more than keywords similar to those found on the first two unnumbered pages of the typescript. Only in the final section, with the heading CINEMA IV, is there greater detail in which Berg describes both the scenic setting and the three stages of the Mountain Trek, as well as the concluding dawn, which serves as a pendant to the beginning of *Night (Nocturne)*.

Monodrama, Dream Sequences

On the second page of his notes Berg referred to his play as a monodrama.[14] Several internal and external voices (He, The Other, the Voices from the Library) engage in conversation or are in conflict within the drama, but there is only one person on stage: "HE reads," and later, reads aloud, closes the book, drinks, falls asleep, dreams. The required stage props are "divan (in front of which is a small table with nightlight, books, bottle with a cup-like glass (?) / in the background stage right the large window. The entire left and middle walls are covered by a huge shelf of books" (Typescript page 3).[15] This is all only "indistinctly" visible. All action and movements happen in a state of dreaming, sleeping, memory, intoxication, or hallucination (alcohol scene; silently scurrying phantoms)—all at night—or on a film screen. The play begins at night and ends with the morning dawn. The basic atmosphere is gloom, darkness, blackness; making light is an important and significant action.[16] The Noises of the Night come from the distance, their source is difficult to establish ("somewhere a door slams"), and when, at the end, in the dawning light, a wide surface finally "reveals" itself to be a window through which one sees "no other image than the sky that appears as a pale gray surface." Before this the window was a film screen on which one could see the mountain trek. Thus, according to Berg's plan, the trek would take place not as stage action but as a projection (*Licht-Spiel*). It is part of the remarkable series of scenic transformations that begin with a "completely darkened rear wall" and a "forest devoid of light or contour" and reaches a climax with another contour-less state, this time in the form of broad, white surfaces in which "snow and sky become one."

As in other expressionistic stage works of this period, including those cited in Berg's sketch, the protagonists, designated only with He and The Other, are not given names, but stripped, as it were, of all personal and individual characteristics.[17] Berg's He is in a certain sense a mirror and counterpart of the Woman in Schönberg's monodrama *Erwartung*.[18] She too has no name, but it is her personal drama that we see on the stage. Her thoughts focus on a male counterpart to whom she speaks without receiving any reply. Berg's He, on the other hand, has a male alter ego with whom he discusses and argues; female figures are present only through the narratives in the Voices from the Library, not as active players.

Both monodramas take place at night and end at dawn. The Woman in *Erwartung*, like Berg's He, is helplessly at the mercy of her thoughts, memories, and fantasies, to which she abandons herself in longing. She wanders in the nocturnal forest, later approaches a house with dark, closed shutters, but keeps her distance and remains outside. Berg's He, by contrast, remains enclosed within the internal world of his room. Movement through time and space takes place only in his thoughts, memories and fantasies, not in reality (he remains *seated* on the stage). The mountain trek at the end—and it is not clear whether it is He who undertakes it—is in any event not real but only on film. The only way out is the view through the window toward the outside world, which is not entered, but is nonetheless visible as a portion of the sky.

Another influence and inspiration from Berg's circle may have been Schönberg's *Glückliche Hand*, whose text with its detailed prescriptions for staging, sets, costumes, and lighting effects was published in June 1911. In scene 2 of the *Glückliche Hand*, for instance, one sees "a soft blue, skylike backdrop. Close to the earth a space, through which yellow glaring sunlight spreads over the stage."[19] The side walls are formed by use of fabric. This set remains fixed until the next scene change. The scene changes take place not with fabric, but with light: "It grows quite dark and immediately thereafter light."[20] Such abrupt scene changes by means of lighting can be traced back to film techniques, especially the crosscut.[21] Beyond that, owing to the small number of spoken, or sung words in relation to the extensive instructions for action, mime, costume, lighting, etc., *Glückliche Hand* has been described as belonging to the "film-related dramas of transformation" (Horst Denkler) in which, following the example of cinematography, "word and sound are integrated with or subservient to the image."[22] However, the addition of music substantially alters the relative balance between word and picture.

Cinema (Excursus)

As we now know, Berg not only regularly attended theater and opera performances but was a frequent patron of the cinema as well. According to his accounts of petty expenses preserved in his papers in the Austrian National Library, he went either alone or with one other person, presumably his wife, Helene, or together with friends and relatives. Moreover, his correspondence with his wife, with Schönberg, and with Webern contains repeated references to his visits to the cinema and specific film titles. In addition, in those newspapers and periodicals Berg is known to have read or subscribed to, prominent authors—even before the First World War—discussed particular films, commented on general film-related matters, including music in silent films, or answered topical questionnaires. Berg knew many of these authors, read their writings, saw their plays in theaters, or set their poems, and they included Peter Altenberg, Ferdinand Avenarius, Franz Blei, Max Brod, Hans Heinz Ewers, Alexander Girardi, Alfred Kerr, Alfred Polgar, Peter Rosegger, Paul Stefan, Otto Stoessl, Ludwig Thoma, Berthold Viertel, Robert Walser, Frank Wedekind, Paul Wegener, and Arnold Zweig.[23]

Berg was certainly aware from his own experience that since the advent of electric light theater productions had begun to incorporate light and shadow, floodlights, static or mobile spotlight beams, as well as colored light. Even on the opera stage there were manifold opportunities for light projection.[24] It is no great leap from here to the use of "moving pictures." In fact, from the very beginning there were links between expressionistic film and drama, including, among other things, "inserting film both as a component of scenic design and as an extension of dramatic action."[25] Most examples, however, date from the period after the First World War.[26] Grigori Kosinzev and Leonid S. Trauberg, for instance, used excerpts from Chaplin films for a production of Gogol's *Marriage* in 1920, and Sergei Eisenstein made his first film, *Glumov's Diary* (1923), for a staging of Alexander Ostrovsky's *Even Wise Men Err, or The Diary of a Scoundrel*.[27] A part of Friedrich Kiesler's stage set for the Berlin and Viennese first performance of Karel Capeks *W.U.R.* (likewise 1923) consisted of films projected with a large iris diaphragm.[28] In Yvan Goll's *Methusalem, or the Eternal Bourgeois* (written 1918/19, German translation 1922) the shoe factory owner Mathusalem sits in his armchair, sleeps and dreams. "We see his dreams flit by as a film on a screen affixed to the window."[29] Max Brod described a similar situation in his contribution to the *Kinobuch* published by Kurt Pinthus in 1913: "There is still another, as yet little exploited technical possibility in which the cinema can be used to project the eerie realism of mere fantasies. Thus it would be possible, if anyone chose to do so, to give a cinematographic depiction of the 'poet at work.' His inspirations arise from the furniture or from the desktop blotting paper, at which he stares in contemplation."[30]

To date, however, there is no indication that Berg (or anyone in his circle) knew this book or the films and plays in question. The topos of falling into a dream state during work or reading can be found elsewhere, for instance, as mentioned above, with Poe. We do not know if Berg was aware of a cinematic precedent for this device when he conceived his own film scene.[31] He could have encountered the association of a window with a film screen—"window on the world"—in contemporary cinema architecture, in which the interior design of many film theaters or auditoriums sought to integrate the projection surface into an actual set design representing, for instance, a veranda door, the window of a house, or a garden structure with naturalistic props.[32] The general tendency toward bringing film closer to theater included extending films to full evening length, recruiting well-known stage actors, or making film-going a festive event similar to an evening at the theater. Moreover, there were countless discussions about film's potential as art, its relationship to the drama, the novel, the epic narrative, or its potential as a medium of factual reportage or documentation.

The first attempts to integrate film into theater and opera productions in the German-speaking world took place as early as 1910, though such experiments were not immediately developed, due to numerous technical difficulties.[33] Berg could very well have read about the 1911 Berlin production of *The Magic Flute* by Georg Graf von Hülsen with its "cinematographic picture" of a waterfall filmed in Switzerland or Hülsen's 1912 production of *Das Rheingold* with its depiction of the gods striding across a rainbow. These productions were widely discussed in numerous articles in specialist journals and newspapers, including Vienna's *Neue Freie Presse*.[34] It is also possible that he could have heard about the Mozart production from Schönberg, then living in Berlin, or Webern, who, on a visit there in May 1911, reported to Heinrich Jalowetz that he was thinking about "looking at this *Magic Flute*."[35]

As a regular patron of the cinema and theater Berg would have been familiar with the practice, typical of the early film era, of presenting dramatic and documentary films as part of a *varieté*-like mixed program. It also became evident that film had upset and transformed the relationship between illusion and reality, as when film actors, as part of the performance, would appear on the stage, or props from the film were integrated into the stage décor.[36] Film, which Robert Walser called "a picture book full of indescribable life," lay claim to its own representation of "actuality," of "reality."[37] But it was a very special kind of reality. "Only in dreams and in cinematic imagination is there a reality without dross," wrote Alfred Polgar in 1911.[38] A new kind of truth was attributed to film. "The natural truth of cinema," Georg Lukács observed in 1913, "is not bound to our reality."[39] Berg's *Night (Nocturne)* raises the question whether the "mountain trek," which is seen only as a film, is to be understood as a part of stage reality or a further variation upon the imaginary dream sequence.

In the fall of 1913 Schönberg alluded to the very same problem in a letter to his publisher Emil Hertzka, in which he mused about a possible film version of *Die glückliche Hand*:

> The basic unreality of the events, which is inherent in the text, is something that they should be able to bring out even better in the filming. [...] My foremost wish is therefore for something the opposite of what the cinema generally aspires to. I want: *The utmost unreality!*
> The whole thing should have the effect (not of a dream) but of chords. Of music. It must never suggest symbols, or meaning, or thoughts, but simply the play of colors and forms. Just as music never drags a meaning around with it, at least not in the form in which it [music] manifests itself, even though meaning is inherent in its nature, so too this should simply be like sounds for the eye, and so far as I am concerned everyone is free to think or feel something similar to what he thinks or feels while hearing music.[40]

Berg may very well have known about these plans and perhaps even the concrete proposals Schönberg presented to his publisher.[41] Nonetheless, Berg's idea of incorporating a filmed presentation of a mountain trek into the stage action at the conclusion of his monodrama is fundamentally different from filming an entire work performed in a theater or studio as Schönberg imagined for *Die glückliche Hand*, as was common practice in operatic films of the era.

It is not clear from the draft of *Night (Nocturne)* whether Berg merely intended to use film in the final cinema section of his play or whether he might have also used it to realize the dreams, memories, drunken fantasies, and related transitions in Parts II and III. Dream sequences and imagery are a central component of expressionistic drama, whose staging frequently incorporated techniques borrowed from film, including crossfade, flashback, etc.[42] The addition of music brings additional, particularly effective means for evoking and depicting dream imagery. In Part III of *Night (Nocturne)* Berg does not simply call for and describe musical means for the "Transition from Memories to Dreams" but stages the entrance—the appearance—of music: "The piano on the left begins to play on its own [...] (perhaps piano offstage)" (Typescript page 100).[43]

At a time when Berg, following Schönberg's compositional advice, was preoccupied with the idea of musical character, he appears to have been interested in fundamental technical questions concerning moving images. In his copy of Strindberg's *New Blue Book* (*Neues Blaubuch*, trans. 1908) he carefully underlined a passage in a section on character delineation:

How many frames does a cinematographer need to film in order to achieve a single movement, and yet the picture still flutters. With every vibration there is a missing link. If a thousand individual frames are necessary to capture the movement of an arm, how many more thousand frames are necessary to describe the movement of a soul. A poet's depiction of people therefore consists of just such a series of abbreviations, contours which are all incomplete and half false.

A true depiction of character is for that reason difficult, nearly impossible; and no one would believe it if one tried to make it entirely accurate. One can only intimate.[44]

Berg's Musical Ideas and Their Sources

In Part I and at the conclusion of the work, two of Strindberg's Chamber Plays, *The Ghost Sonata* and *The Burned House*, are represented with extended quotations, and in the mountain trek, which accounts for almost the whole of Part IV, Balzac's *Seraphita* has left obvious traces. As seen in his letter to Webern above, when Berg first thought of setting to music something from this novel, he had in mind a long symphonic movement, "toward the end of which I wanted to include a boy soprano singing (from above) words from—*Seraphita*." The boy's voice remained and at the very end of the work, following the mountain trek, it was intended to be heard speaking or singing from above: "Oh sweet dreamless sleep (last words) or something similar from Strindberg (or perhaps as if from the top of the bookcase)" (Typescript page 150).

In addition to processing outside impulses into his fragment, Berg also incorporated older compositions that meant something to him. In Part II he intended to include two of his *Altenberg Lieder,* op. 4 (nos. 2 and 4)—or perhaps new settings of the relevant texts?—which he refers to here as "Song in Praise of Rain" and "Song in Praise of Woman." In Part III at the cues "Memory" and "Reminiscences" a piano "perhaps offstage" begins to play on its own "a sonata beginning (D-minor syncopations) and the other." We do not know to which sonata "the other" refers, but the one with D-minor syncopations is probably the fragmentary Sonata IV which, as is well known, provided the basis for the music for the transition between scenes 4 and 5 in Act 3 of *Wozzeck* (bars 320ff.).[45] The first reference to Sonata IV at the transition to Part III is found at the bottom of Typescript page 7. Here Berg adds musical notation: the syncopated accompanying figure in the right hand (in octave transposition) from the first four bars of the sonata (though beginning with an eighth note).

Another idea that appears in *Night (Nocturne)* and was also incorporated into *Wozzeck* is the musical representation of snoring. In his Notes for the Monodrama Berg planned to replicate "snoring, recalling the nights on watch" either in the prologue or Part I, though it is at present impossible to determine whether Berg first conceived the snoring scene for *Night (Nocturne)* or *Wozzeck*. On the same page Berg makes a reference to his military service in Bruck an der Leitha in the remark "Instead of cry, better the horn motive from Bruck."[46]

As a musical dramatic work *Night (Nocturne)* would largely have been shaped by its musical setting. Unfortunately, aside from the few scattered musical examples in the typescript, no other sketches or musical annotations have been found. It is possible, though unlikely, that there are sketches among the *Wozzeck* sources that have heretofore been regarded as material that was rejected or not clearly related to *Wozzeck* that were intended for this work.[47] Nonetheless, *Night (Nocturne)* contains many verbal descriptions of music intended for specific situations and functions, as well as details for the incorporation of various sounds and noises.[48]

NOTES TO THE INTRODUCTION

Notes that have been shortened are so indicated.

1. "Alban Bergs Bühnenstück 'Nacht (Nokturn),'" in *Alban Berg Studien: Rudolf Stephan zum 80. Geburtstag*, ed. Regina Busch and Klaus Lippe (Vienna: Universal Edition, 2008), Publications of the Alban Berg Foundation, vol. 6, 96–208. Appended to the facsimile of Berg's manuscript are three appendixes comparing the draft and clean-copy versions of the play; transcriptions of the notebook pages inserted into the typescript; and an overview of Berg's notebooks, day calendars, and address books between 1913 and 1917.

2. Letter of 3 October 1912, *The Berg-Schoenberg Correspondence: Selected Letters*, ed. Juliane Brand, Christopher Hailey, and Donald Harris (New York and London: W. W. Norton, 1987), 116.

3. Letter of 6–7 October 1912, *The Berg-Schoenberg Correspondence*, 118.

4. Paul Stefan, *Das Grab in Wien: Eine Chronik. 1903–1911* (Berlin: Erich Reiss Verlag, 1913), 130. In his copy of Stefan's book, Berg marked this passage, underlining the "we" several times. It was Berg who later identified Webern as the one who spoke up; see Willi Reich, *Alban Berg* (London: Thames and Hudson, 1965), 31. Paul Stefan mistakenly dated the anecdote from 1910. *(Abbreviated)*

5. It should be noted that Strindberg and Balzac shared an interest in Swedenborg, another writer dear to the Schönberg circle.

6. Letter of 29 July 1912, Wien Bibliothek, Autograph Collection, H.I.N. 185.570. My thanks to Simone Hohmaier (Berlin) for making available materials from the edition of the Webern-Berg correspondence that she is preparing in collaboration with Rudolf Stephan (*Briefwechsel der Wiener Schule*, vol. 4).

7. Here and in the other citations in this extract Berg was probably quoting from the copy of Strindberg's *Vor höherer Instanz: Zwei Dramen* (Dresden/Leipzig: E. Pierson's Verlag, 1899) which is in his library.

8. These two notebooks are part of a larger collection of fifty-eight small, thin notebooks (F21 Berg 479/1–58) that Berg began carrying with him around 1911 to jot down everything from shopping lists and appointments to letter drafts and text ideas. For more information, see Busch, "Alban Bergs Bühnenstück 'Nacht (Nokturn),'" especially the discussion, "Weitere Quellen zu 'Nacht (Nokturn),'" 101.

9. Berg reported the gift of the Dostoevsky volumes in a card to Paul Hohenberg on 26 January 1917 (Library of Performing Arts, New York Public Library, card 64).

10. The copy in Berg's library is Fjodor M. Dostojewski, *Der Jüngling*, trans. E. K. Rahsin (München: R. Piper & Co., 1915).

11. See the notebook in the Berg Fonds, F21 Berg 479/23, folio 9, which corresponds to Typescript page 150 at the words "but not like the beginning," or the inserted notebook, page E3.

12. In such matters, including the way protagonists or scenery are named or listed, Berg may have been influenced by contemporary editions of plays such as those by Strindberg.

13. This page contains the longest handwritten addendum in the entire typescript.

14. For this section and the following discussion on cinema I am grateful to the following for assistance in my research: Klaus Busch, Helmut Lethen, Reinhard Kapp, Günter Krenn, Therese Muxeneder, and Nikolaus Urbanek (Vienna), Horst Denkler (Berlin), Dieter Hertel and Moritz Busch (Bonn), Martin Loiperdinger (Trier), Franziska Sick (Kassel), Jürg Stenzl (Salzburg), and Thomas Steiert (Bayreuth).

15. The scenario in which HE sits alone in his room at night lost in his dreams and hallucinations amid "voices from books [. . .] that gaze down upon me" (T3) is reminiscent of the scenario of Edgar Allan Poe's "The Raven." For Christmas 1916 Berg gave Schönberg a six-volume German edition of Poe's works (*Edgar Poes Werke*, trans. Hedda Moeller-Bruck and Hedwig Lachmann; Minden: Bruns Verlag, 1911–1914), an edition that Berg had in his library. In volume 1 of that edition Berg marked the beginning of "Der Rabe" (The Raven) on pp. 151–58, as well as several passages relating to "The Raven" in John H. Ingram's introductory essay on Poe's life. *(Abbreviated)*

16. Nightlights are a frequent topic in Berg's correspondence with his wife, who had a tendency toward sleepwalking or suddenly springing out of bed, which on several occasions led to serious injuries. For Berg himself, who sometimes suffered from insomnia, a nightlight was a necessary reading aid. There might also be a connection to the first Viennese cabaret, Nachtlicht, which opened in 1906. *(Abbreviated)*

17. See, for instance, the *dramatis personae* in Schönberg's *Erwartung* and *Die glückliche Hand*, as well as in Webern's play *Tot* (Dead) from 1913. *(Abbreviated)*

18. While these two characters are not exact parallels, they are nonetheless complementary. The female protagonist in *Erwartung* is actually more like Wozzeck than the "He" in Berg's *Night (Nocturne)*. One might say that Berg had good reason not to use "monodrama" in his title.

19. Schönberg, *Die glückliche Hand, Drama mit Musik*, in *Der Merker* 2/17 (June 1911): 718. In later printings Schönberg slightly modified these directions to read: "Below, to the left, close to the bright brown earth, a circular space 1½ meters in diameter [. . .]." See Arnold Schönberg, *Die glückliche Hand* (Vienna: Universal Edition, July 1917), 5.

20. Schönberg, *Die glückliche Hand, Der Merker*, 719, 721, and similarly, 718.

21. See Karl Sierek, "Die unterirdischen Kanäle: Zur Beziehung zwischen Musik, Malerei und Film," in the catalogue edited by Stefan Gyöngyösi, *Art of Vision. Zeitfluß 93 Filmfestival* (Salzburg: Kulturverein Zeitfluß, 1993), 88–97. *(Abbreviated)*

Notes to the Introduction to BERG'S NIGHT (NOCTURNE)

22. See Siegfried Mauser, *Das expressionistische Musiktheater der Wiener Schule: Stilkritische und entwicklungsgeschichtliche Untersuchungen zu Arnold Schönbergs "Erwartung" op. 17, "Die glückliche Hand" op. 18 und Alban Bergs "Wozzeck" op. 7*, in Schriftenreihe der Hochschule für Musik, vol. 3 (Regensburg: Gustav Bosse Verlag, 1983), 29. See also Horst Denkler, *Drama des Expressionismus* (Munich: Wilhelm Fink, 1967), specifically chap. 4, "Filmverwandte Wandlungsdramen," 108–36, 110.

23. See the texts and bibliographies collected in Fritz Güttinger, ed., *Kein Tag ohne Kino: Schriftsteller über den Stummfilm* (Frankfurt am Main: Deutsches Filmmuseum Frankfurt, 1984); and Fritz Güttinger, *Der Stummfilm im Zitat der Zeit* (Frankfurt am Main: Deutsches Filmmuseum Frankfurt, 1982), 174. *(Abbreviated)*

24. See Friedrich Kranich, *Bühnentechnik der Gegenwart*, 2 vols (Munich/Berlin: R. Oldenbourg, 1929; 1932). *(Abbreviated)*

25. Nora Eckert, *Das Bühnenbild im 20. Jahrhundert* (Berlin: Henschel, 1998). See the chapter "Theaterdekorationen für den Film," 102–05, 103, as well as the excursus on stage lighting, 106–13.

26. The relevant work by Erwin Piscator, Max Reinhardt, or Ludwig Hörth all date from this period. *(Abbreviated)*

27. See Evgenij Margolit, "Der sowjetische Stummfilm und der frühe Tonfilm," in *Geschichte des sowjetischen und russischen Films*, ed. Christine Engel, with Eva Binder, Oksana Bulgakov, Evgenij Margolit, and Miroslava Segia (Stuttgart/Weimar: Metzler, 1999), 22.

28. See Barbara Lesák, *Die Kulisse explodiert: Friedrich Kieslers Theaterexperimente und Architekturprojekte 1923–1925* (Vienna: Löcker, 1988), 70ff., as well as the illustrations on 77 and 79.

29. Yvan Goll, *Methusalem oder der ewige Bürger: Ein satirisches Drama* (Berlin: Gustav Kiepenheuer Bühnenvertriebs-G.m.b.H., 1961), 4; Franziska Sick, "Yvan Golls surreales Filmtheater," in *Französische Theaterfilme—zwischen Surrealismus und Existentialismus*, vol. 5 of *Medienumbrüche*, ed. Michal Lommel, Isabel Maurer Queipo, Nanette Rißler-Pipka and Volker Roloff, (Bielefeld, transcript, 2004), 39–64; 41, 49–51. *(Abbreviated)*

30. Max Brod, "Ein Tag aus dem Leben Kühnebecks, des jungen Idealisten," in *Das Kinobuch*, ed. Kurt Pinthus (Leipzig: Kurt Wolff, 1914; rev. ed. with introduction by Kurt Pinthus, Zürich: Arche, 1963), 71–75. In his 1909 article "Kinematographentheater," Brod had already proposed the "poet in his study" as a film subject (*Die neue Rundschau* 1/12 [1909]: 319–20, repr. in *Über die Schönheit häßlicher Bilder* [Leipzig: Kurt Wolff, 1913]); see Güttinger, *Kein Tag ohne Kino*, 34.

31. We do not know if Berg was aware of Franz Blei's one-act play *Der Film*, in which stage action concerns the filming of a film, with a staged murder that then actually takes place. The resulting film, however, is not shown on stage. See Medardus (Franz Blei), Prokop (Max Brod), and Sylvester (Erik-Ernst Schwabach), *Das Zaubertheater*, with an introduction by Franz Blei (Leipzig: Kurt Wolff, 1915), 13–29. *(Abbreviated)*

32. See William Paul, "Unheimliches Theater: Die Leinwand als Bühne," in *KINtop 8: Film und Projektionskunst* (Frankfurt am Main/Basel: Stroemfeld, 1999), 117–39. *(Abbreviated)*

33. See, for instance, Kranich, *Bühnentechnik der Gegenwart*, vol. 2, 132ff.; Mildenberger, *Film und Projektion auf der Bühne*, 76ff.; and Dieter Herber, "Die Entwicklung der Bühnentechnik im deutschsprachigen Theater von Ende des neunzehnten bis zur Mitte des zwanzigstens Jahrhunderts und ihr Zusammenhang mit den modernen Inszenierungsformen" (PhD diss., University of Vienna, 1976), 222ff.

34. Regarding *The Magic Flute* see reports by Georg Schünemann, *Neue Musikzeitung* 65/4 (1911); and in *Neue Freie Presse* (21 February 1911). Regarding *Rheingold*, there were newspapers accounts in Berlin, Essen, Leipzig, Mannheim from 1912 (13, 15, 17, and 18 December), and New York on 6 June 1913, as well as by Paul Schwers, *Allgemeine Musikzeitung* (20 December 1912). *(Abbreviated)*

Notes to the Introduction to BERG'S NIGHT (NOCTURNE)

35. Webern to Jalowetz, 15 May 1911, in *Anton Webern: Briefe an Heinrich Jalowetz*, ed. Ernst Lichtenhahn (Mainz: Schott, 1999), 149.

36. Musicians accompanying film might, for instance, receive a light cue from the film itself, perhaps hidden in the scenery. See Michael Wedel, *Der deutsche Musikfilm: Archäologie eines Genres 1914–1945* (Munich: edition text + kritik, 2007), 119; illustration, 200.

37. See Robert Walser, "Die leichte Hochachtung," in *Berliner Tageblatt* (12 November 1927), quoted in Güttinger, *Der Stummfilm im Zitat der Zeit*, 66, 40; Alfred Polgar, "Das Drama im Kinematographen," in *Der Sturm* 1/2 (May 1911), quoted in Güttinger, *Kein Tag ohne Kino*, 60.

38. Polgar, "Das Drama im Kinematographen," in *Der Sturm*.

39. Georg Lukács, "Gedanken zu einer Ästhetik des Kino," in *Frankfurter Zeitung* 58/25 (10 September 1913), quoted in Güttinger, *Kein Tag ohne Kino*, 195–200, 198.

40. Adapted from Erwin Stein, ed., *Arnold Schoenberg: Letters* (London: Faber and Faber, 1964), 43.

41. Berg could have seen or heard something about the music of *Die glückliche Hand* while he was with Schönberg in Leipzig, Amsterdam, and Berlin in March, 1914. "Without yet fully understanding or comprehending them, the scores of *Glückliche Hand* and *Seraphita* constantly hover before me." Letter of 26 March 1914, *Berg-Schoenberg Correspondence*, 204.

42. See Denkler, *Drama des Expressionismus*, 125. *(Abbreviated)*

43. From the very earliest days of film one finds analogies between film and music with regard to dream and reality. Music, it was frequently observed, added another dimension, lending a kind of spatial depth to "flat" film, which, of course, was still silent. *(Abbreviated)*

44. August Strindberg, "Charakterzeichnung," in *Ein Blaubuch: Die Synthese meines Lebens*, vol. 2 (Munich/Leipzig: Müller, 1908), 866–71, 866 (marked by Berg in his copy). *(Abbreviated)*

45. Berg Fonds, F21 Berg 48, folio 9-11. See *Alban Berg, Sämtliche Werke*, vol. 2/2, *Kompositionen aus der Studienzeit*, Part I (Instrumental Music 2): *Einzelne Stücke, Variationen, Sonatenentwürfe*, ed. Ulrich Krämer (Vienna: Universal Edition, 2007), 173–77; with commentary 349. See also Ulrich Krämer, *Alban Berg als Schüler Arnold Schönbergs: Quellenstudien und Analysen zum Frühwerk*, Alban Berg Studien, vol. 4 (Vienna: Universal Edition, 1996), 247ff. Regarding the relationship between the "coda theme" of *Lulu* see 26ff.; and regarding the various versions of Sonata IV, 184ff. Facsimiles of the beginning and end are presented on pp. 248 (folio 9) and 186 (folio 11). Regarding piano sonatas in D minor one should also consider Berg's enthusiastic remarks to Webern about the inclusion of Beethoven's sonata, op. 31, no. 2, in Strindberg's *Rausch* (Intoxication).

46. This motive has yet to be identified.

47. This might involve at most a few pages in the sketchbook F21 Berg 13/II (starting at p. 50).

48. Regina Busch's summary of musical cues and commentary in Berg's *Night/ Nocturne* found on pp. 120–23 of her article is omitted here since all music-related items are to be found in the summary translation that follows.

ALBAN BERG

Night (Nocturne)

The following is an attempt to provide, in translation, a descriptive overview of Berg's various ideas for the individual sections of Night (Nocturne). *This edition is based on Berg's typewritten clean copy and does not include the autograph draft text variants that exist for several of its pages and are discussed in the appendixes of Regina Busch's facsimile edition. Introductory commentary about Berg's texts is given in italics, and the texts are in roman (except for handwritten notes inserted in the typescript, reproduced here in italics). No attempt has been made to reflect Berg's frequent but unsystematic use of red typewriter ribbon. The sources are provided in small type in the right-hand margin. Endnotes, drawing on research by Regina Busch, provide further explanation and bibliographic references.*

The principal intervention has been to break up and distribute Berg's various thoughts from the Preliminary Plan and Notes for the Monodrama (the verso and recto of a single sheet) to their respective sections. The extensive quotations from Strindberg and Dostoevsky in Part I are translated from the German editions of these works that Berg himself used and are today in the library of his Trautmannsdorffgasse residence.

Here, to begin, is a structural overview:

Prologue
  Night. Darkened stage; sound and musical effects
Part I
  Book-lined study
  Confrontation with the Other
Part II
  Reading, falling asleep
Part III
  Dreams
Part IV (split off from Part III)
  Mountain Trek (as film)
Epilogue
  Dawn

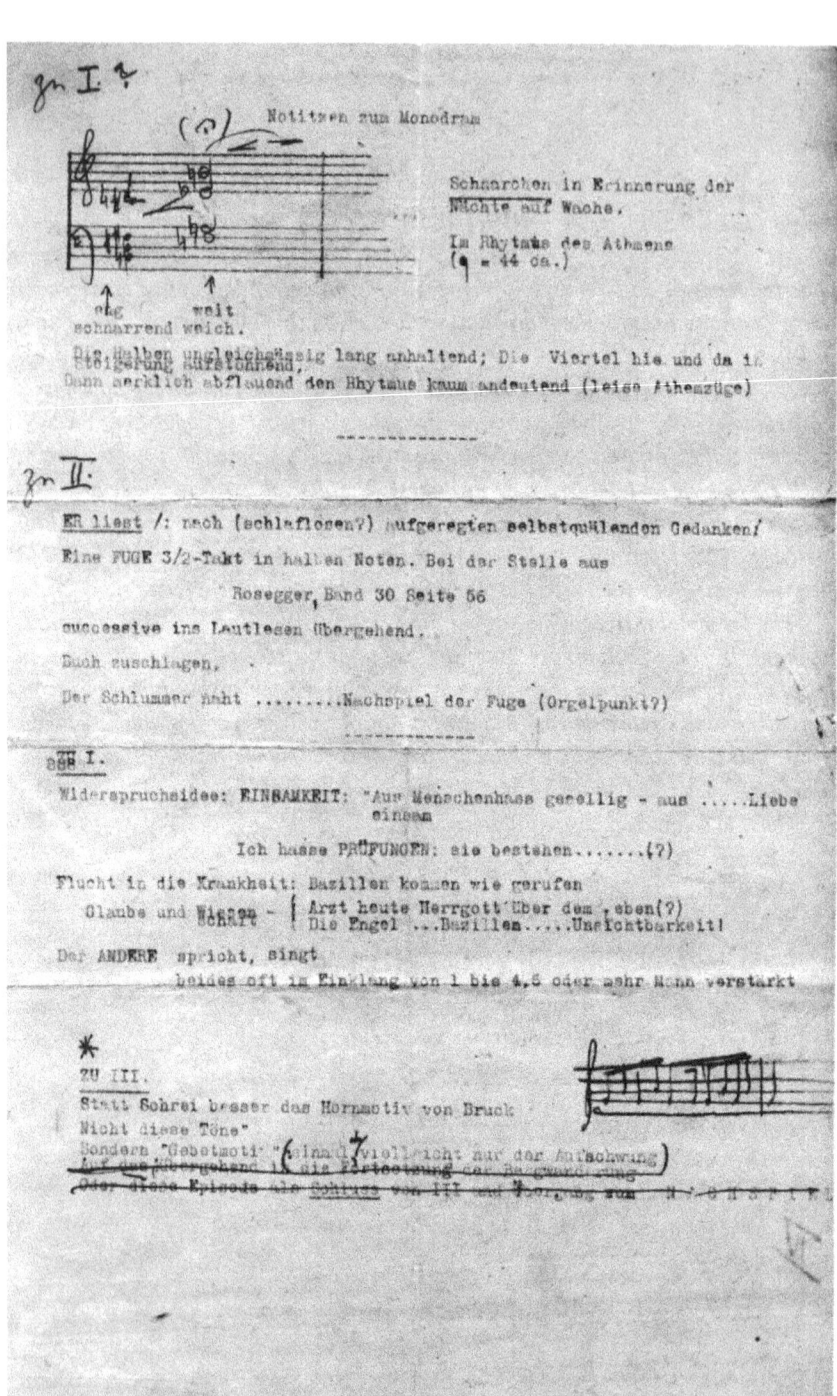

Figure 2. Berg, *Night (Nocturne)*, Notes on the Monodrama.

PROLOGUE

(Noises of the Night? or later?) Here? Snoring?   Preliminary Plan

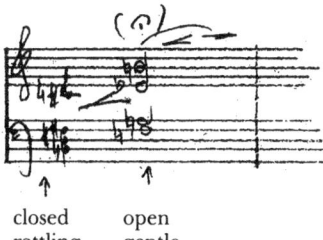

closed   open
rattling   gentle.

Snoring, recalling the nights on watch.   Notes for the Monodrama

In a breathing rhythm ($\quarternote = 44$ ca.)

Sustaining the half notes in uneven lengths; here and there the quarter notes with a moaning crescendo. Then noticeably ebbing with only a hint of rhythm (gentle breathing)

—

PART I

In addition to general notes from his "Preliminary Plan" and "Notes for the Monodrama," Berg devoted ten numbered pages of the typescript to Part I, though it is possible that they represent five separate fresh beginnings for this section.

    Confronting the OTHER (Conscience, second Self or the   Preliminary Plan
        Friend-Enemy, the Examiner....)

    Confession of incompleteness or contradiction

    The OTHER speaks, sings, both often reinforced in unison   Notes for the
    with between 1 to 4 or 5 or more men   Monodrama

Idea of Contradiction: SOLITUDE: "Out of misanthropy convivial—out of .....
                            love solitary
                            I hate EXAMINATIONS: passing them........(?)

                      Escape into illness: bacilli come on cue

            Belief and Science – Physician today Lord over life (?)
                          The angel ... bacilli.....invisibility!

—

NIGHT (NOCTURNE)

I.   Typescript 1

BEGINNING   Sleep ————

Suddenly becoming dark from the lane?) .... a cry of the night!

PEACE   Be calm! Just be calm! Calm yourself my ....
(making light) See how calm I am, my equanimity, etc.

"Are you as calm as you appear? (If you were it would be all up with you!)"

Admission of my constant, hidden anxiety, dissatisfaction with myself, unfulfilled, etc.

"Do you do anything to change that?"

I make sacrifices!

Sacrifice   "Halfway sacrifices! But two halves don't make a whole and 1,000 halfway sacrifices are by no means a whole. And only a <u>complete</u> sacrifice is valid, is a sacrifice, anything else is a concession for the likes of us ?!?!

WISDOM   Is that not philistinism?

GOD   Is that not an excuse?

—

Alban Berg

Typescript Page 2 may represent a fresh beginning.

I. Typescript 2

Thoughts, similar to those articulated by Kraus in the poem "Mythologie."

ARROGANCE   "Aren't these, who call themselves humans, the same living beings we are?" What happens to them? Eradicated!!

Along with the arrogant words one hears the Pharisee quotation: "Lord, I thank you that I am not like them" (quote accurately). In exactly the same rhythm, etc. (The arrogant words must be so chosen that they can stand in for the quotation above), like a 2nd voice (thirds or fifths) from a distance? its source uncertain (or from the Other) Not even heard by the "Other."

I. Who spoke?

At this point the angry question: Who are you then? (you who mock and scold?)

The Other: *I am who you would like to be.*

Less an ideal, something unattainable, or a model that is alive or might live and would thus necessarily be flawed. If you allow it to approach or if I approach you it ceases to be an ideal, has flaws (or) and precisely these you welcome. And you cultivate these flaws and are satisfied with them so that you have no reason to be too dissatisfied with yourself. You keep it at an appropriate distance.[1]

LIE
(perhaps last and stongest accusation!: *fff* "You lie!")   Are you quite conscious of being TRUE? Is it not a lie to be <u>silent</u>, where speaking alone would bring truth to light! Being half, where duty demands being whole?

NIGHT (NOCTURNE)

Typescript Pages 3 to 5 (6 is a blank verso) seem to form a unit that spells out the most detailed description of the opening scene. The text itself is fairly straightforward with few corrections or emendations.

I.

Typescript 3

The Room	Only indistinctly visible: A room, on the left a divan in front of which is a small table with nightlight, books, bottle with cup-like glass (?) In the background stage right the large window. The entire left and middle walls are covered by a huge shelf of books.
The Other:	I: Are you a spirit of higher worlds He keeps o n e secret to himself. Or is it voices from the books that gaze down on me ......[2]
Beginning after the Cry of the Night	Calm yourself (starting to whimper): So just calm yourself! There is nothing to be upset about. There is no thought to torment you, you are not in need of help; nothing can disturb your slumbers for you are not unsettled: *restive soul* No restlessness, dissatisfaction.... Or is it <u>my</u> conscience that speaks from this cry— — — continuation: own peace
Variant:	Address to the Cry of the Night: OH! Cry of the Night why do you disturb my sleep? Half expected, half feared, I meet you (it) trembling in impatience and (simultaneous) pain. You find me prepared!!
One's own Peace!	Why do you disturb me, I, who am so calm?! whom nothing can unsettle, for whom nothing appears unanticipated(?)

Alban Berg

The Other:	Don't deceive yourself. Superficial equanimity. You don't fool me, you don't fool...... An outer layer surrounding your inner self has, through years of practice, become so thick that not a ripple of your constantly agitated inner life breaks through (?) becomes visible

The Other

Typescript 4

Hidden Agitation	Only what is isolated, filtered is let through Tenderness...expressions of joy in daily life the dissatisfaction, longing remain hidden.
Inhibition	But feelings that do work their way through the crust must suffer, atrophy like prisoners (those who die in captivity) The liberated!! They are hidden and what is inhibited does not always break through. Result (also elsewhere: incompleteness!):
	Yourself —— Friend —— Wife —— Your Work ——
	In the end what have you Despair
Earlier?	You believe (you are in control of yourself) you can control the inner self, that is so much stronger, with the outer, whereas you are governed by the cultivation of appearances (so that they appear whole to the world). I s t h a t n o t a p p e a r a n c e ? Nothing should break through this crust! I s t h a t n o t s e l f i s h n e s s, that this crust, this skin not be damaged, be pierced and through that hole the years-long self-imposed, selfish control leak out. Believe me, it has already been pierced.

NIGHT (NOCTURNE)

(perhaps here the 4 points above: friend, wife, etc.)

Everything already now in imperfect form as in the later "Result"

Conflict (Kraus)[3]

Philistinism	Bourgeoisie In their proximity one can be "indecent" without being ashamed of oneself. Comfortable!![4]	Typescript 5
Voices from the Library	e.g. <u>Dostoevsky</u>: A Raw Youth, Part II, Chapter 7 "You love passionately what is lofty and noble, that I'll admit, I see that, but I believe, you only love it from afar, as an ideal.[5] Oh, he is ready to feel remorse, etc...."	
	"Yes, he is perpetually weak, but such weak people are sometimes capable of extraordinary deeds...."[6]	
	"[...] how unsettled was my understanding of the concepts of good and evil"[7]	
perhaps	<u>Lichtenberg</u> on nail-biting.[8] <u>Rosegger</u> instead of later[9] <u>Strindberg</u> *<u>Kraus</u>*	
(Nachts) *Fackel* No. 445/2	Something I cannot get over: that a whole line could be written by half a man. That a work could be built on the quicksand of a character.	

The genuine of the non-genuine is capable of enhancement.[10]

(Den Zwiespältigen [The conflicted])[11]

—

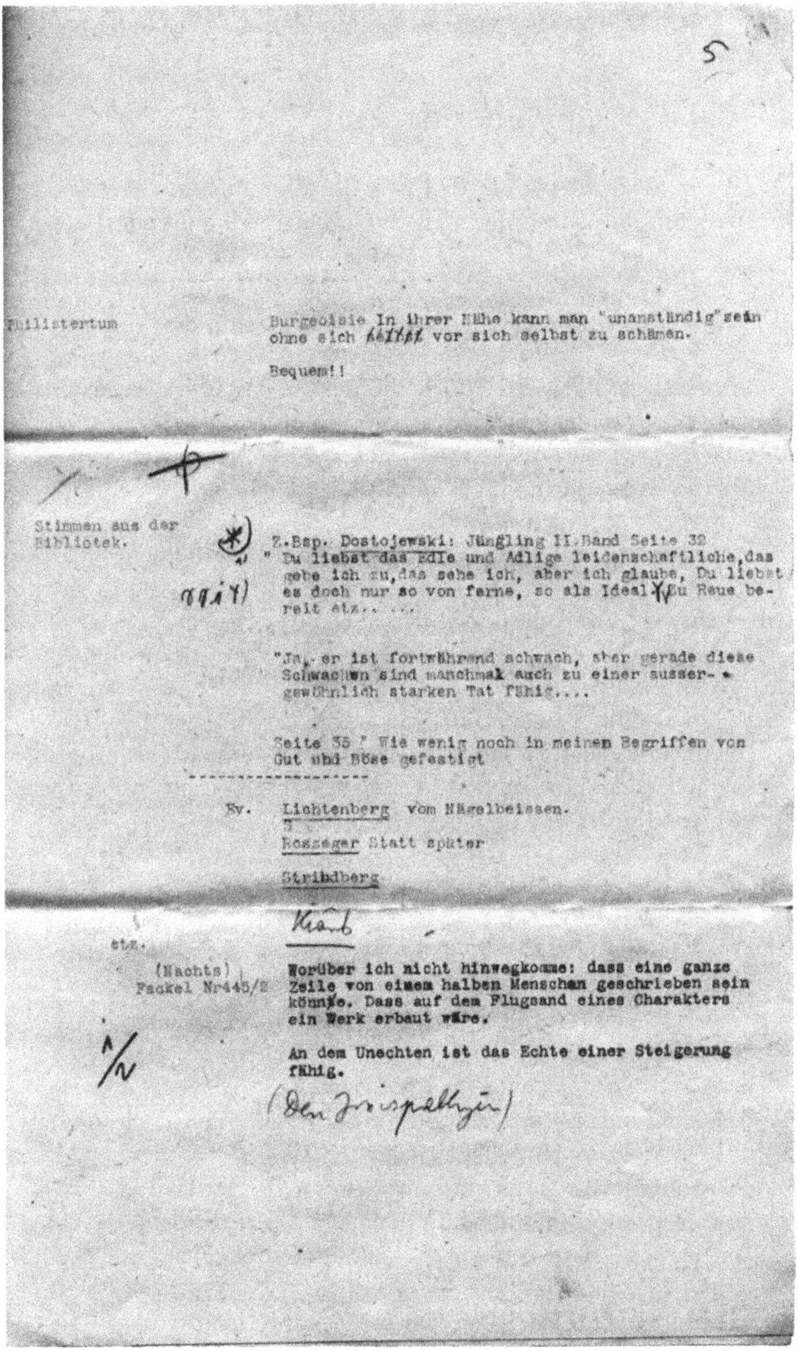

Philistertum   Burgeoisie In ihrer Nähe kann man "unanständig"sein
                      ohne sich **** vor sich selbst zu schämen.

                      Bequem!!

Stimmen aus der
Bibliotek.   Z.Bsp. Dostojewski: Jüngling II.Band Seite 32
                      " Du liebst das Edle und Adlige leidenschaftliche,das
                      gebe ich zu,das sehe ich, aber ich glaube, Du liebst
                      es doch nur so von ferne, so als Ideal. Zu Reue be-
                      reit etz.....

                      "Ja, er ist fortwährend schwach, aber gerade diese
                      Schwachen sind manchmal auch zu einer ausser-
                      gewöhnlich starken Tat fähig....

                      Seite 35 " Wie wenig noch in meinen Begriffen von
                      Gut und Böse gefestigt

                Bv.   Lichtenberg vom Nägelbeissen.
                      Rosseger Statt später
                      Strindberg

etz.
      (Nachts)   Worüber ich nicht hinwegkomme: dass eine ganze
      Fackel Nr445/2 Zeile von einem halben Menschen geschrieben sein
                      könne. Dass auf dem Flugsand eines Charakters
                      ein Werk erbaut wäre.

                      An dem Unechten ist das Echte einer Steigerung
                      fähig.

Figure 3. Berg, *Night (Nocturne)*, typescript page 5.

NIGHT (NOCTURNE)

Typescript page 7 seems to suggest new ideas for the beginning, as well as additional thoughts for the Idea of Contradiction.

I. Beginning: Asthma ...... half breath, half heart,   Typescript 7

        Where does the path lead? Up or down?
        (Ask this question over and over with increasing urgency)

I. Answer (evasively)
HE   at first gently (then later, increasingly) accusatory!

        You want to know the future, though the past is unclear to you and you have no idea how to deal with the present.

        Works wrested from half a mind

        Confrontation between Jewish and Christian (gift for numbers)

II. Or further answer to the question above:

HE.   When I tell you that things are going downhill, or that you're deteriorating, you are outraged and in this outrage there is an element of progress (a turnaround). And you hold this progress against me so often and so vehemently that I appear to be wrong. Do you think I don't see through you?

HE: You have big secrets. Black mark in your life!

I: If so, then it has been expiated.

        To serve, at the very cost of one's personality, the essence of
        life is sacrifice (Dr. Bhs Müller)[12]

        Idea of Contradiction: envied for no reason. Envied without envy.

before IV   Conclusion: Boy's voice from above:
        Either poem from the Ghost Sonata (Gespenstersonate), page 46
        or page 53 "What remains?" "Waiting, Ordeals, Patience"

III   Transition: "MEMORIES," covers face with hands[13]

Alban Berg

*Typescript pages 8 to 11 (12 is a blank verso) consist for the most part of quotations from two Strindberg works, with occasional handwritten commentary in the left margin (indicated here by italics). Because Berg shortens some of his quotations with "etc.," these passages are given here in full based on editions in Berg's own library in which these sections are marked or underlined. The English passages that appear here are based on the German translations Berg used (*Die Brandstätte *and* Gepenstersonate, *Munich and Leipzig: Georg Müller, 1908); page numbers from that edition are provided in the right hand margin below.*

                                                                            Typescript 8

The Burned House

THE STRANGER (slowly). I remember from my childhood....   *Die Brandstätte*, 18
When you are young, you see how things are <u>interwoven</u>: <u>parents, relatives, comrades</u>, acquaintances, servants, that's the warp. Later in life you see the weft. And now the little shuttle of fate weaves the thread back and forth....

Memory
Comfort

THE STRANGER. Whatever form life has taken – I've   *Die Brandstätte*, 20
been rich and poor, up and down, have had shipwrecks
and been through earthquakes – and whatever form <u>life</u>
has taken I've <u>always</u> <u>found</u> <u>a connection</u> and a repetition...
In every situation I saw a consequence of what came
before; whenever I met someone I was reminded of
someone from the past. There are <u>scenes</u> in my life that
have occurred many times so that I've often said to myself:
I've <u>experienced this before</u>. And there are events that
seemed to me downright inevitable or predestined.

THE DYER. What have you done all these years?

THE STRANGER. Everything! I've seen <u>life</u> from all sides and
directions, from above and from below; but always as if it were a
<u>play staged just for me</u>. In that way I've finally been able to
reconcile myself with a part of the past and have gotten to the
point that I can <u>forgive</u> so-called <u>mistakes</u> in others and in myself.

!!

THE DYER. Haven't you <u>forgotten</u> that?   *Die Brandstätte*, 21

THE STRANGER. I haven't forgotten it, but I've <u>forgiven</u>.

THE STRANGER. The <u>memories</u> crowd in upon me....   *Die Brandstätte*, 22

THE STRANGER. You know that we admired each other;   *Die Brandstätte*, 24
we considered our family the best; we had a particular, almost

• 119 •

religious reverence for our parents. Now I had to <u>repaint</u> their faces, <u>strip them naked</u>, drag them through the dust, put them out of my mind. It was horrible! Then they began to haunt me; pieces of the shattered figures reassembled themselves, but they no longer fit....

THE STRANGER. <u>To be young</u>. [. . .] You are no longer master of your own fate, eating other people's food ... Humbug, youth! *Die Brandstätte, 34*

THE STRANGER. [. . .] But let's stop dredging up the past – or we'll wind up back with butcher's ropes and burning switches! *Die Brandstätte, 41*

THE STONECUTTER. It's awful! Isn't life awful? *Die Brandstätte, 42*

THE STRANGER. (covers his eyes) Yes – it – is – awful – beyond – description

—

Typescript 9
THE WIFE. People wrong each other so: they <u>repaint</u> each other, each according to his own image. . . . *Die Brandstätte, 47*

THE STRANGER. And like theater directors they distribute <u>roles</u> to each other; some accept the roles, others reject them, preferring to improvise. . . .

THE STRANGER. I've been <u>across the river</u> but I don't remember anything except that—everything was what it seemed to be! That is the difference. *Die Brandstätte, 49*

THE WIFE. If there is nothing one can hold on to, what can one believe?

THE STRANGER. Don't you know?

THE WIFE. Tell me! Tell me!

THE STRANGER. Grief breeds patience, patience breeds experience, experience breeds hope, and hope cannot be disgraced.

Alban Berg

THE WIFE. Hope, yes!

THE STRANGER. Yes, hope!

THE WIFE. Don't you ever enjoy <u>life</u>?

THE STRANGER. Certainly, but that, too, is an illusion!
I will tell you, sister-in-law: if you are born <u>without blinders</u>
you see life and people as they are . . . and you'd have to be a
swine to thrive in this filth . . . When you've seen enough
stardust your eye turns inward and looks into its own soul.
There's where you'll really see something . . .

THE WIFE. What do you see there?

THE STRANGER. Yourself! But when you've seen yourself,
you die!

THE WIFE. (covers her eyes). [. . .]

THE STRANGER. [. . .] That's a net that humans didn't weave. . . .

THE WIFE. But he is not guilty. *Die Brandstätte*, 50

THE STRANGER. <u>Who is guilty</u>? (Pause)

THE WIFE. No one – – – – – What should I do?

THE STRANGER. <u>Suffer!</u> It will pass! That, too, is vanity!

THE WIFE. Suffer?

THE STRANGER. Suffer! But hope!!

THE WIFE. (gives him her hand). Thank you!

THE STRANGER. And as consolation, take –

THE WIFE. What?

THE STRANGER. That you don't suffer without guilt.

NIGHT (NOCTURNE)

THE STRANGER. [. . . in order to lay this wreath on my parents' grave, on the ruins of my parents' house, on my childhood home! (He says a silent prayer.)] And now out again into the wide world, [wanderer!] *Die Brandstätte,* 52

I.

Typescript 10

<u>Ghost Sonata</u>
Conflict

THE STUDENT. It is strange how stories can be told in two such entirely contradictory ways. *Gespenstersonate,* 12

OLD MAN. [I saved your father from squalor and he rewarded me with all the] terrible hate of <u>gratitude's debt</u> . . .] *Gespenstersonate,* 13

THE STUDENT. Perhaps you made him ungrateful by poisoning your help with unnecessary <u>humiliations</u>.

OLD MAN: To speak about the weather, which we know, to ask each other how we are, which we know? I prefer silence, in which one can hear thoughts, look into the past; <u>silence</u> can hide nothing the way words can! [. . .] *Gespenstersonate,* 42

THE YOUNG LADY. [. . .] Imagine then a <u>nursery</u> as well! *Gespenstersonate,* 57

THE STUDENT. The greatest joy of all. . . .

THE STUDENT. Do you love <u>candor</u>? *Gespenstersonate,* 58

THE YOUNG LADY. In moderation!

THE STUDENT. Sometimes I am overcome with a mad desire to say everything I'm thinking; but I know that the world would collapse if one were truly candid. . . .

THE STUDENT. [. . .] He was surrounded, as we all are, by a circle of acquaintances, which, for convenience sake, he called a <u>circle of friends</u>; naturally, they were a wretched bunch, as most people are. But he <u>needed some sort of circle</u> since he couldn't live alone. Now, one doesn't tell people what one thinks of them, at least not usually, nor did he. He was well aware how false they were and he was *Gespenstersonate,* 59ff

well acquainted with their treachery . . . but he was a prudent
man and well-bred, so he was always polite. But one day he
had a big party. [. . .] There he <u>threw caution to the winds</u> and
in a long confrontation stripped naked the entire gathering,
one after another; laid bare all their duplicity. [. . .]

Ideal!

THE STUDENT. If one is <u>silent too long</u> stagnant water begins
to form. [. . .] I saw a colonel who wasn't a colonel, I had a
noble benefactor who was a bandit. [. . .] By the way, where
can one find virginity? [. . .] Where is beauty to be found? [. . .]
Where can one find loyalty and faith? [. . .] Where can one
find what delivers on its promise? In my imagination! [. . .]

Ghost Sonata continuation

Vampire   Typescript 11

THE STUDENT [. . .] Now I can feel how the vampire in   *Gespenstersonate,* 61
the kitchen begins to suck me dry. [. . .] There are poisons
that <u>dim your vision</u> and poisons that open your eyes—I
was most certainly born with the latter because I cannot
see <u>beauty</u> in what is <u>ugly</u> or call evil good!—I can't! Jesus
descended into Hell [. . .] the <u>thief</u> always gets the <u>sympathy</u>!

(Conclusion of III.)

The redeemer is coming! Welcome, you pale <u>sleep</u>, etc.

THE STUDENT [. . .] and when you awaken again . . . may   *Gespenstersonate,* 62
you be greeted by a sun that does not burn, in a home
without dust; may you be greeted by kin without dishonor,
love without defect. . . . You wise, gentle Buddha, you sit
there and wait for <u>a heaven to emerge from the earth</u>, grant
us patience in trial, purity of will, so that hope is not in vain!

[There is a rustle of harp strings, the room is filled with
white light.]¹⁴

It seemed to me, as I looked at the sun,
that I saw what was hidden;
Man reaps as he sows;
blessed is he who does good.
Deeds done in anger,
are not healed with evil;
comfort well those you have afflicted,

NIGHT (NOCTURNE)

and it will profit you.
Only those who have wronged know fear:
Good is living a blameless life.

[Whimpering can be heard from behind the screen.]

You poor, small child! Child of this world of illusion, of guilt, suffering, and death; the world of endless reversals, disappointment, and pain. May the Lord of Heaven be merciful to you on your journey . . .

[The room disappears; Böcklin's "The Isle of the Dead" appears in the background.]

"And God will wipe away all tears from your eyes; and there will be no more death or suffering, or crying, or pain; for the first has passed."

[From the Isle of the Dead one hears soft, pleasing, melancholy music.]

Nightlight extinguished? (or at III in connection with the "CRY"?)[15]   *Preliminary Plan*

PART II

Turns on light.   *Preliminary Plan*
HE reads [. . .]

HE reads: after (sleepless?) agitated, self-tormenting thoughts /   *Notes for the Monodrama*

A FUGUE $\frac{3}{2}$ meter in half notes. At the Rosegger passage, volume 30, page 56[16]

gradually moving into reading aloud.

Closing book.

Reaching for alcohol/: Idea of contradiction thirsting in drinking: / Alcohol: fatiguing . . . . . easing	Preliminary Plan
Sleep approaches . . . . Epilogue of the fugue (pedal point?)	Notes for the Monodrama
falling asleep	Preliminary Plan

—

Typescript pages 50, 52 and 54, all devoted to Part II, are given here in full.

II. Typescript 50

Songs of praise of

Work

Sleep

Alcohol:

He extinquishes the present
The future becomes easy and light
And fills the past with or full of sweet memories....

M e m o r i e s . . . .
                               Transition!!

II. Alcohol Scene   Typescript 52

Related thoughts. How the spirit makes use of earthly means, has to make use of them in order to speak to us (the chosen have the gift of discovering God in earthly things) Better word!

    Doesn't God's eye peer from the bottom of the cup.

    Does not his breath . . . . women's lips

    Continuing this imagery or analogy (strophic song!?!)

        God's protective hand . . . .

NIGHT (NOCTURNE)

    The power of his loins

Drinking Song!   Notebook page E3
Standing, bending over the goblet, everything entirely *ppp*

II.   Typescript 54

Song in Praise
of the night
Perhaps also I.   1. Sleep (III)

               2. Everything standing on a higher plane

               The thoughts of a dream, of half sleep, how they dissipate
               by light of day... spoken in waking? —in being spoken they
               vanish (no depreciation!)

Song in praise
of the rain   (P. A. song)

Instead of:
"   "   Woman   "   "   "Nothing has come..."[17]

—

PART III

    <u>III</u>.   Preliminary Plan

    DREAM:

    Shapes silently scurrying and slinking past: diagonally across
    the stage
    Dream figures at first light (love?) then ever gloomier

Choirs

  I   ⎡ Somewhere a door slams, a window casement swings
        ⎢ back and forth in the wind = noises of the night
        ⎣ train in the distance . . . .

    Screeching voice: Where is the beat?!!!!

Alban Berg

"Not these tones": flight into the mountains – – – cinematographically

Suddenly interrupted (as an aftereffect of the preceding terrifying dream figures)

Perhaps the Dream-CRY brought about through the crackling of the extinguishing nightlight

Calming . . . . . prayer and . . . . . .

Notes for the Monodrama

Instead of cry, better the horn motive from Bruck

"Not these tones"

Rather "prayer motive" (perhaps only once, perhaps only the upbeat)[18]

Typescript pages 100, 101r and 101v, all devoted to Part III, are given here in full.

III.   Typescript 100

Memories Lights

Perhaps
transition   Reminiscences: We went through the . . . . Night
from
Memories
to Dreams

    (The piano on the left begins to play on its own)

    Sonata beginning (D-minor syncopations)

    (Perhaps piano offstage)

    and the other

NIGHT (NOCTURNE)

<u>Transition</u>: Church attendance, an altar with 1,000 candles looming out of the gloom of a church

together with that the thought of school

Perhaps transition from Memories to dreams

<u>Dark</u> memories: school: The Catalog
                             The Professors.
(see also next page)

The way over the bridge!

III. Dreams Memories (of an erotic nature?, Scents,   Typescript 101r

School!!! Examinations, poor memory for numbers, dates, equations with many unknowns. . . . . .

$$x = 23$$

Men's voices (fugue, or canon: use of the timbral color of voices all sounds (*Twwwwenty thrrree* etc.)[19]

→ women's eyes (see II. Drinking scene)
Armpits: the vestibule of passion's temple . . . .

Conclusion: Nightmares unbearably intensified.   Typescript 101v

Women (coarse, plump, overly voluptuous, ugly???) wallowing in a wild round dance. In between, from above, heavy, waving, billowing, dark Bordeaux-red plush curtains in giant folds, likewise taking part in this round dance, again and again, becoming ever more closely entangled, entwined. Swarms of women emerge out of this mass of material, giant folds, only to be immediately swallowed up by the darkness. Again and again new combinations (also musically) At the climax of this monstrously swollen nightmare, sudden, startling awakening (night cry, complete extinction of the nightlight?)

?
Here:
Where is
the beat
?

Completely shaken: M e m o r i e s *(for the 2nd time)*

Alban Berg

"Longing"   Transition to IV (Mountain Trek)

You pale sleep!

The originally unnumbered notebook pages, now titled E1 through E3, contain references related to church visits (Typescript page100) as well as dreams and memories (Typescript page101v):

God? Notebook page E1
Memory dreams
like a side altar, dimly lit by candles, in the deep gloom of
a gothic church (at first only individual points of light, only
gradually recognizable. Moving quite slowly in front of it,
a few shadowy, completely silent figures (priests and
ministrant), the latter swinging an incense vessel so that   Notebook page E2
the view is increasingly obscured by smoke only to
disappear entirely at the sound of the ministrant's bell
(a 5-voice, brightly repeated ringing), that is, after making
way for the next scene (lane?)   Notebook page E3

PART IV

It appears that what is now Part IV was extracted from Part III since in Berg's Preliminary Plan a handwritten IV *in the left margin is all that indicates the following as the starting point of a new section.*

Gradual reemergence of the "MOUNTAIN TREK" Preliminary Plan
(cinematographically)
Ever higher and lighter
   Until entirely white, that is, the pale light surface, now
grown quite white, gradually reveals itself to be the large
window in the background (with the window's crossbars, or
multiply divided pane) through which the pale gray morning
becomes visible through no other image than the sky that
appears as a pale gray surface — similar to that leaden quality
of morning sleep. . . . .

NIGHT (NOCTURNE)

Typescript pages 150r and 150v give a detailed description of the cinematographic depiction of the Mountain Trek, while Notebook page E19 suggests a possible musical realization of the Mountain Trek:

Following the first scene of the mountain trek, after   Notebook page E19
the forest darkness, the clearing with heather,
heather singing in wordless coloratura, spirit
of the flowers and thicket

CINEMA IV   Typescript 150r

Emerging quite imperceptibly from the completely darkened
rear wall is the shadow of an image that only with
difficulty can be recognized as a thick forest devoid of light
and contour.

Very gradually something like a path leading out of this
wilderness becomes visible. (A completely neglected primeval
Styrian forest (mainly coniferous forest) with toppled, uprooted
trees, through which, and only with great difficulty, one
might make one's way toward any kind of clearing. This forest
and the path gradually grow lighter and more ordered and
finally leads to a gently inclining mountain pasture.

Phase I . The mountain-range in relationship to the earth

    Noises from the earth (cowbells)

Ascending with dreamlike speed (or through interruptions caused by the above noises from the earth)

Phase II. The mountains down below

    Highlands, plateau trek

The plains no longer visible, in the midst of the highlands
but not in the picturesque high mountains

Then, the "Cry of the Night," but not as at the beginning,
but rather as if from a distant interruption. Cut, sudden
darkness and when the screen is again visible:

Phase III. The mountains in relationship to the sky

    In the mountain peak, deep in snow, ever higher, ever fewer
contours! Broad white surfaces, snow and sky become o n e.
The blinking white grows softer, dull light gray like the
morning sky of the city. Imperceptibly a shadow, contours,
the silhouette of the window crossbars become visible on
the screen so that the window becomes clearly recognizable

    At the rear of the room, which is enveloped in <u>very subdued</u>   Typescript 150v
morning dawn. The furnishings are once again visible,
though in contrast to the opening scene, without any flickering
restlessness, without color, a calm that has left behind life
(pulse, the lowered temperature of the cooled human body)
as an expression of morning sleep.

    "O sweet, dreamless sleep" (last words) or something similar
by Strindberg (or perhaps as if from the upper reaches of
the bookcase /: boy's voice: /)

—

EPILOGUE

The epilogue is mentioned by name, without description of contents. However, an unnumbered page, D (Diverses), contains the following remarks:

V a r i o u s

The strings are out of tune within me	Played in the orchestra
	(Play a sweet melody with out-of-tune strings.
A string snaps within me	Make a string break.)

NOTES

1. Berg suggests the possibility of beginning this section with the first Dostoevsky passage, quoted on Typescript page 5.

2. Berg suggests this line could appear on page 5 after the word *comfortable*.

3. In this handwritten note at the bottom of the typed text Berg refers to the poem "Den Zwiespältigen" (The conflicted) by Karl Kraus to which he alludes again on Typescript 5 and 10.

4. Here, in the open space after the word *comfortable*, Berg suggests inserting the line from page 3 "Or is it voices from the books that gaze down on me . . . . ."

5. Dostoevsky, *Der Jüngling (A Raw Youth)*, trans. E. K. Rahsin (Munich: R. Piper & Co., 1915), 2:32. In a handwritten note Berg suggests that the quotation above might be incorporated into a passage on page 2 after the words, "I am who you would like to be."

6. Ibid., vol. 2, 33.

7. Ibid.

8. Regina Busch has suggested that this may be an allusion to an aphorism (K 270) drawn from Georg Christoph Lichtenberg in which Lichtenberg discusses nail biting as a sign of man's instinctive striving toward self-cultivation. *Schriften und Briefe*, vol. 2, *Sudelbücher II, Materialhefte, Tagebücher* (Frankfurt am Main: Zweitausendeins, 1998), 445.

9. See Part II on pg. 123 as well as note 16 below.

10. This and the preceding aphorism are drawn from Kraus, "Nachts" (Aphorisms), *Fackel* 18/445–53 (18 January 1917): 3–19.

11. This is a handwritten reference to Kraus's poem "Den Zwiespältigen" (The conflicted) in ibid., 148–49.

12. The reference to Dr. Müller is unclear.

13. The two handwritten notes in the left margin—"before IV" and "III"—suggest that Berg may have intended to insert the boys' voices singing from above just before Part IV and the stage action and musical example at the beginning of Part III (see Typescript 100 and 101r, 101v).

14. Berg did not type out the stage directions given here in square brackets; they are added here for orientation.

15. Besides exploring this passage as a possible transition to Part II, Berg apparently also entertained the idea of using it for Part III.

16. In his copy of this Rosegger volume, a collection of essays titled *Höhenfeuer: Allerhand Beleuchtungen mit Sternen und Laternen*, Berg has marked—given here in curly brackets { }—a portion of the last paragraph of the essay "Love and Marriage" (pp. 44–56) in which Rosegger discusses the divine nature of carnal love between a man and a woman: "The love between man and woman understood and felt in this sense [. . .] I emphatically agree with all those who sense the spirit of God in earthly love {and who ennoble sensual joys with spiritual love. When this spiritual love is present in full measure, all pleasures are enhanced, they remain constant, and the desire for indissoluble union comes automatically. False love fears marriage, genuine love seeks it, indeed, genuine love is already in itself a union made in heaven that only death can part.}"

17. Berg is referring to two Peter Altenberg texts he set in the *Altenberg Lieder*, op. 4. The first: "After the summer rain did you see the forest?!?! / All is glitter, quiet and more beautiful than before – –. / See, good woman, you too sometimes need summer rain!" (Peter Altenberg, *Neues Altes*, 64). The second: "Nothing is come, nothing will come, / for my soul – – –. / I waited, waited, ah, waited –. / The days will slip stealthily –. /And in vain flutters my ashen-blonde silken hair round my pallid countenance / – – –." (Peter Altenberg, *Neues Altes*, 60).

18. Crossed out on Notes for the Monodrama are the following: "At the changeover to the continuation of the mountain trek / Or this episode as conclusion of III and transition to EPILOGUE."

19. (*drrrei, uuuuuund ZZZZwanzig, etc.*)

Berg and the Orchestra

ANTONY BEAUMONT

From Biber to Berg: A Little History

The art of orchestration, in the sense that it concerns us here, dates back to the last decade or so of the seventeenth century, to the time when composers began assigning individual parts (other than the ground-bass) to specific instruments or instrumental groups. Despite a steady growth in contrapuntal and textural complexity, art music was still almost as close to nature as folk music, strings were still strings,[1] a trumpet just a trumpet.[2]

During the Classical period, radical changes in texture and line went hand in hand with a sharper focus on orchestral brilliance, on virtuosity of the group rather than of the individual. As orchestras grew in strength, continuo instruments could no longer provide the necessary harmonic backbone. Though Haydn continued to direct from the keyboard, even in his "London" symphonies of 1791–95, the continuo group had long since been replaced by a pair of horns supported by violas (sometimes in two parts), together with one or more bassoons. Optional extras included flutes, oboes, and clarinets and trumpets, also usually in pairs. Apart from the added melodic and coloristic interest afforded by extra wind players, the entire group could be employed to fill out *tutti* passages. Hence, in French- and German-speaking countries it became customary to designate the complete complement of woodwind, brass, and percussion as *Harmonie*.

The *Harmonie* of Haydn and Mozart had its shortcomings. Horns and trumpets, restricted to the upper partials of a given fundamental, could be used only in music that strayed not too far from the tonic key. Hand-tuned timpani were subject to similar limitations. Nevertheless, with these comparatively primitive instruments, inherited from our hunting fathers, eighteenth-century composers sought and found whole new worlds of orchestral sound.

Throughout the nineteenth century, orchestras expanded in size and compass. Mozart and his contemporaries had already added trombones to the brass and extended the woodwind from the low C_2 of the contrabassoon to the high g^4 or a^4 of the piccolo.[3] Mendelssohn, Berlioz, and the young Verdi added the unwieldy bass ophicleide, later supplanted by the *cimbasso* (contrabass trombone) and, ultimately, the bass tuba. To offset the dry acoustic of Italian theaters, Rossini and Donizetti brightened their scores with pairs of piccolos, high clarinets, and ample use of "Turkish" percussion. Berlioz found ways of involving horns in passages of rapid modulation by using up to four transpositions at once (e.g., in the Queen Mab Scherzo from *Roméo et Juliette*). To cover a wider range of pitches, he also introduced extra pairs of timpani (*Symphonie fantastique*, Requiem, etc.).

While most virtuoso composer-performers continued to write music tailored to their own technical strengths and weaknesses, Beethoven stood for subservience to the musical idea. In answer to a complaint by the violinist Ignaz Schuppanzigh that a passage in the Opus 95 quartet did not lie under the fingers, he retorted: "When the spirit speaks to me, and I write it down, do you think I could give a damn for a wretched fiddle?"[4] Pitch, rhythm, and speed, he implied, must be liberated from the physical limitations of fingers, mouths, and lungs.

As if in answer to his call, instrument making developed more rapidly during the course of the nineteenth century than ever before or since. This was the age of the great pianoforte builders, of Buffet and Heckel, who revolutionized the mechanism of the bassoon, of Boehm, who did the same for flutes and clarinets, of Sax and Gautrot, who patented the saxophone and sarrusophone families, of Blühmel, Stölzel, and Sattler, who perfected the valve mechanism of the chromatic horn, of Mustel, the celesta builder, and many others.

Some composers were reluctant to accept the innovations, others did so unhesitatingly. As early as 1835, Halévy called for valve trumpets in the score of *La juive*, and in 1868 Ambroise Thomas included a saxophone in his opera *Hamlet*. Brahms, on the other hand, even in his last orchestral work, the Double Concerto, op. 102 (1887), was still writing for natural horns and trumpets. Richard Strauss included a quartet of saxophones in the *Sinfonia domestica* (1903) and a heckelphone in *Salome* (1905), but never broke with the tradition of writing for horns with changing transpositions.

Nor, for all his innovative spirit, did Richard Wagner. One of his concerns, as far as orchestral sound was concerned, was homogeneity. To this end he conceived a new family of instruments, the tenor tubas. Built in two sizes, they extended wide-bore brass timbre into the bass register, closing the range gap between horns and bass tuba. Wide-bore sound now covered five octaves, from the contra F_2 of the contrabass tuba to the high f^1 of the *Waldhorn*. Two further instruments built to Wagner's specifications, the bass trumpet and the contrabass trombone, similarly extended the compass of narrow-bore brass to nearly six octaves.

Wagner, the pan-European genius—there was no escaping him, and under his leadership the world of music experienced many radical changes, including a completely new aesthetic of orchestration. In the immortal words of Mark Twain, "Wagner is not as bad as it sounds." To most ears, Wagner sounds exceedingly well. His sound was not only widely admired and imitated, it was also applied to the works of his predecessors. For over a century after his death, the orchestral music of all previous eras was customarily heard as if through a Wagnerian filter. Timbres and articulations, dynamic contrasts and expressive range, even concepts of tempo, as applied to the music of Bach, Vivaldi, Mozart, Gluck, Haydn, Beethoven, and Schubert, no longer conformed to what those composers, in their day, had expected or envisaged.

Berlioz was the first to specify minimum strengths for his string sections. Others, including Wagner, followed suit, and in larger cultural centers the orchestras soon boasted permanent bodies of sixty string players or more. Against these forces the balance in *tutti* passages could be maintained only by reinforcing the woodwind section and strengthening the brass. The outcome, in a Europe grown fat on colonization and industrialism, was a new opulence: soft-edged, vibrant, well nourished. As if to match the new threshold of industrial noise, orchestras reached out for, and achieved, a higher dynamic ceiling than ever before.

In the first half of the twentieth century, courageous souls such as Otto Klemperer and Hermann Scherchen strove for leaner, more athletic timbres, particularly in Bach and Mozart. Likewise, many of the composers who shunned the ideology of Bayreuth strove for greater transparency and sharper contours. Nietzsche had written, "Il faut méditerraniser la musique" and found his ideal antidote to Wagner in the pellucid orchestration and lithe rhythms of Georges Bizet.[5] Nevertheless, in professional circles post-Wagnerian opulence remained the norm.

In the Vienna of the later nineteenth and early twentieth century, the ideals of sound and style represented by Gustav Mahler and his *Philharmoniker* still corresponded largely to the model of Bayreuth. Nevertheless, the Viennese added nuances of their own: cosmopolitan versatility in style paired with Austrian grace and elegance, rhythmic elan controlled with the accuracy of a watchmaker.

It was with these sounds and impressions in his ears that Alban Berg received his musical education.

Breaking with Tradition

Customarily, the craft of musical composition was handed down from one generation to the next in a process of learning by doing. Opera or ballet composers worked seasonally or temporarily in commercial or court theaters, composers of sacred music stood in the employ of the church. They began as volunteers or apprentices and rose, if fortune smiled on them, to the rank of Master (Kapellmeister, *maestro di capella*). Those who wrote for orchestra came into contact with orchestral sound, either as instrumentalists or conductors, every day of their working lives. Those who wrote for voices worked regularly with singers, and themselves knew how to sing, sight-read, play from a figured bass, and accompany themselves at the keyboard. Aptitude was of the essence. The road to a distinguished career was open only to those with a virtuoso command of at least one instrument.

Other than in nineteenth-century Russia, where the social contract forbade the upper classes to engage in below-stairs activities such as professional music making, the "gentleman composer," with little skill as an instrumentalist and little or no experience of professional music making, was a rare bird.

When Berg enrolled in Schoenberg's composition class in 1907 he was, to all intents and purposes, such a "gentleman composer." He was a capable pianist, but no virtuoso. He had composed a respectable body of lieder, but none revealed the dazzling talent of a young Mendelssohn or Korngold. Since he played no orchestral instrument, he had no inside experience of a symphony orchestra or even a string quartet. Having never worked in an opera house, he knew the capabilities of the singing voice chiefly from his domestic circle. The *convenienze ed inconvenienze teatrali* were familiar to him only from the auditorium, from the *feuilletons* of the Viennese critics or the diatribes of Karl Kraus in *Die Fackel*. The young Berg was uncommonly receptive, alert, and discerning. But his role in the musical, dramatic, literary, and artistic life of Vienna was that of a passive observer.

Where then did he acquire the skill, practical experience, and wisdom to write so utterly convincingly for the orchestra? Who taught him to stretch every instrument, from piccolo to contrabass, from accordion to xylophone, to its individual limits? How did he learn to model his musical ideas so masterfully to the voice, to make demands on singers such as could be met only by the exceptionally gifted? Who or what nurtured his feeling for music drama, his infallible sense of timing, contrast, and color, the play of human emotions?

Certainly, he learned much from Schoenberg, and in a comparatively short time. The rest must have come from tireless study of theoretical writings and printed scores, from his ability to observe the minutest of details, an exceptionally retentive memory and an inborn talent for organization. Presumably he learned the rudiments of musical theory at school, presumably he also kept in touch with instrumentalists among his contemporaries and friends, quizzed them on the capabilities of their instruments and observed them in action. These aspects of Berg's early life are not well documented. The fact remains that with his first orchestral work, the *Altenberg Lieder,* op. 4, the world witnessed the birth of a new Pallas Athene, bursting forth from the forehead of his Zeus-like spiritual father, Arnold Schoenberg, fully armed.[6]

Apart from his studies with Schoenberg, which covered not only the basics of theory, harmony, and counterpoint but also practical matters such as notation, score reading, and orchestration, Berg's personal process of learning by doing was largely theoretical. Thanks to commissions from Universal Edition, he was able to familiarize himself with every detail of three exceptionally complex and expansive orchestral scores: Schreker's *Der ferne Klang*, for which he prepared the vocal score in 1911; Schoenberg's *Gurrelieder*, for which he not only prepared the vocal score but also published a detailed thematic analysis (guide); as well as Schoenberg's tone poem *Pelleas und Melisande,* op. 5, for which he prepared a "brief thematic analysis." Although in these earlier works Schoenberg was still following the orchestral road paved by Wagner and widened by Richard Strauss, Schreker's approach broke fresh ground. The "far-off sound" of *Der ferne Klang* and the glowing, iridescent colors of *Die Gezeichneten* owe more to the innovations of the French post-Wagnerians than to Wagner or Strauss. For the sheer vision of his orchestral writing and his technical ability to translate that vision into notation, Schreker outstripped them both.

Schreker and Zemlinsky, Bartók and Kodály, Szymanowski and Janáček, Holst and Vaughan-Williams, Bax and Bridge—all these and many more found strength in their fight against the stifling influence of Wagner and his followers in the subtle timbres and elusive rhythms of Debussy and Ravel. Many German intellectuals, who mistrusted their neighbors west of the Rhine, habitually disregarded or deprecated French trends in music, literature, and the visual arts. Between Austria and France there was no such atmosphere of resentment. Contact between the two capital cities was direct and immediate.

The influence of Paul Dukas on progressive composers in Vienna was equally profound. His opera *Ariane et Barbe-Bleue* (1899–1906) received its Austrian premiere at the Vienna Volksoper under the baton of Zemlinsky on 2 April 1908. "At a higher level than ever before in French opera," wrote the critic Elsa Bienenfeld, "the work presents complete motivic development of all themes, and is formally designed in a fashion foreign even to the theater of Debussy."[7] Dukas worked with relationships between key and color inspired by the *Farbenlehre* of Goethe and developed techniques of motivic variation akin to those of Schoenberg. He commanded a vivid yet pellucid style of orchestration and knew to fashion even the most complex textures in such a way as to maintain perfect clarity. The coruscating textures and flawless architecture of *Ariane* must have appealed strongly to Schreker, who assisted the production as chorus master. The discipline and logic of the score, which placed intellectual rigor at the service of emotion, would have appealed the more strongly to Berg.

On the eve of the premiere, Zemlinsky sent a cable to the composer in Paris, countersigned by Schoenberg, Berg, and Webern. For lack of documentation, theories of a further influence of Dukas on the Second Viennese School must remain speculative. An anecdote may serve as substitute: on 19 April 1925, Zemlinsky conducted Berg's *Wozzeck* fragments in Prague. Berg heard of the event only after it had taken place. To make amends, Zemlinsky took the impromptu decision to repeat the work four weeks later, in his presence—as curtain raiser to a staged performance of *Ariane et Barbe-Bleue*.

The influence of Schreker on Berg is well documented, not least because of Berg's involvement in the publication of *Der ferne Klang*. In a word, the connection brought forth little fruit. Adorno drew a parallel between the "twitter machine" opening of Berg's first Altenberg song and the opening bars of Schreker's *Die Gezeichneten*, only to retract with the observation that if a parallel could be drawn, then only on the surface:

> The similarity of the idea behind the sonoral design with that of the opening to the prelude of Schreker's *Gezeichneten* is striking, except that Berg's work, surely written earlier, goes much further in its use of dissonance than Schreker with his polytonally clouded triads; seldom, however, is a certain affinity between the two as palpable as it is here. The differences are all the more relevant. Here as there it is a case of mixed sonority [*Mischklang*]. Schreker's sound virtually eradicates the individual colors in its shimmering totality, they are perceptible only as momentary reflexes within a homogeneous sound. The nature of Berg's mixed sonority, on the other hand, which is indebted to the color piece in Schönberg's Op. 16, is such that while the simultaneously juxtaposed colors likewise blend into a whole, they at the same time remain unhomogeneous, independently layered: mixed sound without mixture. It is no mere analogy to periods in painting to call Schreker's technique late-impressionistic, Berg's early Expressionistic. The introduction to the first Altenberg song is far more profoundly infused with the idea of chamber music than is Schreker's conception, in which, according to Schreker himself,

the orchestra is to sound like a single instrument. By contrast, Berg's compositional approach and overall technique exhibit, at least in his earlier works, a decided tendency toward the dissociative, extending even to his instrumentation. His sound, like his motivic-thematic organization, yearns to return to its component elements. Planned disorganization becomes organization; such clear-cut intention transforms those eighteen instrumental bars into something other than the chaos they initially appeared to be.[8]

The operative word—*organization*—comes in the closing sentence of this quotation. To which one might add: *emotional discipline*—Berg's greatest strength and Schreker's most obvious weakness.

From Mahler, Berg learned to integrate the banalities of the street and the dancehall into his scores: the "Schrammel" band and out-of-tune piano of *Wozzeck*, the jazz band and barrel-organ imitation of *Lulu*, the heart-rending *Ländler* in the first movement of the Violin Concerto, the elegant tango in *Der Wein*. Had Mahler known the score of Berg's Three Orchestral Pieces, op. 6, he would have disapproved of its complexity, which stood in total opposition to his own ideals of clarity and concision. Likewise, the soft edges of Berg's later scores, which originate in the time-honored tradition of writing for horns and bassoons in close harmony, have little in common with the luminance and transparency of Mahler.

Berg may have despised Richard Strauss, but that did not prevent him from borrowing when it suited him. A case in point is the moan of the contrabass in the dormitory scene of *Wozzeck* (Act 2, sc. 5). The idea originates in *Salome* ("Es ist kein Laut zu vernehmen," rehearsal number 305ff.), where Strauss uses single eighth notes, pumped out *sforzando* by solo contrabass on a high B♭, to create an atmosphere of urgency and foreboding. In Berg, the same note (high A♯) is elongated to a full quarter note with *crescendo* and *decrescendo* fork, and to heighten the effect of otherworldliness the instrument is muted. After his own fashion, Berg creates no less tense an atmosphere than Strauss. Set against the creepy background of a wordless male-voice chorus, his contrabass sounds plaintive, forlorn, timeless.

Comparable borrowings can also be traced to Zemlinsky's *A Florentine Tragedy* and *The Dwarf*, scores that Berg knew well and admired greatly. But these and other influences are small touches on a giant canvas. It would be doing Berg an injustice to look for far-reaching influences on his unique concept of orchestral sound. He learned where he could, distilled the essence of many influences—and went his own way.

Itinerary with Detours

The orchestration and dramaturgy of the *Altenberg Lieder* diverge from Schoenberg's guidelines in several essential points. To the end of his days, Berg remained fundamentally true to the precepts set down in this work. It may therefore be helpful to examine these divergences in some detail.

- Whether in a tonal or freely atonal context, Berg divides up pitch content between orchestral groups and individual instruments in such a way as to create small, continually shifting islands of tonal or quasitonal harmony, based on perfect fifths, triads, sixth chords, and triadic seventh chords. Schoenberg, in contrast, relishes the abrasiveness of fourths, sevenths and ninths and goes out of his way to obliterate diatonic thinking from his music.
- In his atonal music, Schoenberg customarily avoids the octave; according to his laws of composition with twelve notes, octaves are strictly forbidden. Thereby he excludes that interval from which all else evolves, the first upper partial of the harmonic sequence, the interval closest to nature. With single-octave bass lines, which unite the cello and contrabass in an infortuitous and disaster-prone unison, his later orchestral scores are deprived of this fundamental element of musical acoustics. Webern followed Schoenberg all the way, at least in his middle period and late works. Berg never did, not even in those works that employed twelve-note technique.
- When setting a piece of poetry or prose, Schoenberg's prime concern is to sound out the psychological undertones. His forms emerge from reading between the lines, as expression of the perceived message. Berg's approach is more dispassionate. He divides a poem or operatic scene into architectural units, and assembles these in such a way as to articulate their expressive and dramatic qualities. Thereby he uncovers unexpected musical substructures: palindromes, rondos, sonata forms, inventions. Orchestral colors then serve to clarify and articulate those forms.
- Neither Berg nor Schoenberg possessed any great gift as performers. Perhaps for that very reason they both delighted in virtuosity. But where Schoenberg's music endorses Beethoven's retort to Schuppanzigh a thousand times over, Berg is a model of consideration and courtesy. In extreme cases, such as the third movement of the *Lyric Suite*, he worked intensively with the performers to ensure that every note lay under the fingers. Even if "the spirit spoke to him," he did indeed "give a damn"—as in the first tavern scene of *Wozzeck*—even for the most wretched of fiddles.

- Where Schoenberg's choices of color and hue are determined largely by the inspiration of the moment, Berg works more systematically. In his first published compositions, the Piano Sonata, op. 1; the Four Songs, op. 2; the String Quartet, op. 3; and the Four Pieces for Clarinet and Piano, op. 5, he handles each instrument as an orchestra in itself. How many colors, he asks, does a concert grand, a clarinet, a violin, a cello, or a soprano voice have to offer? He takes each instrument in his hands, like a precious object, inspects it from every angle, then draws up—mentally, if not on paper—a table of resources. These are distributed according to their relevance to specific parts of the musical argument, or the musical argument is so designed as to lend itself to a particular resource.

Digression I: Berg and Bruitism

The *Altenberg Lieder* stretch this system to its limits and beyond, notably at the point, toward the close of the first song, where Berg calls for two unusual effects—lightly sliding a finger of the left hand up a violin string (*quasi-flageolet*) and drawing the bow across the bridge of a contrabass—both superimposed upon a static harmonium chord. These experiments with unpitched noise may have been influenced by the Futurists. Their touring exhibition, which had been admired and decried in London, Paris, Berlin, and Brussels during the spring and summer of 1912, reached Vienna on 15 December of the same year, at the very time when Berg was adding finishing touches to his score. "Compared with *this* art," Busoni wrote of the Futurist sculptors, "Schoenberg's *Pierrot lunaire* is lukewarm lemonade."[9] In Vienna, the exhibition was shown at the Schwarzwaldschule, the very place, as it happens, where Schoenberg had held his composition classes. On show were paintings by Umberto Boccioni, Giacomo Balla, Carlo Carrà, Luigi Russolo, and Gino Severini. Together with the composer Francesco Ballila Pratella, Russolo represented the musical wing of Futurism and was rated by far the more radical of the two. In 1913 he published his manifesto on Bruitism, *L'arte dei rumori* (The art of noises) and began composing for an ensemble of *intonarumori* (noise intoners).[10]

Although Berg was intensely occupied with correcting the performing materials for the *Gurrelieder*, due to be premiered on 23 February 1913, he is unlikely to have ignored so provocative and well publicized an event as the Futurist exhibition. The day after the exhibition opened, Julius Korngold, critic of the *Neue Freie Presse,* brought Futurism into his discussion of Frederick Delius's symphonic poem *Paris:*

Now and then, the brazen turbulence of a great, self-indulgent city is captured in noise, in juxtapositions and confusions of sounds. . . . Futurism, too, is reflected, or rather anticipated, in music of this kind. The point of intersection is found in heterophony. . . . Is it not interesting that one of the Futurist pictures attempts to apply the "principle" [of multiple imaging] to a Parisian nightclub?[11]

As Korngold pointed out, the second act of Schreker's *Der ferne Klang* also used multiple-imaging techniques akin to those of the Futurists.[12]

Russolo's concept of Bruitism, the use of noise as musical material in its own right, could be understood as an antidote to the ever-increasing refinement of the post-Romantics. Yet Russolo was by no means the first to advocate the use of noise in musical scores. Turning the clock far back, Bruitism of a kind had already featured in the music of Jannequin and Biber; Leopold Mozart played with the notion in his *Toy* Symphony and *Musical Sleigh-ride*, Beethoven included cannon fire in *Wellington's Victory* and Lortzing a gunshot in the overture to *Der Wildschütz*, to cite but a few examples. Wagner's operatic scores include notated parts for such *intonarumori* as anvils and hammered shoe soles; Strauss domesticated the rattle in *Till Eulenspiegels lustige Streiche* (1895) and the wind machine in *Don Quixote* (1897); Mahler, in his sixth and seventh symphonies (1904 and 1905), revealed the poetry of cowbells. Even the *Gurrelieder* include noise-producing devices, a rattle and some iron chains, in the scene of the Peasant (Part 3: "Deckel des Sarges klappert und klappt").

Russolo's manifesto, which propagated a music consisting solely of noise, arrived on the scene a little too soon; furthermore, he proved to be a composer of little distinction. His ideas were taken up to better effect by George Antheil and Edgard Varèse, and his influence reached as far as Dada, the "Warsaw Autumn" composers of the 1960s (notably Penderecki), John Cage, and the *musique concrète* of postwar Europe and America.

As for Berg, the inclusion of unpitched noise in the first Altenberg song was by no means his last venture into this most un-Viennese area of artistic speculation. Bruitism of a kind also occurs in the fourth clarinet piece, op. 5, where the pianist pounds out the three lowest notes on the keyboard *con tutta forza*. The hammer blows in *Reigen*, the third of the Orchestral Pieces, op. 6, are customarily interpreted as an homage to Mahler, but could equally well be interpreted as a further salute to Bruitism. The first of the Opus 6 pieces opens with Berg's most elaborate use of organized noise, a veritable birth of order out of chaos, in which isolated notes and chords (including the notorious high E♭ of the tenor trombone) emerge from a jumble of unpitched percussion. For this, Berg had no need of *in-*

tonarumori or other unusual instruments. The facilities offered by a standard orchestral percussion section were all he required.

He must soon have recognized that Bruitism was incompatible with a music based entirely on pitch manipulation. In *Lulu* he identifies the sound of an electric doorbell as a combination of vibraphone and triangle. Thereby the concept of Bruitism is turned on its head, noise becomes real music with specified pitches. In the process, Berg imbues his score with a fine touch of Wedekind-inspired Surrealism.

Reception

Considering the exquisite craftsmanship of Berg's mature compositions, it is hardly surprising that they have always been of particular interest to theoreticians and analysts. After all, Berg himself published numerous analyses, both of his own music and that of others, and from his published writings we can glean as much about his musical thought processes as from the compositions themselves. Taking their cue from these publications, several distinguished musicologists have attempted to disentangle the most complex and intriguing aspect of his music, namely its pitch organization.

With the help of simple analytical data, such as can be gleaned from any well-written program note or CD booklet, the ear can follow Berg's larger-scale formal and thematic outlines with relative ease (it is this, above all, that places him above Webern, and indeed Schoenberg, in the affections of the musical public). However, even a listener with a retentive mind and an acute ear will have difficulty in apprehending structures and pitch relationships of greater complexity "on the fly" during performance. The simplest of palindromes, as in the third movement of the *Lyric Suite*, the ostinato of the *Lulu* Symphony or the second section of *Der Wein*, eludes the ear almost completely. The same goes for the retrograde of a twelve-note row. Our brains possess only limited capacity for processing retrograde acoustical data. Try deciphering a tape of text running backwards, or even spoken word for word in reverse order: given the appropriate commands, a computer processor can accomplish the task in a split second. Like so many other figures of musical architecture, the palindrome is an inherently inhuman device.

In performance, then, Berg's pitch organization remains largely unfathomable. But that, as he explained in a lecture on *Wozzeck*, is what he intended:

Ladies and gentlemen, when you attend the performance of my opera *Wozzeck*, I would like to ask you to *forget* all the theoretical and aesthetical points about the music that I have attempted to explain to you.

With rhythm, it is a different matter. It is far easier to apprehend the variative processes applied to the *Hauptrhythmus* in the second tavern scene of *Wozzeck* or the "Monoritmica" in Act 1 of *Lulu* than to follow the pitch organization of those same scenes.[13] Even the retrograde of a rhythm can usually be recognized as such.

When it comes to instrumental or vocal timbre, the ear is more reliable than any machine. Just as the eye can differentiate between considerably more than the 16.7 million colors available to the standard computer, the ear can distinguish between timbres—whether primary or compound— far more precisely than any machine. Listen to a high C sung in turn by Callas, Caballé, Nilsson, and Tebaldi or a simple scale passage played by Francescatti, Menuhin, Oistrakh, and Szigeti. With little hesitation, cognoscenti will be able to identify them; anyone with a reasonably good ear will at least recognize that they differ. Science, on the other hand, cannot measure and calibrate such parameters. To define the attributes of an individual performing artist in words or numbers is cumbersome and error prone.

Similarly, the sound of a musical composition is less accessible to analysis than its structure and substance. Perhaps this explains why analysts have expended less column space on Berg's orchestration than on any other aspect of his craft. Adorno, who was not only a philosopher and sociologist but also a composer and practical musician, is the notable exception. In his book on Berg, he often dwells on aspects of orchestration and timbre. And when it comes to *Wozzeck*, the orchestration is given pride of place. Reading between his lines, one can perceive that the economy and transparency of *Wozzeck* contributed largely, if not decisively, to its acceptance and lasting success.

> The orchestra makes the music real in the Cézannesque sense of *réaliser*. The entire compositional structure, from large-scale division to the tiniest capillaries of motivic development, becomes clear through color values. Conversely, no color is used that does not have a precise function in the delineation of musical continuity.[14]

Intuition

Some people dream in color, others in black and white. The same goes for composers. Intuitions of pitch and rhythm are domains in which logic does not rule, and over which creative artists themselves have no control. Sometimes an intuition is accompanied by a timbre, or is itself nothing but timbre; at other times, timbre has no part in it.

Once the raw material has manifested itself—whatever machinery of the subconscious may have set that process in motion—the composer takes control. Colors begin to emerge, at first often subliminally. What happens next depends on the medium. Music for a solo instrument or small ensemble can be "orchestrated" with relative ease, as it emerges on the paper. In the case of a full orchestral or operatic score, before it is fleshed out with tempo markings, textures, dynamics, stage directions, etc., the score is normally assembled in skeleton form, as a short score (*Particell*).

Brahms was known to complete a short score down to its last detail before deciding on the instrumentation (an extreme case is the Piano Quintet in F Minor, op. 34, also published as the Sonata for Two Pianos, op. 34b). On the other hand, there can be little doubt that he conceived the expansive horn theme in the Finale of his First Symphony—to cite a random example—with that instrument in mind, and no other.[15]

Reger would write down the complete musical text of a new work before adding markings of phrasing and dynamic. Nevertheless, nuance played as important a part in his concept of a work as any other aspect.

In the imagination of a composer, the parameters of a musical composition often evolve concurrently, or near-concurrently, spreading like concentric rings on water. Berg was blessed with such an inner ear. There can be little doubt that timbres asserted themselves at an early stage in the gestation process. The task of writing out the full score was then largely a matter of precisely defining his vision, note for note and bar for bar. Where other composers disfigure their short scores with afterthoughts, corrections, erasures, and all manner of extramusical graffiti, Berg's bear witness to a love of order and a fastidious eye for detail. As culmination of a tortuous process of seeking and finding, they are models of calligraphic elegance.

We cannot be certain whether Berg's first drafts were associated with specific instrumental colors, nor can we know precisely how his first notation of an idea corresponded to the form in which he had conceived it ("Every notation," writes Busoni, "is, in itself, the transcription of an abstract idea. The instant the pen seizes it, the idea loses its original form").[16] Soma Morgenstern recalls that Berg usually worked at the piano, often letting his fingers wander idly over the keys in search of ideas.[17] How did his inner ear react to these impulses? Abstractly, in the black and white of ivory and ebony? Judging by the rich color sense that Berg applied to his piano writing and the ease with which his keyboard writing translates into orchestral terms, most of his spontaneous intuitions must have come to him "in color." As a hypersensitive soul, he was probably incapable of playing a single note on the piano without imagining the snarl of a muted trumpet, the *Echoton* of a clarinet or the pure, rounded tone of a French horn.

It is time to choose a random example and examine it in some detail.

The First Measure of Wozzeck

Example 1. *Wozzeck*, Act 1, sc. 1, measure 1.

Berg describes these chords as "introductory." Perhaps they should be defined as the introduction to an introduction, for the drama does not begin until the curtain rises in measure 4. It could be that these two chords, taken on their own, came to Berg as one of his first intuitions for the music of *Wozzeck*. Together with the ensuing three measures they constitute an introduction not simply to the opening scene, but to the entire drama. Like any well-made overture, they presage all that follows.

Taken on their own, the string chords stand as a motto, and it is in this function that Berg quotes them verbatim, complete with percussion, in Act

2, sc. 2 of *Lulu* (m. 1095ff.), to underline Alwa's remark, "Über die liesse sich freilich eine interessante Oper schreiben" (about her, of course, one could write an interesting opera).

1. A Little Analysis

The first chord spans a major fourteenth, from e to d^2. Rearranged in rising sequence, its pitches cover steps 1, 2, 3, 5, and 6 of the D-minor scale. The second chord spans an augmented fifth, from g to $d\sharp^1$. Rearranged in rising sequence, its pitches cover steps 1, 3, 4, 5, and 7 of the G-sharp minor/A-flat minor scale. Douglas Jarman has pointed out that this second chord verticalizes the leitmotif associated with most of Wozzeck's entrances and exits.[18] Here its first appearance is illustrated, the pitches drawn from the scale of E-flat minor:

Example 2. *Wozzeck*, Act 1, sc. 3, measure 427.

The *glissandi* in Example 1 form a terrace of descending intervals, none of which occurs twice:

1. Vl. / 1	diminished octave (= major seventh)	8/7
1. Vl. / 2	minor sixth	6
2. Vl.	diminished fifth (= augmented fourth)	5/4
Vc.	minor third	3
Vla.	major second	2

Hence, Berg invests his opening bar with two kinds of universality:

- The chords are bounded by the tritonal axis D–G♯–A♭: diametrical opposites on the circle of fifths.
- The five *glissandi* are arranged in such a way as to cover every interval within the compass of an octave, in a manner that anticipates Berg pupil Fritz H. Klein's "all-interval" row of 1921.

During the course of Act 1, sc. 1, these opening chords recur three times, in different octaves, diversely orchestrated and, in all but one instance, rhythmically modified.[19]

- Measure 24: strings, rhythmically unaltered, one octave higher, *mf*; percussion as in measure 1 (*pp—p*):

Example 3. *Wozzeck*, Act 1, sc. 1, mm. 23–24.

- Measure 58: horns and tuba, rhythmically altered, one octave (partly two octaves) lower, *mf–crescendo–diminuendo*; no percussion:

Example 4. *Wozzeck*, Act 1, sc. 1, mm. 58–60.

- Measure 153, second segment: five woodwind instruments, rhythmically altered (note repetitions), original pitch, *mf*; no percussion:

Example 5. *Wozzeck*, Act 1, sc. 1, measure 153.

A third kind of universality is furnished in the opening measure by assembling a complete chromatic set. The string chords cover ten of the twelve semitones; on the upbeat to the second measure the oboe adds an eleventh (C-natural), and half a measure later the bassoon adds the twelfth (F-sharp):

Example 6. *Wozzeck*, measure 2 (with upbeat) and measure 3.

With the first three notes of measure 2, the oboe restates the upper segment of the second string chord, C♯–D♯–B, in horizontal array; the fourth pitch of measure 2 shifts the putative tonal center to an area between G-sharp minor and G major. The bassoon, with a *Drehfigur* bounded by the tritone E♭–A, marks out a corresponding territory between D major and D minor.

In these two measures, Berg assembles a quintet of woodwind instruments—oboe, English horn, clarinet, bass clarinet, and bassoon—that are deployed in the first thirty bars of the scene as obbligato instruments. The same quintet features again in a corresponding, palindromic passage toward the end of the scene (mm. 153–72). The obbligato instruments enter one by one, after a fashion described by Adorno as Berg's "Kapuziner" technique.[20] Their entries are staggered at intervals of 8, 13, 19, and 24 sixteenth-note beats.

On the last sixteenth-note of measure 3, elements of D minor and G-sharp minor combine to form a chord of ambiguous leading-note character (Example 7). It serves as fulcrum between the all-embracing pantonality of the introduction and the C-sharp minor/B-flat minor axis that underlies much of the ensuing music in scene 1.

Example 7. *Wozzeck*, measure 3, last chord; measure 4, English horn at sounding pitch.

2. The Gesture

The ear construes the *glissando* as a falling major seventh, indeed Berg marks the first violin line as *Hauptstimme* to ensure that this interval is highlighted. In combination, the major seventh and its attendant *glissando*, which folds in on itself like the leaves of some insect-eating plant, constitute a characteristic musical gesture.

As musical archetype, the falling seventh traces its line of descent via Schumann, Berlioz, and Liszt to Bach, Mozart, and Beethoven—perhaps even further still.[21] Although in *Wozzeck* the interval does not transcend the bounds of a single octave, it recalls the cry of Kundry, plummeting from the highest, most strident register of the soprano voice to its lowest, most guttural:

Example 8. Wagner, *Parsifal*, Act 2.

From there, it is but a small step to the scream of the Empress in *Die Frau ohne Schatten* (1914–18) . . .

Exmple 9. Richard Strauss, *Die Frau ohne Schatten*, Act 3 (study score, p. 486). Copyright ©1946 by Boosey & Hawkes Ltd.

. . . and hence to the blood-curdling scream of Marie as Wozzeck plunges his knife into her throat:

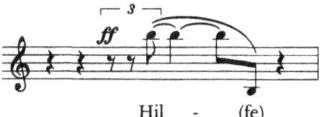
Example 10. *Wozzeck*, Act 3, sc. 3, measure 103.

In a sense, then, the opening measure of *Wozzeck* can be read as a stifled pre-echo of Marie's death cry. In Berg's subconscious the idea may have been inspired by a work of Zemlinsky:

Example 11. Zemlinsky, String Quartet no. 2, op. 15, mm. 6–9 after rehearsal number 65. Copyright ©1916 by Universal Edition A.G., Wien, © Renewed. All Rights Reserved. Used by permission of European American Music Distributors LLC, U.S. and Canadian agent for Universal Edition A.G., Wien.

Like much of the chamber music written by the circle of composers close to Schoenberg, Zemlinsky's Quartet has a hidden program. Central to that program is the figure of his sister Mathilde, Schoenberg's first wife. Within a dramatic framework bordering on hysteria, successive episodes depict Mathilde as a disheveled and downcast Elektra, abandoned and isolated; we hear her children playing unconcernedly at her side, learn—if indirectly—of her desperate love for the painter Richard Gerstl and of his suicide. The drama slowly subsides, and the work closes in a mood of wistful optimism.

Zemlinsky's Second Quartet was premiered in Vienna on 9 April 1918 at a concert of the Rosé Quartet. Subsequently, it featured three times in programs of the Verein für musikalische Privataufführungen.[22] Berg, as secretary of the Verein, would have known it well and heard every one of these performances.

In this context, it is therefore edifying to compare a brief passage from Zemlinsky's Quartet with the moment when Wozzeck begins to suspect Marie's infidelity (Act 2, sc. 1, mm. 96–98; Wozzeck: "Was hast da?" Marie: "Nix"). On paper, the similarity is scarcely apparent, but to the ear the gestures are one and the same:

Example 12. Zemlinsky, String Quartet no. 2, op. 15, mm. 5–8 after rehearsal no. 115. Copyright ©1916 by Universal Edition A.G., Wien, © Renewed. All Rights Reserved. Used by permission of European American Music Distributors LLC, U.S. and Canadian agent for Universal Edition A.G., Wien.; and Berg, *Wozzeck*, Act 2, sc. 1, mm. 96–98.

As it happens, the two Zemlinsky quotes are interrelated, with the falling sevenths of Example 11 on the viola, *tremolando sul ponticello*, moving in contrary motion to the fivefold gesture of first and second violin:

Example 13. Zemlinsky, String Quartet no. 2, op. 15, mm. 5–8 after rehearsal number 115. Copyright ©1916 by Universal Edition A.G., Wien, © Renewed. All Rights Reserved. Used by permission of European American Music Distributors LLC, U.S. and Canadian agent for Universal Edition A.G., Wien.

Hence, these cross-references reveal a hidden link between Wozzeck's entrances in Act 1, sc. 1 and Act 2, sc. 1. As such, they define the significance of the opening bar more precisely, as subconscious foreboding of an irrational jealousy and its tragic consequences. Schoenberg once observed that "it is *impossible* for a person to have only *one* sensation at a time. One has *thousands* simultaneously."[23] With the simplest of means, the opening bar of *Wozzeck* arouses these thousands of sensations.

3. The Instrumentation

Try playing the first two chords of *Wozzeck* on the piano. They sound quite different. The dreamlike quality of the opening chord, its *crescendo* awakening and metamorphosis through the *glissando* into a muffled scream—all this is lost in translation. It seems unlikely, therefore, that Berg would have lighted upon this particular idea at the keyboard. The gesture, together with its accommodating chords and distinctive timbre, must have sprung directly from his imagination onto the manuscript paper.

With woodwind or brass instruments, the measure would sound quite different. Bearing in mind that the first section of the scene is dominated by a quintet of obbligato woodwinds, it would have been logical—and perfectly possible—to open the scene with those instruments. The *glissandi* would have been less practicable, more of a smear than a slide. Moreover, a woodwind chord needs to be articulated, whereas a string entry, played on an up-bow in the upper half of the bow, drifts in as if from nowhere. That, evidently, is what Berg intended.

It would also have been perfectly possible to score the chords for muted brass (three trumpets and two trombones, or a *Mischklang* of muted trumpets and horns). Both the *crescendo* and the *glissando* would have been manageable, but here too the soft attack would be lost, and the entire character would be radically different.

The only viable alternative to Berg's solution would be to reverse the voices, with either violas or cellos on the top line. On the cello, the *glissando* from d^2 to $d\sharp^1$ would make a stronger effect, since the entire span would be covered with one finger on the A- or D-string. On the violin, the effect can be made only by sliding down the D- or G-string, whereby on the D-string the last few millimeters of *glissando* (from f^1 or g^1) would be omitted or, at best, simulated. (Since G-string tone is not stipulated, that possibility can be disregarded.) The reedier timbre of the viola or fluty timbre of the cello would have changed the overall character of the bar quite radically.

In a word, Berg's is not the only solution, but it is the simplest and most telling.

This entire discussion is based on the assumption that Berg *orchestrated* his music, i.e., he reviewed all the options open to him and weighed them, if briefly, before choosing the most appropriate. Had his working methods in any way resembled those of Mahler, he might even, after a few trial performances, have changed his mind. The soft opening fanfares of Mahler's First Symphony, for example, were originally scored for muted horns; in the definitive, four-movement version they were transferred to clarinets. Mahler's vision was evidently not as precise as Berg's, and needed to be corroborated in performance. For Berg, once a work had been published and performed, he rarely saw any need to change or revise it.

Naturally, this did not rule out the possibility of afterthoughts. Comparison with the short score of *Wozzeck* indicates that the side-drum and cymbal entry in the opening bar were added later.[24] As a rule, Berg notates unpitched percussion entries in his short scores on hand-ruled, one-stave lines. In this instance, the cue is not included:

Figure 1. *Wozzeck*, facsimile of opening measure (short score).

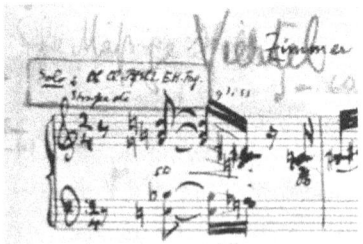

In a lecture written in 1929, Berg discussed this percussion entry in some detail:

> Before the drama begins, there stand two introductory string chords. Between the one chord and the other the side-drum

plays a soft, swelling roll, intended to underline the crescendo of the 1st chord into the 2nd. The idea was conceived purely instrumentally, i.e. from a musical and acoustical standpoint. When I first heard it, I realized to my great surprise that I could not have alluded to the military milieu of the play more tellingly and concisely than with this side-drum.[25]

Strictly speaking, the *crescendo* needs no reinforcement (where would we stand if Berg had underlined every *crescendo* in his score with percussion; where, for that matter, would the singers stand?) To the listener, the side-drum roll is likely to awaken military connotations only if viewed, with hindsight, as presaging the passage at the end of Act 1, sc. 2 (mm. 298–301, "Die Sonn' ist unter, drinnen trommeln sie"), where Berg calls for several military drums offstage "at a great distance," stipulating that they play *ff*, but far enough away as to sound *pp* in the auditorium (Mahler stipulates a similar chiaroscuro effect for the "Fernorchester" in *Das klagende Lied*).

In his lecture, Berg makes no mention of the suspended cymbal on the second chord, struck with an unspecified (presumably wooden) stick. But then, unless followed by a stroke on the bass drum, as in Marie's "Tschin Bum" (Act 1, sc. 3, rehearsal number 330 and following) or the music for the Animal Trainer and his Clown in *Lulu* (Prologue, 2nd measure after rehearsal number 5, passim), the cymbal stroke adds little or nothing to the military character.

Digression II: The *Seven Early Songs*

In the orchestral version of his *Seven Early Songs*, Berg uses the same side-drum roll, *crescendo* from *pp* to *p*, to completely different effect. It occurs twice (with no accompanying cymbal stroke) in the sixth song, "Liebesode" (O. E. Hartleben), and is stretched in both instances over a whole bar (plus eighth-note *crescendo* upbeat). In both instances, the *crescendo* is followed by a *decrescendo*. Though the material is substantially identical—a tiny dose of Bruitism, as in the *Altenberg Lieder*—context and gesture are entirely different. The first entry, mm. 7–8, illustrates the word *Sommerwind* (summer wind) and coincides with the last syllable of that word; the second (mm. 21–22) echoes the phrase "Träume des Rausches" (dreams of rapture), exploiting the dual meaning of the word *Rausch* as "rapture" and "rushing" or "rustling." With one and the same effect, the listener is transplanted into surroundings as far distant as can be imagined from the parade grounds and marching bands of *Wozzeck*.

At face value, the *Seven Early Songs* were published to satisfy the demand for new works from the now celebrated composer of *Wozzeck*. Berg may have chosen them not only for their individual qualities, but also because he could still recall, in his mind's ear, the timbres and colors with which they had been conceived over twenty years earlier.

Percussion is used sparingly and almost entirely for illustrative purposes. The *pp–p crescendo–decrescendo* side-drum roll features again in the seventh song, this time to underline the words "von deiner tiefen, tiefen Lust" (of your deep, deep desire; rehearsal number 26), and is repeated once, at a slightly higher dynamic level (*p–mp*). In the first song, a soft roll on the bass drum anticipates the word *schattenschwarz* (shadow black; one measure after rehearsal number 19), and in the closing bars of the fifth song an irregular series of strokes on a suspended cymbal (doubled by harp or celesta), ten in all, suggest the chiming of a clock: "wie leise die Minuten zieh'n" (how silently the minutes flee; rehearsal number 18).

Any occurrence of the number 10 in a work of Berg's in or after 1925 sets alarm bells ringing, for this was the secret number of his beloved in Prague, Hanna Fuchs. Considering the overtly erotic character of all seven poems, it is not inconceivable that the orchestral version of the *Seven Early Songs*, despite the dedication to Helene Berg, was in fact intended for Hanna. Had the fifth song comprised 23 measures, or included the number 23 (Berg's secret number) in some other parameter, the symbolism would have been perfect. But the fifth song is only 22 measures long. The sixth, "Liebesode," comprises 24 bars. Taken together, these two songs add up to 46 bars (23 x 2). All seven songs were composed between 1905 and 1908, long before Frau Fuchs entered Berg's life. The orchestral version was completed in 1928, at a time when the relationship had entered a critical phase. Despite solemn vows to the contrary, Hanna revealed the clandestine relationship to her husband. To read any particular significance into these numbers would be stretching the point. So we must leave those ten chimes hanging in the air like a question mark—which is how they sound.

Could it be that the chimes also reveal the significance of the cymbal stroke in the first bar of *Wozzeck*, a marking of time, an anticipation of the Captain's admonition, "Langsam, Wozzeck, langsam . . . ! Eins nach dem Andern!" (Slowly, Wozzeck, slowly . . . ! One thing after another!)? If so, then the wheel of circumstance can be turned still further. At the end of Act 2, sc. 5, Wozzeck, beaten and exhausted, utters a variant of those words: "Einer nach dem Andern!" (One man [person] after the other!) And those words in turn are a forewarning of Marie's impending murder. Just as the chords can be read as a premonition of her death, so can that one soft cymbal stroke.

Unlike Webern, who possessed a genius for instrumental transcriptions, Berg was a reluctant arranger.[26] The score of the *Seven Early Songs* is therefore rare, in that Berg resolved for once to "orchestrate" in the classical sense of the word.[27] In contrast to the idiomatic orchestral transcriptions of Debussy ("Le jet d'eau" from the *Cinq poèmes de Baudelaire*, opening sections of *La boîte à joujoux*) and Ravel (*Le tombeau de Couperin*, *Une barque sur l'océan*, *Don Quichotte à Dulcinée*, Mussorgsky's *Pictures from an Exhibition*, etc.), Berg rarely allows the listener to lose sight of the original piano textures, perhaps because his piano writing was itself orchestrated in the sense described above, that is, conceived in instrumental colors and notated as the piano reduction of an imaginary orchestral score.

Whatever the case, the orchestrations betray their keyboard origins in that almost every chord includes some form of ictus to reproduce the effect of a hammer striking a piano string. To this end, Berg doubles woodwind lines with pizzicato strings (e.g., mm. 1–5 of the first song), reduced sometimes to pizzicato double basses or celli (e.g., mm. 1–9 of the third song), or with the harp (e.g., last three measues of the first song, mm. 1–3 and 7–8 of the second song). Sometimes, on the other hand, the original piano part is entrusted entirely to the harp, while the harmony is spread out over winds and strings (e.g., mm. 9–13 of the first song) to reproduce the effect of the sustaining pedal.

For any competent arranger, these techniques are stock in trade. Nevertheless, Berg fulfills the assignment with scrupulous attention to detail, coupled with his highly developed sense of relevance to the context, color, balance, and sheer sensual beauty.

The most remarkable aspect of these orchestrations is their extrinsic organization:

- The full complement of instruments participates only in the first and the last songs.
- The second song is scored for a chamber ensemble of fifteen instruments (though not the same fifteen as in Schoenberg's First Chamber Symphony and Act 2, sc. 3 of *Wozzeck*).
- The third song is scored for strings only, with each string group subdivided throughout into one solo and one *tutti* line.
- The fourth song omits the clarinets, bass clarinet, bassoons, and trumpets, and reduces the horn section from four players to three.
- The fifth song omits the strings, reduces the horn section to two, and calls for just one trumpet and one trombone.
- The sixth song omits the flutes, oboes, and trombones, and calls for just one trumpet.

With the intention of imposing order on an implicitly chaotic world, Berg thus molds his orchestration into a loosely symmetrical arch form: the first song finds its reciprocal in the seventh, the third in the fifth.

Further organizational parameters are the chosen schemes of key, natural phenomena, and time (day/night, season, passing of time). Apart from the last two songs, major alternates regularly with minor. The first song finds its reciprocal tonality (relative minor) in the sixth, and the fourth in the fifth. As in the first bar of *Wozzeck*, the last two songs stand at diametrically opposite poles on the circle of fifths, here F-sharp and C.

The first, second, third, and sixth poems are by nature nocturnal; the fifth and seventh diurnal; the fourth depicts a transition from day to night. Four of the poems make express use of flower symbolism, but only one makes specific reference to a living creature, the nightingale.

1. "Nacht" (Night)	three sharps: A major	Night; Flora
2. "Schilflied" (Song amongst the reeds)	four flats: F minor	Night; Flora
3. "Die Nachtigall" (The nightingale)	two sharps: D major	Night (Spring); Fauna
4. "Traumgekrönt" (A crown of dreams)	two flats: G minor, with *maggiore* conclusion	Day, then Night; Flora
5. "Im Zimmer" (Indoors)	two flats: B-flat major	Day (Autumn); Passing of Time
6. "Liebesode" (Lover's ode)	three sharps: F-sharp minor	Night (Summer); Flora
7. "Sommertage" (Summer days)	three flats: C minor, with *maggiore* conclusion	Day (Summer); Passing of Time

The wonder of it all is that to the innocent ear this zeal for order—a network of intrinsic connections following an irregular, extrinsic plan—neither obtrudes nor militates against the artistic sensibility of each song in its own right.

To highlight the principal themes of the cycle—memories of erotic bliss, unrequited yearning—Berg may have been tempted to devise some flowery title. But then, if he revitalized and orchestrated these songs as a fresh token of love for Hanna Fuchs, which seems plausible, he had every reason to publish them under a neutral or objective title.

Returning to Wozzeck...

Not surprisingly, in a score of which every note and every musical parameter is precisely placed within a globally organized network, the scoring of Act 1, sc. 1 of *Wozzeck* is as carefully thought out as that of the *Seven Early Songs*. In fact, it is done with even greater care, particularly with regard to symmetry. The basic principle can be summed up in one word: obbligato. In a sense, Berg's use of obbligato instruments can be understood as a salute to tradition. It reminds us of Mozart's virtuoso quartet of woodwinds and strings in *Die Entführung aus dem Serail* (Constanze's C-major aria, "Martern aller Arten"), the whooping trio of horns in Beethoven's *Fidelio* (Leonore's recitative and aria, "Abscheulicher... Komm, Hoffnung"), the somber cello that accompanies a lonely king in Verdi's *Don Carlo* (Philipp's aria "Ella giammai m'amo"), and of a perplexed Emperor in Strauss's *Die Frau ohne Schatten* (Act 2, sc. 2, "Falke, du wieder gefundner").

Needless to say, Berg also breaks with tradition. Firstly, the obbligato instruments are not spotlighted, and the innocent ear does not necessarily register their prominence: a) because their contribution is sometimes embedded in the overall texture; b) because Berg does not allow the predominance of an obbligato to preclude equal or even stronger emphasis on other instruments. Secondly, not every obbligato contribution is continuous. Thirdly, some contributions are brief, others more extended (the length of obbligato passages varies between six and forty-four measures). Fourthly, the choice of instruments is at times unconventional and changes, often abruptly, from one episode to the next:

Measures	*Instrument(s)*
1–29	oboe, cor anglais, clarinet, bass clarinet, bassoon
30–50	timpani, bass drum, side-drum, and harp
51–64	solo viola
65–108	three flutes,[28] celesta
109–14	contrabassoon
115–26	four trumpets
127–32	four horns
133–36	four trombones
137–53	*tutti* strings
153–72	oboe, cor anglais, clarinet, bass clarinet, bassoon

Each instrument or instrumental group makes its obbligato contribution in turn, until the entire orchestra has presented itself: a reversal of the time-honored commedia dell'arte practice of parading all the actors across the stage before the drama begins. The list of obbligato intruments includes a "joker," namely the solo viola. By rights, if Berg allowed one stringed instrument a solo "break," he should have offered every other principal string player an equal opportunity. But life is unfair, and in this instance dramatic necessity takes precedence over equal rights for all. Of particular note is the cadenza-like passage for contrabassoon, whose lavatorial contribution aptly illustrates the Captain's concept of morality. To comply with the palindromic nature of the closing bars, the quintet of woodwinds, to which the curtain had risen, returns to wind it down.

Here, as in everything he wrote, Berg seeks and finds the best of *all* worlds.

NOTES

1. In reaction to a critic's lavish praise of the "silken" strings in a performance of a Haydn symphony, Stravinsky allegedly observed: "Haydn's strings should sound like strings, and not like silk."

2. Gustav Mahler described the high trumpet in his Seventh Symphony as "a tormented struggle with the sublime . . . shrieks intermingling to form a chord of the Universal Symphony." Quoted in Henri-Louis de la Grange, G. Weiss et al. *Gustav Mahler: Letters to His Wife* (London: Faber & Faber, 2004), 306.

3. Octaves in this essay are represented using the Helmholtz system, i.e.: ascending from the C below middle C up, pitches are given with lowercase letters (c, d, e, etc.) and superscripts start with c^1 at middle C; descending the three octaves below that pitches are given, respectively as: uppercase, then uppercase with subscripts (C_1 or C_2).

4. Adolf Bernhard Marx, *Ludwig van Beethoven: Leben und Schaffen* (Heidelberg, 1859; repr. Hildesheim: Georg Olms Verlag, 1979), 2:46. In the original—"Glaubt Er, daß ich an eine elende Geige denke, wenn der Geist zu mir spricht, und ich es aufschreibe?"—the text, though well known, is usually misquoted. Marx writes of Schuppanzigh's protest in connection with an "F-minor Quartet op. 59," presumably a typographical error.

5. "*Il faut méditerraniser la musique*: ich habe Gründe zu dieser Formel. Die Rückkehr zur Natur, Gesundheit, Heiterkeit, Jugend, Tugend!" Friedrich Nietzsche, "Der Fall Wagner," in *Werke*, ed. Karl Schlechta (Munich: Carl Hanser, 6th rev. ed., 1969), 3:907.

6. At least, the world might have witnessed it, had anyone taken the trouble to take note. The complete cycle remained unperformed until eighteen years after Berg's death.

7. Elsa Bienenfeld, *Neues Wiener Journal*, 3 April 1908.

8. Theodor W. Adorno, *Alban Berg: Master of the Smallest Link*, trans. Juliane Brand and Christopher Hailey (Cambridge: Cambridge University Press, 1991), 64ff.

9. Letter from Busoni to his wife, dated "(Paris, le), 23. Jn. 1913," in *Busoni: Briefe an seine Frau*, ed. F. Schnapp (Erlenbach-Zürich/Leipzig: Rotapfel-Verlag, 1935), 279.

10. The instruments devised by Russolo bore onomatopoeic names such as *crepitatore, gorgogliatore, rombatore, ronzatore, scoppiatore, sibilatore, stropicciatore,* and *ululatore*. See also John C. G. Waterhouse, "Futurist Music in Historical Perspective" in *Futurismo 1909-1919*, exhibition catalogue (Newcastle upon Tyne, 1972), 93–104.

11. Julius Korngold, *Neue Freie Presse*, 16 December 1912.

12. The concert had been conducted by Schreker.

13. *Wozzeck*, Act 3, sc. 4, Universal Edition study score, 419–35.

14. Adorno, *Alban Berg*, 86.

15. Johannes Brahms, Symphony no. 1 in C Minor, op. 68, fourth movement, m. 30ff.

16. Ferruccio Busoni, *Sketch of a New Aesthetic of Music*, in *Three Classics in the Aesthetics of Music*, trans. Th. Baker (New York: Dover, 1962), 85.

17. Soma Morgenstern, *Alban Berg und seine Idole*, ed. Ingolf Schulte (Lüneburg: Klampen, 1999).

18. Douglas Jarman, *The Music of Alban Berg* (London/Boston: Cambridge University Press, 1979), 59.

19. Ibid.

20. "Berg's music, in all the lush opulence of its variety, cannot support naked contrast, the unmediated juxtaposition of opposites—as if the assertion of musical opposites might grant individual elements an existence incompatible with the metaphysical unpretentiousness, the fragile ductus, of all Bergian musical design. One can illustrate this Bergian manner—manner in the larger sense of Mannerism—with the children's game in which the word 'Kapuziner' is disassembled and put back together again: Kapuziner – Apuziner – Puziner – Uziner – Ziner – Iner – Ner – Er – R; R – Er – Ner – Iner – Ziner – Uziner – Puziner – Apuziner – Kapuziner. That is how he composed, that is how all of his music plays in a Capuchin tomb of whimsy, and his development was essentially a development toward the spiritualization of that manner." Adorno, *Alban Berg*, 3.

21. See Antony Beaumont, *Busoni the Composer* (London: Faber & Faber, 1985), 343.

22. Zemlinsky's Second Quartet was performed at propaganda concerts of the Verein on 11 and 23 May 1919 (Feist Quartet) and at a regular concert on 20 June 1919. It was also included in the fourth concert of the Prague Verein, which Berg did not attend, on 14 March 1920.

23. Arnold Schoenberg to Ferruccio Busoni, undated letter (August 1908), trans. in Antony Beaumont, ed., *Ferruccio Busoni: Selected Letters* (London: Faber & Faber, 1987), 389.

24. Berg Fonds, Music Collection, Austrian National Library, F21 Berg 14.

25. Alban Berg, "'Wozzeck'—Vortrag von 1929," in *Glaube, Hoffnung und Liebe: Schriften zur Musik* (Leipzig: Reclam, 1981), 270.

26. See Antony Beaumont, "Schönberg's 'Verein' and Its Orchestra," in *Arnold Schönbergs Wiener Kreis*, Report of the Symposium 12–15 September 2000, *Journal of the Arnold Schönberg Center* 2, ed. C. Meyer, Vienna, 2000.

27. Apart from his arrangement of the Adagio from the Chamber Concerto for violin, clarinet and piano, his piano reduction of the two movements with voice from Schoenberg's Second Quartet, an adaptation for string orchestra of three movements from the *Lyric Suite*, and a transcription for salon orchestra of Johann Strauss's waltz *Wein, Weib und Gesang*, Berg made no orchestrations or arrangements. This seems all the more surprising in view of his commitment to Schoenberg's Verein für musikalische Privataufführungen, which relied for its programs on a steady supply of transcriptions and arrangements.

28. Between mm. 75 and 97, the flutes "step down." During these measures Berg deploys all four flutes. Although their contribution is just as prominent as in mm. 65–74, it is not marked as obbligato.

"... deinen Wuchs wie Musik": Portraits, Identities, and the Dynamics of Seeing in Berg's Operatic Sphere

SHERRY D. LEE

> Dear Master and Teacher,
> I forgot to send you with my last letter the copy of a large essay on you and Webern, which I wrote for the American magazine *Modern Music*, and which you will perhaps find pleasing. In enclosing it here, I would like to append a request. *Modern Music* would like one photograph each of you and Webern to complement the essay; but not one from real life, rather one of a *portrait*. Do you own one of the picture by Schönberg depicting you? If it were available, I would be most grateful to you for sending it . . .
> —Theodor Adorno to Alban Berg

In the brief note above from Theodor Adorno to Alban Berg, which dates from 1931, the primacy accorded by the American magazine's request for a painted portrait over a photographic likeness is striking.[1] True, a painted portrayal was still accorded something of an elite status over the wider public accessibility of the snapshot. Berg's own work at the time testified to the continued artistic interest in portraiture: he was well into the composition of his last opera, *Lulu*, in which a portrait plays a key role. But by this date, the status of the painted portrait as a naturalistic likeness of the individual had faced repeated opposition. Photography itself had of course posed one significant challenge. The importance of realism and truth in the portrayal of subjects was a mark of the nineteenth century's growing emphasis on scientific objectivity, and photography seemed to guarantee the sought-after possibility of a precise, objective likeness of the individual. Not only was the photographed portrait apparently more true than the painted one, but it was more efficient and less expensive and widespread well before Berg's time.

A second challenge to the status and authority of the painted likeness arose within Berg's lifetime in the form of artistic abstraction, and the corresponding denigration of the mimetic mode that had always been fundamental to the role of portraiture as a naturalistic portrayal of individual likeness. "More fundamentally," as Joanna Woodall explains, "the early twentieth-century rejection of figurative imagery challenged the belief that visual resemblance to a living or once-living model is necessary or appropriate to the representation of identity."[2] But perhaps the most important challenge to portraiture in the years preceding Adorno's letter to Berg arose from shifts in the understanding of the individual subject and its representation. For, throughout its history, the portrait had traditionally been presumed to capture not only the surface likeness of its subject but the essence of the sitter's identity. By the end of the nineteenth century, though, the presupposition of a transparent relationship between visible, external appearance and a hidden, inner self had been seriously undermined. And in Berg's world, the very notion of subjective identity had been fundamentally called into question.

It has become almost a cliché to characterize the Vienna of the late nineteenth and early twentieth centuries in terms of crisis, and indeed the city was marked by features of social, political, economic, and cultural instability and rupture—a European capital in turbulent transition under the pressures of modernity. It is Jacques Le Rider's contention that the processes of modernization, which "cast doubt on collective cultural identities, and also on individual subjective identity," were nowhere more acutely felt than in early twentieth-century Vienna, and that "the crisis of the individual, experienced as an identity crisis, is at the heart of all the questionings we find in literature and the humane sciences" in that milieu.[3] Berg lived in a culture whose overwhelming concern with the vulnerability of the subjective self and the instability of inner and outer identity was as evident in the artist's studio as in the psychoanalyst's consulting room.

At a time when modernity cast doubt on the nature of individual subjective identity, the genre of the portrait, in which that identity was traditionally represented, could not but be questioned; its persistence among artists in Berg's Vienna is a sign of the urge to depict the pressures on the subject within the Viennese modernist milieu. The very breadth of what Richard Brilliant describes as "the oscillation between art object and human subject," which "gives portraits their extraordinary grasp on our imagination," demonstrates how varied—even fragmented—was the Viennese artistic response to the modernist cultural moment.[4] For example, what Carl Schorske termed Klimt's "asocial portraiture" of women from Vienna's social elite evokes "the dominion of the environment over the person of the subject," in which naturally and even sensitively portrayed faces are trapped within rigidly two-dimensional surfaces of artifice and pattern.[5] Subjectivity and interiority retreat behind abstractly designed surfaces, to which the tension of psychological states has been transferred in the form of conflicting shapes and patterns. Oskar Kokoschka sought the opposite, a vital and dynamic portraiture that conveyed psychological truths through intimations of gesture, facial expression, and bodily tension:

> When I paint a portrait, I am not concerned with the externals of a person—the signs of his clerical or secular eminence, or his social origins. . . . What used to shock people in my portraits was that I tried to intuit from the face, from its play of expressions, and from gestures, the truth about a particular person. . . . A person is not a *still* life.[6]

The distorted treatment of face and body in Egon Schiele's brutal self-portraits gives uncompromising expression to the extremity of the subjective condition, whereas in Schoenberg's own Expressionistic self-portraits, the body retreats behind the priority given to the gaze—especially in the *Brown* and *Green* self-portraits and the famous *Gaze* images of 1910—in which identity resides precariously in a fearful interiority. "Before anything else," asserts Jean-Luc Nancy, "the portrait looks. [. . .] Its 'autonomy' gathers and restricts the painting, even the entire face, in the look."[7] The gaze of the subject looking out from Schoenberg's mirror-canvases surely eclipses in intensity that of the onlooker, for whom the image is disturbing not because of a lack of resemblance, but because of its presumed resemblance to a self. The stark condition of subjectivity is recognizable in the absence of the possibility of actually recognizing the subject of the image. In the words of Nancy, "resemblance has *nothing* to do with recognition."[8] Yet self-resemblance remained the goal of most of Schoenberg's self-portraits during and in the decades beyond this Expressionist moment.[9] And in his naturalistic portrait of Berg, referred to in Adorno's letter, resemblance takes on a quality of play for the viewer who recognizes, in its pose of elegant nonchalance, both Berg himself and his physical resemblance to Oscar Wilde (Figure 1).[10]

Adorno remarked on this resemblance, too, and the reference to Wilde is no mere digressive anecdote. In fact, Wilde's image as a public personality and an artist, and his literary and dramatic works, played no small part in a modernist ethos in which self-image, identity, and the conflicted relation between the two was a central concern. It is hardly necessary to reassert here the prominence accorded in Berg's sphere to Wilde and his works, which were translated into German literally dozens of times in the

Figure 1a. Schoenberg's portrait of Berg, c. 1910.

Figure 1b. Portrait of Oscar Wilde, signed "Aubrey Beardsley" but almost certainly a forgery.

decades following his death. *Salome* made an early and far-reaching impact, from its German premiere in Berlin in 1901, through its Viennese premiere at the Volkstheater the following year, to its operatic incarnation by Strauss in 1905. Unswervingly admired by Karl Kraus, Wilde epitomized an engrossment with image and appearance and a correspondence between art and life.[11]

With characteristic subtlety and richness Wilde explored the motifs of portrait and mirror, self-image and destructive gaze, themes that recur often and in various guises throughout his oeuvre. One of the most fascinating aspects in the Wildean perspective is the conflation of portrait and mirror image. "The first image was a portrait," comments Woodall, invoking the reflected image of Narcissus in the pool.[12] Not surprisingly, narcissism is a frequent trope in Wilde's poems, parables, dramas, and stories, in which art more often than not takes on the role of a mirror—not of life but of the spectator, as Wilde said. From this moment onward, the possibility is always present that the portrait acts also as a mirror, and that the mirror reflection's relation to identity and truth may be as problematic as that of the painted representation. Not long before he featured the portrait in *The Picture of Dorian Gray* (1890) as the visual trace of the ongoing conflict between outer appearance and inner essence, Wilde probed that theme in his little parable "The Birthday of the Infanta" (1889), wherein the mirror image of the self is at first unrecognizable and, when it is recognized, becomes an object of horror and revulsion. An ugly, deformed little dwarf, so innocent of cultured refinements that he has never seen a mirror, performs for the amusement of the pretty Infanta on her birthday. Later, naïvely imagining her laughter at his awkward dancing as a sign of her affection for him, he wanders through the palace in search of her, and his chance removal of a drapery reveals a large mirror. His belated recognition that the hideous monster in the glass is really himself breaks his heart, and he dies.

Nearly twenty years after Wilde's little tale was first published, Vienna was treated to a ballet-pantomime performance based on it, staged in the Kunstschau Garden Theater in 1908, and danced by the Ausdruckstanz duo of Grete and Elsa Wiesenthal to music by Franz Schreker. Peter Altenberg's enthusiastic response in print testifies to its resonance among Vienna's modern artists and aesthetes.[13] The effectiveness of its idea of outer unloveliness at odds with inner selfhood was just as keenly appreciated by Alexander Zemlinsky, who wrote to Schreker some years later requesting an opera libretto on the subject of "the tragedy of the ugly man."[14] Schreker wrote the libretto, but became so engaged with it that he asked his friend to relinquish it so he could set it himself. The result, Schreker's *Die Gezeichneten*, premiered in 1915. But the theme stayed with

Zemlinsky, who ultimately returned to Wilde's tale of the tragic little dwarf. His opera *Der Zwerg* finally appeared in 1921.

Georg Klaren, Zemlinksy's librettist for *Der Zwerg*, altered the Wilde text more than a little for its operatic incarnation, giving it a particularly Viennese tint by overlaying it with a gloss of psycho-sexual pathology that evinces the influence of Otto Weininger's notorious *Geschlecht und Charakter*.[15] But the central dramatic crisis remains the dwarf's traumatic confrontation with his uncanny self/other in the mirror, a theme reflected as much in the composer's score as in the text and dramatic action. Zemlinsky did exploit some play with leitmotific construction and inversion that musically suggests the textual idea of mirroring and reflection, identity, and otherness. Perhaps even more effectively, he utilized harmonic language in a way that engages with the sense of uncanniness that gives his drama its potent effect. By giving dramatic prominence to passages that place familiar tonal harmonies in striking nonfunctional juxtapositions, he was able to evoke an audible experience of uncanny disorientation from within the texture of the music itself: the familiar is estranged, as the self becomes other.[16] These effects, combined with features such as the dramatic employment of a relentless ostinato conveying inescapable recurrence, are among the most vivid strokes in Zemlinsky's operatic portrait of damaged selfhood. It made an extraordinarily strong impression on Berg, who wrote to his wife that some of the most intense moments of the drama were so harrowing as to be "nearly unbearable."[17] The painfulness of personal ugliness was, in Christopher Hailey's words, "a tragedy Zemlinsky knew firsthand," and as Leon Botstein has noted, "autobiographical parallels in *The Dwarf* do not require a stretch of imagination" for a composer who was notably small in stature and unattractive by conventional standards.[18] Alma Schindler's description of him as "a hideous gnome" is only the cruelest sketch of his often-caricatured appearance, rendered by a woman he loved who was powerfully attracted to him for a while but ultimately rejected him.[19] Yet it is misleading to imply that the opera's impact relies solely or even substantially upon an understanding of it as a self-portrait of its composer. When viewed merely as a personal document, the work shrinks, its significance pales. What is lost is the very real sense in which this reckoning with the mirror participates in the wider sphere of artistic works, many influenced more or less directly by Wilde, that explore issues of selfhood through a play of image and identity.

In *The Picture of Dorian Gray*, Wilde went further, reimagining the temporal possibilities of the portrait's existence as self-image and reflection of subjective identity. In the novel as in the earlier fairy tale, self-image remains key, but it is transferred from the medium of the mirror reflection to that of the painted portrait, and so to the realm of art. The novel makes a crucial connection between mirror and portrait, which seem at first to be different types of images. But Dorian's portrait, through some mysterious affinity between life and art, becomes a sort of mirror. In the first weeks following its completion, he is enchanted by it, in awe that it is really his own image, and that he is really so beautiful, so physically perfect. "Morning after morning he had sat before the portrait, wondering at its beauty, almost enamoured of it, as it seemed to him at times. [. . .] Once, in a boyish mockery of Narcissus, he had kissed, or feigned to kiss, those painted lips," Wilde tells us, evoking the notion of the picture as reflection.[20] It is on the night that Dorian's cruelty to Sibyl Vane drives her to suicide that he first notices a change in it, "a touch of cruelty in the mouth." His horror gives way first to curiosity and then to a kind of excited pleasure. The picture, and not he himself, bears the consequence of his sins; in the years to come, it will age and wither, but he will remain youthful, handsome, and most important, free of the signs of corruption, with which the portrait instead will be marked. As Dorian realizes, "This portrait would be to him the most magical of mirrors. As it had revealed to him his own body, so it would reveal to him his own soul."[21] While the symbolic aspects of Wilde's novel thus postulate an imaginative shifting of the boundaries between art and life, they also challenge the boundaries separating the visual, spatial art of painting from the temporal art of literature. For Wilde created in the medium of words the image of a painting that, in defiance of its nature as visual art, changes over time—and this task was itself something that only a temporal art such as literature could accomplish. "That literature and painting could not exchange their roles was the idea which *Dorian Gray* would alter," Richard Ellmann says, "by bringing together [. . .] the exalted moment and its disintegration."[22]

So Vienna became preoccupied with the ways in which the image of the subject, whether mirrored self-image or portrait, reflected or falsified a subjective interiority that may or may not be visually accessible through the image itself. And these themes, which exceed the boundaries of the artist's canvas to proliferate throughout the literature and drama of the era— from Peter Altenberg's aphoristic word-portraits of beautiful women and young girls in the 1900s and 1910s to Franz Werfel's drama *Spiegelmensch* of 1921 and beyond—are manifest also within contemporary opera. Indeed, the centrality of opera's participation in the artistic exploration of central themes of Viennese modernism can hardly be overemphasized. Canonic studies of modernist culture in Vienna—such as those by Allan Janik and Stephen Toulmin, Schorske, and Le Rider—tend to focus primarily on literature, paying less attention to music in general and very little to opera in particular. Still, they do not fail to recognize the devotion of the upper and middle classes to music and the theater in a city where the performing arts made front-page news. "By the end of the century," Schorske observes, the Viennese populace "manifested more genuine enthusiasm for these arts than its counterparts in any other city in Europe."[23] Only in a city where opera was a primary focus of cultural attention would a figure such as Mahler, for example, have achieved such prominence. As director of the Hofoper, he was undeniably a central public personage, whether he was being lauded as a cultural hero identified with everything progressive or vilified in the anti-Semitic press. The occupancy of that podium and the happenings on that stage were truly important matters. A list of Viennese composers who directed their energies toward opera composition would be lengthy indeed, and would include Julius Bittner, Ernst Krenek, Franz Schmidt, Hans Gál, and Egon Wellesz in addition to Schoenberg, Schreker, Zemlinsky, Korngold, and Berg. In short, opera played a vital role in Berg's Vienna as the musical-theatrical genre in which subjectivity was both seen and heard, staged in spectacle and sound.[24]

Berg's *Lulu* orbits within a wider constellation of operas that use the conceit of a reflected image or portrait to play on the dynamics of looking, seeing, and being seen.[25] The opening of Puccini's *Tosca*, for example, plays repeatedly on the contrasts and contradictions between portraits as supposed likenesses and the nature of individual appearance. The pious blond woman whose prayerful devotion furnishes a model for Cavaradossi's portrait of the Magdalen is a disguise for concealing an escaping prisoner in the chapel. Cavaradossi's own explicit comparison between her portrait and the miniature one of Tosca he carries suggests that his art secretly combines the physical charms of both women. And Tosca's jealousy over the model's beauty is matched by her discomfort at the look of the portrait, in which the eyes seem to mock her; she will feel better if the portrait's eyes are changed from blue to black, so that she can see it instead as a kind of self-reflection. Perhaps closer to Berg in the German operatic sphere is Max von Schillings' *Mona Lisa* (1915), in which da Vinci's historical work of art, and the notoriously enigmatic "look of the portrait," is the catalyst for a sensationalist drama of sexual jealousy and murder. The comic tone of Kurt Weill's *Der Zar lässt sich photographieren* (1928) is a marked contrast to such melodrama, but the gun hidden in the camera associates death with the taking of a likeness, and the "shooting" of the portrait photo is framed by a play of seduction and attempted murder.[26]

In all these works, portraits and likenesses shed traditional connotations of transparency and true portrayal, pointing instead to concealment. These dynamics are no less evident in the lively operatic arena in Vienna where, as Schorske has noted, everything that was vital in Austrian culture was bound to find expression on the stage.[27] In *Lulu*, Zemlinsky's *Der*

Zwerg, Franz Schreker's *Die Gezeichneten*, and Erich Wolfgang Korngold's *Die tote Stadt*, the workings of the themes of identity and self-image, of gaze and reflection, are as diverse as the subjects depicted in their onstage portraits. The following discussion employs shifting perspectives from which to regard the spatial and temporal dimensions of the viewing and listening experience, and the play of looking and recognition among characters, performers, and audience in the opera house. In each work, the visual image encapsulates multiple tensions between appearance and identity in a web of sexual and psychological complexity. Simultaneously, it prompts a critical examination of the musical engagement with the visual trope in opera. The dramatic interaction of sight and sound has far-reaching implications for the musical dialectic between space and time, the visual moment, and its sensual unfolding.

This space-time relationship is central to Adorno's examination of both visual art and music in his 1965 essay "On Some Relationships Between Music and Painting."[28] His deliberations on the possibility for convergence between the two art forms begin from the argument that despite their seemingly obvious modal distinction, music existing solely in time and painting in space, both elements inhere in both art forms in a state of dialectical tension. In asserting the constitutive relationships of painting to time and music to space, Adorno's discussion implies commonalities in the way both arts are not only constructed but experienced. Richard Leppert comments on Adorno's essay in his work on the representation of musical performance in visual art. The image that depicts the performing gesture aims to capture "the now-time of the performance moment," he says, and the visual rendering of music as a human engagement with the experience of time is a reminder that "temporality is a fundamental category of what constitutes both modernity and modern self-reflexivity about the nature of selfhood."[29] Alongside the observable image of the individual, then, temporality is also fundamental to the constitution of identity.

As Leppert's focus on performing gesture suggests, the human body forms a crucial connection between temporal and spatial dimensions in both the visual and musical spheres. The performing body is the means of realizing music within space and time. Similarly, the body and its gestural language, which form the very content of the portrait image, are the link between identity as physical appearance and a lived experience of the self. This in turn is significant for a consideration of the meaningful interaction of imagery and music within opera, wherein the dynamics of seeing and hearing are intertwined in the theatrical experience: its effects and meanings are produced both aurally and visually. An opera that centers on the presence of a portrait onstage simultaneously exhibits to its audience the bodies that perform its music, and draws attention to the act of looking at the image of the subject on display: the audience looks, and the onstage characters look as well—as Linda and Michael Hutcheon note, in this special instance, "they see as we see."[30] And the portrait looks back. The portrait may have been at home on the Viennese operatic stage ever since Mozart's *Die Zauberflöte*, wherein the beauty of Pamina's painted image is a transparent signifier of her virtue; but by Berg's time, when the tradition of portraiture had become as fractured as the identity of the individual subject it portrayed, its operatic presence had become more problematic.

In choosing Georges Rodenbach's symbolist novel *Bruges-la-morte* (and its dramatic adaptation *Le mirage*) as the libretto source for *Die tote Stadt* (1920), Korngold hit on an evocative scenario in which a painted portrait plays a central role.[31] A husband, Paul, grieves obsessively for his dead wife, Marie, pure and sainted in his memory and in the shrine of images and mementos he has constructed; the pretty and seductive dancer, Marietta, appears so like the departed beloved that she seems to be her double, even a revenant. Paul's guilty dream-fantasy of a passionate but conflicted affair culminating in the murder of Marietta dissolves into his waking reconciliation with his loss and the past. A particular time dimension of portraiture is clearly evident in *Die tote Stadt*, which revolves around Paul's obsession with Marie's painted portrait. This time dimension is an inherent part of the traditional social role of the portrait, whose primary function in no small measure is to provide a temporal illusion of continued presence: to render present the absent or dead subject. "The role of the portrait," comments Nancy, "is to *look out for* the image in the absence of the person, regardless of whether this absence results from distance or from death [. . .] it brings back from absence, and it remembers in absence. As such, then, the portrait immortalizes; it renders immortal in death."[32] In the room Paul has dedicated to his wife's memory—occupied by relics including a plait of her hair—Marie's portrait serves precisely this traditional function of making present the dead sitter, of prolonging her presence in her absence. But its significance within the opera is more complex and contradictory.

Korngold's stage directions imply that there is more than one image of Marie present onstage. Paul has filled her room with mementos, including numerous photographs. Within these surroundings the portrait is given a special status, and it is notable that Marietta, when she first enters and gazes around at the photographs in the room, sees only "lovely women [. . .] other women you have loved"; yet a little while later, when she sees the painted portrait, she recognizes *herself*, and her recognition is immediate. This is one instance in which the opera goes further than the book in transforming what was, in Rodenbach, only a powerful resemblance between dead wife and living dancer, into an actual identity between the two. Korngold specifies that both Marietta, and the Marie of Paul's vision who emerges from her portrait to speak to him, be sung by the same soprano. This doubling of roles—a dramatic technique which, significantly, framed Schilling's *Mona Lisa*, and which Berg was to utilize to a much greater extent in *Lulu*, with far-reaching consequences—amounts here to an identity between the portrait-likeness and the living likeness of Marie in Marietta's form: in Paul's vision at the end of Act 1, they do not merely resemble one another, but are literally the same person.[33] The Marie that steps through the painting's frame after Marietta's departure is both Marie and Marietta; Paul hears Marie's voice when Marietta sings, because it is literally the same voice—and the audience hears it, too.

Traces of the *Unheimlich* can be felt in this episode not only because the portrait becomes doubly animated, but because the opposite is also true: the image depicts the still-living woman as a dead one. It serves both as a kind of uncanny mirror and a permeable boundary between the dead and the living. In looking at the two, both possibilities are present at once, and it is the second possibility that is realized in the opera's penultimate scene when Paul murders Marietta. As the Hutcheons note, the opera's "uncanny conflation of the living and the dead is made possible by the ability of the staged phenomenal image [the portrait] to conflate *what is* and *what is not*."[34] Ultimately, this identity between portrait and individual (although ostensibly a different individual than the one originally portrayed) has two important consequences, which are, not surprisingly, intertwined. The first, perhaps unexpected, is that viewing the female characters via stereotypically dichotomous gender roles becomes complicated, in a manner particularly characteristic of Viennese perceptions of women that were shaped by the widely influential misogynist theories of Otto Weininger, wherein all women are viewed as essentially and completely sexual.[35] The other result is that the static, painted portrait acquires a uniquely heightened temporal existence. These two possibilities come together through musical performance.

Carmen Ottner numbers *Die tote Stadt* among a veritable crowd of Viennese operas composed during the first decade of the twentieth century that center on the representation of female characters of two distinct types: the "femme fragile," who is "pure, innocent," and the "femme fatale," typified by "fallen maidens, demonic, mysterious, power-obsessed women with at times exotic flair."[36] According to Ottner, these opposed types are clearly formulated in Korngold's opera. Both the name of Marie and her enshrined position present her as a kind of madonna, and Paul's repeated references to her pure and elevated nature reinforce this suggestion. And Marietta, with her sensual behavior and her multiple lovers, is clearly "the typical femme fatale;" as Ottner says, the "crucial character difference" is communicated from the moment of Marietta's entrance.[37] Apparently, nothing could be more obvious than this dramatization of the clichéd gender roles in which those often-critiqued Viennese conceptions of femininity were rooted. Yet the nature of Marie's portrait itself calls this polarity into question. She is pictured as a performer. Her pose, holding a lute, implies a musical performance, and not a sacred one. This imagined performance is realized within moments of the first unveiling of the curtained portrait. Marietta has only been onstage a few moments when Paul begins the process of visually framing her as a living image of his deceased wife. He first drapes Marietta's shoulders with the shawl worn by Marie in her portrait and, flattered at his interest in her appearance, Marietta runs to look at herself in a mirror; seeing her thus, Paul actually calls her by his wife's name. He then hands her the lute, making the resemblance to the portrait complete, and she laughingly asks whether he is an artist looking for a model.

At this point Marietta executes an explicit musical performance: the "Lautenlied," the opera's most popular excerpt, is ostensibly a sad old song known to both her and Paul from the past (Example 1). Her performance

Example 1. Erich Wolfgang Korngold, *Die tote Stadt*, Act 1, sc. 5 (rehearsal no. 58), opening strophe of the "Lautenlied" (Korngold, *Marietta's Lied zur Laute*, © 1920 by Schott Music, Mainz - Germany, © Renewed 1948. All Rights Reserved. Used by permission of European American Music Distributors LLC, sole U.S. and Canadian agent for Schott Music, Mainz - Germany).

Example 1 continued

is not over when this sentimental song concludes, however, for she begins to dance, continuing to accompany herself with Marie's lute and singing of the physical passion and ecstasy she experiences while dancing. As she spins around the room—both repelling and enticing Paul, who is at once enthralled and scandalized at her seeming desecration of Marie's chaste image—she accidentally brushes aside the curtain covering Marie's portrait, and confronts, with some shock, what seems to be a picture of herself.[38] Marietta's performance, which involves both singing while self-accompanied on the lute and dancing, engages the body and in turn implicates the portrait in the corporeality of musical performance. It brings the image from the static spatial realm of the painted canvas into the dynamic temporal one of musical sounding, and emphasizes a passionate physicality that is latent in the still depiction of the woman holding the lute, poised to play and sing. It is only a slight stretch to suggest that this exhibition of sensual vitality actually causes the subsequent effect of animation, in which Marie magically steps out of her portrait's frame a moment after Marietta leaves the room. The work of art that depicts a musical performance is animated by the living manifestation of that very performance.

In this manner Korngold composes the portrait's living embodiment in a way that calls its implied significance into question. Through the identity between the painted portrait as mimetic imitation of the dead woman and the live woman as fleshly imitation of the lifeless painted image, both women are objectified as performing and eroticized bodies. Marietta's musical performances reflect back on the idealized construction of Marie, whose "sacred" memory becomes tinged with the secular and the profane; she is ultimately yet another performing woman on display. So it is too simple to regard the portrait and the live woman as objectifying an age-old dichotomy of feminine roles, purity or wantonness, wife or whore, because the play of identity between image and live embodiment conflates the two, calling at least one—the characterization of Marie as chaste wife—

into question. Not only does this dual portrayal through portrait image and live musical performance resist the classification of each character via one feminine stereotype or the other, but it calls attention to both views of femininity as *images*, semblances on display for the male gaze. That gaze implicates the viewing and listening audience as well.

The performance of the "Lautenlied" has further implications, as recognized by Benjamin Goose's examination of its status as a closed number suited to, and destined for, extraction and popularization in the commercial markets of sheet music and early recordings.[39] Goose highlights the contribution of the song's overtly sentimental quality to its dramatic context, wherein it can serve as a commentary on "Paul's susceptibility to contrived emotions."[40] But its banal yet emotionally manipulative quality also makes it apt material for performance by a female character like Marietta, whose allure for Paul resides in surface appearance and sensual affect. Further, the lute song's commercial aspects and aspirations implicate the "sacred" image of Marie as part of the contemporary marketplace. Yet the music of the "Lautenlied" breaches its commercial frame, just as Marie, in Paul's hallucination that closes Act 1, defies the bounds of frame and canvas and steps out of her own image to address her husband. When the lied's music recurs near the end of the opera, and Paul's recall of the melody with new words signifies his reconciliation with the past, it crosses the boundary between a momentarily foregrounded gesture of explicit performance and a signifying element of the opera's overall thematic texture.

Just as significant, though, is Goose's recognition of the song's pretensions to an uncomplicated, folklike style, which allowed it to participate in the commercial vogue for folk and folk-type song in early twentieth-century Germany. The song's "ostentatiously simple" structure and harmonic language are crucial elements aligning it with contemporary conceptions of folk music that evoked a purer, simpler past.[41] The quality of pastness of the "Lautenlied" can convey more than one effect. As Goose suggests, its markers of folklike simplicity play a role within the dramatic context by supporting Marietta's assertion that it is an "old song," lending veracity to the idea that Paul also knows it and can, with some small effort, recall it from memory and join her in singing its second verse. But when considered in the context of its performance by a character whose role encompasses that of *Doppelgänger* or revenant as well as a living woman, the song's suggestions of time past become part of the *unheimlich* quality of the scene, the effect of which is particularly evident with the recurrence, the return, of the song at later moments in the opera. Considered in its chromatic, often dissonant surroundings within the work, the song's diatonic simplicity renders it a kind of musical revenant from a less-complicated tonal past. Its effect conflates nostalgia with a frisson of the uncanny. Even from its first instance it bears the marks of a return of the repressed, and thus its dramatic and musical significances are multiplied, extending even beyond those cultural and commercial significations that Goose so insightfully uncovers. So the "Lautenlied" ultimately functions as a musical analogue of the portrait of the dead woman with the lute. And, as with the portrait, the lied functions through a recognition of the necessary perspective of the audience, as onlookers and listeners. As the picture becomes both an uncanny reflection and a liminal surface between static image and dynamic embodiment, dead sitter and living presence, so the lied refracts time and acts as a permeable boundary between presence and pastness. Both shatter their frames.

A similar claim might be made for Schreker's *Die Gezeichneten*, which takes up the theme of artistic image through the temporal art of music and attempts to transform both spheres through a music that claims space as its own medium. Its central character, Alviano, is ugly and deformed but a seeker of art and beauty, with a sensitive soul; his handsome friend Tamare is wildly unscrupulous, a ravisher of women. They both desire Carlotta, an artist who has a lovely face but suffers from the inner physical weakness of a diseased heart. She rebuffs Tamare's advances but is drawn to Alviano, in whom she sees a fascinating artistic subject. The feature of his external appearance that interests her is his gaze, through which she glimpses a sense of an inner existence. Despite his suspicions that she is mocking his deformities, she persuades Alviano to come to her studio and sit for a portrait. There, she declares that she loves him, and his wild happiness at being loved at last brings to his eyes the ecstatic expression Carlotta desires to capture in paint. By the next day, however, the portrait finished, she has lost interest in him, and succumbs fatally to the temptation of Tamare's violent seduction.

Die Gezeichneten seems to bear an even stronger resemblance to *Dorian Gray* than to Wilde's fairy tale of the ugly dwarf and the heartless princess that Schreker had set a few years earlier. *Dorian Gray* contains all the elements of transgressive sexuality, flouting of social mores in pursuit of hedonistic pleasure, and meditation on art and artists and their relation to their subjects that find their way into *Die Gezeichneten* but are surely not present in "The Birthday of the Infanta." The crucial similarity to Wilde's novel is especially evident in the opera's central focus on the painted portrait. Schreker came by his interest in portraiture quite naturally, for his father and two brothers made their living through portrait photography. His father in particular was a well-known and distinguished photographer of members of the aristocracy and social elite, both within the studio setting—in Budapest and then in Vienna—and in a range of European capitals through which he traveled. Album collections of his hand-colored photographic portraits, including a series of women of Hungarian high society, are records of artistry as well as of his enterprising skill with what was then a relatively new technology.[42] In *Die Gezeichneten*, however, Schreker showed himself more interested in portrait painting as an artistic probing of the psyche than in the technological realism that photography promised. Both Alviano and Carlotta pursue artistic expression of inner states and desires. Alviano funds the creation of a fantastic island paradise where beauty and sensual pleasures abound. Carlotta describes herself as a painter whose goal is to depict the hidden existence of her subjects. "I paint pictures," she says. "Animals and people, trees and lakes—the sky, the light—but I prefer to paint—souls."[43]

Schreker's unusual stroke here is to make his central artist figure a woman—a character unique in his own oeuvre in this respect. At a time when women's struggle for admission into the Académie des Beaux-Arts in Paris was recent news, and women artists in Berlin could attend the Zeichen- und Malschule des Vereins der Künstlerinnen but were excluded from the government fine art schools by official policy, Schreker's woman artist appears a rather bold modern figure.[44] Peter Franklin notes that the composer "empowers her . . . with artistic talent."[45] Yet her talent remains circumscribed by historical limits. Portraiture, historically perceived as a purely imitative rather than imaginative art, had long been considered more suitable for women painters than more elevated genres of painting; if women ostensibly lacked the rational capacity for the kind of abstraction required by, for example, history painting, they might still possess a mimetic ability.[46] Yet even within this frame of acceptability, the female portrait painter's action and position was always potentially transgressive, since European codes for feminine social behavior historically dictated that it was improper for a woman to aim a direct and prolonged gaze at a man. As both Angela Rosenthal and Tamar Garb have noted in studies of women artists from the eighteenth and nineteenth centuries, the female painter as portraitist appropriates the power of the gaze, turning her male sitter into passive object, and therein lies a danger.[47] Like the music lesson, the portrait studio is historically coded as a site of seduction, and the conception of relation between artist and model has long been tinged with the erotic. "Schreker's Carlotta was both Virgin and Whore," realizes Franklin. "She paints the hesitant, unbelieving Alviano's portrait, literally holding him in thrall to the female gaze while talking him out of his repression into an ecstasy of love."[48] Schreker's portrait of the artist is not easy to decipher, and Franklin's assertion of her dichotomous character suggests some of its complexity. Her artistic and emotional investment in the inner, unseen qualities that both characterize her own hidden physical stigma and form the subject of her creative work also suggest her personal depth, and make plausible her attraction to Alviano's inner self, visible to her through his gaze despite his surface appearance. Yet by the end of the opera she has become unmistakably a Weiningerian woman, whose complete surrender to sexuality overrides not only rationality and morality but lofty intellectual or creative ideals. Thus what initially appears to be a unique feminine role in opera, the woman as artist with creative gifts, regresses into a negative gender stereotype that falls back into the restrictive feminine roles often assigned to women in modernist Viennese culture. In truth, Carlotta's position is conflicted in its historical associations from the start, even before her betrayal of Alviano for the dangerously seductive embrace of Tamare has taken place.

Nevertheless, a great deal is invested in the images Carlotta paints; they have implications for the musical evocation of both time and space in a way inherently modern. Her art is not solely concerned with portraits of others' souls, but mirrors her own inner self as well. Carlotta does not only paint portraits like the one of Alviano, in which the facial expression is expected to capture inner emotion, she also paints hands. Further, these hand images—at least one in particular, but perhaps all—are symbolic *self-portraits* with distinct psychological connotations, which Carlotta herself explains as she speaks with Alviano in her studio. She tells a story of a woman friend of hers, another painter, and the revelation near the end of the scene that she has really been speaking of herself comes as no surprise. After briefly describing several of her paintings, she lingers over the description of the "strangest" of them. This rather disturbing image depicted a pale hand, like that of a dead person, grasping something that could only be glimpsed as a faint glow.

Carlotta's symbolic hand paintings reflect an inspiration that Schreker drew from Schoenberg, whose oil painting titled *Hände,* an Expressionist depiction of hands clasping at a small, bright object, dates from before 1910. Some three decades later, after seeing a performance of *Die Gezeichneten*, Schoenberg gifted his friend Schreker with a watercolor version of the image in recognition of the latter's symbolic gesture.[49] The image of a hand grasping a light evokes ineffability as well as force, the embodied and the incorporeal. Curiously, Carlotta describes this visual image in terms of muted sound, the light "like a silent lament, like stifled whimpering tears and a restrained cry of deathly fear, like a suppressed cry for release." When Alviano inquires as to the meaning of this picture, Carlotta offers two interpretations, both involving sublimation on the part of the artist. First, she suggests that the painter had never experienced love, and feared it; then she explains that the painter was driven by a pain that was not emotional but physical. All her life she had been ill with a weak heart; the painful spasms she experienced were, she fantasized, like a cruel hand that gripped and crushed her heart to death. As Carlotta triumphantly throws away her brush, the portrait of Alviano complete, she is overcome by a weak spell and staggers, clutching at her heart. When she grasps an easel near her for support, its cloth covering slips away, revealing a painting of a pale, long-fingered hand with a reddish light shining through its fingers. Thus the painting and both its possible meanings refer (perhaps a little too obviously) to Carlotta's own inner self. Her art, then, encompassing portraits of others' souls and her own, is deeply implicated in a Wildean ethos in which art both reveals and conceals hidden psychological and moral truths, about its subject *and* its author. In Schreker's opera, as in Wilde's novel, the outward appearance conceals the inner being, for better or worse, yet this inner being is mirrored in the painter's art.

The crucial moments of recognition in *Die Gezeichneten*, *Die tote Stadt*, and *Der Zwerg* all come about seemingly by accident, with the chance brushing aside of a curtain and the unexpected unveiling of the image that gives rise to a shock for onlookers both onstage and in the audience. Schreker's music accompanying the moment of revelation of the mysterious hand painting has a mimetic quality: the motion of rising and falling sixteenth notes imitates the motion of the drapery slipping from the canvas, while a high, soft, sustained chord that fixates on the revealed image is like an analogue of Alviano's gaze, and ours. A fermata on this chord fixes the instant of recognition for a moment of undefined length, as though the sound were arrested by the sight itself, and the music immobilizes the passage of time while the realization of the hidden truth unfolds (Example 2). Here, the music itself takes on the temporal quality Adorno prized in successful painting, in which the sensation is that of "a passage of time that is holding its breath."[50] Such deliberately mimetic moments are not regular occurrences in Schreker's music, but this one's vivid encapsulation of the

Sie hält sich, um nicht umzusinken, an einer Staffelei an, die, mit einem Tuch verhängt, im Hintergrunde steht. Das Tuch löst sich an einer Seite los. Man sieht ein Bild; eine Art Totenhand, aus der ein roter Schein schwach hervorleuchtet. (To keep from falling, she grasps an easel that stands in the background, covered with a drapery. The drapery slips to one side. A painting becomes visible; a kind of dead hand, from which a red glow is shining weakly.)

Example 2. Franz Schreker, *Die Gezeichneten*, Act 2, sc. 2 (2 mm. before rehearsal no. 830), the revelation of the painting. Copyright ©1936, 1996 by Universal Edition A.G., Wien/UE 5690. All Rights Reserved. Used by permission of European American Music Distributors LLC, U.S. and Canadian agent for Universal Edition A.G., Wien.

visual experience in sound is surely deliberate in its musical-temporal reflection on the opera's larger theme of outer appearance and inner essence. A painting of a hand holding a hidden object embodies a paradox of representing what is concealed, what cannot be seen. It invokes a grasping at the ineffable, an attempt to hold the disembodied; it might even be said to reach toward the state of music itself.

The whole studio scene is musically constructed around a series of recurring elements; in this respect Adorno compared it directly to scenes between Lulu and Alwa in Berg's *Lulu*.[51] Possibly the scene's most interesting structural aspect is the reappearance of a substantial portion of the opera's opening prelude, featuring one of Schreker's most evocative sonorous textures, whose initially wordless effusion seems to be lent dramatic concretion when it materializes within the studio setting. The opening music of that prelude is notable first for its singular timbral quality, which makes use of the string harmonics, harp, and celesta that often give the Schrekerian sound an iridescent quality; additional touches of the triangle are like flashes of brightness from within a suffused glow. But this phantasmagorical timbral impression is given dimension by its combination of harmony and rhythmic texture, almost at the micro-level. Arpeggiated D-major and B-flat-minor triads oscillate rapidly, falling in turn on slightly stronger or weaker sub-pulses, their swift alternation giving rise to a "flickering" effect that Adorno termed the "Schrekerian chiaroscuro," a quality of light and dark aptly described as a "shimmer" (Example 3).[52] Indeed, Adorno's "Schreker" essay of 1959, drawn from a lecture he delivered on radio, is filled with metaphorical evocations of the visual and spatial character of the Schrekerian sound. For Adorno, who attended a performance of *Die Gezeichneten* as a teenager, the radio talk was in part a return to this youthful experience, viewed belatedly through the dialectical lens of critical theory. What is clear is that the musical experience made a profound impression on him, one diminished yet not entirely lost decades later, but the source of which he had come to question. Berg's use of the term "kitschy" to describe Schreker's dramatic writing suggests that his view of Schreker's art may have been somewhat equivocal.[53] Berg's student Adorno, hearing in Schreker's music both kitsch and the promise of a utopia, was troubled by the perception of a music that aspires to the sensual quality of space and forgets its own essence as time.[54] The realm of alluring and effervescent sound, the idea of a *Klang* that "proves too elusive to grasp and then disappears," both symbolically postulates exaltation and its own dissolution, and, as Adorno recognized, hovers transgressively on the border between the temporal and the spatial.[55] Through this very liminality Schreker's music openly registers its own ineffability.

Example 3. Schreker, *Die Gezeichneten*, opening prelude (mm. 1–2) (Vienna: Universal Edition A. G., 1916).

Even before the success of *Die Gezeichneten*, Berg had felt the influence of the evocative timbral-spatial qualities of the Schrekerian sound as he worked on the piano score of Schreker's *Der ferne Klang* in 1911. This influence is felt almost immediately in the orchestration of Berg's *Fünf Orchesterlieder nach Ansichtskartentexten von Peter Altenberg*, composed in 1912. The aesthetic qualities of Altenberg's brief postcard texts engage simultaneously with a spatial preoccupation with the visual image and a temporal awareness of the fleeting quality of the glance, the momentary perspective afforded by the snapshot. In "Rokoko," for example, a feeling of interminability—"I have waited, waited, oh, waited"—is contrasted a few lines later by an abrupt termination—"suddenly everything is over"—and in between comes the evocation of endless space—"You gazed meditatively out beyond the bounds of all."[56] Altenberg summons in words the effect Adorno described as the dimension of temporality that is captured by the successful work of visual art, "in which what is absolutely simultaneous seems like a passage of time that is holding its breath."[57] The brevity of Altenberg's texts encapsulate the essence of a postcard, its quality of seizing an ephemeral moment. And yet the texts dilate on that moment, even if briefly, making it into a temporal as well as a visual-spatial experience of the subject being depicted. Furthermore, the quality of recurrence implied in the collector's repeated perusal of his stash of images speaks to their temporal continuity, to the way in which the visual image holds on to and prolongs the passing moment. While Berg's famously brief settings convey the poetic sense of momentariness, they hold in suspension the spatial quality through their sumptuous timbral dimensions and their very fullness. Given their richness, they ought to be longer. The implication of extension is present in the unhurried unfolding of so much material in so little time. As is well known, Schönberg criticized the *Altenberg Lieder* rather sharply.[58] But as a visual artist, he should have been better able to appreciate the finely tuned tension between the sonorous evocation of vast spaces—"Über die Grenzen des All"—and the fleeting experience of the vanishing glimpse.

Adorno singles out the orchestral introduction to the first of the *Altenberg Lieder* for a direct comparison with Schreker's music in *Die Gezeichneten* (although he misses the possible influence of the earlier *Der ferne Klang*):

> The similarity of the idea behind the sonoral [sic] design with that of the opening to the prelude of Schreker's *Gezeichneten* is striking, except that Berg's work, surely written earlier, goes much further in its use of dissonance than Schreker with his polytonally clouded triads; seldom, however, is a certain affinity between the two as palpable as it is here.[59]

More than once Adorno pointed out similarities between Berg's music and that of Schreker; in one instance he claimed that this comparison had been shown him by Berg himself.[60] Almost invariably the resemblance has to do with timbral and sonorous-textural qualities.[61] Where such characteristics in Schreker always seemed to point toward the privileging of space over the temporal dimension of structural development, Adorno also discovered a spatial perception within Berg's structural and formal musical processes. He recognized a sense of space, and of the visual, in both conception and realization, as he reminisced on Berg's compositional procedures and their results:

> He laid out plans, which became ever more complicated, according to quasi-spatial symmetrical relationships. His propensity, too, for mirror and retrograde formation may, apart from the twelve-tone technique, be related to the visual dimension of his responses; musical retrograde patterns are anti-temporal, they organize music as if it were an intrinsic simultaneity. It is probably incorrect to attribute those technical procedures solely to the twelve-tone technique; they are derived not only from the microstructure of the rows, but also from the overall plan, as if from a basic outline, and as such they contain an element of indifference toward succession, something like a disposition toward musical saturation of space. . . . Much as Berg belonged to the tradition of thematic work and developing variation, that is, to a thoroughly dynamic kind of composition, his musical manner nevertheless had something peculiarly static about it, hesitantly marking time.[62]

The most important distinction, for Adorno, between this sense of space in Schreker and in Berg, is that, in the music of the latter, the static quality is held in a kind of dialectical suspension with the dynamic impulse of development in time. Although the above quotation was made in general reference to Berg's oeuvre, certainly it is nowhere more apt than in the case of *Lulu*, wherein the static and spatial techniques of mirror and retrograde patterns and forms, as much as the sense of space invoked by Berg's richly variegated timbral canvas, has direct resonance with the theme of appearance at the heart of the drama.

In Act 2, scene 2 of *Lulu*, Alwa sings a sensuous and impassioned praise of Lulu's physical beauty, likening portions of her body to musical genres and forms, and imagining, as he sings, her figure as music: "deinen Wuchs wie Musik." It is one of the principal moments in the opera that lends weight to the perception of Alwa, the composer, as Berg's own self-portrait. But this idea of a musical rendering of Lulu's physique was evident from the opera's very first scene. Realizing Lulu's form as music was precisely Berg's task in this opera. This task he carried out in numerous ways, beginning from the moment that the audience in the opera house joins the characters onstage in witnessing the painting of the portrait of Lulu.

It is well known that Berg was deeply impressed by Karl Kraus's 1905 lecture delivered in Vienna before a performance of the second of Wedekind's Lulu plays, in which both Kraus and Wedekind played roles. According to Kraus, "Her portrait, the picture of her painted when at the height of her beauty, plays a more important role than Lulu herself."[63] Given the obsession in Viennese culture with the indeterminacy of the relationship between inner and superficial identity, and indeed with the very nature of selfhood, it seems worth noting that Kraus's statement, if only incidentally, implies a distinction between Lulu "herself" and the painted image of her—the significance of her identity, her selfhood, is perceived to be eclipsed by that of her image. The portrait unquestionably has a central role in Berg's operatic version of Wedekind, appearing and reappearing throughout the work from the first scene to the last. Berg provides a musical analogue to the portrait image in the form of what George Perle called the "picture chords." Silvio José Dos Santos refers to this material instead as the "*Bild* motive," following the references in Berg's own sketches and conveying a broader sense of the significance of the motive apart from a specifically chordal presentation. Citing the constant presence and pivotal position of this motive throughout the opera, Dos Santos argues in favor of a relationship of identity between Lulu and her portrait, which, as "a representation of Lulu's beauty," is ultimately significant for "Lulu's own sense of self-identity."[64] This argument for identity is in contradiction to the separation between self and image implied by Kraus. Dos Santos's thoroughgoing analysis of the motive's pervasiveness throughout the score, in one form or another, convincingly demonstrates its central role in Berg's presentation of the ways in which Lulu's character is *seen*. All analysts who confront the work must grapple with the recognition that the character's appearance, however prominently displayed, gazed at, discussed, admired, even parlayed as part of her downfall, does not fix her identity in any way, nor make it remotely transparent. For the portrait is a semblance, an illusion—in it, Lulu is a character, and she is known to have different portraits, in which she is different characters.

And there are so many portraits of Lulu in the opera. The Painter has painted at least two, and one, which we do not see, he has sold for a good price: this one portrays Lulu not as Pierrot but as a Dancer, which is of course the very role she takes up in Act 2. But the relationship between the Painter's depictions of her and her identity is dubious, to say the least. Lulu, in frustration, draws Schön's attention to the falseness of the Painter's perceptions of her, saying that he does not even "see" her—that is, who she really is: "He is blind, blind, blind!" Also unseen within the opera are the pictures that Lulu gave to the Marquis, which he in turn sent to the procurer of the Cairo brothel; in one of them, he reveals, she was posing as Eve in front of a mirror. But the film at the heart of the opera also contains her image, in the forms of her silhouette on the wall of her prison cell and her mirrored reflection in the surface of the dustpan, and these are the very opposite of the ideal and imaginary painted depiction in their gritty, sordid reality.[65] Arguably, the escaping Lulu in disguise is another portrait. This one is painted during the film by the Countess Geschwitz, who creates a plausible and yet false likeness of herself on and of Lulu's body somewhat in the manner of Paul when he dresses up Marietta: as Lulu says later, Geschwitz "used all her art" to make them look like each other. With the visual contents of the film, Berg brings the assumed artifice of the painted portrait into proximity with the presumably greater realism and hence authenticity of photography and mirror image: Lulu on film, Lulu's dustpan reflection. These images that presuppose truthful, direct presentation rather than re-presentation according to artistic perspective, highlight the tension between differing qualities of image; but neither type of picture, whether "real" or imaginary, can any longer be supposed to give access to interiority, to the self beneath the surface. Each portrait is "Lulu *as*," and as such is always "as-if," remaining semblance rather than representing identity. Yet Dos Santos's discussion and analysis establishes clearly the inextricable link between the *Bild* motive and Lulu's *appearance* in all its various guises, even if the nature of the connection between appearance and identity remains opaque and refuses to be fixed. The effect of multiple images and portraits of Lulu, along with her multiple names of Nelly, Eva, and Mignon, is echoed in the famous doubling of character roles, which Berg took well beyond the doubling in Korngold's opera, conflating the identity of several crucial figures in the drama.[66] By this means the composer utterly destabilizes appearance as a representation of identity.

If the portrait presents Lulu as Pierrot, Berg's music presents her in yet another guise, which is most apparent in moments such as Lulu's Lied—Lulu as soprano. Dos Santos is justified in complaining that the far-reaching significance of the *Bild* motive has been somewhat neglected by scholars in favor of a focus on other sections of the music, especially Lulu's Lied.[67] Yet the reason that the lied has so often been taken as a significant emblem for analytical consideration of the nature of her identity within the work is that, in it, she makes an explicit claim to identity found nowhere else in the opera. "I have never in the world wished to appear as other than what I've been taken for," she sings, "and no one has ever taken me for other than what I am." With these words, the lied makes a remarkable claim to identity between appearance and essence that dialectically reaffirms *and* contradicts the significance of her portrait (which clearly does show that she can be taken for—and represented as—other than what she "is"). It is extraordinary not merely because its untruth is so apparent, nor because it comes from the mouth of an operatic character who seems to embody enigma, whose identity seems anything but apparent, but because of the way it seems so at odds with its own context: an opera in which the illusory, the play of appearance, is so apparent on the surface of the work. Its paradox is that it manages to make this truth claim in the most artificial means possible: coloratura excess that displays the cultivated singing voice, as Adorno suggested, like a circus character, a tightrope walker, holding in suspense the virtuosity of execution and the illusion of effortlessness.[68]

The understanding of appearance as inextricable from illusion, rather than from identity, is at the heart of the opera, as its opening frame of the circus makes clear, and this play of appearance is manifested musically throughout the work. This is nowhere more evident than in the film and its music at the work's center point, wherein illusion is a product of both space and time. Its visual and musical elements are calculated to highlight the temporal illusion that gives the second half of the opera its appearance as a mirror image of the first. Throughout the work the sense of temporality—encapsulated in Berg's direction that Lulu's Lied be performed "in the tempo of a heartbeat"—is formally unfolded and revoked in the large scale and moment to moment. This becomes particularly audible in isolated passages, such as the distillation of Berg's compelling constructive principle of rhythm into the ostinato of the Monoritmica; but it can be heard (and seen) especially in the retrograde at the work's core. Indeed, the music of the interlude accompanying the silent film makes the dialectics of reality and illusory appearance, and of temporal progress and reversal, readily apparent to the ear as well as to the eye. In its narrative and technical structure, the film advances the drama at an accelerated forward pace, encompassing many months' worth of events within a few minutes. Simultaneously, it enacts the illusion of temporal reversal, turning backward on itself. Even more precisely than Berg's carefully calculated sequence of filmic imagery, his music makes this reversal apparent through its precise palindromic structure. Musical retrograde structures are not always readily audible, but this one is easily heard, and deliberately so. The striking clarity and conspicuousness of its aural appearance reveals the technical means of creating the illusion of the reversal of time, especially at its still center. There, Berg not only declines to conceal the joint between forward and backward to create a seamless flow but emphasizes the turning point with a fermata, an indefinite suspension of musical temporality that in the narrative encapsulates an entire year of ennui, in the reality of the performance experience is relatively brief, and in theory is infinite. Bracketed by Lulu's image, her shadow and her own gaze at herself, is it the sonorous analogue of a mirror that reflects, or of a painting, one which "seems like a passage of time that is holding its breath"?

In November 1927 Berg wrote to Adorno to ask his advice in selecting his second opera libretto: he was interested in Wedekind's Lulu plays and also in Gerhard Hauptmann's *Und Pippa tanzt!*—which one did Adorno think would be best?[69] Nearly two years earlier, they had corresponded about the possibility of setting the Hauptmann play. Tellingly, what Adorno thought promising in it was "the manner in which naturalism and unreality are enmeshed." Yet he advised against setting it at that time,[70] and was consistent in his later support of Wedekind's Lulu instead.[71] "I cannot say with certainty," he admitted, "whether it was I who first pointed him toward *Lulu*, as it now seems to me upon reflection; in such cases it is easy to err out of narcissism."[72] He continued to follow Berg's progress in composing the opera through their correspondence, and it is little wonder that he remained so invested in the work when he wrote his later reminiscences of his beloved former teacher and friend. "In *Lulu*," says Adorno, "the self—from whose point of view events are seen, from whose perspective the music is heard—steps visibly onto the stage."[73] The reference here is not to the title character at all, but to Berg, as part of a mention of the opera's gesture of self-quotation. He compares the practice to that of a medieval painter who includes "his own self-portrait as a minor figure in a religious painting," a self-reference that asserts the portrait's illusion of presence, the capacity for temporal continuity that incorporates the self into history. The suggestion that the work is more a portrait of the artist than of its ostensible subject draws it back into the sphere of Wilde and *The Picture of Dorian Gray*, a copy of which Berg owned and from which he copied quotations into his personal notebooks aptly titled "On Self-Recognition."[74] As the portrait painter in Wilde's novel asserts near the opening of the narrative, "Every portrait that is painted with feeling is a portrait of the artist, not of the sitter."[75] Later, he seems to change his mind: "It often seems to me," he says, "that art conceals the artist far more completely than it ever reveals him."[76] But there is no contradiction here, for any modern portrait, including that of Lulu, both reveals and hides its subject. The play between what is seen and not seen, between appearance and identity, is its essence.

NOTES

1. The letter cited in the epigraph is from Theodor W. Adorno to Alban Berg, 20 January 1931, in *Theodor W. Adorno & Alban Berg: Correspondence 1925–1935*, ed. Henri Lonitz, trans. Wieland Hoban (Cambridge: Polity, 2005), 178. The journal article Adorno refers to is "Berg and Webern—Schoenberg's Heirs," *Modern Music* 2 (January/February 1931): 29, 38. In the end, this article did not use portraits. *Modern Music*'s usual practice was to utilize artworks to illustrate its articles, so it is not this request in particular but the magazine's preference for painted images in general that is notable, at a time when the use of photographs was much more common.

2. Joanna Woodall, "Introduction: Facing the Subject," in *Portraiture: Facing the Subject*, ed. Woodall (Manchester, UK: Manchester University Press, 1997), 7.

3. Jacques Le Rider, *Modernity and Crises of Identity: Culture and Society in Fin-de-Siècle Vienna*, trans. Rosemary Morris (Cambridge: Polity, 1993), 27, 1.

4. Richard Brilliant, *Portraiture* (Chicago: University of Chicago Press, 2004), 7.

5. Carl Schorske, *Fin-de-Siècle Vienna: Politics and Culture* (New York: Vintage, 1981), 270.

6. Oskar Kokoschka, *My Life*, trans. David Britt (New York: Macmillan, 1974), 33.

7. Jean-Luc Nancy, "The Look of the Portrait," trans. Simon Sparks, in *Multiple Arts: The Muses II*, ed. Simon Sparks (Stanford, CA: Stanford University Press, 2006), 242.

8. Ibid., 229.

9. Although many of Schoenberg's paintings, including self-portraits and other subjects, were produced during a concentrated period, roughly 1908 to 1910, he continued to produce drawings and sketches (some watercolors), including numerous self-portraits, through the ensuing decades. The latest self-portrait in the catalogue raisonné of the Arnold Schönberg Center is a watercolor dated 1944.

10. This portrait of Wilde, while almost definitely not by Aubrey Beardsley, contains some interesting reflections of other, "authentic" images: the head-on-hand attitude of Wilde echoes that of a well-known photograph of Wilde from the 1880s; the leaning pose, elbow on a high piece of furniture, resembles that of the Pierrot figure in the second of Beardsley's illustrations for *Pierrot's Library* (1896); and the image on the back wall recapitulates the central figure in the repressed version of "The Toilet of Salome," from Beardsley's illustrations for Wilde's *Salome* (1894). According to Mark Samuels Lasner, some among the many forgeries of Beardsley's works are fraudulent copies of his own drawings, others are outright fakes, and some—like this one—present a kind of "pastiche" in assembling various elements of existing Beardsley images. See Lasner, *A Selective Checklist of the Published Work of Aubrey Beardsley* (Boston: Thomas G. Boss Fine Books, 1995).

11. Several significant contributions have been made to the subject of Wilde's reception in Germany and Austria. See, for example, Rainer Kohlmayer, *Oscar Wilde in Deutschland und Österreich* (Tübingen: Niemeyer, 1996); Patrick Bridgwater, "Oscar Wilde and Germany: Germany and Oscar Wilde," in Bridgwater, *Anglo-German Interactions in the Literature of the 1890s* (Oxford: Legenda, 1999); Joseph Bristow, ed., *Oscar Wilde and Modern Culture: The Making of a Legend* (Athens: Ohio University Press, 2009).

12. Woodall, "Introduction: Facing the Subject," 1. Le Rider emphasizes the centrality of the figure of Narcissus in Viennese modernism. He explores the type of Narcissus in Viennese representations ranging from Freud's theories to Hofmannsthal's writings and beyond as a "hero of modern life," an individual response to "feelings of isolation, the fragility of the subjective self and the instability of inner and of superficial identity." See Le Rider, *Modernity and Crises of Identity*, 60, 1; see also chap. 4, "Narcissus," 60–72, and chap. 5, "Crises of Masculine Identity: Schreber, Weininger, Hofmannsthal," 77–100, including references to Wilde.

13. Peter Altenberg, "Gartentheater in der Kunstschau," in *Bilderbogen des kleinen Lebens* (Berlin: Reiss, 1909), 123–25; repr. in *Das grosse Peter Altenberg Buch*, ed. Werner J. Schweiger (Vienna and Hamburg: Zsolnay-Verlag, 1977), 321.

14. As quoted by Schreker, excerpted in Haidy Schreker-Bures et al., *Franz Schreker, Österreichische Komponisten des XX Jahrhunderts* 17 (Vienna: Österreichischer Bundesverlag, 1970), 22.

15. The nature of these changes is already well documented. See esp. Uta Wilhelm, "Zum Einfluß der Theorien Otto Weiningers auf die Figurenkonzeption in Alexander Zemlinskys Einakter *Der Zwerg*," *Archiv für Musikwissenschaft* 54/1 (1997): 84–89.

16. For a detailed analytical discussion of the strategic employment of such harmonic effects within the opera that draws upon Richard Cohn's theory of the uncanny nature of hexatonic polar relations, see Sherry Lee, "The Other in the Mirror, or, Recognizing the Self: Wilde's and Zemlinsky's Dwarf," *Music and Letters* 91/2 (2010):198–223.

17. Letter from Berg to Helene Berg, 22 November 1923, in *Alban Berg: Briefe an seine Frau* (Munich: Langen-Müller, 1965), 526.

18. See Hailey, "Alexander Zemlinsky: *Eine florentinsiche Tragödie* Op. 16 (1916) / *Der Zwerg* Op. 17 (1921)"; and Leon Botstein, "Opera and Oscar Wilde," *American Symphony Orchestra Dialogues and Extensions*, 2001–2002 Season, 9 June 2002, http://www.american symphony.org/season.php?season=2001-2002.

19. Alma's comment is cited by Antony Beaumont in *Zemlinsky* (London: Faber & Faber, 2000), 27.

20. Oscar Wilde, *The Picture of Dorian Gray*, in *The Complete Works of Oscar Wilde* (New York: Barnes & Noble Books, 1994), 88.

21. Ibid.

22. Richard Ellmann, *Oscar Wilde* (London: Penguin, 1988), 294–95.

23. Schorske, *Fin-de-Siècle Vienna*, 8.

24. The influence on Berg of the theme of mirror image as expressed in Werfel's drama is discussed by David Schroeder in "Berg's *Kammerkonzert* and Franz Werfel's *Spiegelmensch*: Mirror Images in Music and Literature," in *Encrypted Messages in Alban Berg's Music*, ed. Siglind Bruhn (New York and London: Garland Publishing, 1998), 67–90.

25. The theatrical portrait had wide currency outside the theater and opera house as well in the form of images of actors and singers, very often costumed as their most famous roles, which not only frequently decorated the foyers of performance venues (and still do today), but were sold as postcards. I am grateful to Christopher Hailey for this observation. For some documentation of the portraiture of opera singers from the nineteenth century through much of the twentieth, see *The Oxford Illustrated History of Opera*, ed. Roger Parker, (Oxford and New York: Oxford University Press, 1995), and *The Great Opera Stars in Historic Photographs*, ed. James Camner (New York: Dover, 1978).

26. Strauss's Wildean *Salome* may not contain a literal portrait, but few know better than the princess of Judea the power of the gaze, from the first scene—"Why does the Tetrarch look at me . . . ?"—right through to the last: "If thou hadst looked at me," she tells the head of Jokanaan, "though hadst loved me."

27. Schorske, *Fin-de-Siècle Vienna*, 327.

28. Adorno, "On Some Relationships Between Music and Painting," trans. Susan Gillespie, *Musical Quarterly* 79/1 (Spring 1995): 66–79.

29. Richard Leppert, "Music, Gesture, and the Embodiment of the Utopian Imagination," keynote address delivered at Royal College of Music, London, 24 April 2009.

30. Linda Hutcheon and Michael Hutcheon, "The 'Phenomenal Image' in Opera," *South Atlantic Quarterly* 104/1, Special issue on "Music, Image, Gesture," ed. Bryan Gilliam (Winter 2005): 67.

31. Arne Stollberg emphasizes the importance of recognizing that Rodenbach's dramatic adaptation of *Bruges-la-morte*, titled *Le mirage*, is really the principal source for

Korngold's libretto rather than the novel itself. See *Durch den Traum zum Leben: Erich Wolfgang Korngolds Oper "Die tote Stadt"* (Mainz: Are Edition, 2003), 95.

32. Nancy, "The Look of the Portrait," 235.

33. Stollberg queries the dramatic-psychological ramifications of this explicit conflation between the two women and its distinction from the suggestion in the source novel. See *Durch den Traum zum Leben*, 97–98.

34. Hutcheon and Hutcheon, "The 'Phenomenal Image' in Opera," 72.

35. Weininger's notorious racist and misogynist views may seem too exaggerated to be cited as reflections of Viennese attitudes of his time, yet Chandak Sengoopta's *Otto Weininger: Sex, Science, and Self in Imperial Vienna* (Chicago: University of Chicago Press, 2000) highlights not only the widespread influence of Weininger's *Geschlecht und Charakter* (1903) but its foundation in wider fin-de-siècle Viennese thought, recognizing that the treatise was "so rooted in its times and molded so fundamentally by the currents of Viennese intellectual life and cultural politics that the text simply defies comprehension if examined in isolation from its epoch" (2).

36. Carmen Ottner, "Frauengestalten in der österreichischen Oper: Zum Schaffen der bedeutendsten Komponisten ab der Jahrhundertwende bis in die Dreißiger Jahre," in *Kundry & Elektra und ihre leidenden Schwestern*, ed. Silvia Kronberger and Ulrich Müller (Salzburg: Verlag Mueller-Speiser, 2003), 145.

37. Ibid., 164

38. This performance must not only be heard but *watched*. Marietta's accidental uncovering of Marie's portrait as she dances around the room is described not in sung text but in stage directions only; the moment of recognition is incomprehensible unless the audience *sees* what Marietta sees and experiences the same moment of recognition.

39. Benjamin Goose, "Opera for Sale: Folksong, Sentimentality, and the Market," *Journal of the Royal Musical Association* 133/2 (2008): 189–219.

40. Ibid., 218.

41. Ibid., 198. Goose also notes the song's underlying artifice, recognizing that it is less simple than it appears.

42. On the pursuit of the art and business of portrait photography through two generations of the Schreker family, see Marcella Stern, "Die Dynastie der Atelierphotographen Schreker," in *Franz Schreker: Grenzgänge, Grenzklänge*, ed. Michael Haas and Christopher Hailey (Vienna: Mandelbaum, 2004), 36–37.

43. "Ich male Bilder. / Tiere und Menschen, / Bäume und Seen—/ den Himmel, das Licht—/ doch am liebsten / male ich—Seelen."

44. See Tamar Garb, "The Forbidden Gaze," *Art in America* 79 (1991): 147–51, 186; and J. Diane Radycki, "The Life of Lady Art Students: Changing Art Education at the Turn of the Century," *Art Journal* 42/1 (Spring 1982): 9–13.

45. Peter Franklin, "Franz Schreker, Die Gezeichneten," *Opera Quarterly* 23/4 (2007): 491.

46. See Shearer West, *Portraiture* (Oxford and New York: Oxford University Press, 2004), chap. 6, "Gender and Portraiture"; and Angela Rosenthal, "She's got the look! Eighteenth-century female portrait painters and the psychology of a potentially 'dangerous employment,'" in *Portraiture: Facing the Subject*, ed. Woodall (Manchester, UK: Manchester University Press, 1997), 147–66.

47. See Rosenthal, "She's got the look!" and Garb, "The Forbidden Gaze."

48. Franklin, "Franz Schreker, Die Gezeichneten," 491.

49. Both images can be viewed online in the "Impressions and Fantasies" section of the catalogue raisonné of Schoenberg's paintings and drawings in the archive of the Arnold Schönberg Center, http://www.schoenberg.at/index.php?option=com_joomgallery&func=viewcategory&catid=2&Itemid=339&lang=en.

50. Adorno, "On Some Relationships Between Music and Painting," 67.

51. Theodor Adorno, *Alban Berg, Master of the Smallest Link*, trans. Juliane Brand and Christopher Hailey (Cambridge, UK: Cambridge University Press, 1991), 64n.

52. Theodor Adorno, "Schreker," in *Quasi una Fantasia: Essays on Modern Music*, trans. Rodney Livingstone (London and New York: Verso, 1992), 136.

53. For example, as communicated in a letter to Schoenberg around the time of *Der ferne Klang*, see *The Berg-Schoenberg Correspondence: Selected Letters*, ed. Juliane Brand, Christopher Hailey, and Donald Harris (New York: W. W. Norton, 1987), letter of 8 May 1912.

54. See Sherry Lee, "A Minstrel in a World Without Minstrels: Adorno and the Case of Schreker," *Journal of the American Musicological Society* 58/3 (2005): 639–96.

55. Adorno, "Schreker," 134.

56. Berg selected the five texts he set from the "Texte auf Ansichtskarten" in Altenberg's *Neues Altes*, 1911. Arved Ashby has discussed the subtle qualities of voice and use of grammar in Altenberg's texts that contribute to a sense of ambiguity in their temporal implications; see Ashby, "Singing the Aphoristic Text: Berg's *Altenberg-Lieder*," in *Encrypted Messages in Alban Berg's Music*, ed. Siglind Bruhn (New York and London: Garland, 1998), 191–226, esp. 200–203.

57. Adorno, "On Some Relationships Between Music and Painting," 67.

58. Some discussion of Schoenberg's critical disapproval of the work is found in Kathryn Bailey, "Berg's Aphoristic Pieces," in *The Cambridge Companion to Berg*, ed. Anthony Pople (Cambridge: Cambridge University Press, 1997), 83–110; and Christoph Khittl, "The Other Altenberg Song Cycle: A Document of Viennese Fin-de-Siècle Aesthetics," in *Encrypted Messages in Alban Berg's Music*, 137–56.

59. Adorno, *Alban Berg*, 64. When Adorno writes "polytonally clouded triads," he is referring to larger dissonant chords composed of superimposed triads. It is doubtful he is claiming that Schreker's idiom is "polytonality," however such a term might be defined. Nick Chadwick also notes Schrekerian features in the *Altenberg Lieder*; see "Franz Schreker's Orchestral Style and Its Influence on Alban Berg," *The Music Review* 35 (1974): 29–46.

60. In the "Afterword" to the translation of Adorno's monograph on Berg, editors Juliane Brand and Christopher Hailey note Adorno's indication, in his essay "Im Gedächtnis an Alban Berg," that Berg had pointed out to him a similarity between a moment in *Wozzeck* and Schreker's musical style. See Adorno, *Alban Berg*, 142; the reference in Adorno's essay can be found in the *Gesammelte Schriften* (Frankfurt am Main: Suhrkamp, 1970–86), 18:498.

61. It is worth noting that more recent studies of Schreker's music have sought to go beyond the stereotypical view of the composer as a purveyor of sensual sonority first and foremost, by analytically engaging with elements of structure that suggest further parallels with Berg's structural techniques. See, for example, Ulrike Kienzle, *Das Trauma hinter dem Traum: Franz Schrekers Oper "Der ferne Klang" und die Wiener Moderne* (Schliengen: Argus, 1998), and Janine Ortiz, *"Feuer muss fressen, was Flamme gebar": Franz Schrekers Oper "Irrelohe,"* Schreker Perspektiven 1, ed. Christopher Hailey and Ulrike Kienzle (Mainz: Are Musik Verlag, 2008).

62. Adorno, *Alban Berg*, 14.

63. Karl Kraus, "Die Büchse der Pandora," *Die Fackel* 182 (June 1905); trans. by Celia Skrine in Douglas Jarman, *Alban Berg: Lulu* (Cambridge, UK: Cambridge University Press, 1991), 104–5.

64. Silvio José Dos Santos, "Ascription of Identity: The *Bild* Motif and the Character of Lulu," *Journal of Musicology* 21/2 (Spring 2004): 269.

65. Depending on the production, there may be other portraits in the film: in Graham Vick's Glyndebourne production of 1996, the film prominently featured Lulu's "mug shot" taken on her arrest for Schön's murder, followed by a series of crime scene photos of Schön's body, and later in the hospital, X-ray shots. It is interesting to note that the portrait in this

production does not represent Lulu as Pierrot—a not uncommon deviation from Berg and Wedekind in recent productions—but as a conflation of the "serpent" she is identified with in the Prologue, and as Eve, as the painter of the portrait views her: she poses wearing a pair of snakeskin pants and holding a bitten apple. In relation to the mug-shot photo and the crime scene shots in Vick's film version, Woodall's comments about the nineteenth-century rise of photography for portraiture and identification are pertinent: "The objectivity attributed to photography [also] quickly led to its use in the identification or investigation of criminal, insane, diseased, orphaned and otherwise 'deviant' individuals. This was because the camera objectified the sitter and the photographic technique tended to record imperfections and physical idiosyncrasies which were, according to the idealist precepts underlying honorific portraiture, indicative of the accidental and animal elements of humanity." Woodall, Introduction, *Facing the Subject*, 6–7.

66. In Schreker's *Der ferne Klang* there is also a potential for doubling of character roles—suggested by the assignment of the same voice types to characters not simultaneously present onstage—and some recent productions have realized this possibility.

67. Dos Santos, "Ascription of Identity," 269. The article goes on to interrogate the question of "who Lulu is" as queried by Donald Mitchell, George Perle, Leo Treitler, Judy Lochhead, and Karen Pegley; see 270–71.

68. Adorno, *Alban Berg*, 130–31.

69. Letter from Berg to Adorno, 30 November 1927, in *Theodor W. Adorno & Alban Berg: Correspondence*, 112–13.

70. Adorno to Berg, 30 January 1926, in *Theodor W. Adorno & Alban Berg: Correspondence*, 46.

71. Adorno's written response to Berg in favor of Wedekind over Hauptmann as a libretto source has been lost, but Adorno's discussion of it in his monograph on Berg is corroborated by Berg's reference to it in a letter to Soma Morgenstern. See Adorno, *Alban Berg*, 26; and Henri Lonitz's note in *Theodor W. Adorno & Alban Berg: Correspondence*, 113–14.

72. Adorno, *Alban Berg*, 26.

73. Ibid., 7.

74. Susanne Rode-Breymann discusses the contents of Berg's notebooks "Von der Selbsterkenntnis," including passages from Wilde, in *Alban Berg und Karl Kraus: Zur geistigen Biographie des Komponisten der "Lulu"* (Frankfurt am Main: Peter Lang, 1988).

75. Oscar Wilde, *The Picture of Dorian Gray*, 21.

76. Ibid., 94.

"Remembrance of things that are to come": Some Reflections on Berg's Palindromes

DOUGLAS JARMAN

The basic postulate of twelve-note technique—that having arranged the twelve notes of the chromatic scale in a particular order the composer is free to use this ordering in its original, its inverted, its retrograde, and its retrograde inverted forms—is now so generally known and accepted that those of us who listen to or think about this music rarely pause to question it.

That a row can be inverted, that is turned upside down, is an understandable assumption: we are all familiar with thematic material being inverted in tonal music, although, given the nature of the diatonic scale and the hierarchy of relationships involved, such inversions usually have to be modified to form what are called "tonal inversions." The idea that a row can be played backwards (retrograde), or backwards and upside down (its retrograde inversion), is much more peculiar. Whether it remains in some ways recognizable in retrograde and retrograde inversions has been a matter of some discussion, but hardly anyone seems to have asked where the idea came from.

In his 1941 article "Composition with Twelve Tones" Schoenberg cites only one (somewhat unconvincing) precedent for such a procedure: the last movement of Beethoven's F-Major Quartet, op. 135, in which he regards one figuration as being a decorated form of the retrograde inversion of the "Muss es sein?" motive that opens the movement.[1] Schoenberg dismisses any potential criticism of his analysis with the comment that "the last century considered such procedures as cerebral and inconsistent with genius. The very fact that there exist classical examples proves the foolishness of such an opinion."[2]

But how did the idea originate? Retrogrades, or palindromes (in which the original and its retrograde are juxtaposed without any intervening passage or section) are, after all, hardly common in music of the Baroque and post-Baroque periods. The *Musical Offering* includes one cancrizan (or crab) Canon a 2, in which the two canonic voices start at the same time but one is the retrograde of the other; there is the Minuet al Rovescio of Haydn's Symphony no. 47 (which reappears in Piano Sonata no. 26 and the fourth violin sonata); and a similar Minuet in C Major for keyboard by C. P. E. Bach, as well as the passage in the finale of the *Hammerklavier* Sonata, in which Beethoven treats the fugue subject in retrograde. But otherwise—apart from an extraordinary example in Schubert's *Die Zauberharfe*, to which Brian Newbould first drew attention in 1992, and which is perhaps the only retrograde in the whole of nineteenth-century music—there are almost no other examples in the music of the Baroque, Classical, and Romantic periods with which the composers of the Second Viennese School would have been most familiar.[3]

The precedents usually cited in this context are the works of the Netherland composers of the Ars Nova, the most famous of which is Machaut's *Mon fin est ma commencement*. In his article "Retrograde, Inversion, Retrograde-Inversion and Related Techniques in the Masses of Johannes Obrecht," R. Larry Todd identifies five Obrecht masses in which "an addition to be heard in the original form of the Cantus firmus is also stated in retrograde, arranged in inverted order or, by combining the two properties, presented simultaneously in inverted and retrograde forms."[4] Noting that "even before Obrecht's time composers practiced techniques such as retrograde inversion in addition to the more common retrograde and inversion" and that "of the three procedures retrograde motion appears to have been the first to be widely cultivated," Todd cites three crab canons from the fourteenth century, a later fourteenth-century source that includes a palindrome, a Credo from the Old Hall manuscript that includes a retrograde, and two early fifteenth-century examples, in addition to one work by Dunstable, one by Dufay, and six by Busnois.[5]

Webern, of course, was well acquainted with the music of this earlier period. His doctoral dissertation, an edition of Heinrich Isaak's *Choralis Constantinus*, was completed in 1906 (in the middle of his four-year period of study with Schoenberg) while he was also studying at the University of Vienna with Guido Adler, whose special area of expertise was Renaissance music. Book 2 of *Choralis Constantinus*, for which Webern was responsible, certainly contains a number of crab canons (to which Webern himself draws attention in his introduction to that volume). It is unclear, however, how familiar Schoenberg and Berg were with this music, or indeed how much of this material was available at the time. There had been an interest in medieval music from the 1780s onward but, as Daniel Leech-Wilkinson has shown, knowledge of the fourteenth century remained almost entirely blank until the 1890s when the *Denkmäler der Tonkunst in Österreich* published the pioneering work of Friedrich Ludwig and Johannes Wolf.[6]

That Schoenberg had some knowledge of this music is evidenced by a curious little piece titled *Eyn doppelt Spiegel u. Schlüssel-Kanon für vier Stimen gesetzet auf niederlandische Art*, as well as by the cancrizans of "Mondfleck" in *Pierrot lunaire*.[7]

Berg's knowledge of this earlier music is less clear; indeed, there is no indication that Berg had any interest in music before the Baroque. He may have discussed Isaak with Webern, and he would certainly have known Webern's *Five Sacred Songs*, op. 15, and the *Five Canons on Latin Texts*, op. 16, of 1924 (although there are no crab canons in these works). And though the *Thema* and the subsequent variations of Webern's Symphony, op. 21, are palindromic, that work was not written until 1927, by which time Berg had composed the Three Orchestral Pieces op. 6, *Wozzeck*, and the Chamber Concerto, all of which—to greater or lesser degrees—include palindromes or retrogrades.

The one work that includes a retrograde that we can be certain Berg knew intimately is *Pierrot*, a work in which (significantly) the cancrizans of "Mondfleck" have a textual, extramusical significance since they symbolize the impossibility of Pierrot discovering and brushing away the spot of moonlight on his own back.

Retrograde movement can take a number of different forms. The cancrizan canon in Bach's *Musical Offering* consists of two voices, each of which is the other backwards, played simultaneously. There are no such canons in Berg's output.

In the Obrecht masses the retrograde is applied to the basic structural element of the music—the cantus firmus—in a way that is comparable to it being applied to the basic structural element—the note row—of twelve-note music. But in fact Berg, unlike Schoenberg and Webern, rarely uses retrograde row forms as part of his normal musical language. There is one example of Berg employing a retrograde row in a sketch for *Lulu* and one sketch for a passage in the last movement of the Violin Concerto that Berg's numbering indicates as a retrograde (although the latter is a curiosity since the retrograde of the row of the Violin Concerto is identical to a cyclic permutation of the inversion and thus has no separate identity). Elsewhere, however, Berg only uses retrograde forms as part of a larger retrograde or palindromic structure and for specific extramusical reasons.

Another form of what might be considered a retrograde is that in which sections of music reappear in reverse order, although the music itself does not run backwards. Thus in Hindemith's *Hin und Zurück*—in which a trivial domestic incident leads to a husband shooting his wife and then, following his expression of remorse, the sequence of events is reversed to the original situation, and connubial bliss is restored—the music of the second half is not a retrograde of the music of the first but consists of short sections (4 bars, 6 bars, 9 bars, etc.) of the original repeated, but juxtaposed in reverse order. Although it ends with a strict retrograde of its opening bars, such a structural retrograde forms the basis of the Prologue to *Lulu*.[8]

True multivoiced retrogrades (as in the Haydn Minuet al Rovescio) when whole sections of music run backwards, are for obvious reasons rare in tonal music and hardly more common in earlier music, but are peculiarly characteristic of Berg's music.[9] Extensive palindromes occur in the Sextet of Act 1, sc. 3 and the Film Music Interlude of Act 2 of *Lulu*, and also in *Der Wein*, all note-for-note retrogrades (with minor exceptions to be discussed later). The central Adagio movement of the Chamber Concerto is palindromic but heavily decorated and with some parts omitted in the second half. Elsewhere we find not palindromes, with the two halves juxtaposed around a central turning point, but large-scale retrogrades in which the original and its retrograde are separated by an intervening section, as in some scenes of *Wozzeck*; the Allegro misterioso of the *Lyric Suite*, where the sixty measures of the original are separated from its shortened retrograde by the Trio estatico; and the Praeludium of Three Orchestral Pieces, op. 6.

Where did Berg get the idea that in music, the most temporally dependent of all the art forms, one could turn whole and substantial passages (the *Lulu* Film Music is 69 measures long, the Chamber Concerto's Adagio 240 bars long in all) backwards? Whether or not he discussed these things with Webern, or indeed with Schoenberg, it seems unlikely that his use of palindromes came from a knowledge of the Netherlanders.

What do Berg's retrogrades signify and what do they tell us about both his conception of time and his ideas about how time is experienced? It is not my intention, nor am I qualified, to discuss the concepts of time prevalent in late nineteenth- and early twentieth-century thought, although it is clear that the Newtonian idea of an absolute, objective time, in which the flow of time remains unaffected by anything that happens in the material world—in which "absolute, true and mathematical time, of itself, and from its own nature, flows equally without relation to anything external"—had been progressively undermined from the late eighteenth century onward.[10] Philosophers from Kant, who argued that space and time were part of the subjective apparatus of understanding, to Bergson had questioned the idea of objective absolute time; scientists and "a whole generation of experimental psychologists and clinicians in the late nineteenth century" were already investigating the nature of subjective time.[11] Even before the publication of Einstein's special and general theories of relativity, in 1905 and 1916 respectively, overturned classical theory, the "thrust of the age was," in the words of Stephen Kern, "to affirm the reality of private time ... and to define its nature as heterogeneous, fluid and reversible."[12]

Kern gives two examples of contemporary inventions that he claims could have led to time being seen as reversible: Edison's invention of the lightbulb in 1879, which, if hardly capable of reversing time, had the ability to blur the distinction between night and apparent day; and the cinema, a medium in which time could be brought to a standstill, slowed down, speeded up, and turned backwards. The cinema is, of course, of some significance when discussing Berg: not only do we know that he was an enthusiastic filmgoer but we have in the palindromic Film Music of *Lulu* a visual quasi-retrograde associated with a strict musical retrograde followed by a scene Berg indicates as "quasi Zeitluppe"—as though in slow motion.[13]

A number of commentators have drawn attention to the links between Berg's musical techniques and philosophical and mystical thought at the turn of the nineteenth and twentieth centuries. Writing specifically about retrograde and circular form in Berg's music Robert Morgan relates what he calls "Berg's cyclic conception of time" to Nietzsche's concept of "eternal recurrence"—the belief that "all events are destined to repeat themselves through eternity."[14] To Nietzsche not merely the acceptance of but the wish for the eternal return of all events—a return that gives meaning to the constant transience of time—was the ultimate affirmation of life:

> What if some day or night a demon were to steal after you into your inner loneliness and say to you "This life as you now live it and have lived it, you will have to live once more and innumerable times more. . . ." Would you not throw yourself down and gnash your teeth and curse the demon who spoke thus? Or have you once experienced a tremendous moment when you would have answered him: "You are a god and never have I heard anything more divine."[15]

Berg admired Nietzsche and, like all of his and the previous generation, was deeply affected by Nietzsche's ideas, though Nietzsche was not the only source of such theories about time. Indeed, the concept of time as moving in recurring cycles was a common feature of much mystical and quasi-scientific thought in the late nineteenth and the early years of the twentieth century. The works of Giovanni Battista Vico (1668–1744), whose *Scienzia nuova* had proposed that society progressed toward perfection through a series of recurring cycles, had been rediscovered during the course of the nineteenth century. A similar concern with the idea of cyclic time is evident in the theosophy of Helene Blavatsky and Annie Besant, which promulgated a mixture of beliefs derived from Hinduism, Buddhism, and the supposed forgotten wisdom of the ancients; the anthroposophical writings of Rudolf Steiner; and the esoteric teachings of G. I. Gurdjieff and his pupil Peter Ouspensky. Such writings were widely read and had enormous influence in both Europe and America at the time.

Similarly, quasi-scientific writings of the same period attempted to show that all the important events in natural life followed a law of periodicity based on a certain significant number. The Viennese biologist Paul Kammerer claimed to have demonstrated that the law of periodicity extended to chance events, arguing that it was "a fact" that unlucky occurrences never came singly but always in twos or threes;[16] the Berlin nose and throat specialist Wilhelm Fliess held that all events in natural life were determined by the numbers 23 (for men) and 28 (for women);[17] and according to the Viennese Hermann Swoboda the determining number of all things was the number 7.[18]

Numerology also played an important role in many of the esoteric and mystical beliefs of the period in which, again, the number 7 also played a particular, significant role. In Blavatsky's *The Secret Doctrine*, in which man's life cycle is described as "interminable in its duration of successive incarnations of rebirth," and in the writings of her colleague Annie Besant, the number 7 related to the organs of the human body, which were believed to have correspondences in the seven colors, the seven known planets and the notes of the diatonic scale.[19] Above all, 7 was the number of stages in human development, highest of which, according to Besant, were the sixth, the spiritual soul that was usually unrealized in man as he then existed, and the seventh, a spark of impersonal divinity that was the fundamental selfhood of all beings and so was unrealized in all but a handful of people. Steiner's anthroposophy, in which reincarnation was also a necessary part of human evolution, likewise posited seven cosmic cycles, each of which was divided into various subcycles also based on the number 7.

Berg, with his well-known interest in numerology and the occult, was undoubtedly familiar with and interested in such quasi-mystical ideas.[20] We know from his letter to Schoenberg of 20 June 1915 that he saw Fliess's theories as lending support to his already existing belief in the significance of his fateful number, the number 23.[21] Moreover, Paul Kammerer was a personal acquaintance,[22] Helene Berg was deeply involved in mystical writings, and many of his friends and colleagues in the Schoenberg circle—including Schoenberg himself—were either theosophists or interested in theosophy.[23]

Among the most frequently cited nonmusical sources of the twelve-note system, of the idea that "a musical creator's mind can operate subconsciously with a row of tones regardless of their direction," is Balzac's *Séraphita*, a work based on the writings of Swedenborg.[24] Rudolf Steiner gave two lectures about Swedenborg in 1915; Blavatsky called him "the great Swedish Theosophist"; and Berg, Schoenberg, and Webern all particularly admired Balzac's novel about the philosopher's ideas.

Schoenberg himself refers to the Balzac novel in the article "Composition with Twelve Tones," where he states that "the unity of musical space demands an absolute and unitary perception. In this space, as in Swedenborg's heaven (described in Balzac's *Séraphita*) there is no absolute down, no right or left, forward or backward."[25]

The high regard in which the members of the Second Viennese School held Balzac's novel (to modern minds almost unreadable) is well known and the importance of its interpretation of the teachings in Swedenborg's *Heaven and Hell* on the thought of these composers has been discussed by many writers. As their letters show, Swedenborg's ideas—or perhaps more correctly, Swedenborg's ideas as reflected in the writings of Balzac and Strindberg since it is unclear how familiar they were with Swedenborg's own writings—were an abiding interest of the Schoenberg school. Both Schoenberg and Berg had plans at one time to write works based on *Séraphita;* both toyed with the idea of setting Strindberg (neither of them did but Strindberg's *Jacob Wrestles* was an influence on Schoenberg's own *Jakobsleiter*); and Berg's Christmas present to Schoenberg in 1912 was "a few volumes of Balzac."[26]

Among the commentators discussing Berg's music in the light of *Séraphita*, John Covach has seen Berg's use of palindromic structures as being associated with the spiritual transformation undergone by the figures of Wilfrid and Minna in Balzac's novel, and as "part of a larger concern in his music for addressing an alternate mode of temporality." Thus for Berg, according to Covach, "Balzac's *Séraphita* suggested that music concerned with evoking the higher spiritual realms must also somehow disrupt our normal sense of temporal unfolding."[27]

A belief, or at least an interest, in such things was not confined to Vienna or Austro-Germany but widespread through Europe and America, not least among artistic circles, and an inherent part of the intellectual outlook of the period. Examples of the influence such ideas had on the artistic output of the last years of the nineteenth century and the early decades of the twentieth are numerous. W. B. Yeats, who had read A. P. Sinnet's "Esoteric Buddhism" and addressed the Hermetic Society on such matters in the 1880s, was deeply influenced by theosophical ideas; in 1926 Franz Werfel, the brother of Hanna Fuchs Robettin to whom the *Lyric Suite* is secretly dedicated, planned to write a theosophical novel, a fictional life of Helena Blavatsky; in England, J. W. Dunne published *An Experiment with Time* in 1927, a book that had a wide readership and influenced at least two of the plays of J. B. Priestley; Mary Lutyens, the youngest daughter of the architect Sir Edwin Lutyens, chaperoned Besant and C. W. Leadbeater's protégé Krishnamurti on his theosophical travels.

Although James Joyce seems to have taken a more skeptical attitude, satirizing both Yeats and Madame Blavatsky in *Ulysses*, he was nonetheless aware of the work of Vico and made reference to the idea of cyclic recurrence.[28] The last, incomplete line of *Finnegan's Wake* links back to the first line of the work, and when, in the brothel scene of *Ulysses*, Stephen Daedalus plays the piano he "repeats once more the series of empty fifths"[29]—the endless cycle of fifths that, since it eventually covers all the notes of the diatonic scale to end where it began, represents "the ultimate empty return."[30]

Given such a context it is difficult not to believe that the fragment of the cycle of fifths that accompanies the Captain's mention of "Ewigkeit"— eternity—in Act 1, sc. 1 of *Wozzeck* and the structural role assigned to the number 7 in the opera (Berg's own op. 7) are not also a reference to such generally widespread beliefs.[31]

As the above makes clear, all these systems of thought—whether philosophical, metaphysical, or mystical—saw recurrence as positive, offering the possibility of development, of attaining a new level of consciousness and of progressing from the less to more perfect, since, in the words of Robert Morgan's summary of Nietzsche's "eternal recurrence," "only through dissolution and decay [. . .] are change and thus ultimately rebirth possible."[32] Morgan cites, in this respect, the return at the end of the work of the opening bars of the Berg Violin Concerto when "the final two measures include a return to the arpeggio of the concerto's opening measures (retrograded in that they return in reverse order) so that the music recalls, in the very moment of its dying out, its moment of initiation."[33]

Morgan is, I think, correct in his interpretation of this passage as one "of acceptance and reaffirmation."[34] Adorno, who was Berg's pupil, voices a similar view of the end of the concerto, though he does not specifically mention the closing bars but sees the use of the Bach Chorale in the final Adagio not "as mere poetic design or even as a concession to a formula of reconciliation" but as bearing "a trace of that which music at its Bachian heights once infused into the chorales accompanying mortals through a gateway into darkness so complete as to be capable of kindling the final light."[35]

Although it is difficult to see all such "circular" returns in Berg in so positive a light (the reminiscences of mm. 5–6 and 38–39 of the Allegro giovale first movement of the *Lyric Suite* hardly suggests either reaffirmation or acceptance in the context of the last movement's Largo desolato, mm. 36–37 and 38–39), it is, in any case, important to distinguish between strict retrograde or palindromic motion and the kind of returns we find in the final bars of the Violin Concerto. Morgan equates the two, suggesting that Berg's fondness for ending a piece with a reprise of the music with which it began is in some way comparable to his use of retrograde motion. In fact, the two are, I suggest, quite distinct compositionally, experientially and hermeneutically, as is evidenced by the lengths to which Berg goes to make the listener aurally, and anyone reading the score visually, aware that the central turning points of his retrogrades and palindromes are in some way special mysterious moments, moments of "musical black-magic."[36]

In the Film Music ostinato of *Lulu*, Act 2, the turning point is marked by a pianissimo ascending arpeggio figuration on the piano, which, over a held *pp* chord, ascends to its highest note and then pauses before starting to run backwards (Figure 1).

In *Der Wein* an ascending, arpeggiated first inversion B-major triad on harp, over a held F-major chord, is followed by a pause and a single low C♯ on piano before beginning its return (Figure 2).

In the Chamber Concerto an ascending arpeggio figuration in the highest register of the winds crescendos to fortissimo and, over soft brass chords, gives way to a high figuration on solo violin over twelve repeated low C♯s on the solo piano (the piano's only entry in the movement). The halfway point of these piano notes—after the sixth C♯—marks the moment at which the retrograde starts (Figure 3). Hans Ferdinand Redlich, aware of the almost magical significance of these moments, has referred to the low piano notes that mark the turning point of the Adagio of the Chamber Concerto as "12 mysterious chimes . . . which ring in the hour of musical ghosts."[37]

Berg is also careful to ensure that all three scores present a visual picture that draws attention to the musical symmetry. In *Lulu* and *Der Wein* the turning points of the palindromes come at the center of a single bar and, in the manuscript, both are laid out so that this bar is in the center of the page, flanked on either side by the symmetrically corresponding bars. In the Chamber Concerto the turning point comes at the end of a bar—between, as it were, the end of one bar and the start of the next. In Berg's manuscript the final bar of the first half is the last bar of a left-hand page, and the first bar of the second half is the first bar of the facing right-hand page. As the facsimile of Berg's manuscript in Figure 3 shows, the various textual inscriptions—the annotations on either side of the piano's six bars and above the double bassoon part; the indication of the double bassoon's lowest note ("Des"; D♭); the change from "Kfg. setzt fort" (contrabassoon goes on) in the oboe part at measure 358 to "Kfg. Fortsetzend" (contrabassoon continues) at measure 363, etc.—are also incorporated into this symmetry so that the two pages as a whole form a single symmetrical picture. Also significantly, the right-hand of the two pages shown in Figure 3 is the only page in the whole score in which Berg omits the conventional brackets that elsewhere couple the staves of instrumental "family" groups —the piccolo and flute staves, the oboe and English horn staves, etc.

George Perle has pointed out how Berg marks the exact midpoint of the *Lulu* Film Music by an unconventional notation of his own invention

Figure 1. *Lulu*, Act 2, mm. 685–90 (Film Music Interlude).
See next page for copyright information.

Alban Berg, *Lulu*. Copyright ©1964 by Universal Edition A.G., Wien. © Renewed. All Rights Reserved. Used by permission of European American Music Distributors LLC, U.S. and Canadian agent for Universal Edition A.G., Wien.

Figure 2. *Der Wein*, mm. 137–45.

in which the fermata sign, representing the year Lulu spends in jail, stands between the half-note of the first half of the bar and the half-note of the second half of the bar.[38] An equally novel inscription appears in the manuscript of the Chamber Concerto Adagio, at the center of which Berg writes not ♩ = 48 but ♩ = on the left and = 48 on the right page so that the two = signs themselves become part of the symmetry.[39] The first published edition of the Chamber Concerto was an opalographic facsimile of Berg's manuscript; so keen was he to ensure that the two pages at the central turning point of the palindromic Adagio were facing each other and formed a mirror symmetry that he wrote a note to the person in charge of producing the edition asking that, against all publishing convention, the score should start on a left, rather than a right-hand page.[40]

The prevalence of such large-scale palindromes and retrogrades, and the musical and orthographic care expended on them, make it clear that such constructions have a particular significance in Berg's music. In pieces like the Haydn Minuet al Rovescio and Bach's cancrizan canon the writing of such retrogrades are a display of technical skill. In Berg, I suggest, they have a different significance. If, as Morgan claims, the return of the opening material of the Violin Concerto at the end of the work is a symbol of reaffirmation, Berg's palindromes and strict retrogrades are, on the contrary (as I have argued elsewhere), symbols of negation.[41]

Adorno has observed that musical retrogrades are, by their nature, "anti-temporal."[42] At the center of each palindrome time comes momentarily to a standstill (the central point of the *Lulu* Film Music has the indication "a complete standstill" above it) before the music reverses itself and runs, inexorably, back to its starting point. In effect, it wipes itself out as though it had never been, denying its own existence and returning to a point at which it restores the status quo ante.

In *Lulu* such palindromes are a reflection of the dramatic situation or of the text; in the Sextet of Act 1, sc. 3, people rush into Lulu's dressing room to discover the reason for her faint and then leave again; the Film Music depicts Lulu's arrest, trial, and imprisonment, and then her escape from prison. Even the smaller palindromes in *Lulu*, embodied in the larger ongoing passages of music, have a similar significance: the short palindrome at mm. 680–81 of the Monoritmica in Act 1, sc. 2, for example, symbolizes the verbal negation implicit in Schön's sentence, "I didn't come here to create a scandal; I came to save you from a scandal."

In the instrumental works, as has become clear as a result of recent research, such palindromic reversals reflect the negation implicit in aspects of the autobiographical programs.[43] In his Berg book, Adorno suggests that Berg's propensity for "mirror and retrograde formations may . . . be related to the visual dimension of his responses."[44] Yet, as someone who

Figure 3. Chamber Concerto, Adagio, mm. 356–60.

Figure 3 continued, mm. 361–65.

knew about the secret program of the *Lyric Suite*, Adorno was also aware that the retrograde of the opening section of the Allegro misterioso, following the Trio estatico, had a significance that was more than purely visual or purely formal and hints as much in his description of the piece:

> The reversal of the sequence of events is quite literal, beginning with the last note and ending with the first; only a middle section is excised. The trick finds its justification in the idea: nothing could capture more drastically the sense of hopeless confinement than the circular closed form.[45]

What Adorno did not know, and what we now know from George Perle's discovery of the annotated *Lyric Suite*, is that the negation of the first part of the movement symbolized by this retrograde section is specifically indicated by Berg in the annotation that stands at its head: "Vergessen Sie es"—Forget it![46]

In discussing *Lulu* Adorno had an overt plot line, rather than a secret program, on which to base his observations, and his reading of the Film Music recognizes the symbolic nature of the palindrome: "The film music—the work's caesura and its innermost reflection—is in strict retrograde: time passes and revokes itself and nothing points beyond it but the gesture of those who love without hope."[47] Adorno's readings of the palindromes of *Der Wein* and the Chamber Concerto, however—works for which he has no dramatic scenario and no knowledge of the secret programs—avoid discussion of, or even hinting at, their possible symbolic, extramusical, significance. Of *Der Wein* he simply notes that mm. 141ff. are a "complete retrograde of the second scherzo half."[48] The retrograde of the Chamber Concerto he attributes entirely to structural considerations:

> The disposition of the Concerto as a whole initially precludes a development section since, of course, the Rondo functions as a development of both the first and second movements. By the same token, any traditional kind of development in the Adagio itself is ruled out by that movement's thematic wealth and by the quasi-developmental character of the third theme. [...] Simple or varied repetition of the exposition without development [...] was not possible because of the considerable length of what according to the formal design would constitute the exposition (mm. 241–330). [...] This situation: no development, no repetition, and yet the need for formal balance and coherence, automatically invoked, as it were, the expedient of a retrograde of the entire exposition. As in many of Mahler's movements—the Adagio of the Ninth Symphony—the retrograde nature

of the form as a whole is meant to effect a closure no longer guaranteed by the formal scheme of music whose very fibre is unsuited to that scheme.[49]

Recent revelations have shown us that both *Der Wein* and the Chamber Concerto have programs with which the palindromes of both works are closely associated. The significance of the palindrome at the center of *Der Wein* is made clear by Berg himself in his letter of 4 December 1929 to Hanna Fuchs Robettin:

When I sang of wine, as I did this past summer, whom else does it concern but you, Hanna, when I say (in "The Wine of Lovers"): "Come sister, laid breast to breast, let us flee without rest or stand, to my dreams' Elysian land" and these words die away in the softest accord of B and F major! What follows after that can only be the song of "The Wine of the Solitary." Aye, that I am and that I remain.[50]

The program of the Adagio of the Chamber Concerto, which was unknown until unraveled by Brenda Dalen, is concerned with the illness and death of Schoenberg's first wife Mathilde, the musical cipher of whose name, along with a modified quotation from Schoenberg's *Pelleas und Melisande*, appears at a number of points in the movement.[51] Having become ill in June 1923, Mathilde died of a tumor on the adrenal gland on October 18 of the same year. As Dalen has shown, although Berg began work on the movement "in the late Spring or early summer of 1923" there is "little reason to believe that in Autumn 1923 the Adagio would have advanced beyond m. 46" and "it is in fact possible to establish a direct link between her death and the genesis of the turning point" which "clearly came to symbolize" to Berg Mathilde's death.[52] In hermeneutic terms, Dalen's interpretation of the turning point of the Chamber Concerto Adagio—with its frenetic, high wind figurations rising to a piercing fortissimo before the low, bell-like C♯s on the piano—coincides more with our experience of this passage than does John Covach's suggestion of it invoking a spiritual transfiguration. Dalen's reading is confirmed by Berg's annotations in the manuscript first draft of the movement, in which the bars leading to the turning point have the words "Hilfe! Hilfe!" alongside them.

Retrogrades involve the listener's perception and awareness of temporal events in a different way from the kind of cyclic returns found in the Violin Concerto. Formal circularity—"the tendency to end movements, scenes, or entire compositions with a reference to their opening measures" or "some other critical formal moment," which Morgan sees in the *Seven Early Songs* and "roughly a third" of subsequent works—makes its effect by calling on the listener's memory; we recognize the recurrence of something we have already heard.[53] We do not, however, remember things backwards and we cannot remember things that we have not yet heard.[54] Discussing the return of the Prelude as the Postlude at the end of Act 1, sc. 1 of *Wozzeck*, Morgan draws attention to the "complex amalgam of forward-directed and retrogressive elements" and what he refers to as "the dialectic between continuous development and uninterrupted forward progression on the one hand and thematic return and formal articulation on the other."[55] As a composer Berg was fully aware that the way in which we experience and perceive a retrograde is not the same as the way in which we experience a repetition: that is, the "being" of a repetition is not the same as the "becoming" of a retrograde, and whatever the visual symmetries of Berg's palindromic constructions on paper, they are not experienced as temporal symmetries in the same way. The Film Music of *Lulu*, the last and in some ways the most sophisticated of Berg's palindromes, illustrates the extent to which he was careful to structure the piece in such a way that it retained its sense of forward directed movement throughout.

The Film Music Interlude is an ostinato based for the most part on a continuous regular sixteenth note movement (the few exceptional bars lead to the central turning point). On the largest scale, the first half of the Interlude consists of a series of increasingly intense crescendo and diminuendo gestures, characterized by different lengths, registral range, and instrumental timbre. The passage at mm. 663–69 for example, is scored for strings, harp, and piano accompanied by a side-drum roll and defines a *p* < *f* > *p* shape, with the strings playing *am Griffbrett* after the central *forte*, and with the following bars scored for wind while single string lines only pick out important notes. This half culminates in a tutti, a *fortissimo* brass chord, and a statement of the opera's *Hauptrhythmus*. Following this climax the dynamic level gradually descreases, the orchestration is progressively reduced, the tempo markings indicate a slowing down (*poco rit., Schon langsamer, Noch langsamer*) while the regular sixteenths slow first to triplet and then to duplet eighth notes. The gestural clarity of each of the constituent passages and the momentum generated by the constant eighth note movement in this first half are, in themselves, enough to ensure that the sense of directed forward movement is maintained in the retrograde second half, which, having gradually picked up energy (*poco a poco animato*), becomes decreasingly intense as it progresses.

With the exception of the unchanged statement of the opera's *Hauptrhythmus* from the climactic measure 680 on its return at measure 694 (the only element of the first half of the Interlude that is not reversed in the second) the Film Music is an almost exact palindrome in every respect—pitch, rhythm, dynamics, register, orchestration—and the few exceptions (all of them enumerated by Morgan) are, as Morgan observes, designed to promote this forward-directed motion and, in the final bars, to "lend the close more weight and cadential solidity."⁵⁶

But within this overall shape Berg also takes pains to ensure that the thematic and rhythmic material is such as to be aurally recognizable when it returns in retrograde. The main thematic component of the Interlude is the four-note basic cell of the whole opera shown in Example 1, a symmetrical figuration of which the retrograde is identical to its inversion

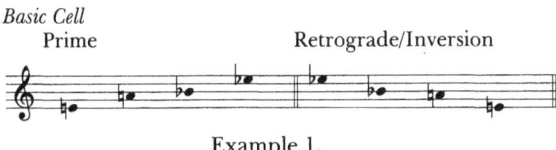

Example 1.

(which we have heard many times in the opera before this point) and is thus easily recognizable. Similarly, the music that opens and closes the Interlude is the five-note figure shown in Example 2. The retrograde of this figure differs from its inversion by only a single note, while the central turning point itself presents overlapping versions of both the basic cell and its inversion and is introduced by similarly overlapping versions of ascending and descending versions of the chords associated with Lulu's portrait (the so-called *Bildharmonien*), the retrogrades of which are again audibly related to their inversion (see Figure 1).

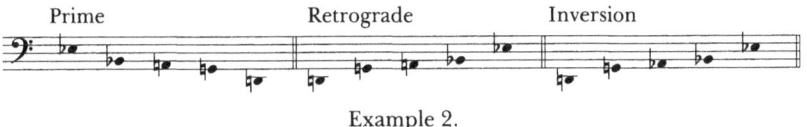

Example 2.

The compositional problem posed when writing a passage of music backwards, however, has less to do with pitch than with duration—whether one reverses a duration from the point at which it starts (the attack point) or the point at which it ends (the release point). Example 3 below illustrates the difference.

Example 3a shows the *Hauptrhythmus* (RH) of the Chamber Concerto in traditional notation; Example 3b shows the same rhythm with the duration of each note indicated in sixteenth notes, the attack points marked by downward stems and the release points marked by asterisks; Example 3c shows, in traditional notation, the rhythm produced by retrograding the attack points; and Example 3d shows the rhythm produced by retrograding the release points.

Example 3 a–d.

In the palindromic second half of the Chamber Concerto Adagio Berg simply writes the durations of the RH statements of the first half backwards (as Messiaen does when writing a "non-retrogradable rhythm"), reversing the release points of the original. The more intricate rhythmic structure of the final Rondo ritmico of the work, however, led him to consider the problem more carefully.

The results of Berg's work on the Chamber Concerto and the solution to the problem can be seen in the Allegro misterioso of the *Lyric Suite* and the Film Music from *Lulu*. In both the note rows are presented as notes of equal durational values and the rhythmic patterns are determined by extracting certain notes from the row—a procedure that ensures that the retrograde of a passage reproduces the attack points of the original. Thus, at mm. 670ff of the Film Music of *Lulu*, the winds present six different note rows as equal sixteenths. All six rows are at a level at which the notes of the basic cell, E–A–B♭–E♭, occur in the same order and are picked out by the strings and piano, the rhythmic patterns of the statements of the basic cell resulting from the position these notes occupy in the different rows.

The six rows and the rhythms of the basic cells produced by applying this procedure to both the prime and retrograde rows—that is, as they appear in the first and second halves of the Interlude respectively—are shown in Example 4.

Allowing that the absolute duration of the last note of a rhythmic pattern is by its nature ambiguous and can be extended without affecting the overall rhythmic pattern, the example demonstrates that in five of the six rows the rhythms of the basic cell produced by both the prime and retrograde forms are identical. The single exception is the row associated with the Schoolboy (Example 4d). In this row, note 1 of the basic cell derived by extracting

Example 4 a–f. *Lulu*, Act 2. The Prime forms to the left of the bar line derive from mm. 670–74 of the Film Music Interlude, and the Retrograde forms to the right, from mm. 700–704.

the notes from the prime form is a sixteenth note shorter and note 3 a sixteenth longer than that derived from the retrograde. In addition, the rhythms produced by extracting the notes of the basic cell from the prime and retrograde forms of the Basic Set are identical with those produced by applying the same procedure to the two forms of Alwa's row (Example 4c).

Consequently, when this passage appears in retrograde at mm. 700–704 it not only presents the basic cell in what we recognize as its inverted form but also presents the different versions of the cell in a form rhythmically identical to those in the first half of the Film Music. The second half of the Film Music thus not only maintains a sense of directed, forward movement but audibly functions as a recapitulation of the material of the first half.

In *Der Wein* the material approaching the turning point consists of diatonic and quasi-chromatic scales and tritone figurations, all of which maintain their identity as inversions or quasi-inversions when played backwards, as do the chromatic scales extracted from the rows of the Allegro misterioso of the *Lyric Suite*.

Even in the Adagio of the Chamber Concerto, in which the retrograde second half is a radically modified and decorated version of the original, some passages act as "markers," designed to make us audibly aware of what is going on. The solo violin passage at mm. 277–80, for example, in which a descending whole-tone scale is progressively transformed into a diatonic, a chromatic, and eventually a quarter-tone scale, not only has a clear gestural overall shape we recognize when turned backwards but the return of the distinctive quarter-tone passage as an ascending figuration at mm. 441–44 alerts us to the retrograde nature of the passage.

I have argued elsewhere that Berg's retrogrades and palindromes represent a fatalistic view of life since, having reached their central turning point, their course is compositionally predetermined.[57] Berg's annotations on the *Lyric Suite*, his comments on *Der Wein* and the secret program of the Chamber Concerto Adagio make clear the negative, fatalistic symbolism inherent in the palindromic structures of these works.

Although *Wozzeck* has no large-scale palindromes comparable to those of *Lulu*, the *Lyric Suite*, *Der Wein*, and the Chamber Concerto, it has many small ones, all of them linked to the subject of the nature of time, a topic that lies at the heart of that opera. The transitory, fleeting nature of time—which so terrifies the Captain—is the central subject of the first scene of *Wozzeck*, while the Doctor's attempts to vanquish time through the immortality his dietary experiments will bestow on him is one of the topics of Act 1, sc. 4.

In Act 1, sc. 1 the concept of time moving in circles is expressed textually by the image of the endlessly turning mill wheel while the Captain's mention of eternity is symbolized musically by a fragment of the "endless" cycle of fifths that accompanies it (the same cycle of fifths that Stephen

Daedalus plays in *Ulysses*). The idea of circular time is also inherent in the structure of this scene, where passages from the opening Prelude return in retrograde in the Postlude, so that the scene closes with the same word with which it began, "Langsam," sung to the same tritone. It is, as Berg himself said, a scene "in which nothing happens."[58]

Elsewhere in the opera, palindromic figurations are associated with Wozzeck's mental instability and the terror of his existence—notably in variations 7 and 12 of Act 1, sc. 4. In variation 12 Wozzeck describes the toadstool rings in the field and the strange, ominous messages he believes they contain. Perhaps significantly, given the theosophical and anthroposophical associations of the number 7, both variations consist of a single 7/4 measure and the number plays an important structural role in the opera (Berg's own op. 7) as a whole. Trapped in an inescapable cycle of time, the characters of *Wozzeck* inhabit a mechanistic universe. It is, as the mechanically repeating ostinati that represent the croaking of the toads around the pool before and after Wozzeck's death demonstrate, a universe that continues on its predetermined course untouched by the human tragedy that unfolds.

At the center of *Wozzeck* lies Act 2, sc. 3, in which Wozzeck confronts Marie with his knowledge of her infidelity. As in *Lulu*, this central turning point is marked by a retrograde. In this case the music that leads into it (mm. 363–66) leads backwards out of the scene (mm. 406–11) and into the following interlude.

Perhaps the most curious and arcane palindrome in *Wozzeck* occurs between the end of Act 2 and the opening of Act 3. Act 2 ends with four bars of silence: two bars, both of which have fermata signs, during which we are presented with a static stage picture, and two bars *a tempo* during which the curtain falls. Act 3 begins with two bars of silence. During the first the curtain rises and during the second, marked by a fermata, we are presented with a stage picture before the music starts. There is no tempo indication at the start of Act 3, only the marking ♩ = ♩, a marking that must mean the quarter note of these opening bars of Act 3 is equal to the quarter note of the final bars of Act 2. Since the last four bars of Act 2 are in 2/4 and the first two bars of Act 3 are in 2/2 the first bar of Act 3 is therefore—as Berg's additional annotation indicates—the same length as the last two bars of Act 2, and the second bar of Act 3 (with the fermata sign) is the same length as the third and fourth bars (also with fermata signs) at the end of Act 2. We are thus presented with a precisely notated retrograde of silence—a retrograde that "restores the status quo ante" in that it returns us to the action following the intermission.

Like the last movement of the *Lyric Suite* the music of the last scene of *Wozzeck* reaches no real end. It simply stops. Adorno observes of the *Lyric Suite* that "the viola alone remains, but it is not even allowed to expire, to die. It must play for ever, except that we can no longer hear it."[59] Berg drew attention to the passage at the end of *Wozzeck* commenting, "Although the music steers again into the cadential haven of the final chord it almost looks as though it could go on. And it really does go on! As a matter of fact, the initial bars of the opera could easily link up with these final bars and thereby close the circle."[60] Again, Robert Morgan regards this ending as a sign of hope saying that "precisely at his moment of expressive nadir there is hope of renewal."[61]

Notwithstanding his interpretation of the similar ending of the *Lyric Suite*, Adorno also sees the ending of *Wozzeck* as positive:

> The music contracts and counts the minutes to death. Then it precipitates the orchestral epilogue. In the *Kinderszene* at the end it is so distantly reflected as the blue sky in the depth of a well shaft. This reflection alone suggests hope in *Wozzeck*.[62]

Despite the absence of large-scale palindromes comparable to those in other works of Berg, the numerous small retrogrades and palindromes and their consistent association with the subject of time in *Wozzeck*—as well as the similar associations of such techniques elsewhere in Berg's music—suggest a more negative interpretation. The circular structure of the work—the linking up of the end with the beginning—is inherent in both the subject matter and the musical structure of the opera. To Nietzsche, as to the theosophists, the Swedenborgians, and the other metaphysical and esoteric, quasi-mystical thinkers of Berg's time, a way out of the unproductive cycle of recurrence was only possible if the individual could achieve a level of consciousness that made possible the recognition of potential for change. There is no such sign of hope in *Wozzeck*, nor, by the end of the opera, have the social conditions of "Wir arme Leut" changed. The music returns to the beginning, the orphaned child takes his father's place, and the tragic cycle begins again.

NOTES

The title of this essay is taken from Ecclesiastes 1:11: "There is no remembrance of former things, / Nor will there be any remembrance of things that are to come / By those who will come after."

1. Arnold Schoenberg, *Style and Idea*, ed. Leonard Stein, trans. Leo Black (London: Faber & Faber, 1975), 220.
2. Ibid., 223.
3. Brian Newbould, "Schubert's Palindrome," *19th-Century Music* 15/3 (Spring 1992): 207–14.
4. R. Larry Todd, "Retrograde, Inversion, Retrograde-Inversion and Related Techniques in the Masses of Johannes Obrecht," *Musical Quarterly* 64/1 (January 1978): 50–78, 51.
5. Ibid., 52–53.
6. Daniel Leech-Wilkinson, *The Modern Invention of Medieval Music* (Cambridge: Cambridge University Press, 2002), 17.
7. Schoenberg's canon is reproduced in *Arnold Schönberg Gedenkausstellung 1974*, ed. Ernst Hilmar (Vienna: Universal Edition, 1974), 148.
8. Douglas Jarman, *The Music of Alban Berg* (London and Boston: Faber & Faber, 1979), 187–89.
9. Newbould, "Schubert's Palindrome," 208, cites Byrd's motet *Diliges Dominum* as one of the rare examples of a "true multi-voiced" palindrome.
10. Isaac Newton, 1687, quoted in Stephen Kern, *The Culture of Time and Space 1880–1918* (Cambridge, MA: Harvard University Press, 2003), 11.
11. Ibid., 22.
12. Ibid., 34.
13. Berg's diagrammatic scenario of the *Lulu* Film Music is reproduced in George Perle's *The Operas of Alban Berg*, vol. 2: *"Lulu"* (Berkeley-Los Angeles: University of California Press, 1985), Plate 7.
14. Robert P. Morgan, "The Eternal Return: Retrograde and Circular Form in Berg," in *Alban Berg: Historical and Analytical Perspectives*, ed. David Gable and Robert P. Morgan (Oxford: Oxford University Press, 1991), 146, 147.
15. Friedrich Nietzsche, *The Gay Science*, trans. Walter Kaufmann (New York: Vintage Books, 1974), 341.
16. Kammerer's *Das Gesetz der Serie* was published in Stuttgart/Berlin in 1919. Both Kammerer and Fliess, and their relationship and influence on Berg, are examined in Wolfgang Gratzer, *Zur "wunderlichen Mystik" Alban Bergs* (Vienna-Cologne-Weimar: Böhlau Verlag, 1993), 175–91.
17. Ibid., 186.
18. Swoboda published three volumes on the topic in the early 1900s: *Die Perioden des menschlichen Organismus in ihrer psychologischen und biologischen Bedeutung* (1904); *Die kritischen Tage des Menschen und ihre Berechnung mit dem Periodenschieber* (1909); and *Das Siebenjahr: Untersuchungen über die zeitliche Gesetzmäßigkeit des Menschen*, vol. 1, *Vererbung* (1917). See Gratzer, *Zur "wunderlichen Mystik" Alban Bergs*, 176.
19. Helena Blavatsky, *The Secret Doctrine*, Theosophical University Press, online edition vol. 1, sect. 16, 636, www.theosociety.org/pasadena/sd/sd-hp.htm
20. Gratzer remains as giving the most thorough and detailed account of Berg's fascination with numerology and esoteric thought.
21. *The Berg-Schoenberg Correspondence*, ed. Juliane Brand, Christopher Hailey, and Donald Harris (New York–London: W. W. Norton, 1987), 248–49.

Notes to "REMEMBRANCE OF THINGS THAT ARE TO COME"

22. Alma Mahler was Kammerer's assistant for a short period in 1911. Kammerer's pamphlet *Über Erwerbung und Vererbung des musikalischen Talentes* (Leipzig: Theod. Thomas Verlag, 1912) is dedicated to "Gustav Mahler's Frau und Kind." According to Gratzer, *Zur "wunderlichen Mystik" Alban Bergs,* 189, Kammerer was also Berg's rival for the hand of Helene Berg.

23. Kandinsky's theosophical beliefs, his association with the Schoenberg circle and his extensive correspondence with Schoenberg are, of course, well known.

24. Schoenberg, *Style and Idea,* 223.

25. Ibid., 223.

26. *Berg-Schoenberg Correspondence*, 135ff.

27. John Covach, "Balzacian Mysticism, Palindromic Design and Heavenly Time in Berg's Music," in *Encrypted Messages in Alban Berg's Music,* ed. Siglind Bruhn (New York: Garland Publishing, 1998), 5–29, 8, 16.

28. "Have you found those 6 brave medicals [. . .] to write *Paradise Lost* at your dictation? [. . .] I feel you would need one more for *Hamlet*. Seven is dear to the mystical mind. The shining 7 W.B. called them." James Joyce, *Ulysses* (London: Bodley Head, 1960), 235; "Hiesos Kristos, the magician of the beautiful. [. . .] The life esoteric is not for ordinary persons. Mrs. Cooper Oakley once glimpsed our very illustrious sister H.P.B's elemental." Joyce, *Ulysses,* 237.

29. Ibid., 261.

30. Stuart Gilbert, *James Joyce's "Ulysses"* (Harmondsworth: Penguin, 1963), 69n.

31. On the structural role of the number 7 in *Wozzeck* see George Perle, *The Operas of Alban Berg,* vol. 1, *Wozzeck* (Berkeley and Los Angeles: University of California Press, 1980), 128ff.

32. Morgan, "The Eternal Return," 147ff.

33. Ibid., 148.

34. Ibid., 149.

35. Theodor W. Adorno, *Alban Berg: Master of the Smallest Link,* trans. Juliane Brand and Christopher Hailey (Cambridge: Cambridge University Press, 1991), 1.

36. Hans Ferdinand Redlich, *Alban Berg: The Man and His Music* (London: John Calder, 1957), 113.

37. Ibid., 113.

38. Perle, *Operas of Alban Berg*, 2:150, discusses the extent to which Berg's wishes were followed in the full and piano scores that were originally published.

39. Berg's wishes concerning the notation of this central turning point are followed in the recently published Alban Berg *Sämtliche Werke,* vol. I/5, 1, and in the Philharmonia pocket score (Phil. 561) based on it; they are partly followed in the previously published score (Phil. 423).

40. An opalographic facsimile is one made from sheets of glass onto which the pages of the score have been photographed.

41. Jarman, *The Music of Alban Berg,* 237–41.

42. Adorno, *Alban Berg,* 14.

43. Since we know of no program for the Three Orchestral Pieces, op. 6, the harmonic retrograde of the Praeludium may or may not be an exception to this statement. I am grateful to Christopher Hailey to drawing my attention to the fact that, at one point, Berg planned to make *Wozzeck* the first of a trilogy of operas, the second of which, *Vincent,* was to have been based on a five-act play by Hermann Kasack about the relationship between Van Gogh and Gauguin. Berg's sketch for the trilogy (Austrian National Library, F21 Berg 70/2) shows that the opera was to have been in two acts, the second of which was to have been the retrograde of the first. Berg's plans never got any further, so it is impossible to know how the musical retrograde would have related to the dramatic structure.

44. Adorno, *Alban Berg,* 14.

45. Ibid., 110.

46. George Perle, *Style and Idea in the "Lyric Suite" of Alban* Berg (Stuyvesant, NY: Pendragon Press, 1995), 40.
47. Adorno, *Alban Berg*, 124.
48. Ibid., 119.
49. Ibid., 100f.
50. Constantin Floros, *Alban Berg and Hanna Fuchs*, trans. Ernst Bernhard Kabisch (Bloomington: Indiana University Press, 2001), 56.
51. Dalen's paper, originally presented at the annual meeting of the American Musicological Society in Cleveland, 6 November 1986, appears in an expanded version as "'Freundschaft, Liebe, und Welt': The Secret Programme of the Chamber Concerto," in *A Berg Companion*, ed. Douglas Jarman (London: Macmillan, 1986), 141–80.
52. Ibid., 160.
53. Morgan, "The Eternal Return," 138ff.
54. Hans Keller has argued that "the unprejudiced or re-educable ear [. . .] will not be all too surprised to learn that, historically or genetically, retrograde motion can be shown to be more 'natural' than inversion" and that "inversion was an artifice logically erected upon the structural lessons learnt from employing the more spontaneous thought process of retrograde motion." Hans Keller, "Knowing Things Backwards," *Tempo* 46 (Winter 1958): 14–20, 16; repr. in *Hans Keller: Essays on Music*, ed. Christopher Wintle (Cambridge: Cambridge University Press, 1994), 144–50, 146. The example which purports to demonstrate this, however, consists of a decorated ascending major scale so that, perceptually, what is technically a retrograde is recognized as a tonal inversion.
55. Morgan, "The Eternal Return," 119.
56. Ibid., 137.
57. Jarman, *The Music of Alban* Berg, 241.
58. As quoted in Redlich, *Alban Berg: The Man and His Music*, 268–69.
59. Adorno, *Alban Berg*, 113.
60. As quoted in Redlich, *Alban Berg: The Man and His Music*, 264.
61. Morgan, "The Eternal Return," 149.
62. Theodor Adorno, "Die Oper Wozzeck 1929," trans. Nikolaus Bacht, in Nikolaus Bacht, "Music and Time in Theodor W. Adorno," (PhD diss., King's College, London, 2002), 43.

1934, Alban Berg, and the Shadow of Politics: Documents of a Troubled Year

INTRODUCTION, TRANSLATIONS, AND COMMENTARY
BY MARGARET NOTLEY

Toward the end of 1934, Clemens Krauss was on his way out as director of the Vienna State Opera. Alban Berg was angling for Erich Kleiber, whose primary appointment was in Berlin, to succeed him. In a letter of 20 November to the latter conductor, Berg offered his thoughts on the possible candidates, including Kleiber himself:

> To be sure, I don't know yet whether your membership in the N.S.D.A.P. is an obstacle or not. That must be carefully explored. But ultimately everyone concerned has some sort of snag [*Haken*].[1] Walter is a Jew, Busch is seen as red, Böhm may be in a similar situation as you are. Thus remains only . . . Kabasta! And let us hope we'll be spared that![2]

In short, the political climate in Vienna put almost every candidate at a disadvantage. Oswald Kabasta, a favorite of some members of the Austrian regime but not well regarded as a musician in most other quarters, was the only conductor with no apparent political liability. Bruno Walter was Jewish, Adolf Busch was viewed as Marxist, and Karl Böhm may already have become a Nazi—like Kleiber, Berg was assuming. When he replied to Berg's letter on 22 November, Kleiber was vehement in insisting that he "was *never* a member of the N.S.D.A.P.*," the asterisk corresponding to a footnote that said "never as well had the intention of becoming one! ! ! Despite repeated requests!" He continues in the letter, "I always sympathized with the *national* movement—but now I can no *longer follow* it *into the realm of the "race question"*—because I am in possession of an artistic conscience, thank God."[3]

These unpublished passages from correspondence between Berg and Kleiber illuminate the politicization of musical life in Vienna; they also reveal Berg's priorities. Kleiber vigorously denied any inclination toward anti-Semitism and thus toward Nazism. Yet Berg, who himself never displayed any sympathy for Nazism, was willing if necessary to accept Kleiber's affiliation with that party. Opportunities in Germany had increasingly dried up during 1934, hence Berg's focus that fall on instating a conductor at the Vienna State Opera House who would perform and advocate for modernist music, including his own.

When Hitler first assumed power at the end of January 1933, Berg and musicians associated with him had not known whether the regime would last or what the general hostility to modernist music of the Nazi cultural apparatus might mean for each of them. Recent research has indeed underscored that choosing, say, to write twelve-tone music did not necessarily lead to suppression or other kinds of reprisals by the Nazi authorities. To be sure, that spring Berg began to receive letters announcing canceled performances of his music in Germany; at about the same time the Prussian Academy of the Arts placed Arnold Schoenberg and Franz Schreker on leave. But musicians whose futures were not decided by the Nazi regime tended to temporize. Even Kleiber, though no admirer of Hitler and an outspoken proponent of modernist music, was willing to remain at the Berlin State Opera for the time being. In a postcard of 26 December 1933 he asked Berg for an update on his second opera, *Lulu*, the premiere of which had long been planned for Berlin, and also noted, "One of the leading journalists of the current regime is a great, great *Wozzeck*-Berg admirer!"[4] At that point virtually everyone in the groups that included Berg was playing a waiting game.

Kleiber and Berlin had been crucial for Berg's career, beginning with the sensational premiere of *Wozzeck* in 1925. He, along with his teacher Schoenberg and his friend Anton Webern may have identified themselves as the "Vienna School," but their native land offered few opportunities for them as composers. Berg had looked elsewhere, and especially to Germany, where Kleiber continued to play a key role in his many successes. With the ascendancy of Nazism, Berg came to realize that he could no longer depend on German performances of *Wozzeck* to sustain his comfortable life as a celebrated artist.

Early in 1934 the scant number of orchestral performances of modernist music in Vienna dwindled further. Most of these performances in "Red Vienna" had been connected to the Austrian Social Democratic Workers Party, either directly through its cultural affairs office or through ties between that office and the International Society for Contemporary Music. After the bloodbath in February, the Social Democratic Party and most of its cultural activities were banned (see Table 1 at the end of this essay). Berg had to be resourceful. When the precariousness of Krauss's situation became apparent in the fall of 1934, easing Kleiber into Krauss's position as director of the Vienna State Opera became one of Berg's goals.

That 1934 would be the critical year in both Vienna and Germany for Berg and others in similar situations was of course not immediately apparent to them. Indeed, they were slow to recognize that culture and politics had become intertwined in Germany during 1934; in Vienna the relationship between the two remained more fluid. The point of no return for Kleiber came after he conducted Berg's arrangement of Symphonic Pieces from *Lulu* on 30 November—this performance was the occasion for the letters cited above—and then, with the press paying full attention, resigned his position in Berlin. During the climactic events in November and December, Berg's former student Willi Reich would represent him in Berlin. But those events were the culmination of a succession of dismaying events throughout the year, including the rejection of the opera *Lulu* by Berlin authorities in the spring.

The documents compiled here concern people and events in both Vienna and Berlin. In discussing the situation in Vienna, I focus especially on Reich, upon whom Berg depended in various ways. Berg was spending most of his time in Carinthia so that he could work in relative quiet on *Lulu*. Certain kinds of assistance had to do with Berg's absence from Vienna and involved Reich in carrying out mundane chores for him. Reich worked as a pharmacist and a journalist while also completing a doctorate in musicology. Sometimes he sent books and newspapers to Berg's country home and, at other times, medications and ointments. On more serious occasions, Berg called on Reich for the kinds of help that show a deep level of trust in him.

By the fall of 1934 Reich and the composer Ernst Krenek, along with another former student of Berg, the critic Theodor Wiesengrund-Adorno, now resident in Frankfurt, were the core writers for *23: Eine österreichische Musikzeitschrift*, a Viennese music journal modeled after Karl Kraus's *Die Fackel* and published by Reich between 1932 and 1937. During the final years of his life Berg took a keen interest in *23*, and though he did not write for the journal, Reich did send copy to him for his scrutiny and advice, which Berg provided in abundance.

I concentrate here on unpublished correspondence between Berg and Kleiber and Berg and Reich as well as other underutilized collections: letters between Berg and several editors at the Viennese music publishing firm Universal Edition, and articles by Herbert F. Peyser (see Table 2 at the end of this essay). Peyser, a music correspondent for the *New York Times*, lived in Europe for over a decade until the Anschluss forced him to leave. He did not hesitate to give blunt assessments of performances or to note the political significance of events that actors in the events were sometimes hesitant to articulate in public.

The sources and colleagues I have chosen serve to elucidate the efforts of Berg and his circle to grasp and adjust to rapidly changing circumstances. They allow us glimpses of the human and sometimes less than heroic actions of the composer and his associates at a time when politics cast an ever longer shadow over musical life.

December 1933 to February 1934: Concerns and Undue Optimism

All of these first documents were written shortly before the civil conflict in Vienna. No one foresees that particular calamity, but there is a sense of general crisis. In what was starting to emerge as a pattern in Berg's professional life, Bavarian Broadcasting had referred to him (and Webern) as Jewish. Berg responded by sending a letter asserting and providing documentation of his "100 %" Aryan-German extraction.

Peyser, back in "semi-Asiatic" (read: "half-Jewish"?) Vienna after a year in Germany, more accurately assesses the situation in Berlin than Heinsheimer and Kleiber do. Berg and his allies believe that they can quell rumors about his "non-Aryan" roots through proper documentation, but also that a Berlin premiere of *Lulu* will be possible (despite the "cleansing" of the repertory that has already caused performances of *Wozzeck* to be canceled). And a letter by Reich refers to translating Mussolini's writings.

Peyser's attitudes toward musical events in Vienna do, however, resonate with comments by Reich and Berg. All three note the poor quality of Lehár's opera *Giuditta* and the adulatory reviews by Viennese critics. Reich and Berg discuss chastising one of them, Joseph Marx, in *23*. More ominous is the mysteriously delayed premiere of Krenek's opera *Karl V*. A concert by the Kolisch String Quartet that included contemporary music offers a bright spot.

Letter from Alban Berg to Bavarian Broadcasting, 20 December 1933

Dear Sirs,[5]
I just learned that in one of the most recent Austria addresses the speaker, an Austrian gauleiter,[6] used the occasion of Vienna Ravag's concert hour on 6 December to characterize as Jewish composers the two being performed, namely me and Anton von Webern, and to draw conclusions from that about lacking Aryan- and Germanness.[7]

Assuming that it will also not be pleasant for Bavarian Broadcasting to disseminate obvious untruths, I allow myself to point out an incident unfortunate not just for me and to express my surprise that neither the Austrian gauleiter nor Bavarian Broadcasting is aware that Anton von

Webern comes from old Carinthian landed gentry and that I, too, am of "100 %" Aryan and German extraction.

As can be seen from the enclosed family tree (which I am of course in a position to certify with documentation), not only my grandmothers but also my great great grandparents are Aryan. I have not been able to trace it any further back. That my forefathers beyond these two centuries were also Aryans is, however, to be assumed from the fact that all of my great great grandparents were Catholics, indeed, that among them was an attendant at the Bavarian court. It follows also from the German sound of all their names and from the birthplaces of my great grandparents that I am of German extraction (or rather 5/8 German [*reichsdeutscher*] and 3/8 German-Austrian extraction). This fact incidentally agrees with the additional fact that part of my relatives live in Germany and indeed—here one must say "of all places"—in Munich, Nuremberg, and Augsburg, where folks will have been not a little surprised by the news of my Jewish extraction disseminated by an Austrian—again, "of all people." They will have been no less surprised than my many, many friends living in Germany as well as men there in leading positions in theater, music, and radio who would never have conceived such an absurd idea. Indeed, all of them—except the gauleiters and apparently even the gentlemen of Bavarian Broadcasting (who otherwise would never have left such things uncontested)—know that as a member of the Prussian Academy, I cannot be a Jew or of Jewish extraction.

Dear gentlemen, I do not know how you feel about this "authorization" of an untruth. I cannot, however, hide the fact that in my opinion there is only one position that accords with the German spirit and Aryan uprightness: to tell the *truth* from now on.

I leave it to the gentlemen of Bavarian Broadcasting to find the proper way to do this and sign with the expression of
greatest respect

Herbert F. Peyser
Vienna Revisited: Contrasts of Artistic Activities in Days before Internal Strife
Dated 25 January, published 18 February 1934, *New York Times* (excerpt)

The watcher of the musical skies, suddenly translated from the present jail and cemetery atmosphere of Berlin to the comparative serenity of Vienna, is instantly struck by the multiplicity and the standard of tonal dispensations in the general neighborhood of the Opern-Ring and the Schwarzenberg Platz. His elation, to be sure, is not shared by some of the more hard-boiled Viennese, who complain that the musical life of their "semi-Asiatic" city is heading for perdition, that the opera is hopeless and that concerts are dying of dry rot.

Possibly after I have been here another three months I may be howling in the same key, but from my first fortnight in this genial environment I have definitely obtained what in good Broadwayese is known as a "kick." And after a year in Germany in its most Aryan resplendence, I had almost forgotten what a musical "kick" felt like.

A hasty consultation of the operatic bills shortly after I had been deposited on the Ringstrasse revealed that the Staatsoper held in store for the next few days performances of "Manon," "Rienzi," "Otello," "Simon Boccanegra," the "Ring," the "Last Judgment" (Margaret Wallman's imaginative choreographic drama, with Handel music) and the world première of Franz Lehar's latest contribution to the joys of existence, "Giuditta." "Karl V," the first operatic work which Ernst Krenek—sweet singer of the once scandalous but now forgotten Alabama Jonny and his stolen "Strad"—has turned out in years, was down for public exposure on Feb. 26.

But a few days later rumors of a postponement began to circulate, and one fine morning the papers carried the news that the Krenek opus would be put off until May or, peradventure, October. Various reasons were hinted at, among them the great difficulties of this highly modernistic affair, which had already been in rehearsal for some time. But I have it from a very trustworthy source that it was less the technical difficulties of "Karl V" which causes embarrassment than its political implications, and that the thing is much likelier to be shelved altogether than to be given either this Spring or next Fall.

[. . .]

I went to "Manon" with pleasant anticipations, but fled in dismay when I heard Margit Angerer, the embodiment of amateurishness (but the wife of the wealthy storage and moving man Schenker), attempt "Je marche sur tous les chemins" (or whatever the German text calls it). I should also have liked to flee from Lehar's "Giuditta," over which they made a terrible advance pother in Vienna. With this four-hour-long "music comedy" the composer of "The Merry Widow" for the first time in his extended and prosperous career crashed the gate of the Staatsoper and heard the holy Vienna Philharmonic play his tunes. I presume I could write three columns about the piece, as all the Viennese critics did, if I were so minded, but with the best will I cannot see the need of a long obituary.

Possibly "Giuditta" will turn up in some American theatre some day, but it will have to stand a good deal of plastic surgery beforehand. The book has a thin plot, vaguely reminiscent of "Carmen," but is desperately poor "theatre," and it is astounding that any one [sic] of Lehar's experience should have accepted it. The music—pseudo-grand opera at one minute and stale operetta the next—is typical Lehar, but a Lehar badly written out and repeating himself. Of course, there is the usual fill of larmoyant and slushy "heart songs" for Richard Tauber, who, with Jarmila Novotna, heads the cast. But those people who anticipate in "Giuditta" another "Land of Smiles" had better curb their expectations.

* * *

In the course of two weeks I have heard in Vienna more distinguished concerts than during all of the previous six months in Berlin. Each of these events deserves comment far more circumstantial than I have space to give it—particularly the intense, fiery and uplifting performance given by Fritz Busch at the Konzerthaus of Beethoven's "Missa Solemnis," which in ardor of conception and in virtuosity of choral accomplishment surpassed any presentation of this work I have ever heard. Herr Busch, who has not appeared here in years, has never, within my recollection, risen to such proud heights.

A spirit of consecration and a beauty transcending words rested, likewise, upon two recitals of Beethoven sonatas given in the Musikverein Saal by Artur Schnabel. One of the mysteries of Mr. Schnabel's supernal playing lies in the fact that one can scarcely isolate the elements of its lofty enchantment. Less memorable but still decidedly worthy of notice was the first Viennese recital of a young Polish pianist, Boleslav Kon, who will bear close watching. He has abundant technique, brilliance and power, though the imaginative and poetic vein is not yet conspicuously developed in him. By way of chamber music there have been concerts by the venerable Rosé Quartet, which is to disband at the close of this season, and by the incomparable Kolisch foursome, which I admire more intensely with every hearing.

The venomous Hitler propaganda aimed by the German press and radio against Austria is now actively striving to disrupt the musical life of Vienna. No means are too despicable or mendacious for the Nazis to employ in pursuit of their ignoble ends. One of the latest targets of these attacks has been the distinguished American-born contralto, Sarah Cahier, for years a member of the Vienna Opera and even today an object of great public affection in the Austrian capital, where she is still active in concert life and a member of the faculty at the State Academy. A writer in Hitler's Völkische Beobachter recently clamored that "the American Jewess (sic) Mme. Cahier, is actually teaching in German Vienna." When the singer addressed to the paper a letter declaring that she was not a Jewess, the author of the article replied: "You were associated at the State Opera with the Jew Gustav Mahler, and you have sung his music. That is enough for us!" He added further that if she wished the Völkische Beobachter to retract its statement "she would be compelled to produce documentary proofs that she was not a Jewess!"

Letter from Willi Reich to Alban Berg, 24 January 1934 (excerpt)

Dear Herr Berg![8]

You have perhaps missed my coverage of some Viennese events (Giuditta, the Krenek affair). It was only excessive work on the Mussolini proofs that kept me from writing.

Lehar's work is the biggest rubbish that was ever performed in the opera house. In every respect a failure: Nowotna is the only bright spot but does not save the thing. Everybody agrees that it is trash, and ticket sales have already slackened; all the more wicked therefore the fawning critiques, which we'll get busy on for "23"—especially the one by Marx that you saved for me. The conclusion is the biggest piece of presumptuousness of the century.

The Krenek affair is still very much in the dark. I sense monstrous mean tricks there; he is perhaps somewhat more optimistic. At the moment Krenek is in Switzerland; maybe more will be known after his return. Great material is in the offing for "23" there as well. [. . .]

Letter from Alban Berg to Willi Reich, 26 January 1934 (excerpt)

[. . .] On Saturday evening I will envy you: Kolisch Quartet: Webern.

I listened to Giuditta for two acts, then had had enough.[9] [. . .] Marx's review the height of vulgarity. Lately in general he is becoming more and more shameless and in other respects the successor of J. K., to whom, however, he cannot hold a candle with regard to either intellect or character.[10] (*The* style! ! !) With good reason: for he is indeed performed increasingly often (on Ravag almost daily) and soon will be *the* composer who has the corner on *recollections of Austria*. [. . .]

Letter from Hans Heinsheimer to Alban Berg, 26 January 1934 (excerpt)

Dear Herr Berg![11]

Just back from Berlin, I would like to report briefly to you. Herr State Conductor Kleiber was unfortunately not in Berlin, since he is conducting in Doorn today on the occasion of dear Kaiser Wilhelm's 75th birthday![12] I was told this by everyone with pleasant and suggestive amused smiles.

By chance on the day before my arrival Stuckenschmidt had been with Herr Tietjen, who told him that LULU would definitely be performed in the State Opera. Your letter to the Bavarian Broadcasting, which you unfortunately withheld from me and which I read at Rufer's home, as well as your family tree were already at the State Opera.[13] As soon as a performance can be considered, we will be able to take a now greatly simplified path to gaining permission. This path is Herr Prime Minister Goering's direct decree.

[. . .] Many things can of course change again before autumn, but the trend is unconditionally to support truly modern art and to counter over and over again the suspicion of [Nazism] being a reactionary movement. [. . .]

Letter from Willi Reich to Alban Berg, 29 January 1934 (excerpt)

[. . .] The next issue will appear as quickly as possible and get through all of the accumulated polemical material. I will take on Marx very thoroughly; I already have a plan there.

We will also bring up the opera questions (Giuditta, Karl V, etc.).

You were right to envy me concerning the Kolisch Quartet. It was splendid and what is most encouraging, almost completely sold out. [. . .]

Letter from Erich Kleiber to Alban Berg, 3 February 1934 (excerpt)

Dear Friend,[14]

I didn't have time before today to answer your letter. I was interested and encouraged to hear that you will be finished with "Lulu" in the spring or fall. I of course do not have to tell you how much I am looking forward to this work by you. I shall do everything to prepare the ground here for you and the performance. In any case I would be very grateful if I could receive the definitive version of the libretto soon. You can make some notes for me at the beginning, in the instrumentation, about the individual singer's type and function, kind of voice, special requirements, etc. [. . .]

Your letter to Bavarian Broadcasting is excellent, and I will pass along the copy you sent to the place that seems suitable to me.

Regarding your documented family tree, I ask that you by all means have a notarized copy of this prepared. Here there are very many—rightfully or unrightfully—"would-be" composers who would all too gladly damn as "racially alien" anyone with a bit more talent than they have. I will emphatically support Berlin having the honor of giving the premiere of your new opera. If, however, I see that it is encountering difficulties, I will use my vacation time next year and *study* and *conduct* the opera for you wherever you would like. But it would be such a disgrace for Berlin that I do not believe they would expose themselves to this. And so mark this well: *I will conduct the premiere even if it is in Klagenfurt!* (Which I don't believe!) [. . .]

April to July 1934: Rejection and New Plans

The first document in this group dates from a few weeks before the Berlin authorities turned down *Lulu* based on the libretto that Berg had sent at Kleiber's request, and the last document happens to have been written two weeks before another major crisis in Vienna. With German support Austrian Nazis attempted a putsch that culminated in the assassination of the Austrian chancellor, Engelbert Dollfuss, and ended only when Mussolini sent troops to the Brenner Pass, for Austria had signed a pact with Italy and Hungary four months earlier.

Well before Italy came to Austria's rescue, Reich had undertaken the translation of Mussolini's writings that comes up a number of times in his correspondence with Berg. While conducting research in Italy for a dissertation on Giovanni Battista (Padre) Martini, he had developed an enthusiasm for Fascism and Il Duce.[15] In 1934, with Hitler in power in Germany and Red Vienna in disarray, other Viennese musicians who regarded themselves as modernists were also reorienting themselves in an increasingly threatening environment. For this group the vital difference between the two totalitarian governments is easily discerned. Nazi Germany regarded their "atonal" compositions as "musical bolshevism," whereas Italy seemed to have a place for their art and had not yet enacted anti-Semitic policies. Thus even as performances of Berg's music were disappearing in Germany, performance possibilities began to open up in Italy. Although a Fascist state since 1925, Italy was the site for a number of international music conferences during Mussolini's rule, including three of the yearly festivals of the International Society for Contemporary Music: Venice in 1925, Siena in 1928, and Florence in 1934. At the Florence festival, the Kolisch Quartet performed three movements of Berg's *Lyric Suite*, but only after the protracted negotiations that Berg refers to obliquely in the first of three letters to Reich, the main focus of which is Richard Strauss.

A British journal, the *Monthly Musical Record*, had asked Reich to write an article for an issue conceived as a tribute to Strauss on the occasion of his seventieth birthday. In the first letter to Reich Berg expresses an attitude toward Strauss that is consistent with comments elsewhere by him and others in his circle: Mahler was the true progressive; Strauss was concerned with mere outward effect. The second letter makes Berg look petty, but it is unlikely that he thought Reich would act on his deplorable suggestions, and Reich of course did not. In the third letter Berg shows a more likable, self-deprecating aspect of his character. Reich had suggested that he consider a preeminent soprano of the day, Dusolina Giannini, for the title role in *Lulu*. His response was this: shouldn't he therefore ask Caruso to sing the role of Alwa, the male lead in the opera? Grandiosity does not loom large among Berg's personal shortcomings.

Together, Reich's British commission and a reference to overtures that he was making to the *Wiener Zeitung* highlight his efforts to become a more mainstream journalist, necessary because he had a family to support. These efforts meant that Reich did not carry through on the promised polemic against Marx in *23*. Perhaps Yella Hertzka, the widow who was heir to Universal Edition, which published *Anbruch*, quit worrying about ill effects of Reich's contributions to *23*, which Berg alludes to in the third letter. Ultimately Reich's greater respectability would allow him to work on Berg's behalf around the time of the Berlin premiere of the *Lulu* pieces. This is the score that Berg refers to having "plunged into" in the third letter.

The fourth and fifth letters, written by two of Berg's editors at Universal Edition, directly address that arrangement. Shortly before the Berlin authorities rejected *Lulu*, Otto Klemperer had approached Berg about conducting an arrangement of music from the opera, most of which Berg had completed only in short score. After the rejection, Berg and Kleiber conceived the plan of premiering the Symphonic Pieces from *Lulu* in Berlin. This created some awkwardness because Berg and Heinsheimer had already implicitly made a commitment to Klemperer. Stein offers a rationale for why Berg should go ahead and choose Kleiber instead. He also tries to assuage the composer's hard feelings about difficulties he is experiencing concerning a performance at a festival planned for September in Venice.

Stein had known Berg since their student years, so naturally he had a more cordial relationship with him than Heinsheimer did. Like Kleiber, Stein was one of the few people who used the intimate form of address with Berg, whereas Berg and Heinsheimer tended to relate to each other on professional terms. Heinsheimer's letter reports on a meeting in which he had showed Klemperer and another conductor, Fritz Stiedry, the first three movements of the Symphonic Pieces from *Lulu*.[16] As the letter from Stein indicates, Heinsheimer had allowed Berg to retain the text for "Lulu's Lied" as it stood after first asking him to alter it: Berg had been uncharacteristically firm about this matter.[17] But in his own letter Heinsheimer expresses outrage about the composer's suggestions regarding the first movement, the Rondo, the music of which is sung by Lulu and Alwa in the opera. For performances of the entire Rondo within the Symphonic Pieces, Berg had offered three alternatives. It could be performed completely without singing voices, in which case instrumental phrases given in brackets were to be played. A tenor and a soprano could sing from the place at which in the opera speaking and degrees of rendering text that lie between speaking and singing give way to full-blown lyricism. Finally, a tenor *or* soprano could sing the concluding section, Alwa's Hymn, the most graphically lewd passage in the entire opera.[18] Berg had also suggested that Alwa's Hymn could be published as a separate tenor aria to promote the opera.[19] For self-evident reasons, Heinsheimer rejected that idea and, of the possibilities Berg offered for performances of the entire Rondo, found only the first one acceptable. Berg readily acquiesced to Heinsheimer on this.

Letter from Alban Berg to Willi Reich, 22 April 1934

Dear Herr Reich. Thanks for the letter of the 19th. Yesterday I sent off 57 Schillings 60 to you. Thanks! —Thanks as well for the pictures of Bokor. Very nice—but no Lulu. Tomorrow evening I'll hear her at length on the radio. Am eager. In this instance the up-and-coming prima donna Carol Reich seems much better suited to me! A lovely picture![20] — Marx article enclosed. — I very much look forward to your arrival in Carinthia. — Is your Mussolini translation actually official now? I *continue* to remain silent. I am curious about the result of your overtures to the Wr. Zeitung. Don't expect too much! — That the Viennese chapter also wrote to London seems *to me as well* not very proper. In the end the people from the I S.f.K.M.A. (Dent, Casella, etc.) will still be angry with *me*.[21] But this is *completely between us*!

I will congratulate Karl Kraus. You should certainly go to the Kraus evening on Sunday the 29th.[22] Please report! How gladly would I subscribe to the 4 Shakespeare volumes by him. —But—"he who has no money!" ... High summer has turned into a dreadful fall.

Now to Strauss: a few too many introductory and general things in comparison with what really should be said about Strauss.

About the symphonic poems one could for example also say how powerful their *theatrical* descriptiveness is. This even already about the melodrama: Enoch Arden. —

If you write about a logical development, you should first of all say that he has *brought* music in general—and even *his own* in truth *no further*. What was achieved by him in his early years (which, placed against Wagner, was indeed scarcely *musical* progress), was maintained nearly for decades, and only the technique, the adaptation of these devices to everything *later*, still undergoes development. For example, that with his gigantic orchestra surging and kept continuously in motion, the singing voices are nonetheless still audible (preference for the highest register of the soprano, long notes, etc.) or the extension musically on the so-called resting points. Perhaps worthy of mention is the comparison with Meyerbeer! —

That *all* works (even the less inspired) are not, as with other masters, masterpieces! At the same time, whenever no inspired ideas have occurred to Strauss (thus permanently after Rosenkavalier), no masterpiece has come into existence—because precisely all that which otherwise develops in a master (even when *inspiration* diminishes with age), in the case of Strauss does *not* develop.

This also explains why really only the half-dozen beloved songs are *good* and the others—if one ever gets to hear them: rubbish. How different with *masters*—even if only a few songs by them are always repeated. The 3, 4 dozen others by Brahms or Mahler, Schönberg or Wolf are just as significant as the popular ones.

In conclusion it should be mentioned—to treat him with dignity in all respects: yet none of the *real* masters has shown such a *downward* turn later in life as Strauss (since his 50th year at least). *Everyone* (except those suffering from mental illness) has *grown* until death (Verdi, Beethoven, Bach, etc.) (not to speak at all of those who died *young*!) or *remained* at their highest point in the last decade (Wagner)—

Something else: how little *in general* can be said about a *development* of music in Strauss; one sees, for example, how he has not brought even dance music *further*. His Rosenkavalier waltz is only a *Johann Strauss* waltz taken higher in outward technique. How different are the waltzes of Brahms. Or the minuets of Beethoven, Mozart—*that* is development. With Strauss, music really stagnates in the Wagner epigonism of the 1890s (except that he was by far the most talented of all the epigones, Hausegger, Schillings, Humperdinck, etc., and naturally also the personally most singular). That Brahms actually left no trace on Strauss speaks also for this Wagner-Liszt epigonism (a few melodic turns of phrase do not count), and Brahms is therefore *in many respects more modern*—than Strauss, there, namely, where Schönberg first started. (Compare the splendid Schönberg articles by Erich Schmid in the Schweizerische Musikzeitung!)[23] Mahler in turn developed in a completely different way—but *how* he developed. Even a blind person indeed sees and hears this,

which is indeed also the reason that after such a long time the final Mahler still has not succeeded as much as the first 4 (5) symphonies.

This is all confused, dear Herr Reich, but perhaps *stimulating*. —

What do you hear from Berlin? Let us hope good things.[24]

Cordially your Berg

Could you call the police to find out the seriousness of the punishment when someone (in an automobile) does not have a driver's license with him? —[25]

Letter from Alban Berg to Willi Reich, 28 April 1934

Yesterday I heard "Heldenleben"! The "theatrical descriptiveness" that I wrote about yesterday is completely, tremendously obvious here—often to the point of *musical* senselessness.[26] —

It would be good if you (without anyone noticing the spiteful intent) were to quote some facts (musical, of course!) from which emerges that Strauss is by no means such a prototypically German, Aryan composer. Perhaps something will occur to you (e.g. the Mendelssohn influence, Hofmannsthal, Salome, etc.)[27]

Cordially
your Berg
Enclosed the height of vulgarity and foolishness.[28]

Letter from Alban Berg to Willi Reich, 12 June 1934

Thanks for your letter, dear Herr Reich!

I plunged immediately into the score, hence my silence.

Thanks for the tip about Giannini. But by the same right for Alwa you should have recommended to me—Caruso!

Enclosed Marx. Show it to Frau Hertzka and then you should say to her, *who* harms the *publishing firm* and new music. *Marx* or *you*? The Neues Wiener Journal or 23?

Incidentally, you will see from the enclosure how one dares to write about Strauss in *Germany* (and how *splendidly*). You thus need not have been so very careful—I believe—in your article.

This in haste. Soon more from your
Berg

Letter from Erwin Stein to Alban Berg, 1 July 1934

My dear Alban! *I* am not in favor of Klemperer (as perhaps you have already noted).[29] He views the Lulu pieces apparently *only* as sensation. If you can get out through your not being ready with the score, you'll certainly spare yourself not only the risk of the American premiere under Klemperer, but also the dilemma on account of Kleiber. Heinsheimer's arguments are almost always dictated by a completely superficial and immediate opportunism. One should not take him too seriously. He deals regularly with Klemperer and that's why he is ambitious to secure the premiere for him. But, as Hh. himself says, Kl. (these two names, which, as you see, I am very fond of, are horribly long!) apparently changed his mind rather anxiously after looking through the score.[30] These idiots and cowards shiver today again if something falls outside the customary framework. What has

Klemperer had success with up to now: with many classical works and of the modern ones, Stravinsky, Casella, Krenek, Janacek (Sinfonietta). As an interpreter, he altogether lacks, however, the temperament that one unconditionally needs for your music. I am pleased that you expressed yourself so decisively about the text question regarding the Lied. About that and about the questions concerning the premiere in general we had a lively discussion. There was a conflict of authority there because the pieces, as promotion for the opera, fall in part under his purview.[31] — Perhaps Kleiber will not have the nerve to perform the vocal piece. You have certainly anticipated that. And Hh. *may* indeed be right that in the end the performance will be forbidden to Kleiber. Then he will be all the more obligated to you and will add it as soon as he can do so (Brussels, Italy). *In the worst case* the premiere will then be in Prague under Talich on January 9.[32] —In short, I believe that you should give the premiere to Kleiber. Through the tempo of your work you have that in your power.

As far as Venice is concerned: that is of course very annoying, and it is perhaps right not to let the matter drop. But I do not see in what manner the publishing firm could intervene. One will certainly not receive a straightforward answer. It is of course something else if you yourself as the invitee with whom there has been repeated correspondence write to the people. One could still get the better of them but apparently only from the side from which they want to force you out, from behind the scenes. Frau Mahler would have to do that; I understand, however, that this is unpleasant for you. It doesn't help to want to be amicable; these people (Krauss? Casella? they are difficult to pin down) have a battle position against you, and they know why. Good music exposes bad, as do the interpreters of it (Wozzeck at the Vienna Opera). But dear Alban, be comforted and don't take even the Venetian festival so seriously. Working on your Lulu score is, to put it mildly, a million times more important. Your work is already finding favor; that happens by itself, even if it does not go as quickly as one would like and time after time one cannot comprehend the difficulties and obstacles.

What do you say about the events in Germany?[33] I don't believe that everything will happen again now in the way that Hitler would like. That was only a beginning.

Many heartfelt greetings to both of you from us three
your Erwin
Ansermet intends to perform not only the Lulu pieces but also the Wein aria.[34]

Letter from Hans Heinsheimer to Alban Berg, 11 July 1934

Dear Herr Berg,[35]

Yesterday I had the opportunity to show the Rondo to Herr Klemperer and Herr Dr. Stiedry together, and both looked through it. On this occasion Herr Klemperer informed me that he would not perform Lulu's Lied under any circumstances, that he refuses to conduct such a text. He considers this to be impossible in a concert hall. You see then that it is not just Klemens [sic] Krauss who has arrived at the point of view against which you have struggled so much.

As it now stands, both Klemperer and Stiedry think that this version of the score—in which either a tenor and a soprano or just the soprano may sing, or song is omitted altogether and the orchestra alone plays and includes the bracketed passages—that such a version is highly impractical and confusing. Either it is an opera scene, in which case one must perform it as such, or it is a self-contained piece of music, in which case the text only confuses. Both are unconditionally of the opinion that the piece must be printed with the text omitted, thus as in the third possibility presented by you: leave out the brackets, thus print everything, even the bracketed music, and leave out the entire text and the stage directions.

Today I had a very long discussion about this matter again with Stiedry, who certainly stands much closer to your work than Klemperer does. He advises you most urgently to follow this advice. Conductors, critics, the public, everyone would become confused by this thoroughgoing ad libitum, and it would be a great shame for the piece. When we at one time advised you to arrange the score insofar as possible so that it could be used for opera and concert, we naturally thought that it was a matter of orchestral pieces and Lulu's Lied, thus of interludes, preludes, etc., as well as the film music. We obviously thought that it was a question of four orchestral pieces and a single piece for orchestra and soprano, which one could omit as an option. Now it appears that this first piece is a large, full-size opera scene, and I can scarcely describe to you the dismay with which both of these conductors looked at the score and that made them fear the worst for the wider dissemination of the work. In addition, your suggestion that Alwa's Hymn could also be sung by a woman and in fact by the one who sings Lulu's Lied seems very problematic, as we cannot at all imagine that this detailed description of the punctus puncti can be given instead in a concert hall.

Esteemed dear Herr Berg, there was never talk that this Lulu Suite would contain complete scenes of the work and bring together the most offensive passages in the text. We can only warn you in the most urgent and serious manner to stand by your commitment. We obviously had no idea when we suggested to you that if possible the score for the suite might be prepared so as to be usable for the opera. We hereby formally withdraw this suggestion and replace it with the proposal that we indicated above:

> to print the score without text, thus in the arrangement that you yourself have already proposed for the eventuality of omitting the vocal part.

We do not know if the two pieces you have yet to send are likewise opera scenes or, like the film music, purely orchestral pieces. Herr Klemperer has in any case already stated that he will forgo the performance if here it is also a matter of opera scenes. Even Stiedry thinks that many conductors will have misgivings about introducing singing voices, if, that is to say, they know about it. Even he advises urgently to refrain from that and to publish the pieces as if they were really proper orchestral pieces. Later, once the opera is published or performed, will still be time to show people that it was actually meant differently.

If this text problem is added as well to the extraordinary difficulties of the music, the dissemination will in fact be complicated in the extreme. We can therefore only ask you in the most deeply felt and urgent manner to agree to the arguments and considerations presented here. We await your further news and sign with best regards

P. P. Heinsheimer

September to October 1934: The Venice Festival and New Political Developments in Germany and Austria

This section includes excerpts from a speech that Hitler gave in early September, one purpose of which was to advocate eliminating Gothic-style typeface. Berg makes a comically tangential pun on this passage in an exchange of letters with Alfred Kalmus at Universal Edition immediately before traveling from Carinthia to Venice to attend the Festival Internazionale di Musica. During the summer he had worked out the problems of having his orchestral song *Der Wein* performed at the festival. The organizers had stipulated that the invited composers were to conduct their own works in the planned concert, and Berg had insisted that he was not a conductor; in the end Hermann Scherchen conducted.[36]

As a way of further promoting Berg's music in Italy while supplementing his personal income, Reich wrote an article in Italian for the arts periodical *Pan*, edited by Ugo Ojetti. At Reich's request Berg had sent two photographs and an excerpt from *Lulu* in short score; one photograph was published along with the excerpt.[37] Berg refers to Reich's article in the fourth document, a letter to him from mid-October. In the same letter he instructs Reich to send to Kleiber program notes that they had collaborated on for the Berlin premiere of the Symphonic Pieces from *Lulu*. During the summer Berg had asked Reich to write these notes but came close to ghostwriting them himself. The purpose was to guide interpretation, since he had had to remove most of the words from the music. Because of the venue and the pressure he was under when he completed the libretto, he misrepresented the opera as a morality tale, when it is something much more troubling, ambiguous, and interesting than that.[38]

Also in the same letter, Berg suggests his pleasant surprise at having discovered that the *Neues Wiener Journal*, for which the composer Joseph Marx had worked as a critic for some time, had hired another critic whom he considered to be an ally: Friedrich Deutsch or "F. D." (Earlier Berg had asked Reich whose name the initials stood for.) Berg also renews his request for the latest edition of Arnold Schering's famous *Tabellen zur Musikgeschichte* and then in a characteristic display of loopy humor, proceeds to parody Schering's approach. As in certain other music-history textbooks, Schering makes parallels, often pointless, between musical events and other kinds of historical events. Berg imagines the book ending with the 1934 assassination of Dollfuss in one column and two trivial events in the other: Strauss's not attending the Salzburg Festival and Marx's "Japanisches Regenlied" receiving its (fictional) 738th performance. In fact, Schering concludes with Hitler's rise to power in Germany and other events of 1933.[39]

One purpose of the letter was to comment on the galleys of a forthcoming issue of *23* that Reich had sent to him. Excerpts from the article that Berg singles out for praise appear here as the final document. Krenek, a prolific and gifted writer as well as an esteemed composer, was the author of this highly polemical piece. Using the pseudonym "Austriacus," he was reacting to the Nazi infiltration evident in Austrian cultural matters despite the strong anti-Nazi stance apparent elsewhere in the government's rhetoric and actions.

Krenek had reentered the Catholic Church, the presumed foundation of the new Austria, in March 1934. For several years in the mid-1930s he tried to focus on positive aspects of Austria reconceived as a hierarchical Christian *Ständestaat*, a conception promulgated by the government as an alternative to the parliamentary democracy that no longer existed. Krenek had explored related philosophical questions of Catholic-universal humanism in *Karl V*, which had to do with the sixteenth-century Holy Roman Emperor. As later emerged, Nazi influence within the government and, in particular, the influence of the composer and journalist Joseph Rinaldini, caused Krenek's opera to be removed from the schedule of the Vienna State Opera at the beginning of 1934.[40] In a demoralizing turn of events, Marx and Rinaldini had become the highest-ranking representatives of music in the *Ständestaat* by late fall.

Still, in a further demonstration of naïve good intentions toward the new government, for the 1934–35 season Krenek instituted a series of "Austrian Studio Concerts" that programmed works mostly by Austrian composers representing an array of styles. For instance, the first concert, which took place on October 15, celebrated the birthdays of three sixty-year-old composers: with Schoenberg, two much more traditional Austrian composers, Julius Bittner and Franz Schmidt. Also for the fall of 1934, Ravag, the semi-official Austrian radio station, had organized a festival of contemporary Austrian music. In contrast to Krenek's series, this festival, organized by the conductor Kabasta, excluded avant-garde composers. Some of the musicians who administered Ravag at this point, above all a composer named Friedrich Bayer, appear to have been virtually indistinguishable from those in authority in Germany. Krenek targets Ravag and Bayer in the article excerpted here.

Adolf Hitler
Kulturrede at the National Socialist Party Day Rally in Nuremberg on 5 September 1934 (excerpt)

[. . .] Nations come and nations pass away, but the great racial tribes remain.[41] Languages as well as governmental forms have always been suited only to cause confusion, to obscure the traces of common origin, and to erect walls even between those whom nature has created from one substance and in one spirit over thousands of years. And, in particular, written language as the mechanical recording of expressive sounds has contributed more than anything not only to making the common roots of nations unrecognizable but also, in the representation of sounds, to separating languages from each other.

[. . .] The national-socialist movement therefore has two dangers to weather today:

1. It is threatened by the sudden enthusiastic acceptance of those debauchers of art who believe that one may not express a new truth in words customary up until now. That is to say, nervous stammerers, who know as the sole motto for their artistic work only the rule "new at any cost." [. . .] The entire artistic and cultural stuttering of cubists, futurists, dadaists, and the rest is neither racially justified nor bearable to the *Volk*. [. . .] Second [*sic*], however, the national-socialist state must guard against the sudden surfacing of those backward ones who intend to offer an "olde-German

art" as a binding inheritance for the future from the muddled world of their own romantic ideas about National-Socialist revolution. [. . .]

So it has completely escaped them that National Socialism rests on knowledge based in one's blood and not on antique traditions. [. . .] So they offer today train stations in original German-Renaissance style, street names and machine type in typically Gothic letters, song texts freely after Walter von der Vogelweide, fashions after Gretchen and Faust, pictures in the style of the trumpeters of Säckingen, and two-handed swords and crossbows where possible as arms.

[. . .] So as we again allowed a free course for the development of German spirit in the rest of our lives, in art we cannot do violence to modern times for the benefit of the Middle Ages. Your supposed Gothic inwardness fits poorly in the age of steel and iron, glass, and concrete, of the beauty of women and the strength of men, of heads held high and defiant minds. [. . .]

Letter from Alban Berg to Universal Edition, 7 September 1934 (excerpt)

Dear U.E. If you consider it important, please answer this more peculiar than "urbane" letter.[42] I really have no idea who this conductor A. Huber is [. . .] and what Stagma means. Perhaps: state authorized whole-tone machine guns[43] (a designation that does not appear excluded after the most recent *culture* speech of the *Führer*, in which he himself calls for modern spirit with iron and steel—the whole-tone scale perhaps, instead of the Gothic). —

NB. The Preußische Zeitung (Karl Kühne) recently reported "in detail" the approaching "Symphonic Pieces" in Berlin and concluded: "as evidence that the regime (Prime Minister Göring) is not hostile to radical music, do not fail to note the limited (=concert) performance of the work."

[. . .]

Today Frau Hanna Schwarz travels to Venice; we rehearsed with great care and she ought to sing it very beautifully. I apparently won't travel until Saturday. Performance 11 Sept. Conductor? Best wishes, your Berg

Postcard from Alfred Kalmus to Alban Berg, 10 September 1934 (excerpt)

[. . .] Herr Kapellmeister A. Huber of Munich is a salon conductor who would be astonished to receive any of your works, but since he openly cadges scores from everyone, he turned in error also to you.[44] We're giving him an appropriate answer. Your deciphering of the word "Stagma" could almost work; it came out of the combination of Gema and G.D.T. and means "State authorized society for musical performance rights."[45] [. . .]

Letter from Alban Berg to Willi Reich, 19 October 1934

Thanks for your letter of the 16th. Please send no more newspapers! In one or two weeks I'll be in Vienna. Here it is snowing!

Please retain the unused photographs. Which picture appeared in Pan (Ojetti)?

Instead of "chaotic and wild," please: "tumultuous."[46]

Please send your guide to *Kleiber*. You can certainly mention Giannini although he already selected Cebotari some time ago.[47]

I know Deutsch well and am even more astonished than before.

Concerning Schering's tables, *the most recent* edition would certainly interest me. By the way, I imagine it as follows:

1898 Discovery of radium	/	Rinaldini born. —
		Marx decides to compose "Regenlied."
1900 First zeppelin flight	/	Graener takes instruction in harmony. —[48]
		"Regenlied" completed.
etc.	/	etc.
etc.	/	etc.
1934 Dollfuss murdered	/	Strauss does not travel to Salzburg. —
		738th performance of "Regenlied."

Most cordially,
Your Berg

Toscanini's *Wagner* concert *enormously* disappointed me as well.

I must first read the galleys. Should I return them (since your corrections were included)? Then a postcard!

P. S. I just read the proofs. It will be an interesting and strong issue. Only the Réti is weak. In contrast, "Ravag's Message and Austria's Message" has become *even* more convincing and decisive.[49] One would think that it will not remain without repercussions and consequences.

Please, then, a postcard as to when I should return the galleys.

(On the squib "Toscanini Nordicized"):

I do not completely understand your objection. Why should Toscanini be *nordicized* now* if he is *praised* for Nordic clarity anyway. Your objection would apply only if Moser had reproached Toscanini (the sensual epicure) for *lacking* Nordic clarity.[50]

* despite renouncing Bayreuth, etc.

Ernst Krenek
"Ravag's Message and Austria's Message,"
from *23: Eine österreichische Musikzeitschrift*
25 October 1934 (excerpt)

Approximately a year ago we posed here with some concern the question "In which camp is Austria?" and warned about the singular task assigned to the music city Vienna as a consequence of the cultural development in Germany.[51] This past year the response to the question by political Austria was as gratifyingly unambiguous and powerful as was lamentable the vacillating and ambiguous attitude toward it that many cultural factors showed, if we shouldn't perhaps suspect that an answer contrary to the political decision has already been given. A hundred signs speak for this sad likelihood, a particularly clear one appearing to us to be the so-called musical festival that "Ravag" organized on the occasion of its ten years of existence. Nothing is more praiseworthy than the announced effort to show its connection with Austrian musical creativity of the present on this occasion, nothing sorrier than the carrying out of this intention.

At the beginning of the "festival" the official program showed the following names: Otto Siegl, Fritz Schreiber, Hans Holenia, Hans Gál, Egon Kornauth, Robert Wagner, Joseph Rinaldini, Julius Bittner, Friedrich Reidinger. Let us assume from the outset that all the splendid qualities that Herr Kabasta found in these artists' works are in fact inherent in them. We are the last to hold the prejudice that talent and skill are tied to a certain style and tonal language. That the selection made, however, is thoroughly biased and provocative in nature is so patent that the glaring omission from the official introductions of any apologetic or even merely polemical reference to that group of artists missing from the program only aggravates the situation. [. . .]

Without further ado, it can be inferred from the selection that it was knowingly and intentionally carried out against a particular direction in Austrian music. The conclusion must be drawn that the music administration of Ravag, a partially or completely official institution, decided, on its own behalf or that of other authorities, to suppress, if possible, the other orientation in Austrian music today. (The organization of an extremely modest Schönberg celebration can scarcely count as an adequate alibi.)[52] The question must first of all be posed of how such one-sidedness can be reconciled with the repeatedly proclaimed Christian and corporative principle of cooperation. This does not merely guarantee development of all positive strengths but rather virtually summons them in order to realize the ideal image of well-ordered multiplicity on which the scholastic conception of the corporative state is based and through which this is distinguishable from the totalitarian state of mechanical synchronization. (Here we leave aside for the time being the possibility of someone daring to utter the contemptible suspicion that representatives of the new music are not to be valued positively within the tenor of the new state. That someone has nevertheless done this—he is not the only one—and how he was rewarded for this will later be seen.)

If the fact of suppression in itself contradicts the proclaimed reason of state, the situation becomes all the more disquieting when one recognizes that it concerns the same music also being silenced in today's Germany, through which monstrous spiritual and material damage to its creators has increased. The at least partial alleviation of this would seem to be a self-evident task of so well situated an Austrian artistic institution as Ravag is. Here in any case was an outstanding opportunity to confirm that part of the Austrian message which with good reason is spoken of so often in places of authority: namely, to secure the continuity of true German culture and keep it alive for future Germanness as a whole.

One could perhaps charitably interpret the omission by the organs responsible for executing the regime's cultural will as merely a regrettable expression of their artistic inadequacy (although the exercise of a public office ought never to be used to enforce the private taste of those that hold it). Many of their actions, however, steer the objections to their behavior in a completely different, considerably more serious direction.

It has to do here with a piano concerto by Herr Dr. Friedrich Bayer that was originally on the radio festival's program, then removed by its creator because of political concerns, to be inserted finally in the last festival concert. Among other instructive things concerning Herr Bayer is his explanation of "Musical Creation in Vienna" published in an almanac, *Art in Austria*, which appeared in Leoben. "No less than Ambassador Professor Dr. Anton Rintelen" gave the publication his "support," wrote the *Neues Wiener Journal* at the time.[53] —Herr Bayer first of all asserted the existence of a Viennese School, as the "living masters" of which he designated Kienzl, Bittner, Schmidt, and Marx. Then he distinguished a "Young Viennese School of Composers," which is supposed to consist of Armin Caspar Hochstetter, Franz Ippisch, Joseph Rinaldini, Adalbert Skocic, Leopold Welleba, and Othmar Wetchy. The author justifies the selection of these names by the constraint of being able "for now to consider only those artists who have either already 'arrived' or at least been able to draw the attention of a broader public to themselves to a marked degree." Finally he discusses also the "atonalists" who, he rightfully emphasizes, "stand in no usual kind of connection with the Viennese School."[54] (One could say rather that they, the "atonalists," are actually the "Viennese School," since as a group they most show the characteristics of a "school" and are known as such in foreign countries that know nothing about Herr Bayer.) About the nature of these "atonalists," the author discloses with other nonsense the following, for example: "As is well known the apostle of atonal music (as the name already indicates) brusquely rejects every connection of his art with the laws of harmony and melody given by nature. He simply places himself beyond all aesthetic principles (such as melodic construction, sonorous effect, natural architectonic form, etc.) and builds his own system. . . ." So many words, so many immediately recognizable untruths for the middling professional. It is "well known" that the laws of harmony and melody are not given by nature, "well known" that no person rejects any connections. Rather, everyone knows how strictly the logic of the new music can be derived from tradition because it comes from it, "well known" that Schönberg's "melodic construction" may be as precisely established and analyzed as that of Mozart or even Welleba. It is "well known" that one cannot actually place oneself beyond "sonorous effect" if one brings forth tones, since that effect is automatically present, and finally that "natural architectonic form" is nonsense because music does not come from nature but rather is made by humans.

Where this is headed the next paragraph reveals: "Atonality, rootless and alien to the land and the people, stands in the sharpest contrast to native Austrian music." That is enough, and here it is necessary to read *Fraktur*.[55] That is the exact vocabulary and unadulterated mentality of the Third Reich, and it is utterly unbearable to expect that we should allow this to happen to us in Austria. It is absolutely unbearable that a person whose musical work no one takes any notice of utters slanderous abuse against men who for the most part are older than he, who at all times have fulfilled and continue to fulfill their duty to the fatherland with conviction. These are men who for decades have carried out artistic acts with the utmost sense of responsibility, whose worldwide reputation without any doubt is august. These are men who, as the actual "Viennese School," have brought recognition and fame to their homeland in every place not inhabited by barbarians and fools. They could thus very well call upon their compatriots' gratitude or at least protection against disparaging treatment by people who have shown no evidence of objective judgment. These people have yet to prove their right to make judgments about "alienation from the land and the people" through an especially impressive, unequivocal profession of loyalty to Austrian ideas. To Herr Bayer, whose *Germany* Symphony is scarcely to be valued as such a profession and who found it proper during the time of his fatherland's gravest defensive action to represent Austria at the Wiesbaden Music Festival while those more qualified than he had the obvious tact to remain at home—to him we deny this right.[56]
[. . .]

October 1934 to February 1935: Behind the Scenes in Vienna and Berlin

Berg could have spared himself a great deal of trouble if he had settled on Klemperer and the United States for the premiere of the Symphonic Pieces from *Lulu* instead of choosing Kleiber and Berlin. Most likely his initial motives included loyalty to Kleiber and a preference for him as a conductor. As the situation evolved, their shared motives clearly came to include a wish to make a public last stand together in the city that had been the site of stellar successes for both of them. The premiere became an opportunity to inspire a show of support for Berg's music in Germany and to advertise their accomplishments from afar to spectators of the international music scene in Vienna and the world at large.

Although Berg sometimes intimated feelings of helplessness in his correspondence, he was not helpless. In the fall of 1934, as I noted earlier, he was pleased to discover that the *Neues Wiener Journal* had hired Friedrich Deutsch as a critic. Around the same time Reich, who already contributed to music journals elsewhere, began to write for several major newspapers in Vienna; his efforts to become more respectable in the eyes of the city's xcultural establishment were paying off for both of them. In addition to collaborating with Berg on the program notes, Reich would serve as his emissary to Berlin in his absence and write many reviews of the performance. As the premiere approached, Berg worked behind the scenes to manipulate public opinion with two goals in mind: to promote *Lulu* and the arrangement he had made for it and to improve Kleiber's chances of gaining the position that Krauss was leaving at the Vienna State Opera.

Oddly enough, Peyser was a third, probably unwitting ally in these efforts. Berg managed to arrange to have Peyser interview him in Vienna before the Berlin premiere. During the interview the composer may well have planted the idea that he had written the Rondo "as an independent concert number" in an attempt to separate the music from the controversial text. If so, Peyser played right into his hands. In any event, Peyser was as forthright as ever and openly discussed the politically motivated attempt to sabotage the performance by keeping Maria Cebotari from honoring her commitment to sing. In one of several follow-up articles he also emphasized the overt political meaning of the fifteen-minute ovation that Kleiber received.

The documents in this final section include three items by Peyser and six letters from the correspondence between Kleiber and Berg, with a letter from Reich to Adorno as an epilogue to the climactic event. By this time Kleiber wrote much more freely from Brussels, where he conducted frequently; he sent three of the four letters translated here from that city.

Sensing that people above him in Berlin were up to something, Kleiber involved Berg in finding and preparing another soprano, Lillie Claus, on short notice to sing the difficult vocal parts in the third and fifth movements. Before this turn of events he complained at length to Berg about his frustrations with the great conductor Wilhelm Furtwängler, a colleague in Berlin who, he thought, was plotting against him. Furtwängler tried to persuade Kleiber to move the performance from the opera house because of reports that politically inspired demonstrations were planned, the pretext being the subject matter of the *Lulu* libretto.

Kleiber and Berg also discuss the position about to become open in Vienna because of Krauss's imminent but not yet publicly disclosed departure. As further evidence of Alma Mahler's perceived power in Vienna, Kleiber suggests that Berg might contact her about the position, as Stein had also suggested about the Venice performance. But Berg cautions Kleiber about her wide-reaching connections (which included many people in government circles).

Reich most likely wrote the reviews that appeared in the *Neue Freie Presse* and the *Wiener Zeitung*, and also wrote about the event for several music journals.[57] And Berg arranged to be interviewed by Deutsch after the premiere. Deutsch's subsequent article in the *Neues Wiener Journal* indicates he did not attend the premiere, although he does quote at length from a number of favorable reviews by Berlin newspapers, a provocative move.[58] An unsigned appendix to a review by Alfred Burgartz in *Die Musik*, once a first-rate music journal but by then a Nazi mouthpiece, removed any possible ambiguity about the political import of Deutsch's article. The author repeats his quotations of Berlin reviews in the *Neues Wiener Journal*, "one of the wickedest foreign smear-sheets," and calls on authorities to enforce newly enacted censorship laws.[59] Hans Heinz Stuckenschmidt, for one, lost his job in Berlin because of his positive coverage of the concert.[60]

Berg had succeeded in drawing international attention to his arrangement and its premiere, but he did not succeed in obtaining the post at the Vienna State Opera for Kleiber; instead, Krauss assumed Kleiber's place in Berlin. Because Kleiber resigned his position immediately after the premiere of the Symphonic Pieces from *Lulu*, he could not conduct a concert in Berlin that was to have honored Berg's fiftieth birthday with a repeat performance of those pieces. Even if Kleiber had stayed in Germany, performing any music by Berg was impossible at that point; the Berlin premiere itself barely took place. Kleiber was also unable to carry out the performance of the *Lulu* arrangement in Vienna that he mentions as a possible substitute. As Reich indicates in his letter to Adorno, the birthday celebrations in Vienna were muted and involved only small-scale forces, and Berg had begun to study English, most likely because he was thinking about possibilities for performances in the United States and Great Britain. His homeland had let him down; moreover, Germany had officially banned performances of his music.[61]

Ironically, it fell to Kabasta, whom Berg, Kleiber, and Peyser all belittle as a musician in these documents and who appears, moreover, to have been complicit with covert pro-Nazi elements in the government, to conduct the first orchestral performance of the Symphonic Pieces from *Lulu* in Vienna.[62] This finally took place on 11 December 1935, after many performances of the arrangement elsewhere including, besides Berlin, Prague (twice), Geneva, Brussels, London (twice), Boston, and New York (twice). It was the last concert that Berg attended before his death on 24 December.

Letter from Erich Kleiber to Alban Berg, 24 October 1934 (excerpt)

Dear Friend,[63]

I write to you in detail from here because the mail from Berlin, as you know, may well be opened, and some kind of difficulty could arise for both of us.

The situation with your "Lulu" Suite stands as follows:

Furtwängler almost promised me the date and performance, indeed even declared: "if you do not perform it, I would do it." Now the *good man* has suddenly somehow become frightened. [. . .] In short we had a very sharp conversation, in which he wanted to *persuade* me that the pieces be performed 1) not in the opera house (do you notice something, Herr Opera Conductor backs out! !) 2) somewhat—in other words, much—later in the Philharmonic.

I kept completely calm but imparted some truths about the suppression of art to him, and *he* had to yield to me, and it remains for 11/30 in the Opera House. If, however, he should now double-cross me from above and run me down as an inflexible and stubborn colleague (in order perhaps to place himself again in a favorable light),[64] then what could only happen is that it would be forbidden to me from the top down. —And *naturally* I could and would respond to that only with my immediate departure—that would be certain publicity for you and me but no help for the premiere. I do not hope or wish for it to come to that, but I did not want to leave you uninformed about W. F.'s lack of character and would like, in case *something* happens, to know above all that the Austrian public is instructed. Perhaps you'll show the letter—but with the *greatest discretion* to Dr. Reich and speak with him—I'll be here again on Sunday, the 18th of November. [. . .] Tell me quickly in Berlin whether you believe that if it comes to a row in Berlin (and I would then, so to speak, be a "free" man), the premiere could be forced in *Vienna*. The performance here (in

Brussels) unfortunately has to be *without* soloists; what should the order [of the pieces] be in this case? Cebotari will *of course* sing the words for the 5th piece as well![65] [. . .]

Letter from Erich Kleiber to Alban Berg, 17 November 1934 (excerpt)

[. . .] In addition, I will ask today at the Lessing Hochschule whether there is any possibility that Willi Reich could give a lecture there about "LULU" and your musical intentions in it on the evening before the performance.[66] In addition, I would also like to know whom among your native or foreign friends you want to have notified about the premiere by the State Opera.

Regarding all these questions and what you might otherwise have to say to me, I expect to find a letter in Brussels, where I'll be from Sunday, 18 November, at the address *126, Avenue Louise, c/o Wiener.*

Now something else confidential: with me yesterday were two "managers" (= people handlers) from Vienna,[67] who tried to make my mouth water, to aim more for the position of the, as you asserted, shaky Clemens. No one knows better than you do how I stand toward this city and would come wholeheartedly under certain conditions, but I do believe that the other side should show more interest. Could you perhaps prod our dear Frau Alma a little about it? I don't know if she still thinks about me and still believes in me as she once had the appearance of doing. I think that she could do much to clarify this situation. [. . .]

Letter from Erich Kleiber to Alban Berg, [18 November 1934]

My dear—[68]

I have just arrived and find a card and dear letter from you—you cannot imagine how *very* sorry I am that you cannot come.

Today I'll send my correspondence with the god-like Wilhelm to you for your information (and entertainment) as well as that of Reich (in case it becomes necessary to bring the state of affairs out into the open).[69] You will gather from this how well I can "go at it" and how wretched—how minimally god-like a "god-like one" can be. But please *for now* keep strictest confidence (you can show it to Alma; she has a sense for this kind of thing and will certainly (for the time being) be quiet. That the *Prime Minister* himself has decided the matter is new to me.[70] But in any case the first rehearsal was yesterday—2 hours for the strings, 2 hours for the winds and percussion but unfortunately only pieces 2, 3, 4, and 5. *U.E.* has left me in the lurch regarding the material for the 1st (most difficult and longest) piece. Perhaps you are urging *in the same way* that the material be in Berlin at the *very* latest on Saturday. The further schedule of rehearsals:

Figure 1. Erich Kleiber, Telefunken publicity photo, 1935.

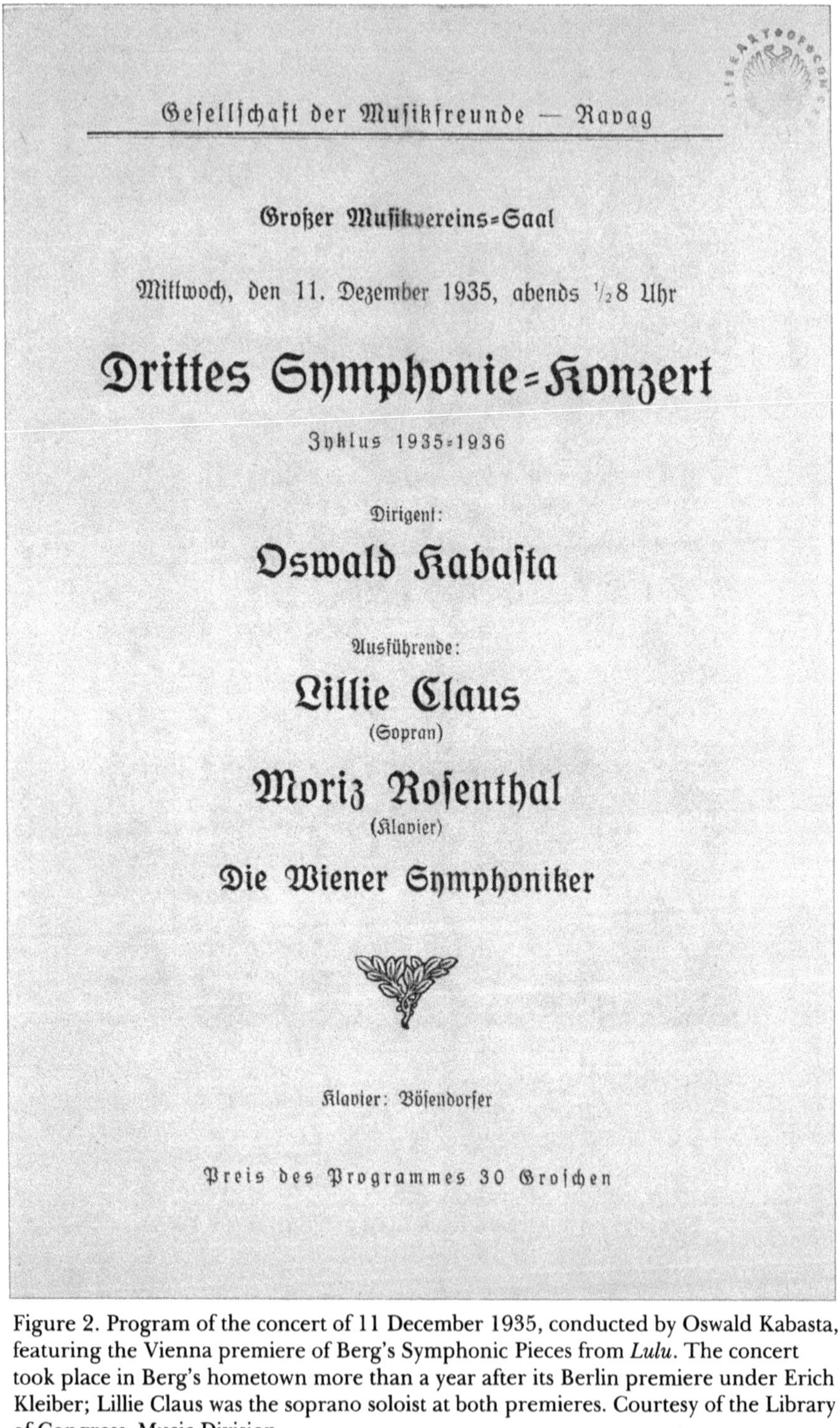

Gesellschaft der Musikfreunde — Ravag

Großer Musikvereins=Saal

Mittwoch, den 11. Dezember 1935, abends ½ 8 Uhr

Drittes Symphonie=Konzert

Zyklus 1935=1936

Dirigent:
Oswald Kabasta

Ausführende:
Lillie Claus
(Sopran)

Moriz Rosenthal
(Klavier)

Die Wiener Symphoniker

Klavier: Bösendorfer

Preis des Programmes 30 Groschen

Figure 2. Program of the concert of 11 December 1935, conducted by Oswald Kabasta, featuring the Vienna premiere of Berg's Symphonic Pieces from *Lulu*. The concert took place in Berg's hometown more than a year after its Berlin premiere under Erich Kleiber; Lillie Claus was the soprano soloist at both premieres. Courtesy of the Library of Congress, Music Division.

Programm:

Richard Strauß:
Ehrenmitglied der Gesellschaft der Musikfreunde in Wien
(Geboren 11. Juni 1864 in München)

„Potpourri"
(Ouverture zu „Die schweigsame Frau")

Erstaufführung

Franz Liszt:
Ehrenmitglied der Gesellschaft der Musikfreunde in Wien
(Geboren 22. Oktober 1811 zu Raiding, gestorben 31. Juli 1886 in Bayreuth)

Konzert für Klavier und Orchester Nr. 1, Es=dur
Allegro maëstoso (Tempo giusto) — Quasi Adagio — Allegretto vivace — Allegro marziale animato

Solist: **Moriz Rosenthal**

Alban Berg:
(Geboren 7. Februar 1885 in Wien)

Symphonische Stücke aus der Oper „Lulu"
Rondo (Andante und Hymne) — Ostinato — Lied der Lulu — Variationen — Adagio (Sostenuto, Lento, Grave)

Sopransolo: **Lillie Claus**

Erstaufführung

Peter Iljitsch Tschaikowsky:
(Geboren 7. Mai 1840 zu Wotkinsk [Gouvernement Wjätka], gestorben 6. November 1893 in Petersburg)

Symphonie Nr. 4, f=moll, op. 36
Andante sostenuto, Moderato con anima — Andantino in modo di canzone — Scherzo, Pizzicato ostinato — Finale, Allegro con fuoco

Figure 2 continued

Monday 26

1st piece 10:00 strings; 11:30 winds, percussion; 1:00 harp, vibraphone, piano alone

Tuesday 27, Wednesday 28, Thursday 29 *and* Friday 30: all—thus 6 rehearsals in all!

(W. F. would burst if he experienced that!)

Before I forget: please tell *Lilly Klaus* that she should keep herself *unconditionally* ready in case something happens with Cebotari (I have a feeling that one could create a *problem* in Dresden, where C. is engaged); one must be aware of *everything*, isn't it true! I *must* absolutely conduct the concert for your 50th birthday (9 February)—if I obtain the necessary rehearsals that I demanded I'd come on your behalf for only the cost of travel and lodging! Or even without that! Don't tell that to Hohenberg right away, but rather let him first make arrangements.[71] I am enthusiastic about the idea and am keeping the days *4–10* February unconditionally free.

This I *must* conduct: 1.) the early songs 3.) 3 Pieces from *Wozzeck* (on purpose) 2.) the *Lulu* Pieces.[72]

Write soon to me here!!

What do you write *there* [*da*]—about Kabas*tà*? Ka-ha-ha-*hà*!

Tomorrow I begin to rehearse the "Rite" (7 rehearsals).

Most cordial greetings to you with your dear wife from your always true Kleiber

The variations (with the Theme at the end!!) and the finale are splendid!! *Truly* you!!!

1st piece I still don't *know*! I have it here with me; learn!! learn!!

I would like to and must become acquainted with Lulu's Lied in its context!!

I have not completely finished the Ostinato yet—at the beginning of the retrograde I must first grasp the other color (sordino) and mood. The rehearsal was not too difficult at all, that is to say, *psychologically*! Present were many of the old *Wozzeck* artists and very interested!![73]

Letter from Alban Berg to Erich Kleiber, 20 November 1934

My dear friend, our most recent letters crossed each other in the meantime, in that your letter came here while mine was already on the way to Brussels.[74] Let us hope that you found it there (also the correspondence card). Indeed, we also wrote about *the same thing*: the Vienna Opera. That is certainly our old, very oldest heart's desire and I think about almost nothing else. For some time thinking was almost useless. But I did not let it out of my sight. I ask that you tell me above all who the managers were. (Whether official emissaries or someone else?) Of course I will speak with

Alma, but even that requires (just between the two of us!!) a certain care and diplomacy, since her relationships and interests are the most *widely reaching* imaginable. But I am thinking also about the N. Wr. Journal and the N. Fr. Presse, where I have very good connections (which could also be drawn on, by the way, for the premiere on the 30th. A report on the state-sponsored premiere, perhaps a review . . .???) I have connections even to the semi-official *Wr. Zeitung*.

To be sure, I don't know yet whether your membership in the N.S.D.A.P. is an obstacle or not. That must be carefully explored. But ultimately everyone concerned has some sort of snag [*Haken*]. Walter is a Jew, Busch is seen as red, Böhm may be in a similar situation as you are. Thus remains only . . . Kabasta! And let us hope we'll be spared that!

You see, for the time being the whole Viennese affair has not gone beyond rumors and there is thus still time to proceed, with caution. But one must use this time! And that I *will* do! But please write now what *you* have to say about the matter. —

P. S. At midday the telegram about the Cebotari cancellation came. Dreadful! I am curious about further details.

I immediately tried to secure Lillie Claus. But!!! Today she has an operetta premiere and will not know before tonight or tomorrow morning whether she will be able to free herself—for *two* days. So I can't give you an answer about this until tomorrow morning. You will have learned from the telegram whether she 1. receives time off at all 2. if yes, whether it is sufficient for you if she is in Berlin on midday of the 29th (perhaps an afternoon piano rehearsal) and therefore can attend only the *one* orchestral rehearsal on the morning of the 30th. She would then leave at night after the performance to travel back to Vienna, thus miss only two performances here in Vienna. 3. if she doesn't receive time off, whether I should try here with another singer, who, I hear, should be *very* suited for it. But *whether* she can undertake this obligation I'll hear also only early tomorrow and either I'll have telegraphed it to you then tomorrow or I'll have said nothing about it. In that case it was also no luck with her.

All of this only to explain my telegram tomorrow, which in the meantime you should have long since received. —

It's good that I have not yet given any hint of our other correspondence.

Once again, most cordial greetings from Berg

Letter from Erich Kleiber to Alban Berg, 22 November 1934

Dear Friend!

I am happy that the matter with Lilly [*sic*] Claus is going according to plan: she will, however, *definitely* be in Berlin on Thursday afternoon, that is to say, at the latest toward evening! ?⁷⁵ —I hope and ask you that *you* will go over everything with her very exactly, that is, that you instruct her in the most thoroughgoing way as to how you want to have it, so that she, so to speak, sings "authorized" by you.

I will leave myself time for a thorough piano rehearsal with her on Thursday evening and perhaps also to rehearse her things twice in the dress rehearsal on Friday morning. The situation with Cebotari, who suddenly was not released (Herr Böhm!!) from *Dresden* for the dress rehearsal (the *only* rehearsal in the theater space!!)—the situation is thus still not completely clarified; she (Cebotari) is supposed to have explained officially in Dresden that the pieces were in any case forbidden, that is, dropped—or so she was supposed to have heard universally in the Berlin administration office (do you notice something, my dear?!). It was then conveyed to me here by telephone from Berlin that under the influence of Böhm and Furtwängler (also Heger, the sweetie!!) she wanted out!—But now the damage is repaired.⁷⁶

My membership in the N.S.D.A.P. is as much a *fable* as the news that I was a Jew, at one time very eagerly disseminated in military circles—I was *never* a member of the N.S.D.A.P.* I always sympathized with the *national* movement—but now I can no *longer follow* it *into the realm of the "race question"*—because I am in possession of an artistic conscience, thank God. In these questions *I* fight much more and more fiercely in Berlin than the (for his Jewish subscribers) "open"-letter-writing W. F.! —⁷⁷

Vienna still scarcely knows me at all as an opera conductor—*I* can wait! —
I will send the names of the invitees to Berlin today!
Very cordially as always,
Your Kl.
Greet your wife very nicely, also from "mine"
Write *quickly* to me in Berlin about whom I should place myself in contact with as *correspondent* for the Neue Freie Presse, N.W. Journal, and Wiener Zeitung!! Concerning tickets for the 30th.

*never as well had the intention of becoming one!!! Despite repeated requests!

Letter from Alban Berg to Erich Kleiber, 24 November 1934 (excerpt)

[. . .]I'll be seeing Peyser in the next few days but will be reserved and limit myself to musical matters.⁷⁸ [. . .]

Highly interesting also your "fable" about membership. That is indeed *exactly* the same kind of fable as that of the 135 Wozzeck rehearsals.⁷⁹ It is unbelievable! But that does decisively change the picture and my "pet" hopes have again risen. More about this, too, after the 30th and, incidentally, speak also with Reich about it. He's coming, you see, to the performance in Berlin *somehow*. He writes reviews, by the way, for many foreign newspapers and writes as well for the N.Wr. Journal and Wiener Zeitung and *apparently* also the N.Fr. Presse. About *this last* I'll write more to you as soon as it is firm. [. . .]

Herbert F. Peyser
Berg's "Lulu" wins Acclaim in Berlin
Dated 30 November, published 1 December 1934, *New York Times*

The world premiere of the music from "Lulu," the new opera by the Viennese modernist Alban Berg, based on Wedekind's plays "Erdgeist" and "Pandoras" [*sic*], evoked a demonstration of riotous enthusiasm at the Stadtsoper [*sic*] tonight seldom equaled in the annals of musical modernism.[80]

The success was scored despite the opposition of some high sources of Nazi musical authority and of threats of disorders that made necessary the presence in the Stadtsoper of large forces of secret police.

For nearly fifteen minutes a huge audience numbering many members of the diplomatic corps, which listened with straining intensity cheered, stamped and applauded, recalling to the platform time and again Erich Kleiber, who prepared and conducted the stirring performance, the orchestra of the State Opera, and the Viennese light soprano Lillie Claus.

Singer Kept From Role.

Fraulein Claus had learned a cruelly difficult soprano solo within a few days to replace the singer originally cast for the part, who was prevented from appearing in the hope of sabotaging the performance.

Tonight's frank production of new music by the composer of the sensationalist "Wozzeck" revealed the strength of the popular desire for work that ranks in the Nazi ideology as subversive and Bolshevistic. Herr Berg himself was not present.

"Lulu," which is Herr Berg's first operatic composition since "Wozzeck" and which has occupied him for more than six years, is not yet finished. A few days ago the composer told the *New York Times* musical correspondent in Vienna that he had still at least two months of work to do on the instrumentation.[81]

The five fragments played this evening do not pretend to furnish a picture of the exact sequence of incidents in the two plays, out of which Herr Berg wrote his newest lyric tragedy. They are "merely extracts from a dream world" whose musical formation can be grasped independently of any knowledge of the dramatic happenings in the opera.

They consist of a rondo, an ostinato allegro, a set of four variations on a kind of street tune, constituting interludes between scenes, a soprano aria, and an adagio movement that forms the conclusion of the opera and allows one to hear in one of the most horrendous dissonances ever written the death shriek of the disemboweled heroine and the lament over her mutilated corpse.

Of these pieces only the rondo was written as an independent concert number, and though built upon music that appears in the opera, does not form an integral part of the score.

Marked by Sheer Beauty.

Undeniably the fact is that few modern works show anything comparable to these "Lulu" fragments in sheer beauty, constructive power and authentic emotion.

It is strikingly different music from what Berg wrote in "Wozzeck," though he utilizes some of the same formulas. The haunted, nightmarish atmosphere of the earlier score gives place to moods of another type. There are scarcely more shocks in "Lulu," as far as tonight's concert disclosed it than in Debussy's "Pelléas et Mélisande." It is poetic, tender and generally fine-grained, smooth, fluid and transparent.

As sheer sound much of it is exquisite and it may be questioned whether anyone has blended with such suave and even noble effect the tones of instruments like the saxophone and the vibraphone with that of the remaining orchestral choirs. Certain pages of the long-breathed rondo and in the closing adagio are simply colossal in their workings.

Here Berg has renounced neither his twelve tones technique nor his employment for dramatic purposes of certain learned forms of classicism. But he uses them to a different purpose and to quite another effect than in "Wozzeck."

From the impression derived this evening the question of whether this composer could with virtually the same means turn out a work palpably different from his earlier opera seems to have been answered with a gratifying affirmative.

Herbert F. Peyser
Berg's New Opera
Dated 2 December, published 23 December 1934, *New York Times* (excerpt)

Erich Kleiber could hardly have picked a more psychological moment for the first performance of extracts from Alban Berg's still uncompleted opera "Lulu." With the country in a state of ferment over Paul Hindemith, with Furtwaengler under attack for daring to defend him, it took courage to sponsor within the four walls of Hermann Goering's Staatsoper the latest production of the author of "Wozzeck."[82]

Mr. Kleiber had this courage and his valor was becomingly rewarded. For almost fifteen minutes after the novelty he was cheered, applauded and recalled. The orchestra and an imported soprano soloist shared in the ovation. The composer was not present, but if he had been he would undoubtedly have tasted the savor of glory. However, let there be no mistake. One has to read more these days in the applause lavished by German audiences on infrequent modern works than mere enjoyment of the music or endorsement of the performance. Demonstrations of the sort have an edge of hysteria and recall the times when Italians shouted "Viva Verdi" and meant something else.

How "Lulu" came to be performed in Berlin at this stage is a long story and a dark one—a tale of intrepidity and determination in conflict with jealousy, baseness and an intrigue involving one of the outstanding conductorial figures of Germany. For indefinable reasons the details of the whole business cannot be discussed at the present time.

[. . .]

Yet even a single concert experience of this music persuaded me that, for better or worse, it has feet of its own to stand on. And it is music different from "Wozzeck"—a music of another profile, of bigger scale and longer line, a music which despite transient resemblances is one of different premises, different moods, different affinities. It probably lacks something of "Wozzeck's" sharp concentration and expressionistic quality—a fact doubtless postulated by the nature of its dramatic problem. In place of the spasmodic thrusts and the jagged outlines of Berg's previous opera, there are in such pages as the rondo and the adagio extended melodic spans, unforced continuity, suave contacts.

There is not only fascination in this new music of Berg's, there is emotional genuineness and a sizable measure of beauty, even of nobility. Several of the Berlin reviewers were reminded by it of Mahler. The composer has captured and transmuted overtones of "Tristan" and of Debussy, passing them through the alembic of his own fertile imagination. And there are few shocks in so much as we were given to hear. [. . .]

Herbert F. Peyser
Weingartner in Vienna
Dated 26 December 1934, published 13 January 1935, *New York Times* **(excerpt)**

Felix Weingartner began his term as artistic director of the Vienna Staatsoper two days before Christmas, when he conducted a performance of "Lohengrin." Speaking by the card—or the contract—Weingartner was about three-quarters of a year ahead of time, for he assumes his post officially only next September, and in Basle, where he has long been active, the conservatory, the symphony orchestra and the opera house still have claims on his service. But the sudden and dramatic ejection of Clemens Krauss and the prospective loss of a number of leading singers who want to follow him to Berlin have threatened to leave the Viennese establishment in a parlous state, Something had to be done, and quickly. The Swiss rose nobly to the occasion and virtually gave Weingartner the privilege of being in Vienna as long and as often as he liked prior to the expiration of his Basle commitments. [...]

For all the talk and agitated prophecy about the imminence of Furtwaengler and Kleiber, cooler heads insisted all along and with more or less reason that the former is anything but a born operatic conductor, while so far as Vienna is concerned Kleiber, though a native Austrian, is pretty much of an unknown quantity.[83] Moreover, some feel certain that he once harbored Nazi sympathies, some resent his allegedly "modernistic" orientation and others suspect the purity of his Aryanism. Considering these and innumerable other factors of the situation, the choice of Weingartner and a sort of regency was, perhaps, inevitable, whatever embarrassments it may ultimately lead to. At present nobody can definitely say whether the systematic scheme, so abundantly discussed, of guest conductors like Walter, Toscanini, Busch, Furtwaengler and so on will come to anything. The air is still almost as blue with rumors as it was several weeks ago. Most of these rumors are only thought-fathering wishes.

The plain truth is that, with the prevailing and innumerable cross-currents of political, religious and other conflicting aspirations and intrigues, the Vienna State Opera is really not concerned at all in securing the most capable artistic personnel. Like every State-controlled institution—and particularly those overrun with petty officials and ancient bureaucrats—in countries where posts go pre-eminently by favor, it is looking primarily for people who, directly or indirectly, serve some special interest or tendency. The artistic aspect of this matter is neither here nor there. It is significant that among the candidates for the conductorial position at the Staatsoper mention has been made at one time or another of Oswald Kabasta, leader of the Vienna "Ravag," or radio, orchestra, and other broadcasting functions. Now Herr Kabasta, though a conductor of wholly undistinguished attainments, is known to have strong support in certain potent political circles. It would not greatly surprise those who understand the workings of all this concealed machinery if one fine day in a future not all too remote Oswald Kabasta were translated in the sight of men from the Johannesgasse to the Opern Ring.[84] [...]

**Letter from Willi Reich to Theodor Wiesengrund-Adorno,
1 February 1935 (excerpt)**

Very esteemed dear Herr Doctor Wiesengrund![85]
Many thanks for your friendly letter of the 27th. I of course immediately had *23* sent to Herr Dr. Benjamin.[86] Likewise to Herr Clark, although I don't expect much initiative from him, since he hasn't once answered important letters (I haven't had this experience only with him).[87] The urgent necessity of a counter-organization in the face of Blubo-International is completely clear to me;[88] I also already understand all the possible proposals. I cannot judge, however, whether the opportunity to realize such a project exists in today's circumstances. It seems highly doubtful to me that Schönberg could be won over for such a plan. His five-page circular, which you surely will also have received, allows little hope![89] I'll gladly speak with Krenek and Berg about the matter and then report to you. You will probably see Berg at Wozzeck in London at the end of April.[90] If it is possible for me, I want also to come. I have already secured the travel costs by agreeing to newspaper assignments, and Frau Dr. Scherchen has offered me lodging free of charge. I thus need only about 5–10 pounds in order to be able to stay in London a couple of days. Perhaps I can somehow raise more. —Do you perhaps have an idea whether one could earn something there through a talk (radio, etc.). I would be very thankful to you for a tip.

[. . .]

I don't know whether the Austrian Studio can become the basic unit of a new organization. You ought not to imagine too much in "Krenek's Viennese organization." In reality the situation is such that Krenek and I alone do all the work without the least compensation for the work and the expenditure of time. It appears very doubtful to me that Krenek will be able to continue next year; his time and his nerves are too precious. The whole thing weighs on me less tragically. Anyway, I am completely up in the air and am thinking seriously of emigrating.

I hope to be able to speak with you in detail about everything if I succeed in being able to come to London in April. Perhaps at that time "23" can be placed in the service of the matter, under the protection of Schönberg and as a proper international battle paper.

Admittedly, the newspaper is at the moment in a serious crisis, since it is in truth very much read but only little paid for. [. . .]

It looks rather lamentable regarding the celebration of Berg's birthday. The large orchestral concert with the Vienna premiere of the Lulu-Symphony was called off altogether. Some small chamber music events are taking place: at the Women's Club, with U.E., and with the I.S.C.M., as well as on the radio. The programs are the usual: Lyric Suite, the Clarinet Pieces, Sonata etc. etc. Only with the I.S.C.M. is there something new: the Adagio from the Lulu-Symphony for piano four hands (Steuermann!) and Lulu's Lied. In addition Berg himself arranged the Adagio from the Chamber Concerto for violin, clarinet, and piano. It sounds wonderful and completely unforced. The task gave Berg much joy; otherwise he is rather morose but is learning English diligently. [. . .]

NOTES

1. *Haken* means hook, snag, or catch; *Hakenkreuz* means swastika. Berg is playing on the connection. This excerpt is from a four-page autograph letter (Photostat) held in the Manuscript Collection of the Wien Bibliothek under two numbers: H.I.N. 202.965 (the first two pages) and 202.957 (a two-page postscript); the entire letter appears in the fourth section of this article, "October 1934 to February 1935." The prefix *H.I.N.* always refers to items held in this collection.

2. John Russell, Kleiber's biographer, did not have at his disposal many of the letters that are now available in Viennese archives. Motivated no doubt by a wish to protect the conductor's reputation, and without access to the letter that Kleiber wrote in response, Russell turned "your membership" into "your non-membership." See John Russell, *Erich Kleiber: A Memoir* (1957; repr.; New York: Da Capo Press, 1981), 144. Andreas Razumovsky, who worked with the same primary sources when he "translated" the biography into German, dealt with the problem by omitting that passage in Berg's letter. See John Russell, *Erich Kleiber: Eine Biographie*, trans. Andreas Razumovsky (Munich: Albert Langen and Georg Müller, 1958). The paragraph where it would have appeared is on pp. 165–66.

3. Three-leaf, double-sided autograph letter from Brussels held in the Berg Fonds of the Austrian National Library (F21 Berg 933/40); the entire letter appears below in the fourth group of documents. The prefix "F21 Berg" always refers to items in the Berg Fonds. The asterisk in the original letter cues Berg to another asterisk and a continuation of Kleiber's train of thought that runs perpendicular to the rest of the letter. This way of using all available space is a feature of their letters to each other.

4. Postcard (F21 Berg 933/6).

5. Carbon copy of a one-leaf, double-sided typed letter (F21 Berg 480/357/1); reproduced in facsimile in Alban Berg, *Maschinenschriftliche und handschriftliche Briefe, Briefentwürfe, Skizzen und Notizen: Aus den Beständen der Musiksammlung der Österreichischen Nationalbibliothek*, ed. Herwig Knaus and Thomas Leibnitz (Wilhelmshaven: F. Noetzel, 2005), 164–65. Both Bavarian Broadcasting and the N.S.D.A.P. officially acknowledged that neither Berg nor Webern were of Jewish extraction in letters, respectively, of 26 January (F21 Berg 539) and 30 January 1934 (F21 Berg 1133).

6. This must have been Franz Hofer, who defied the ban on the Nazi party in Austria to serve as Gauleiter for the Tyrol and Vorarlberg in 1932 and 1933 and consequently was imprisoned in Innsbruck. During the night of 29–30 August 1933 three Nazis entered the prison and helped him to escape.

7. The *Wiener Zeitung* of 6 December 1933 lists a performance in the early evening of the two composers' music by Ruzena Herlinger, Rita Kurzmann, and the Galimir Quartet.

8. The Music Division of the Library of Congress holds typescript copies of the correspondence between Reich and Berg. Reich's original letters are in the Berg Fonds of the Austrian National Library; the whereabouts of Berg's original letters to Reich is unknown. The copies in the Library of Congress do not have individual numbers; the typescripts, most likely made by Reich, sometimes include several short items on a page, which would make numbering difficult. Since I worked with these copies and there is no significant additional information to give about physical characteristics of each item, I do not repeat the basic information.

9. Berg must have listened to the opera on the radio.

10. "J.K." is Julius Korngold, who retired as critic in the spring.

11. Double-sided typed letter (one leaf) signed "P[er] P[rocur]a Heinsheimer" (F21 1473/284). I thank Dr. Karl Ulz for explaining the signature.

12. After the defeat of the German Empire in World War I and the subsequent formation of the German Republic, Kaiser Wilhelm lived in exile in Doorn, the Netherlands.

13. Hans Heinz Stuckenschmidt was a critic, Heinz Tietjen was General Intendant of the Prussian State Theaters, and Josef Rufer had been a student of Schoenberg and then his assistant until the composer emigrated from Berlin in 1933.

14. One-page typed letter with autograph insertions (F21 Berg 933/7).

15. The translation appeared as Benito Mussolini, *Schriften und Reden* (Zurich: Rascher, 1934). Wanting to keep some distance between the translation and his work as a journalist, Reich used "Wilhelm" as his first name. Reich wrote about his translation in "Ein Wiener Musiker übersetzt Mussolini," *Anbruch* 17/4 (April–May 1935): 107–9. In this article he refers to working in Italy on his PhD dissertation, "Padre Martini als Theoretiker und Komponist" (University of Vienna, 1934).

16. These are the Rondo, Ostinato, and Lulu's Lied; the remaining two movements are the Variations and the Adagio.

17. See Margaret Notley, "Berg's *Propaganda* Pieces: The 'Platonic Idea' of *Lulu*," *Journal of Musicology* 28/2 (Spring 2008): 106.

18. In the opera Lulu briefly interrupts Alwa's Hymn toward the end. Alwa's words in the hymn are the following: "Through this dress I feel your form like music. These ankles: a grazioso; this charming roundness: a cantabile; these knees: a misterioso; and the powerful andante of desire. How peaceful are the two slender rivals [her thighs] nestling against each other in the knowledge that neither can equal the other in beauty, until the moody ruler of both awakes, and the paired rivals spread apart like two [magnetic] poles. I will sing your praise until your senses are overcome. . . . You have destroyed my reason. . . . Quiet—quiet."

19. See Notley, "Berg's *Propaganda* Pieces," 107, 124–25, 141.

20. Reich had sent photos of the Hungarian soprano Margit Bokor and another singer, Carol Reich. The physical attributes of the singer who would create the role of Lulu were very important to Berg.

21. Berg was clearly irritated when he wrote this letter, so he substituted for *I.G.N.M.*, the German initials for the International Society for Contemporary Music, the acronym *I.G.f.l.m.i.A.*, for which the equivalent in English might be rendered "International Society for Kiss My Ass." In this letter he refers to two members of the society, the English musicologist Edward Dent and the Italian composer Alfred Casella.

22. Every year Kraus, editor of *Die Fackel*, marked his birthday (April 28) with a performance of some sort. In 1934 he turned sixty.

23. Erich Schmid had written a three-part article, "Studie über Schönbergs Streichquartette," for the *Schweizerische Musikzeitung* 74 (1934): 1–8, 84–91, 155–63. Each installment was devoted to one of the string quartets that Schoenberg had at that point composed. Schoenberg and members of his circle traced technical features of his style to the music of Brahms.

24. This reference concerns Reich's personal financial problems.

25. On 30 April, Reich reported that for a first offense the punishment would be minimal: an official warning or a fine of five Schillings.

26. In discussing *Ein Heldenleben,* the tone poem by Richard Strauss, Berg appears to get his *yesterdays* mixed up, since he is here referring to his letter from April 22, six days earlier.

27. Berg is ignobly suggesting that Reich (himself a Jew) emphasize Strauss's musical connections to Jews.

28. Berg must have enclosed a review, as he and Reich often did when they sent letters to each other.

29. Two-page autograph letter not on U.E. stationery (F21 Berg 1399/69).

30. At this point Heinsheimer and Klemperer had seen the scores of only the second and third pieces.

31. Heinsheimer was director of the opera division of Universal Edition.

32. As Reich suggests, Kleiber conducted regularly in Italy as well as Brussels. Václav Talich did conduct the arrangement in Prague on 9 February 1935, Berg's fiftieth birthday.

33. Stein is most likely referring to the so-called Night of the Long Knives, a bloody purge within the Nazi Party, most of which took place on 30 June 1934.

34. Ernst Ansermet conducted the Symphonic Pieces from *Lulu* in Geneva on 16 January 1935.

35. Double-sided typed letter (one leaf) signed "P[er] P[rocur]a Heinsheimer" (F21 1473/341).

36. Richard Strauss presided over meetings in Venice of a Nazi-oriented counterpart to the International Society for Contemporary Music, the "Permanent Council for the International Cooperation of Composers," which had been formed in Wiesbaden in June (see Table 1). On its founding, see Fred K. Prieberg, *Musik im NS-Staat* (Frankfurt am Main: Fischer, 1982), 209–10. Regarding events in Venice that included the performance of *Der Wein* under Scherchen, Herbert Gerigk asserted, "The concerts and the evening of one-act operas gave a compressed view of what has finally been laid to rest in the new Germany." The Symphonic Pieces from *Lulu* had not yet been performed, but performances of Berg's music in Germany were being cancelled. Gerigk, "Musikfestdämmerung: Das Dritte internationale Musikfest in Venedig und die Erste Arbeitstagung des 'Ständigen Rats für die internationale Zusammenarbeit der Komponisten,'" *Die Musik* 27/1 (October 1934): 45.

37. Reich, "Arnold Schönberg e la sua scuola viennese," *Pan* 2/12 (Dec. 1934): 566–74. Designated only "from Lulu," the excerpt, which gives indications of the orchestration, is the beginning of the Canzonetta in Act 1 (mm. 258–62).

38. Notley, "Berg's *Propaganda* Pieces," 115–21, 136–40.

39. Schering, *Tabellen zur Musikgeschichte: Ein Hilfsbuch beim Studium der Musikgeschichte*, 4th ed. (Leipzig: Breitkopf & Härtel, 1934).

40. Claudia Maurer Zenck, *Ernst Krenek—ein Komponist im Exil* (Vienna: Lafite, 1980), 78–80; and John L. Stewart, *Ernst Krenek: The Man and His Music* (Berkeley, Los Angeles and Oxford: University of California Press, 1991), 175–76.

41. *Reichstagung in Nürnberg 1934*, ed. Julius Streicher (Berlin: Vaterländischer Verlag C. A. Weller, 1934), 164–68. Hitler's goal of eliminating Gothic-style typeface lies behind his references to written language in effect separating (Aryan) peoples and to misguided attempts to link Nationalist Socialism to a cult of the Middle Ages.

42. Double-sided pencil autograph (one leaf) held in the Universal Edition Archive of the Wien Bibliothek (U.E. 387).

43. Berg turned "Stagma" into "Stattlichauthorisierte Ganz-ton-Maschin[en]gewehre."

44. Double-sided typed postcard signed "Kalmus" in pencil (F21 1473/357).

45. GDT stands for Genossenschaft Deutscher Tonsetzer (Association of German Composers); GEMA stands for Genossenschaft zur Verwertung musikalischer Aufführungsrechte (Association for Dispensing Musical Performance Rights); the German behind the acronym Stagma is "Staatlich autorisierte Gesellschaft für musikalische Aufführungsrechte."

46. In a draft of the program notes that accompanied a letter of 11 October, Berg used the word "chaotic" to describe the second movement (Ostinato). Reich had cautioned Berg against providing his critics with ammunition and had suggested "wild" instead in a response dated 16 October, to which Berg is in turn responding here.

47. Berg is referring to Dusolina Giannini and to Maria Cebotari, slated to sing in the premiere of the Symphonic Pieces from *Lulu*.

48. The German composer Paul Graener flourished in the changed political circumstances in his country, just as Marx and Rinaldini did in Austria.

49. The article that Berg did not like was Rudolf Réti, "Salzburg—Verheißung und Gefahr," published on pp. 25–29 of the issue.

50. In the entry for Toscanini in his *Musiklexikon* (Berlin: Max Hesse, 1935), 872, Hans-Joachim Moser had described the conductor in these terms: "Gifted with an unprecedented memory and inspired by fanatical faithfulness to the text, T. has for a generation been the leading conductor of the Italian music world (often abroad as well); consistently not a sensual epicure and above all to be admired for the almost Nordic clarity in delineating part-writing." The squib about this entry was removed from the issue of *23*.

51. Further source information for article: *23* 15/16: 18–24.

52. Schoenberg had turned sixty on 13 September. The preceding evening, Ravag broadcast a short concert of his Op. 11 and Op. 19 piano pieces, two songs, and *Verklärte Nacht*.

53. *Kunst in Österreich: Österreichischer Almanach und Künstler-Adressbuch 1934*, ed. Josef Rutter (Leoben: Kunst in Österreich, 1933). By the time that Krenek's essay was published, Rintelen was in prison for his involvement with Nazis in the attempted putsch and the assassination of Dollfuss on 25 July.

54. Krenek is being ironic here, since Bayer had presented a "Viennese School" that bore no resemblance to the composers usually thus designated.

55. Krenek is choosing to ignore Hitler's call to give up *Fraktur* in the speech at Nuremberg excerpted above.

56. Krenek is referring to the yearly festival of the Allgemeiner Deutscher Musikverein, which took place in Wiesbaden in June 1934. See Table 1.

57. The review for the *Wiener Zeitung* is signed "W. R." and that for the *Neue Freie Presse*, "R." Reich also contributed to *Anbruch*, *Schweizerische Musikzeitung*, and *Der Auftakt*.

58. Deutsch [F.D.], "Alban Berg und sein Berliner Erfolg: Gespräch mit dem Komponisten," *Neues Wiener Journal*, 7 December 1934, 5.

59. Alfred Burgartz, "Alban Bergs 'Lulu'-Musik: Uraufführung im Berliner Staatsopernkonzert," *Die Musik* 27/4 (January 1935): 262–63; and in the same issue, "Unsere Meinung: Alban Berg und die Berliner Musikkritik," 263–64.

60. In an undated letter on his Berlin stationery, Kleiber wrote about Stuckenschmidt's dismissal and asked Berg about employment possibilities for him in Vienna (F 21 Berg 933/31). The *New York Times* reported his dismissal on 12 December.

61. Friedrich Geiger, "Die 'Goebbels-Liste' vom 1. September 1935: Eine Quelle für Komponistenverfolgung im NS-Staat," *Archiv für Musikwissenschaft* 59/2 (2002): 104–12.

62. The chamber concert sponsored by the International Society for Contemporary Music included performances of Lulu's Lied and the Adagio arranged for soprano and two pianists.

63. Five-leaf, double-sided autograph letter from Brussels (F21 Berg 933/16).

64. Furtwängler made himself vulnerable by his outspoken defense of Paul Hindemith.

65. Berg surreptitiously inserted some of the text back into the fifth movement.

66. Two-page typed letter with autograph insertions from Berlin (F21 Berg 933/18).
67. Kleiber is making a pun on the word *Mädchenhandler* (procurer), which is conspicuous in Act 3, scene 1 of *Lulu*.
68. Three-leaf, double-sided autograph letter from Brussels dated only "Sunday evening" (F21 Berg 933/38). The exact date is easily determined.
69. Copies of correspondence between Kleiber and Furtwängler from this time (four letters altogether) are held in the Austrian National Library, F21 Berg 3256.
70. Hermann Göring had finally given official permission for the performance to take place.
71. This is Dr. Arthur Hohenberg, a Viennese impresario.
72. Kleiber initially wrote "2" before the *Wozzeck* fragments.
73. Kleiber wrote these postscripts on the top and both sides of the letter's last page.
74. See note 1 for full citation for this letter.
75. See note 3 for full citation for this letter.
76. Robert Heger was a conductor at the Berlin Staatsoper; Karl Böhm was at the Dresden Staatsoper.
77. On 12 April 1933 an open letter by Furtwängler addressed to Josef Goebbels appeared in the *Deutsche Allgemeine Zeitung*. In a limited way Furtwängler challenged the new regime's anti-Semitic policies as these applied to German musicians. Kleiber may well have known that another open letter by Furtwängler protesting the cancellation of Hindemith's *Mathis der Maler* was about to appear.
78. Six-page autograph letter (Photostat, H.I.N. 202.966).
79. Berg was sensitive to comments that his music required an excessive number of rehearsals.
80. The performance took place in the house of the Berlin Staatsoper. Wedekind's second play is *Pandora's Box*.
81. Berg did not in fact finish orchestrating Act 3.
82. Hindemith's opera *Mathis der Maler*, which was supposed to have been produced at the Berlin Staatsoper in the 1934–35 season, had recently been canceled. Furtwängler wrote an article in protest of this action, "Der Fall Hindemith," which appeared in the *Deutsche Allgemeine Zeitung* on 25 November. See Prieberg, *Musik im NS-Staat*, 65–66.
83. Kleiber and Furtwängler appear to have been vying for the position in Vienna. This may explain some of their behavior toward each other.
84. The administrative offices of Ravag, of which Kabasta was music director, were located at Johannesgasse 4b.
85. Three-page typed letter with autograph insertions in the Walter Benjamin Archive, Berlin (1195/5); the original is in the Theodor W. Adorno Archive, Frankfurt a. M. Adorno's father's name was Wiesengrund; he went by "Wiesengrund-Adorno" before dropping his father's name altogether.
86. This is Adorno's friend, the literary critic Walter Benjamin.
87. Edward Clark had studied with Schoenberg and was currently the program director for the music division of the BBC. At the end of this letter, omitted here, Reich added a postscript stating that a package from Clark had just arrived.
88. "Blubo" was Krenek's ironic contraction of Hitler's nationalistic slogan "Blut und Boden" (Blood and Soil). Krenek had written an article for the December issue of *23* about the Venice festival and its aftermath that he gave the sarcastic title "Blubo-International": how could "Blubo" be international?
89. For this letter, dated 25 November 1934, see *Briefwechsel Arnold Schönberg-Alban Berg*, ed. Juliane Brand, Christopher Hailey, and Andreas Meyer, 2 vols. (Mainz: Schott, 2007), 2:539–46.
90. Berg did not in the end travel to London.

Table 1. Selected Events, 1933–1935

Political Events	Events in Music World	Berg's Professional Life
1933 **30 Jan.**: Paul Hindenburg names Hitler Chancellor **3 Mar.**: Engelbert Dollfuss suspends Austrian Parliament	**April**: Schoenberg and Schreker placed on leave in Berlin **Oct**: Schoenberg emigrates, after changing spelling of his name	**April**: Performances of *Wozzeck* in Breslau are canceled
1934 **12–14 Feb.**: Social Democrats resist Dollfuss's ban on leftist political parties, leading to civil war in Vienna **18 Mar.**: Austria signs pact with Italy and Hungary **23 Mar.**: Hitler assumes dictatorial powers **1 May**: Dollfuss turns Austria into *Ständestaat* **30 June**: Purge of Nazi Party: "Night of the Long Knives" **25 July**: Nazis attempt a putsch that leads to Dollfuss's murder but stops when Italy intervenes **2 Aug.**: Hindenburg dies; Hitler is now *Führer* **Early Sept.**: Nazi Party Congress in Nuremberg	**Late Jan.**: Vienna premiere of Krenek's *Karl V* postponed because of right wing pressure **Spring**: Seventieth-birthday celebrations for Richard Strauss **3–9 June**: Annual festival of Allgemeiner Deutscher Musikverein in Wiesbaden **8–16 Sept.**: Venice Biennial includes Berg's *Der Wein* **By Nov.**: Joseph Marx and Joseph Rinaldini represent music world in *Ständestaat* **Dec.**: Clemens Krauss takes Kleiber's position in Berlin	**26 Jan.**: Heinsheimer optimistic about premiere of *Lulu* after visit to Berlin **3 Feb.**: Kleiber asks Berg to send libretto for *Lulu* **23 May**: Furtwängler reports Berlin premiere of *Lulu* will not be possible; Berg decides to arrange some of the music **11 July**: Heinsheimer forces Berg to remove words from the first *Lulu* piece **Oct.**: Furtwängler asks Kleiber to change venue for Berg premiere; Kleiber refuses **30 Nov.**: Berlin premiere of *Lulu* music; Kleiber resigns
1935	**Sept.**: Germany officially bans music of Jewish composers but also of Berg	**9 Feb.**: Muted celebrations of Berg's fiftieth birthday in Vienna; Berlin concert canceled **Dec.**: Vienna premiere of *Lulu* pieces on 11 Dec. is the last concert Berg attends before his death of 24 Dec.

Table 2. Overview of Sources

Group 1, from 1933 and 1934

Letter from Alban Berg to Bavarian Broadcasting, 20 December 1933
Article by Herbert F. Peyser, published 18 February 1934, *New York Times*
Letter from Willi Reich to Alban Berg, 24 January 1934
Letter from Alban Berg to Willi Reich, 26 January 1934
Letter from Hans Heinsheimer to Alban Berg, 26 January 1934
Letter from Willi Reich to Alban Berg, 29 January 1934
Letter from Erich Kleiber to Alban Berg, 3 February 1934

Group 2, all from 1934

Letter from Alban Berg to Willi Reich, 22 April
Letter from Alban Berg to Willi Reich, 28 April
Letter from Alban Berg to Willi Reich, 12 June
Letter from Erwin Stein to Alban Berg, 1 July
Letter from Hans Heinsheimer to Alban Berg, 11 July

Group 3, all from 1934

Hitler's *Kulturrede*, 5 September
Letter from Alban Berg to Universal Edition, 7 September
Letter from Alban Berg to Hans Heinsheimer, 7 September
Postcard from Alfred Kalmus to Alban Berg, 10 September
Letter from Alban Berg to Willi Reich, 19 October
Ernst Krenek, "Ravag's Message and Austria's Message," *23*, 25 October

Group 4, from 1934 and 1935

Letter from Erich Kleiber to Alban Berg, 24 October 1934
Letter from Erich Kleiber to Alban Berg, 17 November 1934
Letter from Erich Kleiber to Alban Berg, 18 November 1934
Letter from Alban Berg to Erich Kleiber, 20 November 1934
Letter from Erich Kleiber to Alban Berg, 22 November 1934
Letter from Alban Berg to Erich Kleiber, 24 November 1934
Review by Herbert F. Peyser, published 1 December 1934, *New York Times*
Article by Herbert F. Peyser, published 23 December 1934, *New York Times*
Article by Herbert F. Peyser, published 13 January 1935, *New York Times*
Letter from Willi Reich to Theodor Wiesengrund-Adorno, 1 February 1935

Alban Berg zum Gedenken:
The Berg Memorial Issue of
23: A Viennese Music Journal

TRANSLATED AND ANNOTATED BY MARK DEVOTO

The first issue of *23: Eine Wiener Musikzeitschrift* appeared in Vienna with a date of January 1932. As its founding editor, Willi Reich (1898–1980), wrote later, its intent was to "sharply oppose" with well-aimed polemics "the corruption that was more and more out of control in Viennese musical life." Reich had proposed the journal in a letter to Alban Berg, his teacher and friend, suggesting various possible titles like *Ausbruch*, *Synkope*, even *Der musikalische Beobachter* (The musical observer)—a barely concealed reference to *Der völkische Beobachter*, the official newspaper of the increasingly powerful National Socialist Party in Germany. Berg wrote to Reich on 12 September 1931: "There is already a crying need for a musical *Fackel*; I've wanted one for 25 years. Ideally I'd write it myself, but then I'd have to give up composing. —— But if *you* wanted to try it!!! We have to discuss this at length. —— Your proposed titles are all pretty bad, but I can't think of any good ones myself." *Die Fackel* was a journal of criticism and satire written and published by the Austrian poet Karl Kraus (1874–1936) and deeply admired by Berg, Schoenberg, and hundreds of Austrian artists and intellectuals who writhed under its lash.

The title eventually chosen for *Fackel*'s musical counterpart had a double reference: to the numbered section of the Austrian press law that required newspapers to publish official corrections of incorrect information previously printed in good faith, and to Berg's own superstitious numerology that associated the number 23 with an important nexus in his own life and music (the *Lyric Suite* being especially important in this regard). The editors of *23* were the attorney Rudolf Ploderer, the composer Ernst Krenek, and Reich as editor in chief, and these three also wrote the greater part of the journal's content, maintaining an aggressive support for new Austrian music and for the Second Viennese School in particular.

Figure 1. Berg's burial, Hietzing cemetery, 28 December 1935; visible on the left are Ernst Krenek and Egon Wellesz.

Ploderer died in September 1933, and thereafter T. W. Adorno wrote with increasing abundance. Though not himself a member of the editorial board, Berg kept close watch on its operations and gave freely of his advice and counsel. Thirty-three numbers of *23* eventually appeared, of which eleven were double issues, before the journal ceased publication in September 1937.

The new journal embraced controversy from its first issue, with "A Korngold Affair in 23 Points," an attack on the conservative Viennese critic Julius Korngold (1860–1945), father of the very successful opera composer Erich Wolfgang Korngold (1897–1957). Korngold sued; Reich lost, then appealed and was acquitted. Today it seems odd that Stravinsky's beloved *Symphony of Psalms* (1930), whose Vienna premiere took place in February 1932, would provoke a harsh reaction in a progressive periodical, but "Strawinskys 'Psalmenkakophonie'" was featured on two pages of the second issue of *23*. A special tribute to Anton Webern for his fiftieth birthday was offered in no. 14, which appeared at the end of February

1934. Thereafter *23* was published irregularly as double issues (one triple), two or three times a year.

The saddest *23* was the Alban Berg memorial issue, nos. 24/25, dated 1 February 1936, which we reproduce here in complete translation. In the *Doppelnummer* that followed, Berg's celebrated radio interview from 1930, "What Is Atonality?" was reprinted, as well as a page of Berg's instant thoughts about Mahler's Ninth Symphony, "the most wonderful thing that Mahler wrote." Only two more double issues appeared after that, separated by nearly a year, and the heart seemed to go out of *23* as the political situation in Austria rapidly deteriorated under the threat of advancing Nazism. The last issue included an excerpt from Reich's just-published Berg memorial volume, *Alban Berg: Mit Bergs eigenen Schriften und Beiträgen von T. W. Adorno und Ernst Krenek* (Alban Berg: With Berg's own writings and articles by T. W. Adorno and Ernst Krenek) (Vienna: Herbert Reichner, 1937), a book that despite its hurried compilation remains one of the most valuable documents of Berg biography and bibliography; it was reprinted in 1963 in an abridged and etiolated edition.

The Berg memorial issue began with a photograph of a casting from Berg's death mask, followed by Willi Reich's tribute to his beloved teacher. Further farewells were offered by Berg's close friends Heinrich Jalowetz, Erwin Stein, Soma Morgenstern, Hugo Winter, and Krenek, along with two lengthy essays by Adorno, writing under the pseudonym of "Hektor Rottweiler." Most of these continued their already distinguished careers into later years. The conductor Jalowetz (1882–1946), a student of Schoenberg and active all over Europe before World War II, emigrated to the United States, where he taught at Black Mountain College in North Carolina until his death. Stein (1885–1958), composer, editor, and writer on music, was also a Schoenberg student; he worked for Schoenberg's Verein für musikalische Privataufführungen in Vienna and then for Universal Edition, where he prepared a performing edition of Berg's *Wozzeck* with reduced orchestration. Eventually he emigrated to London, where he worked for Boosey & Hawkes. Soma Morgenstern (1890–1976), novelist and writer on Jewish subjects, was Berg's literary advisor. Following the *Anschluss* in 1938 he made his way to the United States; his biography of Berg was published only in 1995 as *Alban Berg und seine Idole: Erinnerungen und Briefe* (Alban Berg and his idols: Recollections and letters) (Lüneburg: Klampen). Hugo Winter (1885–1952) was one of the three directors of Universal Edition. He immigrated to the United States and continued to be active in music publishing. Willi Reich left Austria in 1938 and emigrated to Switzerland, where he made a significant career as a musicologist; in 1959 he published *Alban Berg: Bildnis im Wort: Selbstzeugnisse und Aussagen der Freunde* (Alban Berg: By himself and by his friends) (Zurich: Die Arche), and in 1968 *Arnold Schönberg oder der konservative Revolutionär* (Arnold Schönberg or the conservative revolutionary) (Vienna: Fritz Molden). Ernst Krenek (1900–1991), a pupil of Franz Schreker and a prolific composer through his long career, achieved international fame in 1927 with his so-called jazz opera *Jonny spielt auf*; he came to the United States in 1938, taught at Vassar College and Hamline University, and became an American citizen, but after the war he regularly returned to Europe to teach and conduct. Theodor Wiesengrund-Adorno, as he was first known (1903–69), studied composition with Berg and wrote extensively on music, serving as editor of *Anbruch* in Vienna between 1928 and 1931. In 1938 he went to the United States and worked at Princeton and in California. After the war he returned to Germany as director of the Institute for Social Research in Frankfurt am Main, where he was a leader in the so-called Frankfurt School of Marxist philosophers. He published *Alban Berg: Der Meister des kleinsten Übergangs* (Alban Berg: The master of the smallest link) (Vienna: Elisabeth Lafite, 1968), incorporating revised and expanded versions of some of the essays he wrote for *23*. His correspondence with Berg, *Theodor W. Adorno / Berg: Briefwechsel 1925–35*, was published in 1997 (Frankfurt am Main: Suhrkamp; edited by Henri Lonitz).

The entire run of thirty-three issues of *23: Eine Wiener Musikzeitschrift: 1932–37* was reprinted in facsimile in 1971 (Vienna: O. Kerry) with a comprehensive foreword by Willi Reich.

Figure 2. The Berg Memorial Issue of *23*.

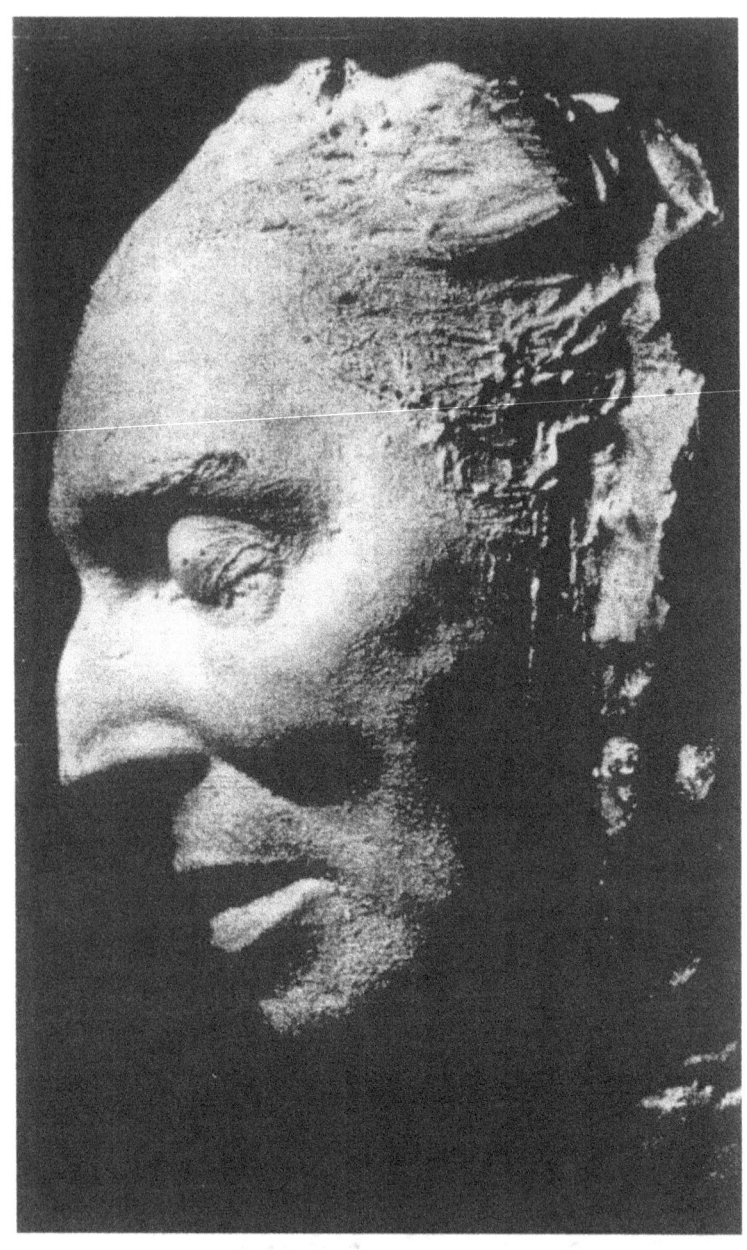

Figure 3. Death mask of Alban Berg taken by Anna Mahler.
This photo appeared in the Memorial Issue of *23*.

> *O glaube, mein Herz, o glaube!* Believe, my heart, O believe!
> *Es geht dir nichts verloren!* You have lost nothing!
> *Dein ist, ja dein,* Yours, yes, yours,
> *Was du gesehnt,* What you longed for,
> *Dein, was du geliebt,* Yours, what you loved,
> *Was du gestritten!* What you strove for!
>
> Gustav Mahler, Second Symphony

Alban Berg

—the following words are for him, our beloved master and friend. That they are uttered certainly needs no justification, save for the fact that this is happening so soon after the catastrophe, at a time when the pain over the horrible event still holds several of us numb in silent loneliness.

Nevertheless, we derive the justification for speaking so soon of Alban Berg from the content of our words and from the general and ceaseless solidarity of this journal with the living man, for this issue is dedicated to the memory of the living man and will speak only of him.— What we have to say in Alban Berg's memory he already knew when he was alive: thanks, a thousandfold thanks for every moment he lived with us and for us, for every smile of his luminous and yet so enigmatic countenance, for every note of his inconceivably concentrated, exalted work!

We wish to provide neither a collection of official necrologies, nor a substitute for a biographical appraisal—although it is hoped that this can soon appear, enhanced by Berg's own words. Our only aim here is to bear testimony: for the man and for what he created. That will be achieved above all by the two more comprehensive articles, the first of which Berg himself was able to enjoy; the others are documents of an unquenchable pain and a pledge of enduring dedication to his work. This is what could be expressed now; the grief for the departed will forever remain locked within our hearts.

Willi Reich

On the *Lulu* Symphony

On 11 December 1935 Oswald Kabasta led the Wiener Symphoniker in the first Austrian performance of the "Symphonic Pieces from the opera *Lulu*." Previously the work had already been heard in Berlin, Prague (twice), Geneva, Brussels, London, Boston, and New York (four times). In this connection we wanted to publish the following notes, set down after the London performance. They were not meant as criticism but as the first sign of astonishment [*Betroffenheit*]. Now they can only greet the one who died.

The Editors

It is necessary to dispense with a comprehensive account of this work because it is so radically conspired from the stage, so irretrievably bound up with the poetic words, that it cannot be completely deciphered in isolation. This is not to imply that this is gestural or incidental accompanying music. Whoever knows anything of Berg's style will expect, from his second opera, completely autonomous, designed-down-to-the-last-detail music—in common parlance: "absolute" music—and will find this expectation more richly repaid than even in *Wozzeck*. But this construction, though far beyond any mere illustration of the spoken drama, is nonetheless organized around its literal meaning as if around a dark nucleus upon which it feeds at every turn. If, even without words, it is a complete construction, it is also one that is closed off. To penetrate its musical mysteries would require more than attending a dress rehearsal, a performance, and familiarity with the score: it would require years of immersion. Rather than engage in such pretensions it is better to record the impressions of a first encounter—which only complete knowledge can eventually rival in significance. The first thing is to identify what is *new* about *Lulu*, even measured against Berg's previous output.

At first glance the *simplification* of Berg's style is striking. It is indeed a simplicity of the most memorable kind: the simplicity of fullness. There is no sacrifice of any of the differentiation of Berg's compositional style; not the slightest concession is made to new-Classic or old-Romantic tendencies; the sound is richer, indeed more radiant and colorful than the faded sound of *Wozzeck*; the harmonic language more graduated, the counterpoint more vibrant. Nevertheless, and paradoxically enough, the impression of simplification remains predominant. Which means that in the new score primacy is given to the demand for *clarity*. This brings Berg into a new constellation with his predecessors: Mahler and Schönberg. From the late Mahler—to which so many of *Lulu*'s lines of connection lead, just as the unfathomable soldier's misery in *Wozzeck* connects to the early Mahler—from the Mahler of the seventh and ninth symphonies comes the demand never to write any voice, doubling, or sound that, by the very nature of its composition, cannot be perceived with absolute clarity. Thus the foreground and background of half-distinct, half-present phenomena disappear; whatever the music contains is wholly perceptible without anything left over. Anything vague or fading is banished, or, if you will, brought into evidence. Nothing perceptibly false is withheld from the discerning ear; and it is the presence of the music in all its fullness that gives the impression of simplicity. If Krenek, proceeding from the relationship to the text, has emphasized the cognitive character of the opera *Lulu*, then it is evident not just in the choice of a text that communicates more through concepts than images, but also in the structure of a music that, just like its beloved Lulu, has wished "never in the world to appear as anything other" than what it has been taken for; and that is precisely why it is never taken for anything other than what it is: music whose substance is so completely at one with its appearance, as only its very subject matter: beauty.

That means an evolution of all aspects of *technique*. From Mahler's principles of instrumentation comes an overall technique of construction. It derives its corrective from Schönberg's twelve-tone method, which Berg adopts in a most specific manner and which is transformed through its intersection with dramatic expression. Roughly speaking one might say that *Lulu* relates to *Wozzeck* as Schönberg's Variations, op. 31, relate to the Orchestral Pieces, op. 16, or to *Erwartung*.[1] Only with Berg, the constructive power works in precisely the opposite direction from Schönberg's. If with Schönberg constructive power devouringly draws every appearance into the very structure itself, as if into its truth, so, in Berg's case, appearance greedily absorbs the constructive essence and transfigures appearance into truth itself. This can be illustrated by the following example: in Schönberg's *Harmonielehre*, in a discussion of new sounds, there is mention that supposed dissonances would lose their terror if they were spaced further apart or at least if the clash of minor seconds were avoided.[2] Schönberg hardly gave this sentence another thought and made his choice of registers and dissonance placement without any concern for their "appearance," but rather solely according to set principles of construction, as, for instance, the constant change of register. With Berg, however, appearance turns into constructive principle, and thus Schönberg's passing thought attains canonical significance for *Lulu*. Schönberg, even in his choral writing, doesn't flinch from the clash of minor seconds, whereas in *Lulu*, even in instrumental passages, they are avoided, or at most used occasionally with specific expressive intent. The result of this kind of texture is a completely fresh sound: that of a highly multilayered harmony, which is always waiting for its twelve-tone chord—indeed draws it in just as Lulu draws in her murderer—and which seems so free of dissonance, sounds so sensuously harmonious, that in London even the colors of Ravel's *Daphnis et Chloé* were pale by comparison.[3]

The principle of wide spacing rules throughout and produces the most extraordinary instrumental effects. At times it seems as though the compositional texture has vanquished the gravity of the orchestra. For instance, at one of the high points of the Rondo—Alwa's music, bars 128–29—violins and three flutes are led *fortissimo* up to high G. As though in ecstasy the music were reaching beyond itself, this high point is outdone and the next-higher B♭ is set on top of it, played by the three clarinets in unison. One might think that in this difficult register and against the luminosity of the strings this highest tone would be diminished in its effect. But the instrumental disposition of the entire passage, especially the doubling of the lower octave in the oboes, is such that the B♭ of the three solo instruments outshines not just the choric G but the full orchestral *tutti*.— Similarly, words cannot describe the way in which the orchestral texture underscores the effect of Lulu's death chord. The clarity and transparency of the orchestral sound becomes an enzyme of expression itself; never before has one felt a twelve-tone chord with such bodily penetration. For never before was there a sonority so obviously a manifestation of variety within unity.

The power of appearance, as clarity and compositional texture, is imprinted as much on the expression of sensuous beauty as on the *compositional* way of thinking. The voices, placed, so to speak, in the light of day, lay claim to the sound-space that was created for them. They wish to move within it; they rise up in long arches and sing out fully. What in the *Wozzeck* style might be called more narrowly expressionistic—the individual sound as an expressive factor—recedes in *Lulu*. Precisely, the mastery in the manipulation of sound draws it completely into the compositional structure; precisely its transparency lets the independent voice come through: as *melody*. Everything has become more maneuverable, more slender, more linear. Only one of the Symphonic Pieces, Lulu's song, is a vocal piece. But to judge by it and by the concluding lines of the Countess Geschwitz at the end of the Adagio finale, the vocal line in *Lulu* is central throughout, it is the human voice that carries the operatic action. Berg's new singing style is most clearly anticipated in Marie's lullaby and in the middle number in the *Wein* aria. It is a *melos* of hovering ecstasy, so to speak. There is no longer any disparity between instrumental and vocal melodic style; as the violins sing, so Lulu's coloratura soprano plays. With unmistakable certainty Berg's vocal style disavows one Lulu—the cliché-ridden "elemental being"—to seize upon that childlike artificial aspect of the figure, in which beauty and mortality are united. In one of his stage directions Wedekind asks that Lulu kiss Alwa "with deliberation"; and this seductive deliberation shimmers over Lulu's music, over the fragile coloratura as an enigmatic picture of a beauty whose nature is fulfilled in the artificial.[4] And snuggling up to this coloratura are contrapuntal lines as transparent as the clothing the Marquis von Keith imagines for his beloved.[5] One might almost suppose that the relationship of this music to the text is like that of clothing to the body: clothing, which reveals a body more beautiful; which, naked, would be veiled by its truth.

The technical—and therein the super-technical—evolution is most clearly evident in the *harmony*. Here the flexibility of the *Lulu* style leads to unforeseen results. Characteristic of early Berg is the technique of imperceptible transformation of sound, the principle of the smallest, almost imperceptible transition. This corresponded to a kind of harmonic *stasis*: it was the art of disguising the harmonic progression while at the same time subjecting it to continuous modification; time stood still, so to speak, in *Wozzeck*, and it is no accident that one of the most powerful places is found at the words "Wieviel Uhr ist" (What time is it); also no accident that an entire scene is constructed around a pedal point and another around the exchange of three chords. In *Lulu*, however, the temporal dimension intrudes, and looking back, the conquest of the temporal dimension appears to be the actual intent of the Chamber Concerto as well as the *Lyric Suite*. The harmony progresses while an extremely precise fundamental awareness is adjoined to the melodic plasticity. Externally this is made clear—similarly to the most recent Schönberg—with a continuo-like accompanimental apparatus of harp, piano, and vibraphone. *Wozzeck* was perceived, so to speak, in a held breath, eternally and simultaneously in a moment, as in the Captain's grotesque words; *Lulu* goes further, like life. It is profoundly revealing when, in one of his performance directives, Berg prescribes "the tempo of the heartbeat" for Lulu's song. If Wozzeck asks what time it is, this music knows, viscerally, the hour at hand. The film music, called "Ostinato" in the Symphonic Pieces, bears witness to this as a striking expression of time-consciousness: rise and fall are captured in musical form with abrupt immediacy. Indeed, it would be incompatible with Berg's sense of form and sensitivity to appearance if the art work were unconditionally surrendered to the stream of time. Just as even here he disdains crass contrasts and spreads out the living in the full panoply of its relationships, so is time construed according to the sense of what happens in it, according to fate's rise and fall, and held together by its rhythm. Accordingly, the form of the film music—the caesura of the work and of its innermost reflection—is a strict retrograde: time passes and revokes itself and nothing points beyond it other than the gesture of those who love without hope.

It hardly needs saying that this sense of form imposes form upon this fragmentary publication, upon these five fragments. They stand in for the form of the whole as only a great torso can. They arrange themselves like a *symphony*: it is as the *Lulu Symphony* that this first-published form will enter public consciousness. Nowhere is the relationship to late Mahler clearer. Five movements: the outer ones, thoroughly symphonic in manner, rather as in Mahler's Ninth, enclose three short middle movements of a distinct "character'—as, perhaps in the Seventh. The opening movement is a broadly conceived rondo—again almost Mahlerian—intricately organized, yet tectonically strictly controlled; of an ecstatic tone that takes the Andante affettuoso of *Wozzeck* and the Trio estatico of the *Lyric Suite* as models but which now for the first time becomes completely free and unfettered. If one searches for "details" nothing more beautiful would serve than the very beginning, the eight bars of introduction, so sad and blissful, as only the promise of beauty can be—these will one day serve as the definitive embodiment of the unquenchable pain that grips us on viewing the beautiful, like Schumann's note of loneliness in the midst of great celebrations. After that, the breathlessly urgent film music, virtuosic as a career, evanescent as a skyrocket, with a deep meditation in between. As a centerpiece Lulu's song, bright and clear as though made of glass, prose of insight and rhyme of the body enfolded in melody. The short variations that follow, drawn from the Casti-Piani scene, are Berg's contribution to musical surrealism. Lulu's decline is harshly portrayed in decayed music; a street song by Wedekind isn't actually varied but is dressed up with extra parts as a domed salon is covered with plaster ornaments; and the putrefaction of a hit song of 1890 illuminates Lulu's last flight with tragic gaslight.[6] The Adagio finale is the death scene. Strangely enough, it is this piece, on first hearing the most striking and accessible of all, that bursts the boundaries of the symphony and appeals inevitably to the stage. For the horror that lives in this music—at its most gruesome, perhaps, in the horn passage at bar 91—can only be borne when the eye is forewarned by the events out of which the music arises. But at that point the music frees itself from the action: free to achieve that fatal reconciliation that is pronounced in Geschwitz's final words.

Hektor Rottweiler

Farewell to Alban Berg

> For there really are only two possibilities of convincing someone of an artist's worth: the first and better way is to exhibit his work; the second, which I am compelled to use, is to demonstrate one's belief in this work to others.
>
> Man is petty! We really should have such a firm conviction that our belief will be immediately communicated. Our ardor for the subject of our veneration should burn so fiercely that whoever comes near must glow with us, must be consumed with the selfsame fire that is holy to us. So brightly should this fire burn in us that we become transparent, that its radiance bursts into the open and shines on him who previously walked in darkness. An apostle who does not glow preaches a false teaching. He who denies the sacred radiance will not carry a godlike image within him. Indeed, the apostle is not illuminated by his own means, but by a light which the earthly body does not recognize as a covering: the light pierces through the covering; but it is gracious, and grants to him, the one who glows, the appearance of one who is self-illuminated. We who are enthusiastic should have confidence that others will share in this glow, will see our light radiating. Others will honor the one whom we worship even without our doing anything about it.
>
> From Arnold Schönberg's address on Gustav Mahler,
> Vienna, 1911

We were standing, once, in a spring thunderstorm at an open grave with Alban Berg. Death had torn Gustav Mahler from us young musicians—he, whose physiognomy banished everything common and without which we could no longer imagine Viennese musical life, indeed music itself; he, who first taught us to hear old music and in his own music had built a new wonderful world that had become our spiritual home.

Our master Arnold Schönberg followed the casket with us; he taught us pure, artistic thought, showed us and the world the way to the musical future, became our friend and taught us friendship. An unbreakable bond, both human and spiritual, united us, we who followed him and who knew why we followed him, no matter where our own paths might lead us even in all weathers, no matter how varied our professions, our personal forms and spheres of expression.

Now—almost exactly a quarter-century after that day of Mahler's burial—we have had to pay final honors to Alban Berg. The brief time span that was granted to his life and works corresponds almost to the day to

Mahler's. Neither had yet completed his fifty-first year when death, with one sudden blow, cut off their intensity-laden work, which they gave freely, with no thought of themselves, to contemporaries who were slow to follow. It is as if Berg's departure served to express his solidarity with this great man, who had become the decisive artistic experience of his life.

We are now left alone and must try to understand just why we had to lose him so early, he who was the most vitally alive of us all!

When I had the pleasure, earlier in the year, of celebrating Berg's birthday with the opening address at a performance of some of his works, it seemed to me that his life and the destiny of his works represented a musical form; like a sonata, whose development had just ended and whose fulfillment—the resplendent repetition of the principal theme—I wished for my friend.

It turned out otherwise. And yet precisely because it turned out so differently from what we wished and hoped for, it seems like a tragic confirmation that this life, the life of a genuine musician, was itself structured like a musical form. For as a principal theme of this life-sonata I believed I might recognize the idea of surprise, the ever-returning, unexpected twist that first disclosed the true meaning of such an apparently uneventful life. On the surface it had been uneventful; he was the only one in our circle who had never uprooted himself from his native city; indeed, he lived and worked from the day he brought his wife home in the same small, quiet apartment in a hidden suburban alley that always seemed to conceal its approach from the visitor; but what he created, what his work radiated and what the world answered in reply, was over and over the most adventurous surprise.

And the last year of his life brought the fulfillment of this idea, but in a fullness that we could never have imagined and will never grasp, a fulfillment that shows exactly what deep necessity steered the life and work of this outwardly so inconspicuously quiet, kindly modest nature.

The last year of his life began with the unremitting work on the instrumentation of his last opera *Lulu*, which was already completed and was to have been ready for performance as soon as possible. But early in the year came an unexpected commission—as it had similarly to Mozart while he was working on his last opera, *Die Zauberflöte*—one that interrupted the planned effort and that in both cases led to the composition of a requiem. In Mozart's case the secret and anonymous commissioner ordered a requiem through a messenger. In Berg's case an American violinist commissioned a violin concerto, though here, too, the true commissioner remained a secret. For Berg, who at first only reluctantly, indeed unwillingly, interrupted his work, had a heart-wrenching experience: the sudden death of a young girl who was his friend.[7] Now he knew what he had to write. He designed the

Violin Concerto as a requiem—unmistakably, by its dedication and by the interweaving of Bach's chorale "Es ist genug! So nimm, Herr, meinen Geist!" in the final movement—a requiem that, just as in Mozart's case, unintentionally became his own.[8] He who otherwise worked very slowly—the composition of *Wozzeck* took many years—wrote this, his last completed work, in six weeks, as though driven in feverish haste. He had hardly finished when he became ill; without sparing himself, he worked further on the full score of *Lulu*, which he had brought sufficiently far that the completion of the missing parts is easily possible, and he was still able to hear the Viennese premiere of the Symphonic Pieces from *Lulu*—then he left us.

Yes, he surprised us again, we who are left behind and impoverished, and we will never completely grasp that we will never again see that noble visage—will never hear that sociable, loving, all-understanding voice again, he who even in his last days of suffering was more interested in our trivial daily concerns than he was for himself, that he is severed forever from this circle of friends.

Heinrich Jalowetz

What a transformation!
So recently bound with us in daily contact as an artist and as a friend,
with us who followed from nearby your creation:
eager to see what new blossoms you put forth,
to bear fruit and to present to us;
anxious, whither the path, on which your genius led you,
on which, astonished and willingly, you followed,
and would in turn have led us;
stirred by your ever-active love, warmth, and sympathy
even for the least significant.
Today this is a totality, torn from us, and we stand before it.
The thousand features, that showed us an ever-changing image,
   are numb.
Your works, which, by the momentum of your effort, seemed
   immeasurable,
found the center of gravity.
And so, too, does the reciprocity of your friendship
dwell, alive, in our memory,
the boundary is drawn.
What remains for us to do?
We can only promise, that we will guard your work,
your wonderful work:
light on our path!

Erwin Stein

In the House of Mourning

He was noble with the nobility of a new age that Peter Altenberg, its great visionary, foretold: the nobility of naturalness.[9]

He had the deepest kinship with nature. She shone kindly on him only seldom. Peering into her chasms, eavesdropping on her demons, he did not transfigure her: he illuminated her with the light of his mind, he clarified her with the light of his tones. Thus his landscape is closely and strictly related to Gustav Mahler's.

Like his teacher and friend Arnold Schönberg he was a faithful guardian and keeper of the great legacy of music, of the tradition of pure forms, of the great builders of music. Incomprehension—here out of malice, there from sheer ignorance—had the cheek to assail both, the pathbreaking and the younger master, new-toners [*Neu-töner*], re-formers, with the anathema "atonal!"

He had fine, gentle, sinewy hands, creative hands, with which one can make the finest things with such precision, so pure, completely without frills. Adolf Loos loved him.[10]

During the life of this kindest, most conciliatory man he loved in art: the belligerent, the strict, the uncompromising, the pitiless. The wittily playful, the striking, the purifying, the condemning, emphatic word was his highest mental pleasure. His esteem for Karl Kraus was downright fanatical.[11]

In well-considered deference five great names are given here. It is entirely in keeping with the spirit of our dead friend: they stand there purely as his legacy. These five names were the stars in his firmament, his guiding lights, and he pondered them not in a distant heaven; they were his household gods, and he lived in their proximity, modestly enough, in order not even to become aware that among these, his stars, he was a star of equal radiance.

Soma Morgenstern

At the Grave

Alban Berg's interment took place on 28 December 1935 at the Hietzinger Friedhof, in a grave of honor dedicated to him by the city of Vienna. Besides the speakers cited below were these: Dr. Ludwig Rochlitzer, for the Society of Authors, Composers, and Music Publishers; Professor Dr. Egon Wellesz, for the Austrian Composers' Union; and Professor Dr. Paul Stefan, for the Association of Viennese Music Critics.

In the name of Universal Edition I bid farewell to Alban Berg.

Among Alban Berg's character traits was a profound loyalty to his friends, and this quality also characterized his relationship to the publisher to whom he entrusted his works. What we returned to him was more than high esteem and honor; we loved Alban Berg, the great musician, the splendid man.

He did not make life easy for himself. In what he created, he was not a man to make concessions; he created and wrote only what he found to be right and good. Without wishing to pronounce a value judgment on his work, let it be said: that which he found to be right and good to release for publication was, and is, good in the best sense of the word. He was his own severest critic.

He confided his works, his life's work, to our care. We will guard them loyally in his spirit. Alban Berg, you great, beloved, noble man, we will never, never forget you!

Hugo Winter

To have to speak here in the name of Alban Berg's friends—what a bitter and difficult task! Words, echoing dully in the sad darkness of this winter day, can be nothing more than a feeble symbol of the lamentation of those struck dumb by the deep, unfathomable sorrow. Thus as he preceded us on earth on the path of art, he now precedes us all too soon into the kingdom of perfection, of true immortality, where, God willing, we will one day see him again.

That the work of our beloved friend will partake of the earthly immortality granted to the creations of a chosen few must inspire us and give us some modicum of comfort. The International Society for Contemporary Music, whose Austrian section I represent in the absence of its president, Anton Webern, and to whose founding membership the dear departed belonged, mourns the loss of one of the greatest of those to whose life work its actions are dedicated. In Alban Berg we have lost not only a master whose works regularly transformed our programs into a true celebration; not only one who gained convinced friends on all sides for new music and led it to world renown. We have also lost a kindly soul who was always ready to help, who through the calm generosity and noble bearing of his character clarified and smoothed over many a difficult situation for us. The most beautiful, the most precious thing he has left to us: his music, awakening us ever and again to living sound, will do its glorious duty as both our elevating solace and memorial to the irreplaceable one.

And now, dear, unforgettable friend, rest gently, until the last trumpet blast, which you have so powerfully conjured in your work, summons us to a new and unknown life—rest in peace.

Ernst Krenek

Dearest Master, dear Berg!
Today your students have their last lesson with you—on this earth.—Whenever we did our harmony or counterpoint assignments, we always thought, with every note we wrote: "What will Berg say about that?"—And as a living community emerged from those hours of instruction, the same question followed us in everything we did. To be worthy of your penetrating, but benevolent judgments, was our law of life.—

Whatever we do in the future we will always ask ourselves: *"What will Berg say about that?"* Always meeting your demands, that must be our life's goal; we give you our solemn pledge, dearest Master Berg!

Willi Reich

Remembering the Living

To find, in grief, the first words in memory of the dead friend: the attempt is paralyzed, for he himself ironically anticipated it. On the long walks he took around Schönbrunn he occasionally had an unfathomable desire to dream up the obituaries that the Viennese newspapers would one day have in store for him. In one of them, he was certain, they would confuse him with a Jewish folk humorist—I believe his name was Armin Berg. In another, a critic we know all too well would croak out a panegyric about "the Bard of *Wozzeck*": "Just like our Schubert, our Bruckner, our poor, unforgettable Hugo Wolf before him, so this one too has now starved to death in his supremely beloved, unappreciative native city, which nevertheless kept him deep in its heart. One more link in the unending chain of the Immortals..." The impossibility of banishing such anguished fantasies of the feverishly wakeful dreamer, dreams that in any case have already been exceeded by the robust stupidity of the survivors, compels my determination to resist and question them: not for the world, which they so accurately reflect, but for the self concealed in them.

Who was it who played such games? All the antitheses with which hasty interpretations make themselves interesting lay ready at hand: knowledge of the world and alienation from it, melancholy and pride, dreams of happiness and addiction to pain, anxiety and the cleverness that defeats it remain intertwined, in this game as in Berg's features: stony, delicate. But no thought of one extreme would be true if it could not also encompass its opposite. Certainly not about Berg's knowledge of the world. To even a chance acquaintance it would have been apparent what assurance the master brought to relationships with the world around him—he who, in demeanor and appearance so like the romantic notion of the artist, ought to have been ecstatically isolated from it. From the aura of his own appearance the artist liked to transform himself magically into the diplomat, the foreign minister of his dreamland; and upright fanatics might take offense that one so radically inclined, who owned up to his opinions so squarely and candidly, could even so (perhaps even on that account) appear a good friend to everyone. The phrase "had no enemies" was the only enemy that could be uttered at the open grave. But even this phrase would come to nothing as, before the quiet power of his nature, it proved itself one last time. For Berg's conviviality was his loneliness.

In truth he was the daydreamer, who looked up with a wearily awakening glance, who bestirred himself with prehistorically broad gestures. After the Berlin premiere of *Wozzeck*, after that dinner party at Töpfer's, where they feted him and he was hardly capable of responding, I remained with him deep into the night, literally comforting him for his success. That a work—even if conceived in the fields, like Wozzeck's vision, and that met his own standards—that such a work could convince a public—was incomprehensible to him; it even seemed to him an argument against the opera. Not once, even for a second, had he identified himself with the prevailing order, and for seconds the power of his loneliness was able to explode all illusory peace. We were once almost ejected from the Vienna performance of Mahler's Eighth Symphony, under Anton Webern's direction, for disturbing the peace. Enthusiasm for music and its interpretation so carried Berg away that he began to talk about them both out loud, as though it were being played for us alone.— Such isolation dominated him not just in moments of exaltation: it was the unbreakable law of his life and I often had to think that nothing real that happened to him ever touched his innermost being. As when, psychologically knowledgeable and as deeply conversant with Strindberg as with the orchestra for *Die glückliche Hand*,[12] and aware of the ever-present possibility of deadly hatred and betrayal even in the most intimate relationships, he drew isolating substance from his own knowledge, yet could at the same time engage with the most casual relationships in the most friendly, even grateful manner; or find something good in a provincial performance, astonished that it wasn't totally bad. He wished for much, but hoped for nothing, so lonely was he, and he who hopes for nothing has little to lose and still less to fear; in the deep knowledge of the man who is hopeless, however, lies the world, open to domination. If there is any truth in the facile comparison between Wagner and Berg, it is situated here, in the Wotan of *Götterdämmerung*. He has once again denied the will of the world. He underbid the negativity of the world with the hopelessness of his fantasy, outwitted it with all the pent-up fullness and essence of Viennese pessimism, anticipated it with mockery and superstition, as in those invented obituaries; thus, true to the Chinese maxim, he could overcome the very hardest with the very softest; thus was he immune by virtue of his own defenselessness, the only armor granted the giant by modernity, and had to die as one outwitted, from a suffering that goes by the name of poison, poison of the solitary, originating in his own blood. Certainly Berg, whose hypochondriac tendencies never yielded to his knowledge of the world, held ready in his fantasy every possible illness: that he succumbed to one he did not anticipate but neglected, that he did not recognize the danger or believed he had overcome the date of the twenty-third—the fateful number of his peculiar Pythagoreanism, the number for which this journal is also named—is the last subterfuge of an existence that only through the ruse of hopelessness could for half a century sustain itself, between sleep and death, in music.

Not just in music, but through music. It is the antidote of the hopeless one, both in the aesthetic shape of Berg's work and in his private existence: both an intoxicant and a means of remaining awake. Thus it is handed down from childhood as a phenomenon of the nineteenth century: playing piano four hands with his sister Smaragda. Berg was certainly not the "last music-dramatist," but certainly the last four-hands player. He pursued the old-fashioned pastime as an artistic technique, and with persistent repetitions stamped music into his memory that perhaps otherwise might not have penetrated him. In addition he made numerous four-hand arrangements, far more than one knows—not only of Schönberg's works but of his own, including the first quartet, and, if I'm not mistaken, the orchestral pieces.[13] Something of this practice of arrangement may have passed into his compositional technique. And just as the music in such arrangements represented, so to speak, "material" for restructuring and rethinking, so too did his own empirical existence. He was no ascetic artist, preserving in all his pieces the full, sensuous cultivation that found its apotheosis in the orchestral euphony of his late works. But this existence, overflowing in sensuous and spiritual nuances, with all the breadth and refinement of his psychology, was only the occasion and "material" for the work: broken, indeed split; he regarded his own concreteness with a strange abstraction, as removed from himself as he was from reality. What Mahler once said about the landscape around the Atter See—that he had composed it completely away—Berg could have said about the landscape of his own soul. He was alienated from himself, which is also to say: objective, at every moment almost a historical presence to himself. Not for nothing did he especially love Proust, who, after Kafka, provided him with his last great literary experience. He treated his person as carefully and carelessly as the musical instrument he was for himself. This may serve to illuminate one of the most puzzling paradoxes of Berg's essence: he was completely egocentric and completely selfless. He spoke and wrote a great deal about himself and his music, most of all about their fate, but without any shadow of vanity, hardly even identical with himself, much more as the biographer of the highly treasured composer Alban Berg; the one who spoke and wrote there, who prided himself not in the least on the work or the fate of that master, followed him like a long shadow, unpretentious, indeed with no sense for pretension. "Only when I'm composing do I think I'm Beethoven, never afterward," he said to me once. For hours at a time and despite protests he would carry the bulky, heavy briefcase of a sickly student, thinking it too heavy for the student. In similar fashion—resignedly—did he carry with him his own work, as well as the stockpile of life that nourished it.

This brings up Berg's relationship to the nineteenth century, a question appropriate to this primacy of work over life. The clichés that seek to make Berg into a late-Romantic and psychologist, a man of individualism and supple artistic expression whose *ultima ratio* is called Tristan, are so pernicious because every element seems to offer willing confirmation, while the decisive difference is to be found in the tendency toward which the elements are directed. First of all, Berg's aesthetic nineteenth century reaches much further than chromatic voice-leading and dominants. He recognized his physiognomic resemblance to Wilde and did not deny it. The similarity reflects what the fin-de-siècle era used to call the artist's nature. The impulse to express his own essence is stronger than the compulsion of a clearly predominant aptitude in the sense of innate facility; both as a composer and as a man Berg was the opposite of Hindemith, whose music he professed to admire for its capacity to "run on and on," only to let himself be convinced, not reluctantly, of the modest value of precisely this attribute. Berg felt himself first of all to be a poet who besides that also composed, the way prodigies may. The colorful artist did not burst out of the chrysalis of the craftsman, did not play the piano like a virtuoso at all, but rather—with good reason—always harbored a mistrust of all composing that grows out of instrumental technique. The *Seven Early Songs* are clearly the music of one who writes poems. The literary sense remains perceptible throughout; not only in the choice of texts and the mastery of the textual arrangement, but above all in Berg's prose; the article against Pfitzner, buried in *Anbruch*, with its analysis of Schumann's *Träumerei*, is probably the greatest piece of musical polemics ever written, the prototype of a legitimate annihilation.[14] Berg's artistic breadth even reaches into the optical. With great seriousness he once told me that he could just as well have become an architect; whoever is familiar with the graphic appearance of his manuscript scores knows how much like floor plans and sketches they are. As a youth he drew a great deal; the title pages of the Piano Sonata and the Op. 2 songs were done by him.[15] Thus the source of material for Berg, that orchestrator of seductively appropriate materials, seems almost accidental. The appropriateness of his materials is the fruit of a painful self-discipline reaching beyond conceptual categories—the fruit of his encounter with Schönberg. This accounts for the small number of works forced out by the master with something like boyish shame; because of this he stopped assigning opus numbers to his works. All of his production, even that written while studying, came slowly—until the uncanny, almost astonishing exception of the Violin Concerto. Never did he immediately find the most comfortable solution, but always, brooding and then with vehemence, the best, which was the most difficult, a vexation to the musicians and to all those who use *l'art pour l'art* as a term of insult, whom he referred to with Karl Kraus's designation, *Kasmader*. He recognized Baudelaire as his forebear, just as Marcel Proust did, and as with Baudelaire the secret of form was for him greater than that of death, form that itself comes from death, and the aria *Der Wein* is not just the most important prolegomenon to *Lulu*, but just as much the terse testimony to the most decisive elective affinity. Its sounds are the only Parnassian sounds in music, not excepting even Debussy, whom he loved; Debussy and Ravel possess, compared with him, a certain harmlessness, which he was first to explode: through chaos, as through form.

That gives a first inkling of Berg's aesthetic nineteenth century. Although he is grounded in its elements, he alters their function. He does not liquidate the legacy of their temporal roots by forgetting and leaping into a radically lost nature, but rather brings them, through his work, to *self-awareness*. The texts of both of his operas belong to that era. But he approaches both as an elucidator and savior, very much like Karl Kraus. Berg composed Büchner as Karl Kraus cited Claudius and Göcking; and the long view with which Kraus defended *Die Büchse der Pandora* awakened the music from *Lulu*.[16] In Berg the nineteenth century aims to survive by collecting itself into a style. There is a note from Wedekind to the effect that *Kitsch* is today's Gothic or Baroque. This sentence, taken in all seriousness, conveys much of Berg's law of form. It is realized in the Casti-Piani variations in *Lulu*, which Berg called "particularly successful." Nothing is more false than taking them for a "parody." Berg hated the very concept of parody, and once snapped at me when I declared the composition of a children's poem to be such. The song pleased him: "That is good music, that is a very beautiful poem, but there's nothing of parody in it." Intensifying appearances into transparency: that is Berg's will, his liberation from his parents, and from that flows the unrestrained seriousness with which he surrendered to appearance, as to its truth.

Berg's tendency toward rescuing appearance in self-awareness, which circumscribes in equal measure both his affinity with and transcendence of the nineteenth century, is possible only through a heightening of the extremes that ultimately tear asunder the bourgeois cultural space of his aesthetic essence. In Berg, the erotically compulsive world of the *Tristan* sphere is increased beyond all private psychology into the chaotic and antediluvian. The giant who awoke in the chasms of the 1880s awakens in them from primeval mountains, and there is no force powerful enough to take away completely the deep sleep of which his first song speaks. The chaos that menaces Berg and that emanates from him, provokes fear and was originally even felt that way: the greatest Schönberg scandal arose because of one of Berg's Altenberg songs. Whoever really knows his music will be aware of its chaotic features at every step. Chaos lurks in the strangely amorphous Mombert song published in *Der blaue Reiter*, in the second movement of his first quartet;[17] it was once allowed to burst out, perhaps completely unfettered, in the March from the Three Pieces for Orchestra, music that is thoroughly monstrous and for which reason is completely suppressed from public consciousness, music whose central function cannot be concealed behind Berg's own interpretation. When he showed the orchestral score to me, I suggested, "That sounds as though Schönberg's Orchestra Pieces and Mahler's Ninth Symphony were being played at the same time," and I will never forget with what antediluvian pleasure Berg's face lit up at what would be a dubious compliment for any other cultured ear. "Yes," he said with a ferocity that buried all johannine[18] sweetness like an avalanche, "here, at last, one should hear what a chord of brass instruments playing eight different notes really sounds like"; as though he were sure that no audience could survive such chords.— If Berg's compositional technique has its starting point in Schönberg's Chamber Symphony, his passion was much more with *Erwartung* and *Die glückliche*

Hand; he was not dissatisfied with any formal deficiency in his own music, but rather that it never again dared to sound completely naked and chaotic. Nevertheless that blind power can still be felt in the street scene in *Wozzeck*, in the Rondo of the Chamber Concerto, and certainly in many places in *Lulu*. For he outwitted rather than "formed" the chaotic substance; that substance, the basis of hopelessness, which was his cunning.[19] My idea about the March, crudely expressed as it was, was not so very wrong; for Berg, to form was always to combine, to place one over the other, to outwit what was disparate, incompatible. Once, when I encountered difficulties reconciling sonata and variation form while composing a quartet movement, he advised me at exactly the critical juncture—and, as it turned out, correctly—to do nothing but bring together contrapuntally two previous variations. This is what he did with the two previous movements in the Rondo of the Chamber Concerto. In this way all Schönbergian structural motives in Berg have become amorphous material, "outwitted." With retrograde reprises he outsmarts time, just as he outsmarts space with contrapuntally juxtaposed forms—as he outwits his interpreters with alternative possibilities that are always provided—among the masters of the new music Berg is the only one who uses the word *ossia*. Berg the constructor is something of the obsessive hobbyist; his music even splits among extremes of models: here stand-still and imperceptible change, there a *perpetuum mobile*; the norm of the Schönbergian root motion [*Fundamentschrittes*] remained foreign to Berg, at least until *Lulu*. Thus did he also use technical things, which he was crazy about, to overcome the chaos in private life: the electric cigarette lighter, the typewriter, the automobile; nothing could excite his sarcasm so much as technical awkwardness; on one long afternoon in the Café Imperial he gave me instruction in writing notes and abundant advice about adjusting a typewriter. All of life's renunciation is recovered through technical cleverness in his work. Berg's music—and here criticism will raise its head for once—can disclaim nothing. It seeks to unify expression and construction; the shock of the chaotic and the ecstasy of sound; autobiographical secrets and objective architecture. Its boundless, hopeless longing for happiness takes musical form in an enigmatic yearning for security: his music seeks to secure itself by doing justice to every criterion, even the most contradictory. He even read with interest the reviews of old Korngold, about whom he was well informed, and said, with the friendliness of a cannibal, that they always gave him a good idea of how it had been.[20] He might have celebrated his personal triumph with a work in which both his nearest friends and old Korngold could have delighted. Such cunning is itself chaotic and mythological; thus did Polyphemus wall in the cave.[21] Certainly, and happily, he did not achieve the security of his work, old Korngold will take no pleasure in anything he wrote, the realm of private relationships will remain private; but as something private, the index of the most objective; astrology will reveal less about the stars, but all the more about Berg's prehistoric being. But much more important than the question of whether in fact his music unifies what he thought to unify is this: which features the mythological cunning engraved into the security of the work itself; what it means for the work that he manipulated the twelve-tone technique until, as it were, one took no notice of it; how even the demands of the nineteenth century were overcome through the dedicated insistence with which Berg held fast to them, holding on to the unbreakable even after the break: Polyphemus as his own Odysseus.

Faithfulness is the ancient companion of cunning; in Berg's nature the two were combined. As a farewell before a long separation, he once sent me a postcard with Alberich's dream-call to Hagen: "Be faithful!"[22] He kept faith like no other; faithful even when he experienced the deepest alienation—and where must he not have known alienation? His renunciation acquired its strength in faithfulness, as did his work; for who would have been more subject to seduction than faithfulness? Ultimately it is faithfulness that led him through and over the prehistoric world into the reconciled light of return; the stony gentleness of the giant transforms itself into that of the apostle, and the powerfully bent figure bears not just the burden of its work and of the ancient past, but bows most deeply under the seed of that which is to come. As his fame took him to Berlin, he reeled through the streets, as though they were too narrow for him; even Vienna seemed to him later like a "sea of stone." Nevertheless he was at home between the rocks and dived under, as into the darkness of birth. Like him, like one who entered the cavern of the subway as if he would have liked to lose himself in the bowels of the earth. But he had grown familiar with it: for, summoning his technique, he rescued from off the gleaming tracks, in front of the roaring train, the living body of a man.[23]

Hektor Rottweiler

A Fresh Justification

When I brought out the first issue of this music journal exactly four years ago, it led off with a "Justification," a special programmatic claim that sought to motivate the existence of the journal; "*We want to rectify!*" as it said then:

"To set right all that happens in the wide circle of the arts and the business of music that is askew, false, malicious, demeaning... We believe that a successful, fruitful, worthwhile criticism and struggle against the pernicious evils of Viennese artistic life can succeed, even from an independent standpoint—above all by means of satire and polemic.

"In our fragmented, standard-less times, the artist has to shoulder a doubly difficult responsibility, for he must give account of the artistic legacy of the past entrusted to him as well as that of the present, and be a signpost to the future as well. But a portion of this responsibility is also assigned to those in whose care artistic achievements and their evaluation is confided—for they have the task of supplying the broad mass of customers with art, and they ought not to suppress or conceal what appears, in this connection, to be necessary and worth knowing.

"Day by day we see that this task is not fulfilled, that official or pretended functions are repeatedly misused. Here we will create change; bring out what was concealed; proclaim new directions; rectify. For this reason we have selected as our leitmotif the rectification paragraphs of the Austrian press law."[24]

With these sentences an aggressive attitude was struck from the very beginning, one directed determinedly toward several of the most important representatives of the Viennese musical press, one that sought to combat them with the announced means. Whether the results aimed for corresponded to the initial expenditure of energy, I am not in a position to judge; but in any case the polemics we engaged in were always justified by the matters they concerned, and legitimized by the absolute independence of the journal and its editor.

Because after January 1934 it was necessary for me to extend my activity as a publicist to Viennese newspapers as well, I accepted that, given the resulting personal connection with Viennese journalism, I should from that moment on (no. 14), avoid even an appearance of conflict by refraining from every polemic in the area of musical journalism, and dealing in the journal only with questions of music and musical politics in which my independence remained beyond all doubt.

As a principal task of the journal I always regarded the advocacy of matters concerning "New Music," realized above all, it seems to me, in the works of Arnold Schoenberg, Anton Webern, Alban Berg, and Ernst Krenek, in such a way that demonstrated not only the significance of those works in light of the present day, but also their connection with the structural principles of the masters of the past and their organic evolution from the basis of tradition. While the journal always remained as precise as possible in its pleadings, from the other side we received only blanket denunciations or had to hear such catchphrases as "cultural Bolshevism," "cacophony," "uprooted internationalism," etc. When this campaign in Austria led ultimately to an open ostracism of a series of significant artists who were excluded from almost all larger performances and otherwise obviously ignored at every opportunity, I considered it my duty to contribute to ending this unworthy state of affairs, especially since it was made plain to me from different sides that the existence and activity of *23* was considered responsible for the intensification of the contrasting views. I sought above all to bring about personal discussions, so that at least we might get information verbally about what concrete, factual objections to the "New Music" were being actually raised. In the course of these efforts I sent the following letter to Privy Councilor Hofrat Professor Dr. Joseph *Marx*:[25]

Vienna, 1 October 1935

Most honored Councilor!

With this letter I permit myself to make the most respectful request of you, that we might, at some near time, confer personally. Although I would have been able to arrange a meeting through the intervention of well-meaning friends, I have preferred to write to you directly, for I have the feeling that the method of direct address will seem more appropriate to you also.

In the conference which I desire I would like to attempt, first of all, to establish more nearly the position which my little journal *23* assumed approximately two years ago respecting your function at the *Neues Wiener Journal*. I believe that in this connection some explanations on my part will be sufficient to dispose of disagreements that, because of unnecessary generalizations, seem to have created regrettable differences between individual groups of Austrian musicians.

I have always given proper respect to the artistic conceptions contained in their musical creations, even when they were different from my own (which indeed belong to quite another category, as the views of one who is himself not a creative musician). In this matter I allow myself to hope that a personal conference with you will result in broad-ranging instruction.

In order to make possible for you an effortless reply, I request that you, most honored Councilor, inform me of your response to my letter, as well as the possible time and place of the requested conference, on the enclosed card.

Most respectfully
Your most obedient
Willi Reich.

Men who obtained, in a way unknown to me, a knowledge of the text of this letter, have described its tone as "undignified." I myself cannot see this, for I chose the tone in order to make it clear to the addressee that nothing remained further from my mind than to overlook his social and official prominence, whereby I, for the sake of the matter, felt it better to risk too much than too little. For that reason I believe that the letter deserved an answer, surely not the attribute "undignified," but up to now, such has not been received. This studied silence I can only regard as the intention to put aside every discussion of the practical bases of the antagonisms involved and to persist in the domain of comfortable general negativity.

With the letter given here a series of attempts has reached its end, attempts that would not have been undertaken had I not considered it necessary to impose a certain limitation on the aggressive methods of the journal for the reasons already referred to, and had they not been repeatedly suggested to me by well-meaning friends. I believe that the sacrifice of the appearance of ambiguity, which I thereby took upon myself, is sufficient to show proof of the futility of such attempts at "communication."

That sacrifice will be taken to heart as a lesson and a warning: now, more than ever, the journal will be devoted to those tasks concerned with exploring the process of compositional creation, with the problems of music criticism, with the social functions of music, tasks that represent the only area about which a factually-based "discussion" is still possible today. To advance these tasks toward a solution seems to us more "dignified" and more worth striving for than defending New Music against accusations that lack, among its attackers, any factual basis.

Willi Reich

[Inside Back Cover]
Several castings are expected to be available for purchase of the Alban Berg death mask taken by Anna Mahler and reproduced in this issue. The proceeds will be devoted to a charitable purpose. Inquiries from those interested will be accepted by the editors of the journal.

NOTES

1. *Erwartung*, op. 17 (1909), is a monodrama (an opera for a single singer) by Arnold Schoenberg, on a libretto by Marie Pappenheim.
2. Schoenberg's *Harmonielehre*, first published in 1911, begins with the sentence "I have learned this book from my students." Alban Berg prepared the index. The third edition (1922) is published in English as *Theory of Harmony*, trans. Roy E. Carter (Berkeley and Los Angeles: University of California Press, 1978).
3. Ravel's ballet, choreographed by Michel Fokine, was first performed in Paris in 1912 by Diaghilev's Ballets Russes; it is the composer's largest and longest orchestral score.
4. The German-Swiss naturalist playwright Frank Wedekind (1864–1918) enjoyed enormous popularity in the intellectual circles frequented by Berg.
5. Wedekind's five-act play, *Marquis of Keith*, was first published in 1901.
6. Wedekind was a noted cabaret singer. Berg made use of the melody of one of his lute songs, no. 10 of a collection of *Lautenlieder*, published posthumously in 1920.
7. Manon Gropius, the nineteen-year-old daughter of Alma Mahler and Walter Gropius, died in the spring of 1935 of poliomyelitis.
8. From Bach's Cantata no. 60, "O Ewigkeit, du Donnerwort"; melody by Johann Rudolf Ahle, 1682. The four notes of the opening phrase of the chorale form three upward whole steps, coinciding with the last four notes of Berg's twelve-tone series in the Violin Concerto.
9. Altenberg (1859–1919) was a Viennese eccentric, a friend of Berg and his wife, a poet and essayist known familiarly as the "Socrates of the Coffeehouse"; his real name was Richard Engländer. He was fond of writing short free-verse texts on picture postcards; five of these were used by Berg in his *Five Orchestral Songs on Picture Postcard Texts of Peter Altenberg*, op. 4 (1912).
10. The Czech-Viennese architect, Adolf Loos (1870–1933), was a pioneer in anti-ornamental styles in architecture.
11. Karl Kraus was a Viennese satirist, playwright, and polemicist (1874–1936) who founded, edited, and largely wrote the journal *Die Fackel* (The torch).
12. *Die glückliche Hand*, op. 18, is an expressionistic opera by Schoenberg composed between 1910 and 1913, to his own libretto.
13. Berg's String Quartet, op. 3 (1910) is dedicated to his wife, Helene. The Three Pieces for Orchestra, op. 6, were written in 1914 and 1915. Berg arranged this complicated work for two pianos, eight hands.
14. Berg's article, "Die musikalische Impotenz der 'neuen Aesthetik' Hans Pfitzners," was first published in *Musikblätter des Anbruch* in 1920 and widely reprinted since, including in English in Willi Reich's *Alban Berg* (London: Thames and Hudson; New York: Harcourt, Brace & World,1965), 205–18. In 1920 Pfitzner (1869–1949), German conductor and composer of operas (*Die Rose vom Liebesgarten*, 1900; *Palestrina*, 1915) and concert music, had published a polemic pamphlet, *Die neue Ästhetik der musikalischen Impotenz*, against the German critic Paul Bekker, with incidental attacks on the composers of the Schoenberg circle; Berg's article is a vigorous rejoinder concerning Pfitzner's notions of inspiration.
15. The amoeboid lettering style on the covers of Berg's Piano Sonata, op. 1, and the Four Songs, op. 2, was drawn free-form by Berg himself, and was later called "Brezel-Schrift" (pretzel writing). The same kind of lettering was used on the door nameplate of his apartment at Trauttmansdorffgasse 27, and in sheet copper on the wooden cross over his grave in the Hietzinger Friedhof.
16. Georg Büchner (1813–1837) was a German playwright and physician, author of *Woyzeck*, from which Berg adapted his libretto. Matthias Claudius (1740–1815) was a German journalist and poet; one of his most famous texts, "Der Tod und das Mädchen,"

was set by Schubert. Leopold Friedrich Günther Goeckingk (1748–1828) was a German poet and epigrammatist. *Die Büchse der Pandora (Pandora's Box)* was the second (1904) of the two Lulu plays by Frank Wedekind; the first was *Erdgeist (Earth Spirit*, 1895). Both were adapted by Berg for his *Lulu* libretto.

17. "Warm die Lüfte," the last of Berg's Four Songs, op. 2, set to poems from *Der Glühende* by Alfred Mombert (1872–1942), marks the composer's first step into near-total atonality. Following the first publication of the songs, this one was reprinted, along with songs by Schoenberg and Webern, in *Der blaue Reiter*, an almanac edited by Wassily Kandinsky and Franz Marc (1912); English edition, in *The Documents of 20th-Century Art: The Blaue Reiter Almanac* (New York: Viking Press, 1975).

18. In the original: *johanneische*. This probably refers to the Gospel According to St. John, regarded among biblical scholars as the most gentle of the four Gospels.

19. In the original: "Denn er hat die chaotische Substanz nicht 'geformt' sondern überlistet; sie, den Grund der Hoffnungslosigkeit, die seine List war."

20. Julius Korngold (1860–1945), influential and very conservative Viennese music critic, father of prodigy composer Erich Wolfgang Korngold (1897–1957).

21. In the Homeric epic, Odysseus is imprisoned in a cave by Polyphemus, a one-eyed Cyclops.

22. *Götterdämmerung*, Act 2, sc. 1.

23. In Berlin in December 1925 for the premiere of *Wozzeck*, Berg happened to be on the subway platform at the moment when a man fell onto the tracks; Berg pulled him to safety.

24. *23: Eine Wiener Musikzeitschrift* 1 (January 1932): 2.

25. The Austrian composer Joseph Marx (1882–1964) was a noted composition teacher and a critic for the Viennese daily *Neues Wiener Journal*.

Alban Berg and the Memory of Modernism

LEON BOTSTEIN

Beyond Schoenberg's Shadow

Few modernist composers have been as posthumously privileged as Alban Berg. His music continues to find a substantial audience worldwide. His work and life have been subject to exhaustive, sympathetic scrutiny.[1] *Wozzeck*'s exceptional success after its 1925 premiere led to widespread anticipation of a completed *Lulu*, spurred somewhat by its "trailer," the Symphonic Pieces from *Lulu*. Despite restrictions on performances of his music after the Nazi seizure of power and hesitancy among many musicians to perform modernist works, Berg's untimely death in December 1935 was an international event. Where his mentor Schoenberg had only achieved notoriety, Berg had become a celebrity. "Atonality still has its prophet," observed Oscar Thompson in *Musical America* in January 1936, three weeks after Berg's death, but "it has lost its pilot." Berg wrote music that "transcends any work of Schoenberg's."[2]

The echoes of Thompson's view that Berg's death left "an unresolved dissonance" remain with us. To many critics in the late 1930s, it appeared that *Wozzeck* would end up as an exception—a modernist work that held the stage more than any other, but succeeded because, brilliantly appropriate to the "almost sadistic inhumanity" of Georg Büchner's text, it magically fit the era in which it was composed. Or was *Wozzeck* a harbinger of a new modernist musical future? Had Berg completed *Lulu*, would it have gained as enthusiastic a response in the more conservative late 1930s? The opportunity to answer that question never came. Although *Lulu* enjoyed frequent productions in its incomplete two-act version, it began to rival *Wozzeck* in popularity only after its 1979 Paris premiere under Pierre Boulez as a completed three-act opera. At the same time, a striking number of Berg's works, notably the Violin Concerto, entered the standard repertory. The "late" Berg—if one can use this category in the case of a composer with a very limited output—has become as frequently heard as *Wozzeck*, the Piano Sonata, and the String Quartet.

Berg's unique place as a modernist embraced by traditional concert audiences has repeatedly attracted notice; comparable acceptance and attachment has eluded Schoenberg and Webern (despite his enormous influence in the 1950s and early 1960s), not to speak of others in the first and second generation of the so-called Second Viennese School.[3] Berg's synthesis of atonal and tonal procedures, his adherence to gestures of Romanticism, and his capacity to integrate classical forms (such as sonata and variation) with programmatic narratives—a skill often associated with the tone poems of Richard Strauss, toward whose music Berg maintained an ambivalent respect—have been adduced as reasons for his popularity.[4] In larger works, both with and without a text—*Wozzeck*, the *Lyric Suite*, the Chamber Concerto, and the Violin Concerto—Berg perfected a subtle interplay and tension between the sequential logic of rigorous small-scale musical forms and extramusical content. The allure of that interplay has only been heightened by the character and frequency of hidden and secret programs that require decoding.[5]

But are the programmatic aspects decisive? Berg's modernism, though rooted in disciplined formal procedures, seems unique in its capacity to achieve an ethical goal dear to Schoenberg and his pupils: the expression, not of mere sentiment but of an authentic, artistic truth about language and life. Using novel methods of pitch aggregation, rhythmic development, fragmentation, contradiction between text and musical form, irony, parody, discontinuity, the grotesque, and an intricate hidden interior of compositional techniques often reliant on tonal expectations, Berg rendered modernism humane. As such, it could be embraced by both the connoisseur and the rank amateur—*Kenner und Liebhaber*—the indispensable audience for concert music and opera.

Key to Berg's success was his choice of the unlikely form of opera as his principal field of endeavor. Opera occupied a central but contradictory place in Vienna and the history of modernism. Insofar as Wagner gave modernism its initial impetus, innovations in musical language, form, expressive rhetoric, and procedures were all tied to opera. But in the generation after Wagner's synthesis of words and music, opera became a problematic arena. Mahler never succeeded at writing one. Despite his reputation as an opera conductor and pioneer in the redefinition of operatic experiences, including stage design, he derided the requirements of the theater. On the one hand opera represented the most popular medium of musical high art, whose cultural significance declined only after the advent of the sound film. On the other, its hybrid nature and the compromising realities of the theater rendered the opera resistant to the achievement of categorical formal aesthetic ideals through music. The opera house and its audience seemed to demand stylistic compromises on behalf of facile comprehensibility.

For Mahler and Schoenberg, the requirements of modernity in musical art permitted no such concessions. Richard Strauss, for whom opera became the key genre in maturity, represented the cynical exploitation of conventional taste and the loss of artistic ideals. Once a figure of admiration, a talent who had been more than an epigone of Wagnerism, Strauss became viewed, after *Der Rosenkavalier* (1911), as a prisoner to the glibly theatrical, a purveyor of sentimentality to philistine audiences, a composer who craved commercial success in the theater.[6] Wasn't opera a mongrel form (to which, for example, Brahms had no evident commitment)? The modernists around Schoenberg took special aim not only at Strauss but at others who in their view had made presumed sacrifices to artistic integrity in their quest to succeed within the operatic medium: the young Viennese prodigy Erich Wolfgang Korngold, for example, and Franz Schreker and Alexander Zemlinsky (not to speak of Puccini). For Schoenberg, trying to locate "authentic" and "true" musical procedures, such as developing variation in an opera, was at best a daunting ambition.

There were minor exceptions, modern operas that merited praise, such as Paul Dukas's *Ariane et Barbe-Bleu* (1907).[7] The two significant opera composers in the first quarter of the twentieth century, however, turned out to be Leoš Janáček and Berg. Of the two, only Berg succeeded in reconciling a wide audience to radical modernist formal ideals. Berg's achievement was even more notable precisely because it occurred in a genre that remained central to Vienna as a bastion of conservative values. From the 1870s until 1938, and particularly at the fin de siècle when the city witnessed the birth of musical modernism, the repertoire and standards of performance at the opera defined the musical politics of Vienna, as the never-ending controversies surrounding it suggest.[8]

Like Wagner's achievement in opera, Berg's can be located in the interior logic of his music. The music is defined by structures ranging from variation to palindromes inaudible except to the most refined and tutored listener. Yet, like Wagner, Berg tightly structures his musical narrative to communicate confidence and not fear. Using contours associated with tonality, albeit in fragments, Berg manages to allay the suspicion of the arbitrary —the sense among listeners that modernist composers are merely playing with them.[9] The critical reaction against modernism was grounded in the belief that, absent tonality, musical events created by modernists were spiteful and random, part of a rebellious conspiracy to undermine order and beauty. Rigorously if not obsessively using small and larger formal structures that demanded a complete, consequential control of pitch and rhythm far more exacting than would be required in conventional tonality, and justifying these through action and words, Berg communicated meaning that circumvented an audience's fear of being taken in by a confidence game.

The appeal of Berg's music has only grown since 1936. When Berg's logical rigor is combined with a lush Mahlerian sound world in operas with riveting narratives about the human condition, the audience, by attaching itself to the narrative text, finds a way to absorb and accept the radical modernism of the music. Berg's gifts as a dramatic composer led him, like Beethoven, to write music that could be understood as having a programmatic dimension, either explicit or implied. The overt meaning of text and action and the hidden programs of the instrumental works continue to frame the perception of the music. In Berg's music the program, by providing a means of justification, puts the listener at ease, the formal rigor of the underlying structure notwithstanding. It persuades through its extramusical intent that Berg's musical choices were specific and necessary to achieve the requisite intense emotion, transmit a particular narrative, and suggest or conceal a confession.

As for scholarly interest, Berg's place in history seems to be expanding, not contracting. Initial contributions to the now massive Berg literature came from witnesses, contemporaries, and pupils—Theodor W. Adorno foremost among them.[10] Helene Berg's long life as a professional and protective widow (she died in 1976) sustained the image of the composer as a blissfully married, gentle and fragile saint. Apart from Adorno's mix of analysis, memoir, and commentary on biography and history, the overwhelming bias in the Berg literature until the late 1980s reveals a single-minded fascination with compositional technique.[11]

Composers between 1945 and 1975 were struggling to find an effective voice for modern music that matched post–World War II modernity. They explored the possibilities inherent in Schoenberg's move in the early 1920s to composition using assemblages of pitches (in his case, twelve-tone rows), as unifying and defining constituents of a work, including combinatorial principles for the manipulation of such rows. With respect to Berg, the priority was to unlock the secrets of how he used tone rows, thematic cells, and other forms of aggregating pitches (and to a lesser extent rhythmic patterning) in a systematic manner within traditional larger compositional forms. Berg circumvented tonality and embraced atonality, but still seemed to remain comprehensible from the vantage point of tonal analysis. Scholars took Berg apart, note by note, to uncover how he managed to be thoroughly modern and yet communicate to the layman drama and emotion as effectively as Puccini and Janáček.[12]

A new phase in Berg reception history began in earnest in the late 1980s and early 1990s. Interest shifted from the intricacies of compositional method to history. Modernism was in retreat. Tonality and rhythmic simplicity and regularity had made a comeback. Understanding Berg's compositional process and method became far less relevant. More than half a century after his death, Berg came to be seen in the context of a sustained Mahler revival and the embrace of neoromanticism and minimalism. He took on the aspect less of prophecy than of history. If Berg was an exception, it was because he was not the starting point of the future, but an idiosyncratic appendage on a glorious past that ended with Mahler.

The late twentieth-century retreat from modernism in music coincided with the unexpected but consonant explosion of scholarly and public interest in the culture and politics of fin-de-siècle Vienna. Gustav Klimt, Oskar Kokoschka, Egon Schiele, Arthur Schnitzler, Adolf Loos, Robert Musil, Otto Wagner, and Karl Kraus became better known in the English-speaking world, filling out the picture of a modernism once defined not only by French, Russian, and English luminaries but, on the Viennese side, primarily by Mahler, Schoenberg, Freud, and Wittgenstein.

This more recent historically focused research and criticism about Berg not only brought up important questions about his extramarital love life, but also the issue of Berg's (and his wife's) attitude to Jews and the Jewish question. As is well known, Jews made up a significant if not dominant part of Vienna's fin-de-siècle cultural elite, which included students, listeners, artists, publishers, managers, and patrons. The Jews in Vienna varied widely, ranging from converts identified as Jews merely by heritage to those who were formally members of the community, the *Kultusgemeinde*. Each group had its own complex linguistic and cultural markers of acculturation.

Although Berg's correspondence with his wife, Helene, reveals his easy offhand use of anti-Semitic stereotypes and the occasional expression of prejudices, his anti-Semitism, such as it was, was entirely common to the Viennese. Helene was perhaps less innocent, as Soma Morgenstern hints in the memoir of his friendship with Berg, but again the issue does not go beyond the realization that neither could have easily become immune from the sentiments that were truly pervasive in the world in which they lived. As a lifelong reader of *Die Fackel*, Berg's devotion and allegiance to Karl Kraus only helped make him more comfortable with the kind of sharp and sardonic repertoire of anti-Semitic sensibilities that no one was more adept at expressing than Kraus. Morgenstern understood this, which explains why the two friends differed on the subject of Kraus.[13]

There is no evidence that Berg's anti-Semitism was anything but benign. Yet he willingly went to considerable trouble to prove, his music and link to Schoenberg notwithstanding, that he was unquestionably Aryan—and this even before it was required by the Nazi authorities in Germany to do so. Furthermore, his dedication to the superiority of the German musical tradition (a conviction he shared with Schoenberg) led him to hope to the end that *Lulu* would have its premiere in post-1933 Germany. He sought not solidarity with, but sympathetic distance from the plight of his Jewish friends and colleagues. He went to the extent of conspiring with Paul Hindemith (naïvely) on how he might take over the master class at the Prussian Academy of the Arts in Berlin from which Schoenberg had been dismissed.[14] Morgenstern wished his friend Berg had shown more backbone and courage, or even common sense of the sort exhibited by Erich Kleiber and Ernst Krenek, two non-Jews who realized that despite their Aryan status, there was little point in trying to do business with the Nazis. The Nazis had no use for Berg's music—and not just because they confused him with Armin Berg, a Jewish composer of cabaret music, a confusion at which Berg poked fun even on his deathbed.[15]

Berg should have realized that his aesthetic commitments made him anathema. The conservative colleagues who ultimately benefited after the 1938 Anschluss—Franz Schmidt and Joseph Marx—were those for whom Berg felt little but contempt. During the war Helene, out of loyalty to her husband's memory, refused to curry favor with the Nazi leadership in Vienna just to get Berg's music performed, even though one such leader, the Gauleiter Baldur von Schirach, was himself a music lover. Nonetheless, Berg's relation to the Jewish question lingered in the mind of Schoenberg. It played a role in Schoenberg's refusal to take on the task of completing the orchestration of Act 3 of *Lulu*. No doubt the Nazis both frightened and horrified Berg. No proverbial moral stone need be cast. But at the same time Berg's willingness to accommodate, though plainly human and ordinary, should dampen enthusiasm for a strain in the literature encouraged by Helene to construct a posthumous halo on his character.[16] Berg was neither a saint nor a hero.[17]

Within the history of Berg scholarship after Helene Berg's death, the first among equals was George Perle. Here was a scholar-composer who through his own search for an effective modern musical vocabulary was attracted to Berg's coherent, rigorous but idiosyncratic approach to composition that both emancipated composers from traditional tonal procedures and yet extended the expressive and communicative potential of music using modern methods. There are few parallels to the close, eloquent, and nearly exhaustive account of Berg's music and career contained in Perle's two volumes on *Wozzeck* and *Lulu*, completed in the 1980s. Together with his discovery of the secret program to the *Lyric Suite*, his critique of the postwar approach to the first two acts of *Lulu*, and his support for the completion of Act 3, Perle's written legacy is an astonishing achievement. In close temporal proximity are the substantial and influential writings of the English scholar Douglas Jarman.[18]

On the historical side of Berg research, the publication of Morgenstern's memoir and letters to Berg, and Suzanne Rode's monograph on Karl

Kraus's influence deepened the understanding of the composer as mirroring a bygone era and a specific place: Vienna.[19] Suddenly this successful disciple of Schoenberg was seen in a quite provincial context. Alongside Schoenberg's cosmopolitan and international modernism, Berg's career and character seemed reminiscent of Schubert's—tied to a city and its outskirts (Hietzing) and, residually, the Austrian landscape. Morgenstern included in the subtitle of his account of his friendship with the composer mention of Berg's "idols." Those so described were two writers (Kraus, Peter Altenberg), one architect (and writer, Adolf Loos), and two composers (Mahler and Schoenberg). All five were residents of Vienna and closely connected to its cultural politics.

Perhaps the most important effect of Morgenstern's memoir was to further distance Berg's achievement from the seemingly overpowering presence of Arnold Schoenberg. Even before he met Schoenberg in 1904, Berg was steeped in the intellectual and artistic life of Vienna and had already allied himself with Altenberg, Kraus, and Loos.[20] But his musical training was rudimentary. The impact of Schoenberg's teaching was transformative: he acquired the craft of composition. Berg never lost his sense of indebtedness and obligation. But he struggled valiantly to maintain his independence of mind without putting his good relations with Schoenberg at risk. This was no small task, given that Schoenberg was at various points abusive, discouraging, overbearing, condescending, envious, suspicious, and cruel.[21] Berg paid a heavy price for staying on Schoenberg's good side—particularly given the endless errands and tasks Berg undertook on his teacher's behalf.

Berg defended himself by skirting every opportunity Schoenberg gave to quarrel. He controlled as best he could the contact he maintained with his teacher after his initial years as a student. Webern was not nearly so adept.[22] Without wavering in his loyalty and admiration, particularly his gratitude for the inspiring tutelage and example Schoenberg provided, Berg was quite shrewd. He balanced flattery, generosity, and attention with distance. It was not hard for him, since he admired the music. Berg, who managed to juggle several lovers in the context of an idealized love relationship with his wife, achieved a comparable result with his mentor. He persuaded Schoenberg of his loyalty without limiting his own behavior.[23] Berg knew that in order to complete *Wozzeck* he had to keep his distance. He saw through Schoenberg enough to discern his master's vanity and the discomfort with his own pupil's success.

Berg's originality and accomplishment using modernist strategies owe to influences that precede, stand apart from, and transcend Schoenberg's influence and example. Much attention has been given Berg's literary passions, some shared with Schoenberg (Strindberg and Balzac) and some not

(Peter Rosegger, Hermann Broch, Kafka, and Altenberg).[24] But the most important contrast—beyond significant differences in social status between the two men—was Berg's simple and perhaps old-fashioned belief about himself, his credo. Berg liked to repeat that only three things really mattered—love, nature, and music. Certainly he was born into and part of a local Viennese and Austrian world in a way Schoenberg was not, on account of Schoenberg's Jewish origins and his family's relatively recent arrival in Vienna. Berg married up, though he did not need to. Helene (née Nahowski) was none other than the beautiful and gifted illegitimate daughter of Emperor Franz Joseph, product of a liaison that predated the legendary Katherina Schratt.[25] Berg's immediate environment from birth to death was familiar and reassuring—periodic economic uncertainties notwithstanding. Nahowski family controversies surrounding a potential musical career, and civic debates regarding the value and purpose of art were mundane and pragmatic, involving income, social standing, opportunity, and respectability.[26]

For Schoenberg, more was at stake in his calling as a composer and the aesthetic controversies of the era because the vocation of the artist held more promise. Art could transcend the material, the mundane, the personal, and the subjective. It was an instrument of ideas and social legitimacy, not mere expressiveness. For a Jew in Vienna, status as an artist, particularly as a musician, represented a unique and rapid route to membership in society, which brought with it security, recognition, and social acceptance that were otherwise impossible. These were all Berg's by birthright. Berg associated his ambitions in music with the personal and the intimate—not the political—and therefore with love and nature, the latter defined primarily by the accessible Austrian landscape.

Berg had not been a particularly stellar student in secondary school. Nonetheless he possessed the ambition to be well read and educated. Like many others he kept a daybook. Berg titled it "Von der Selbsterkenntnis" (On self-knowledge), and eventually filled twelve notebooks.[27] Berg carefully transcribed hundreds of quotations taken from books and anthologies on subjects he cared about and, in many cases, from his systematic reading of Karl Kraus's *Die Fackel*. A few of the entries were aphorisms he wrote himself. During the early years of his studies with Schoenberg, Berg wrote: "For most of mankind, music moves through the legs; in not so many through the hands and arms; even fewer is the number where music goes through the mouth, and fewest of all are those where it moves through the head—but it reaches all humankind through the heart."[28] No such naïve and romantic notion motivated Berg's teacher. Despite the searing drama surrounding the affair Schoenberg's wife had with the painter Richard Gerstl, or the overt subject matter of Schoenberg's orchestral tone poem *Pelleas und Melisande*, or the psychic intensity of the monodrama *Erwartung*, at the center of Schoenberg's artistic project was neither love nor nature, but grandiose ambitions and ideas about the aesthetic and its relationship to truth.[29]

The difference between teacher and pupil, despite enormous overlaps in beliefs and attitudes, can be seen through their contrasting assessments of Mahler. For all his efforts to hide them, Schoenberg retained misgivings about Mahler the composer, although not Mahler the man or artist of principle.[30] Berg had no such reservations. He maintained a lifelong veneration not only for Mahler's music but for the impact it had on its listeners (including himself, Helene, and their friends, particularly Webern). For Berg, Mahler was all about love and nature—and therefore, as for all post-Wagnerians, also life and death. Succeeding as a composer meant following in Mahler's footsteps, not Schoenberg's, as Douglas Jarman astutely observed when commenting on Berg's drift away from short-form works and miniatures during the 1920s.[31]

The key to Berg's success, in his lifetime and after, lies in the composer's tacit yet explicit effort to continue where Mahler left off. Both composers died early, Mahler at age fifty, Berg at fifty-one. Both left unfinished work. Both were tied to Vienna. Both left widows who used to their advantage their status as widows of legendary artists. These coincidences would have attracted a man as superstitious as Berg. But far more relevant is Berg's self-definition as a composer. His views on the power and purpose of music as expressive of nature and love led him, particularly after World War I, to take on the scale and ambition explicit in the late Mahler. Berg's conception of music—though not its particular means—was rooted in Mahler.

In his polemic against the philosophical arguments of the anti-modernist composer Hans Pfitzner, Berg was intent on demystifying the sources and criteria of aesthetic claims. There was no conflict, maintained Berg, between the expressive and emotional on the one hand and the formal, normative logic of musical values on the other. The attempt to appropriate the power of music for pseudo-spiritual special pleading on behalf of beauty and inspiration by arch-conservatives denied Mahler his achievement: the unique synthesis of logical argument and emotional authenticity. Musical values, including beauty and "matters of feeling," or musical potency, were matters of truth about nature and love, and therefore subject to explanation and analysis. Mahler, not Pfitzner, represented the synthesis of logic and emotion, the highest achievement in both the confessional and discursive use of music to tell the truth.[32] For Berg, Schoenberg's music could be considered great because it evoked Mahler (*Gurrelieder*). The heritage of modernism could be traced to Mahler's expressive power and not, as Schoenberg would assert in 1933, to Brahms's compositional logic.[33] Berg's ambition would be to sustain, through modernism, the Mahlerian ethos. The audience he cared most about had once been Mahler's. It included firsthand witnesses of Mahler within his close-knit Viennese world, Alma Mahler first and foremost among them.

Feminine Paradoxes: Alma Mahler and Alban Berg

Attempts to understand Berg as history, not as a prophet or model of normative compositional practice, have helped detach him and his achievement from too close a dependency on Schoenberg and his immediate circle. The resemblance between the impetus and character of Berg's music and Mahler's was not lost on contemporaries. Morgenstern correctly surmised that Mahler had been the composer who most influenced Berg, since for both composers love and nature were indispensable constituent components of the function of music. But there was also a personal link and constant reminder of Mahler's significance: Alma. She kept the flame of Mahler veneration alive within a social circle that included Alban and Helene.

Berg's aesthetic convictions, including his sense of what music ought to be, preceded his first lesson with Schoenberg. Berg's notions of value and truth, and his concept of language and the human character derived less from school than from contemporaries, family, and his own exploration through reading.[34] At the center of intellectual and aesthetic discourse at the turn of the century for all aspiring male artists of his generation in Vienna was an obsessive engagement with the paradoxes of the feminine character.[35] Gustav Mahler epitomized the aesthetic and psychological consequences of the engagement with the seemingly tortuous symbiosis between male and female not only in his music but through his marriage to Alma. She represented the overwhelming connection between sexuality and art, between the erotic and the aesthetic. Alma Mahler, not Helene Berg or later Hanna Fuchs, became for Berg the dominant representative of the feminine paradox. In Vienna, Berg was hardly alone in coming to the conclusion that Alma epitomized the allure and danger of the female. Keenly aware of her seductive powers Alma used her talent and beauty to defend her sense of self. She conquered and dominated the greatest male artists, who pursued her in the hope of defining, dominating, and possessing her. For Alban, this lent her a unique aura.

There was never even a hint of intimacy between Alma Mahler and Alban Berg. Nonetheless her role in his life and career as symbol and friend was pivotal.[36] For one thing, Berg's lover Hanna Fuchs, Franz Werfel's sister, was quasi-related to Alma, who in 1929 finally married Werfel, with whom she had been intimate for years, making Hanna in the end Alma's sister-in-law.³⁷ Alma acted as a go-between, a relationship that lent Berg, psychologically, a quasi-family status vis-à-vis Alma. For Berg, Alma was also a figure of intense admiration, some fear, and critical fascination, though not desire or adoration. Berg's deep attachment expressed itself in genuine devotion and gratitude. Alma believed in him. Alma felt more comfortable with Berg, a respectable non-Jewish Viennese artist, than with her last husband, the Jewish Werfel, much less her friend Schoenberg, with whom there were moments of real tension. Berg respected her judgment and sought no sexual favors from her. In her circle of artists, Berg was one of the few equals—an artist of real promise and a genuine Viennese who was not a Jew. Berg in turn understood and had sympathy for Alma, including her unstable relationship to Werfel, whom Berg could not entirely like or admire, either in terms of manner (especially Werfel's conceits about his own musicality) or his craft as a writer.³⁸

Though Berg's sentiments toward Alma remained filial, they came with a powerful residue of recognition of Alma's allure as a woman. Berg encouraged Helene to cultivate a close relationship to Alma. Ernst Krenek, briefly Alma's son-in-law, was among the first to see in Helene the role of an understudy to Alma in an idealized and essentially mythical construct sustained by both Helene and Alban of the Alma-Gustav relationship, in which Alma took on the indispensable role of muse.³⁹

Figure 1. Helene Berg, Alma Mahler Werfel, Franz Werfel, and Berg, c. 1930

These reasons support the following conjecture: Alma served as the incarnation of Berg's conception of Lulu, and therefore helped define the manner in which Berg edited and combined two Frank Wedekind plays, *Erdgeist* (1895; *Earth Spirit*) and *Die Büchse der Pandora* (1904; *Pandora's Box*), to produce *Lulu*. Berg was a keen observer of human nature. Perhaps, given his penchant for secret programs, he was inspired by the possibilities of fashioning a roman à clef from the Lulu plays, and Alma's life provided as good an opportunity as could be found. His ambition to link his art with life echoed a pattern he observed in Mahler, Schreker, and Zemlinsky, if not particularly in Schoenberg, and helped define the dramatic intent and arc of his longer-form works—not only the operas.

Viewing Berg's reconstruction of the Wedekind texts into the *Lulu* libretto as a roman à clef might take the following speculative form. Alwa, as many have noted, has aspects of Berg himself. Lulu, if modeled after Alma, also possesses hints of Helene. If Lulu is Alma, Schigolch can be seen as evocative of Zemlinsky, Alma's devoted former teacher and lover (who suffered his entire life from her rejection when Mahler appeared on the scene), and residually, in terms of style and manner, of Peter Altenberg, a lifelong admirer of Helene (as well as someone Berg respected).[40]

Dr. Schön, given his pretentious exterior and public prominence, not to speak of his tortured relationship with Lulu, might remind one if not of Mahler himself, then of Werfel and Walter Gropius, two of Alma's lovers and husbands with considerable public careers and prestige whose relationships with Alma were troubled and painful. Berg's double casting of Schön as Jack the Ripper further suggests Berg's own contempt for Werfel and the notion that Werfel, in a manner of speaking, was "killing" her. The Painter, who some have speculated can be connected to Richard Gerstl, who committed suicide after his relationship with Mathilde Zemlinsky Schoenberg ended, is perhaps most directly suggestive of Oskar Kokoschka, who painted Alma into some of his best work and whose representation of her in the painting *Windbraut* became world-famous. Kokoschka also burned a life-sized effigy of Alma after they parted. Countess Geschwitz connects to Berg's lesbian sister Smaragda and her lover Maria (May) Keller, particularly if one looks at the tense Alwa-Geschwitz relationship. One could then speculate that if Berg knew of the Pfitzner-Alma affair, the Prince was a Pfitzner stand-in. Gustav Mahler ends up being represented, symbolically and discreetly, with the speaking role of the Medizinalrat, someone who is literally undone by Lulu's infidelity.

The suggestion of parallels to autobiography and the symmetries between theater and life was already evident in the Wedekind plays, a fact not lost on Berg. In May 1905, when Kraus produced *Pandora's Box*, the character of Lulu could have been understood as evocative of Alma by

Figure 2. Alma Mahler, 1909.

some Viennese. Wedekind's Lulu is a sympathetic character, the incarnation of natural sexuality and charm who exhibits a childlike, narcissistic seductiveness. She is not intentionally cruel and manipulative. Her sexuality leads to madness and destruction among men, but only, as Kraus suggested, as a matter of self-assertion and defense.[41]

Pandora's Box is more naturalistic and less expressionist than *Lulu*.[42] Berg's adaptation of the two Wedekind plays, though retaining qualities of both, streamlined the argument by shifting the focus onto Lulu herself. Despite retaining Wedekind's prologue to *Earth Spirit*, which imagines Lulu as a dangerous snake, Berg's handling of the character distances her from the ethical responsibility for death by simplifying the link between arousal and violence. What remains in the foreground are the fantasies, ambitions, and power of men who see in Lulu a chance to use sexual conquest to cast a woman in their own image. From the moment of Lulu's entrance, her autonomous identity in Berg's version is sufficiently commanding to engender recognition within the listener that she will immediately resist the ambitions of the men around her. The pitch cells of her music, like Lulu herself, are transformed throughout the opera, providing a facet of audible character development absent in Wedekind's treatment.

The hypocrisy inherent in the treatment of women and sexuality, the denigration of the prostitute, and the moral rhetoric of conventional society were Wedekind's primary targets. Berg's ambition was rather to foreground Lulu the person and make her less passive. The music reveals her complexity. Wedekind noted that when he published the first version of his Lulu plays he was genuinely convinced "in his soul" that the play was in support of the "advancement of the highest human ethics."[43] At the core of this claim was his intent to challenge contemporary male conceits and the language of ethical judgment. Lulu has many names in both Wedekind's and Berg's versions because she resists in speech as well as action the male attempt to define her. In Wedekind's *Pandora's Box* Lulu presents the same, unselfconscious sexuality as in Berg's *Lulu*. But through the musical procedures of assigning specific pitch groupings to each character and carefully using leitmotifs, Berg expands and defines the character as a distinct personality. Her wide emotional range, from detachment to passion, is mirrored musically, bringing her closer to the image of Alma than Wedekind's character, who remains imprisoned in a stable archetype of natural female seductiveness.[44]

Furthermore, Countess Geschwitz possesses a function in Wedekind's play far greater than the contrapuntal role she was assigned by Berg. Geschwitz, Wedekind asserted, is the "tragic main figure" precisely because she is a lesbian, and defies the norm. She perceives the corruption of women by men from the outside, immune from susceptibility to men's desire or an erotic attraction to them, recognizing their egotism and feigned strength as well as their vulnerability to Lulu. She loves Lulu and takes on the cause of her protection.[45] Yet she, too, succumbs to the destructive power of the erotic cast in Lulu's female sexuality. In Wedekind, Geschwitz is suggestive of the self-annihilation that comes with the erotic, even when directed inward in the form of narcissism. The parallel Geschwitz offers in Wedekind helped direct his critique of social convention against the criminalization of homosexuality.[46]

Berg's adaptation dispenses with this larger role assigned to Geschwitz while retaining the purity of her devotion to Lulu. The contrast between the two women in Berg is weakened as Geschwitz takes on a subsidiary role.[47] Lulu, through music, becomes less naïve and less of an ingenue; she seems older and more sophisticated than Wedekind's character. In Berg's *Lulu*, a singular life takes center stage, relegating Wedekind's social commentary to the background (the parody of newspapers, the art market, and stock market bubbles notwithstanding).

Berg's choice of title circumvents the specific frame suggested by *Pandora's Box*. Whereas Lulu brings ruin and death, Wedekind treats ironically the biblical and Classical myths that argue that feminine sexuality, left untamed, is the root of evil, intentionally undercutting them. In Berg, there is no hint of Lulu as representative of evil or cruelty. As Carl Dahlhaus noted, the composer removed the passages in Lulu's exchange with Alwa that displayed the most vulgarity and coldness.[48] She has an allure that is recognizable through music. It cannot be suppressed. It resists, albeit not completely, the changes in her character and shape that men seek in order to achieve their own self-reflection.

The musical tension between thematic recognition and transformation parallels the attempts by the Painter, Schön, and Alwa to appropriate Lulu as the vehicle of their own self-realization. At her core, Lulu seeks freedom and love. Through music—Mahler's in real life and Berg's in the opera—Alma and Lulu are central tragic figures who are also the mediums through which art comes into being. Lulu, like Alma, once aspired to be an artist—an ambition Mahler explicitly stifled.[49] The Painter and Alwa succumb to Lulu and become inspired to make art precisely because of her aesthetic sensibilities, not merely as a consequence of her physicality and erotic power, just as Mahler was inspired by Alma, albeit with considerable pain and torment. Alma, like Lulu, willingly played the role of muse to her men, ambivalence and contempt notwithstanding.

This hypothesis of an Alma-Lulu equation takes into account that both Wedekind and Berg pursued a symbolic rather than naturalistic aesthetic in their work. By changing Wedekind's Schwartz—clearly a Jew—into a generic painter, Berg took Wedekind's symbolism further. Turned into a placeholder for the artist who confronts the feminine and her sexuality, the Painter could easily be understood to represent at least one of Alma's former lovers.[50] This surmise is strengthened when one observes that neither Kokoschka nor Gropius, both visual artists, were Jewish. Berg succeeded in replicating onstage the magnetism Alma projected within the circle he and Alma shared, without deviating from Wedekind too sharply.

Both Wedekind and Berg evince the profound ambivalence about feminine sexuality characteristic of early twentieth-century theorizing. At the root of that ambivalence is anxiety about the power of the erotic. Berg's *Lulu,* particularly, shows little inclination to challenge the terms of the debate regarding the superiority of the masculine as a creative spiritual force. Alma Mahler and Helene Berg were as accomplished as any female figures could be while serving primarily as the object of male erotic desire and idealization. Both fit the more complex incarnation of Lulu in Berg's opera. Yet neither Berg nor Mahler had use for claims on behalf of the equality of women. In 1906 Berg copied into his notebooks a quotation from Cesare Lombroso, the influential theorist of criminality and genius.[51] Lombroso argued against women in politics or women in the workforce, claiming that economic and political equality would fuel their aggressive drive and lead to criminality, pulling into the mire an already naturally weak "instinct for the sublime and moral character of women."[52]

The composer left two striking clues in the libretto and the music suggesting the Lulu-Alma parallel. One is well known: Berg turned the character of Alwa in Wedekind from writer to composer. The shift is ironic on several counts, one of them being to remind the audience of the Jewish popular composer named Armin Berg with whom Berg was often confused, much to his considerable dismay after 1933. Alwa, in the opera, composes for the popular theater (as Alwa does in Wedekind).[53] The operetta tradition was dear to Berg, who harbored no snobbery about well-crafted popular music, particularly operetta (Oscar Straus) or folk music. In *Wozzeck* Berg explicitly imitated the ubiquitous waltz (Act 2, m. 481) and prided himself for incorporating an accessible "folksy" character in the work without betraying modernism.[54] If Alwa evokes Alban, then Lulu inevitably takes on aspects of Helene. Alwa's anguish, particularly at the end of Act 2 and in Act 3, are reminiscent of Gustav Mahler's expression of desire, despair, and hopelessness regarding Alma that found its voice in the Sixth Symphony. Berg's use of Mahlerian rhythmic punctuation and repetition of patterns in Lulu support this supposition. Berg even quotes the opening of *Wozzeck* when, in Act 2 of *Lulu,* Alwa talks about writing an opera.

A second clue seems to have largely escaped notice. Berg was a composer of keen literary instincts, as his early songs and *Wozzeck* reveal. The deft arrangement and foregrounding of Büchner's play were inspired strokes of Berg's literary sensibility that shaped the groundwork for the music's capacity to deliver the long dramatic line.[55] The task of paring down Wedekind's texts to prepare a libretto was more extensive and less obvious.[56] The result, both because of Wedekind's writing and Berg's ambition for and conception of the music, was more of a sequential prose narrative with a sustained argument, less of an amalgam of discrete and connected miniatures directed at a single point of dramatic culmination. As a writer Wedekind was far less economical than Büchner. The contrast between the music in both operas was driven in part by stark differences in the literary nature of the texts in terms of character and use of language. Nonetheless, Berg was cautious in changing Wedekind's words. In Act 2, scene 2, Alwa offers Lulu, who has returned from prison, a drink. In Wedekind's play, Lulu asks for "Schnaps," to which Alwa responds, "I have Elixier de Spa."[57] In Berg's text the drink becomes Benedictine.[58] Lulu accepts it and says, "That reminds me of times gone by."[59] Benedictine was well known to those who knew Alma Mahler as her drink of choice. She was, as Berg often observed, a willing and regular drinker of many kinds of alcohol. In her later years Alma was reputed to consume an entire bottle of Benedictine a day. Shortly after Werfel's death, at the end of a huge birthday party for herself, Alma retired upstairs alone for a special moment: to have a glass of Benedictine while reading her former lover Oskar Kokoschka's birthday greeting.[60]

Even more telling is Berg's musical setting of Lulu's line after she accepts the glass of Benedictine, which ranks among the most obvious evocations of late Mahlerian gesture, particularly suggestive of *Das Lied von der Erde*. It is directly followed by Lulu's request to see the painting of her: a material symbol of her aesthetic realization through art. Alwa reminds Lulu of the power of self-representation inspired by the feminine, a reminder that signals the beginning of their first intense love scene. At that moment Alwa takes his dead father's place as Lulu's lover and gives into his passion for her. Not surprisingly, then, the opening of Act 3, which takes place right after the consummation of the Alwa-Lulu relationship, features music reminiscent of a Mahler scherzo, with its grotesque parodies and sharp rhythmic profile. One might even go so far as to suggest that Act 3 suggests the formal patterns of Mahler's Ninth, the work whose manuscript Alma gave to Berg as a gift and the Mahler symphony perhaps closest to Berg's heart.

In Act 3 Alwa more closely mirrors Berg's personal role in protecting and defending Alma in a period of her life marked by unhappiness and decline, and to some extent, an increasing irrelevancy in Viennese cultural and artistic life. Through his own work as a composer Alwa, understood as Berg, reminds Lulu of her past, her crucial role in making his father the editor (Mahler the artist) what he had become. Berg's self-identification as Mahler's metaphorical son, just as Alwa is Schön's son and successor as lover, is deepened by our recognition that insofar as Helene and her role in Berg's life was shaped by his idealized image of Alma, part of Lulu's evolution as a character in the opera derives from parallels between Helene and Lulu. The erotic feminine propels the creative impulse of the male artist.

The music Berg writes in Act 2 until Lulu's spoken recognition of the sofa on which Schön bled to death helps confirm the Alma-Lulu parallel.[61] Berg's writing for Alwa, the tenor role—the tessitura, the length of phrases, and the text setting, as well as the instrumentation—further suggests the tenor writing in *Das Lied*. The whole aspect of the love scene evokes the memory of Mahler. The close of Act 2, which comes quickly, is equally Mahlerian in its drama, suggestive of the Sixth Symphony, the work closely tied to Alma and the obsessive and painful erotic relationship Berg knew Mahler had shared with her.

The question remains whether, as some have suggested, Berg's allusions to Mahler in *Lulu* are meant ironically, to generate distance from Mahler and the conceit of post-Wagnerian late Romanticism. As one scholar has put it, Berg's use of Mahler "parodies a Mahlerian emotional content and undercuts any sense of an emotional authenticity that might attach to the dramatic situation."[62] Perhaps, however, the claim that the Mahlerian style in *Lulu* is not an "authentic" musical language for Berg is a modernist conceit. The drift of late twentieth-century scholarship on Berg has often been propelled by the need to explicate and justify the high modernism of the immediate postwar era as a historical necessity and a justified advance over late Romanticism—entirely in line with the trajectory of the special pleadings of Schoenberg, Adorno, and Boulez, each in their own manner. Could it be that this scholarship simply fails to recognize Berg's debt to Mahler as a composer?[63]

Given the dramatic character and philosophical argument of the Wedekind-Berg libretto (in contrast to the parallel contemporary cases of Richard Strauss libretti that deal with the feminine character and the erotic and romantic connection to men by Hofmannsthal and Gregor), perhaps Douglas Jarman is wrong to characterize Berg's strategy in *Lulu* as subversive.[64] The idea that there is a "disturbing difference" between "the emotional attitude adopted by the music and the nature of the text to which it is set" can be seen as a determination to separate Berg from his own rather old-fashioned ideological and emotional allegiances. The supposition that Wedekind's Lulu was transformed into Berg's Lulu-Alma figure leads us to reconsider Berg's intentions and the relationship of music to text and plot in *Lulu*.[65]

The starting point of that reconsideration needs to be Berg's attitude to what was, for his and previous generations, the foundational text for the consideration of the feminine: Goethe's closing lines in *Faust II*. The last lines of both Wedekind's play and Berg's opera are themselves a satirical commentary on the ending of *Faust*, the very text set by Mahler in the Eighth Symphony.[66] The surface irony is that Geschwitz, a woman, calls Lulu at the end an "angel," a commonplace sentimental rhetorical gesture of idealized affection, otherwise bereft of special meaning. In Berg's version, Wedekind's final word *Verflucht*, a curse or "Damn," is left out. Berg's last word remains Wedekind's *Ewigkeit* (eternity). That word is evocative of the closing lines of *Faust* about the eternal feminine.

In the last scene of *Faust*, various categories of angels carry the immortal soul of Faust upward into what the Female Penitents describe as the "eternal realms" (*ewigen Reiche*). The redemptive force that rescues the physical human being from suffering and offers spiritual bliss is the "eternal feminine," which in turn is the medium for the fulfillment and expression of love.[67] Where Wedekind renders the formulas of Geschwitz's closing expressions of love ironic by the last outburst—"Damn"—Berg leaves the residue of Goethe rather more intact, in line with Mahler's reading of the Chorus Mysticus. The final curse on the Goethe-inspired tradition of idealization fits, since Wedekind's protagonist is Geschwitz, not Lulu, just as Berg's deletion is in line with his own constructs of the feminine as it relates to male ambition.

This should come as no surprise. Berg's sympathetic characterization of Lulu, his staunch loyalty to Alma, and his version of Wedekind's plays derive from his own views on the feminine, sexual love, and desire. These are indebted, insofar as ideas have any proven potency in the formation of character and behavior, to notions Berg developed during late adolescence and early adulthood. He had several sources of inspiration besides Wedekind, including Strindberg, Karl Kraus, and Peter Altenberg.[68] His starting point, like so many others, was Goethe. Quotes from Goethe dominate the notebooks Berg compiled between 1903 and 1907.

But Berg's view of the feminine went beyond Goethe. His attitudes were also as ambivalent, contradictory, and dismissive as those of his contemporaries. In both Wedekind's play and Berg's opera, Lulu is powerful because she mirrors precisely the intense mix of radical idealization, sexual objectification, fear, revulsion, and ambivalence apparent at the fin de siècle.[69] Wedekind's intentions ran more in the direction of exposing the hypocrisy of societal mores and the ludicrous egotism of male conceits. Berg's engagement with the feminine, which was more naïve and less philosophical, centered on love, sexual desire, and male potency as expressed through the making of art. Woman and the experience of desire were essential for artistic self-realization.

But, paradoxically, a woman was inferior. The male was capable of free will and consequently capable of thought, which in the end was higher than love.[70] For Berg, women were not, however, objects of violence and revulsion. As Berg wrote in his notebook, in an attempt at an Oscar Wilde style witticism: "There are two kinds of women: those that are stupid. The others think they are smart."[71] Several years earlier, in the first of his notebooks, Berg added a satirical variation on the closing lines of *Faust*, alluded to at the end of Wedekind's plays and *Lulu*. Berg began with a quote from Ibsen's *Peer Gynt* about how the eternal feminine makes us put our clothes on, or dresses us, a play on the literal phrase about it drawing us closer contained in the German word *anziehen* (to dress). He then graduated to Goethe's line in which the eternal feminine "draws us onward." Berg went on to cite Nietzsche's parody about how the eternal feminine actually pulls us away, distracts us, disgraces us or brings us "down." Then he added his own twist, a reversal on the Ibsen use of the German verb *ziehen*, related to *anziehen*: Berg's joke is that the eternal feminine just makes us "take our clothes off" or perhaps fleece and rob us.[72]

Since in text and plot Berg's *Lulu* is trapped in the world in which Berg came of age, its power for subsequent generations rests increasingly on the music. This is not the case with *Wozzeck*. The operas reveal appropriately distinct compositional and dramatic strategies. In *Wozzeck* Berg's decision to highlight and foreground Büchner's text by retaining a rapid streamlined sequence of tightly constructed short scenes preserved Büchner's argument, even though the order of the scenes in the original play was uncertain.[73] From the early nineteenth century on, the predicament of Wozzeck—an insignificant and helpless character whose spiritual and human needs are crushed under the weight of hierarchies of so-called civilized superiors (the Captain and Doctor) and who faces without resources the competition of superficial values (the Drum Major)—has continued to be relevant. Marie's betrayal, Wozzeck's despair, the murder, and his suicide, leaving the orphan child, readily speak to all future musicians and listeners. Wozzeck's character and existential crisis resonate with us in modernity.

But can the same be said of the manner in which desire, sexuality, and gender are revealed in *Lulu*? The extent to which the argument of the opera is anchored in the discourse of the fin de siècle places the burden of the opera increasingly on the persuasive musical transformation of the somewhat dated symbolic theatrical presentation of love and desire. *Wozzeck* survives as a play to a far greater extent than Wedekind's Lulu plays. And Berg's textual version of *Lulu*, apart from the music, has even less prospect of surviving.

Lulu's Challenge: Sexuality and Moral Judgment

The historically contingent and contradictory but interrelated constructs of female sexuality that Berg adapted had a long history. He absorbed the idealization transmitted through Goethe and Mahler of the feminine as an instrument of male self-realization, redemption, and transcendence. Despite the contradictions and misogyny evident in the Wagnerian extension of that tradition in *Tristan* (a favorite work of Berg's), Berg found in it a model of feminine love.[74] He cited *Tristan* covertly to Hanna Fuchs in the *Lyric Suite*. Berg's reception of Wagner was selective. It sustained his own romantic idealization of the feminine as creating the occasion for male musical creativity and as the ideal object of male self-definition. For all of Mahler's early engagement with Nietzsche, he actually absorbed very little of Nietzsche's skepticism regarding the place and power of women. From Berg's point of view the greatest of Mahler's achievements were tied to the subject of either love or death. These were extensions of the Wagnerian problematic in *Tristan*.[75]

But the formative influences that advanced Berg's perception of the feminine were Kraus and Altenberg. Their views of women in turn owe a debt to Otto Weininger and his famous 1903 book *Sex and Character*. In that tract (a work in turn indebted to Nietzsche), the feminine is clearly understood as an indispensable component of all human beings. Human beings possess in themselves both sexual archetypes, male and female. Men and women share the same sexual drive and are in that strict sense equal. However, although the male and female inhabit every individual, the difference between the two is that the female is "nothing more than sexuality." The female is inferior and dangerous because in principle the male is capable of more than mere sexuality. The male aspect of humanity is superior because the male can achieve self-consciousness and transcend mere physicality. The male, through resistance and struggle, can enter the realm of spirituality, and therefore the aesthetic. The male "has the power of consciousness of his sexuality and so can act against it."[76]

Therefore, man is only "partly sexual," whereas woman is merely sexual. The male has to contain sexuality without renouncing it in order to realize his creative potential. The feminine is at once indispensable and yet dangerous. For Weininger, male and female represent a typology that is expressed differently in each person. The excessively feminine can intersect with cultural traditions and become associated with extreme materialism, rationality, and lack of creativity. Ominously, Weininger's idiosyncratic conception of the Jewish was linked to his construct of the feminine.[77]

Neither Kraus nor Altenberg entirely shared Weininger's point of view, but it gave them a framework for a critique of the way the feminine was understood in contemporary society. Kraus took particular aim at the claims of psychoanalysis that based all human action, including the making of art and culture, on Eros, the erotic instinct. Weininger's views also coincided with Wedekind's critique of the hypocritical societal restrictions on female sexuality. Kraus accepted Weininger's rather than Freud's account of the role of the erotic in the generation of culture by arguing that although the erotic demanded acknowledgment as reflective of the overwhelming priority of nature over culture, it called for resistance. The sexual in both the male and the female was indispensable, but the danger lurked that it would overwhelm the unique potential of the male for thought, language, and art that was, for Kraus, in contrast to Freud, not causally derivative of the erotic.

For Kraus—arguably the thinker and writer who exercised the greatest influence on Berg—woman was, following Goethe, an idealized and essential dimension of pure nature, potentially resistant to the corruption of civilization and modern culture. The feminine therefore possessed the redemptive powers that Goethe celebrated. Less obsessed than Weininger about the destructive potential of the feminine, Kraus was more alarmed at the materialist determinism in Freud's account that reduced art and thought to sublimated primitive erotic impulses. Kraus's own relationship to women was at one and the same time tortured and idealized.[78] But like Weininger he believed that modernity had corrupted nature. Modern culture and society were guilty of suppressing women's sexuality and imposing on it unnatural and inconsistent constraints masquerading as morality. Like Wedekind, Kraus distanced himself from Weininger's extreme dismissal of the feminine as mere sexuality. Yet the male needed to use love to connect to the power of nature and then reach higher into the realm of thought and art.

Another admirer of Wedekind's, Peter Altenberg, whom Berg knew well, went even further. He celebrated the alluring, incipient, and unspoiled sexuality of the female. He lavished praise on the erotic and the beauty of the young female. But his obsessions, following lines suggested by Weininger, reduced the female to an instrument of male self-actualization. Among Altenberg's literary expressions of his vulnerability to the feminine were poems praising the beauty of the young Helene Nahowski.[79] Helene's status as idealized object of Altenberg's attention only heightened Berg's admiration of her and desire for her. Unlike Weininger, Altenberg seemed to have little difficulty with giving in to and expressing erotic desire. But despite clear differences, all three—Kraus, Altenberg, and Weininger—furthered the discourse that had its roots in Parts I and II of Goethe's *Faust*. In the end, for Goethe only the feminine is capable of overcoming the tragic paradoxes of mortality through love, thereby offering the hope of transcendence.

Mahler seems never to have engaged the ideas of Weininger or Kraus, even if one can locate his sense of the feminine and sexuality as consonant with Goethe's idealization. Nonetheless, Weininger's theories (and their roots in Nietzsche) seemed visible to Berg in Mahler's personal and artistic acknowledgment of the feminine as an indispensable, compelling, and at the same time dangerous source of the artistic impulse.[80] The contrast between the music of Mahler and Berg, as well as Berg's debt to Mahler, reflect Berg's recognition of the destructive potential of male creativity in the interplay between sexuality and art. Berg's source was his close reading of Kraus's *Die Fackel*. Lulu's corrosive power and her fate were seen as consequences of the failure of men in the face of her natural sexuality and their own obsessions and desires. Unlike Mahler, Berg was influenced by the ambivalent discourse around him and driven by Wedekind's critical account of the destruction ultimately wreaked on men by their inability to define and subjugate the feminine for themselves.

Appropriately, Jack the Ripper creates the dramatic closure. He has internalized a paralyzing fear of his own vulnerability. His self-revulsion at desire leads him to kill man's life force, which in the cases of Alwa and the Painter framed the purposes of their lives. Geschwitz's plea on behalf of the rights of women may appear ironic in Berg's version, given her comparatively truncated role in the opera, but not in Wedekind's. Yet Berg allied himself with Wedekind and Kraus, for whom conventional morality made the situation far worse. The extreme legal subordination of women and the criminalization of prostitution were deleterious, corrupting genuine ethics and morality. Berg's parody of sentimental romanticism in *Lulu* does not signal his own detachment from a fundamental allegiance to a nostalgic set of conceits regarding the interplay between the erotic and the aesthetic.

Berg absorbed the complex of sentiments encountered largely through Kraus without adding much new of his own. Like Kraus, he idealized a premodern and nostalgic notion of nature and the feminine, and therefore an idealized characterization of love. The spiritual in love emerged from carnal desire but had to lead to creativity. While idealizing the feminine, Berg accepted the notion, mediated through Weininger, that the male is the unique instrument of art, a conceit Mahler shared. It is fascinating to compare Berg's early notebook entries on love and the feminine with his letters to Hanna Fuchs from the 1920s.[81] Berg repeats and replicates his early views and relives the intensity and rhetoric of passion he experienced during the courtship of his wife. Berg's language is nearly identical, as is his conviction that the composer is able to realize the potential of true art only if inspired by the feminine muse through her erotic allure, without succumbing to it completely. In the decades that separate the notebooks from the Hanna Fuchs love letters, little changed in Berg's thinking. A perceptive letter Helene wrote to Alma shortly after Alban's death shows that she understood Berg's dependency as an artist on his own construct of love, desire, and art that drew him to other women.[82]

Who better embodied the creative inspiration of the feminine than Alma Mahler? According to Weininger's categories, her enormous musical talent represented the male side of her being. Yet this talent was overwhelmed by her feminine need to express and realize her sexuality. Because she was a superior woman—graced with a sufficient element of maleness to make her capable of experiencing the aesthetic—her erotic allure was immense. She managed to be the muse and downfall of a legendary line of artists, including the greatest composer of Berg's lifetime as well as such notables as Zemlinsky and Werfel. These were merely the men Berg knew about. Just as he sought to assume Mahler's mantle, Berg also came to see Helene (an inspiration to Altenberg, then to himself) as the next generation's Alma. This explains in part Berg's periodic bouts of jealousy and suspicion as a husband. Morgenstern's suggestion that Berg would have approved of an affair between him and Helene fits Berg's generous, if not admiring view of Alma's mores. In the end Helene was no Alma, and no seductress. Indeed, neither her personality nor her talent ever matched Alma's. Helene's potential as an artist comes closer to Lulu's as dancer than it did to Alma's musical talent. Berg found himself captivated by Helene, but only temporarily. To renew his romantic enthusiasm, Berg went on to add female conquests, ironically replicating Alma's pattern of conquest, without ever feeling vulnerable to Alma herself.[83]

When Berg chose to study with Schoenberg in 1904, he encountered a composer who, although a great admirer of Weininger's, an avid reader of Kraus, and a devotee of Strindberg (whom Berg read closely, and whose reputation for misogyny equaled that of Weininger), had a different view of art and its relationship to the psyche and sexuality.[84] For all of Schoenberg's overwhelming impact on Berg's conception of music, there was very little overlap between the two men's interior psychological impulse for and ideological justification of the making of art. Schoenberg privileged Kraus's notion that making art was an ethical act and that truth was at stake. In art, authenticity confronted the superficiality and corruption of modernity. Music, like language, had to be purified of its romantic and sentimental ornamental overlay. Berg agreed.[85]

However, Schoenberg's interests lay elsewhere. Not even in his most Expressionist period did Schoenberg the composer pay much heed to the *Tristan* problem. The expressive intensity of the love relationship and the role of the feminine in relation to the masculine, even in *Erwartung*, were not his main concerns. On the intersection between art and ideas, Schoenberg was closer to Kraus's position than Berg's. But where Kraus and Berg idealized Nature, Schoenberg was indifferent. The issue of the relationship of language and music, the connection between thought and art, construed philosophically, stubbornly persisted as Schoenberg's primary concerns. Kraus, Schoenberg, and Adolf Loos positioned themselves philosophically as arch anti-Romantics who cherished an idealized version of the late eighteenth and early nineteenth centuries, when aesthetics and ethics were allied and formal logic in art was in the ascendancy, particularly in music and architecture. Although Berg accepted these notions as criteria of craftsmanship, beneath the surface he defined the vocation of composer and artist in terms of the immediate post-Wagnerian era, the era of Mahler and Strauss.

Hidden Influences: Schreker and Zemlinsky

The tradition of writing about Berg's life and career has focused overwhelmingly on the obvious: Berg's debt to Schoenberg and members of his close circle. As a consequence, Berg's links to two other composers who had a decisive impact on him consistently go missing in accounts of his achievement. Like Berg but unlike Schoenberg, both were captivated by the discourse on the feminine that consumed Weininger and Kraus's generation. The first missing link is Franz Schreker, whom Berg knew and befriended, and with whose first great operatic success, *Der ferne Klang*, he was intimately familiar.[86] The second missing link is Alexander Zemlinsky, Schoenberg's brother-in-law and one-time teacher, and Alma's first serious lover and teacher, whose music Berg truly liked.[87]

In 1912, in order to earn money, Berg accepted the task of making the piano reduction of the second and third acts of Franz Schreker's *Der ferne Klang*. The controversy surrounding Berg's realization of that task has been well documented. Although Berg's reduction was deemed too difficult to play, Schreker himself preferred it to the simplified version subsequently prepared by Ferdinand Rebay. Although this episode is routinely mentioned, there seems to have been no serious speculation about what the impact of Berg's close encounter with Schreker's opera might have been. Like many before him, Berg was not above hiding his tracks and artistic debts. He was an adept secret maker and secret keeper. He was also curiously silent about Schreker and even went to the length of declaring *Der ferne Klang* "awful" when he saw it again in the 1920s in Berlin.[88]

Der ferne Klang was a great success upon its premiere in 1912, much to the chagrin of Schoenberg, who openly derided Schreker—the conductor, the man, and the music within his circle (even though Schreker was uncommonly generous and supportive of Schoenberg; the two were on *Du* terms after Schreker conducted the Viennese premiere of *Gurrelieder*

Figure 3. Alexander Zemlinsky, Arnold Schoenberg, Franz Schreker, Prague, 1912.

in 1913, and the composers even traded dedications to each other: *Christophorus* to Schoenberg and *Style and Idea* to Schreker). Key members of Schoenberg's circle, including Berg, maintained good one-to-one relationships with Schreker, their fawning and harsh complaints to Schoenberg notwithstanding.[89] One can argue that Berg learned from the close study of Schreker's first great opera how to compose something Schoenberg never quite figured out how to do: a successful opera. The first clue to the powerful influence of Schreker on Berg can be found in the libretto of Schreker's opera, which the composer wrote himself. It fits squarely into the theatrical and literary tradition that seeks to negotiate the question of the interrelationship of the erotic, the feminine, and male creativity, precise issues that were at the center of the work of Wedekind, Kraus, Weininger, Altenberg, and Berg.

The opera deals with Fritz, a composer, sung by a tenor.[90] He is in love with a Goethe-like figure, not surprisingly named Grete (think of Gretchen in Goethe's *Faust*). She, like Lulu, is the embodiment of unspoiled natural femininity. Fritz, although passionately in love with Grete, leaves her in search of his own creative vision. Schreker followed Weininger closely. In order to achieve his artistic ambitions, Fritz has to prevent Grete from following him: he has to suppress the feminine within himself and transcend mere sexuality. The consequence for Grete is disastrous, and in the second act of the opera she becomes a prostitute (in Venice, a favorite destination and symbol for the Viennese). In a direct parallel to Lulu, Grete is surrounded by multiple suitors and gleefully manipulative of them. Like Lulu, she also assumes multiple names. She struggles, particularly in Act 2, to assert herself against men's efforts to define and appropriate her. When Fritz reappears at the end of Act 2, he barely recognizes her. Grete makes fun of his rhetoric of idealized romantic love. He is in turn horrified and repelled by her status as a prostitute. Schreker, like Mahler before him, was not inclined to do what Wedekind managed so brilliantly, to complicate the character of his female protagonist as a societal symbol. Schreker was further disinclined to render the figure of the male artist more subtle, more in line with Wedekind's characterization of Alwa. Fritz's unreconstructed moral opprobrium is the sort of hypocritical bourgeois morality that Wedekind and Kraus derided.

In Act 3, we encounter Fritz's completed work of art—an opera whose closing act has left him deeply dissatisfied. A destitute and desperate Grete attends the performance. Fritz sees her and is rekindled by his need for her. She goes to him. Their love is reignited, but more as a memory than a reality. Her love cannot redeem Fritz the artist. Through the medium of Grete's love Fritz recovers the will to rewrite the failed last act, but not the capacity. It is too late—and to Grete's horror he dies. An object of love, she is denied the ability to regress into a mediating force of male creativity. Here the *Tristan* model triumphs over Goethe.

But in the end Schreker's sympathies are with Grete. Fritz's moralistic narcissism is not the object of admiration, any more than Grete's suitors are in Act 2. Fritz in *Der ferne Klang* can be seen as consistent with Wedekind's critique of the male construct of the feminine and Schreker's other artist figures in subsequent operas (Alviano in *Die Gezeichneten* and Elis in *Der Schatzgräber*).[91] But just like Alwa, Fritz fails to realize his artistic ideal. He is caught in the web of his own narcissism and inability either to embrace life or find the means to use life to generate art. Berg may have adapted the Wedekind plays along lines suggested by *Der ferne Klang*. Despite evident differences in the musical language of the two works, there are many observable overlapping strategies. First, Berg's orchestration in *Lulu* and indeed *Wozzeck* (the tavern scene in Act 1 of *Der ferne Klang* has a direct parallel in *Wozzeck*) owes much to Schreker's deft use of varieties of string sound, offstage ensembles, and fragments of folk material. In the last act of Schreker's opera, Berg encountered an innovative mixture of melodrama, speech, and singing. The alternation between exotically orchestrated passages, with lush neo-Mahlerian sounds and a nearly ascetic and otherworldly musical sound world, prefigures Berg's *Lulu*.

Second, *Lulu* (though not *Wozzeck*) owes much to the pacing of Schreker's first and third acts. Berg's characterization of Schilgoch is reminiscent of Schreker's representation of the prophetic old woman in Act 1. The way minor characters are handled throughout *Lulu* in ensembles is suggested by parts of Schreker's opera, particularly in the tavern gambling scene of Act 1, the opening conversations of Act 3, and the handling of the suitors in Act 2. One can find ironic echoes of Schreker in the way men address Lulu through music when paying suit to her. Berg also imitated Schreker's strategy of multicasting the same voice in several roles.[92]

George Perle and others have argued that Berg's musical strategy changed between the completion of *Wozzeck* and the writing of *Lulu* and the other late great work, the Violin Concerto. In this process the significance and influence of the Schreker model grew. In *Lulu* the Wagnerian and Expressionist subject matter, dramatic surface, and structure are directly suggestive of Schreker. The music is more continuous, as is the drama. Starting with *Wozzeck*, and even more prominently in the film music for *Lulu*, Berg appropriated one of Schreker's signature skills, the use of long orchestral interludes. The extended orchestral essay in Act 3 of *Der ferne Klang* is the model, structurally, for the *Lulu* Film Music that narrates instrumentally Lulu's incarceration.[93]

Finally, by turning Alwa into a composer, Berg aligns the lead tenor role in *Lulu* with Fritz. One entirely unintentional connection between the two works is that the fictional Fritz fails to complete to his satisfaction the last act of his intended masterpiece, an opera titled *Die Harfe*. In the case of Berg, such a failure would become an unexpected fact of his life and musical career.

The second influence on Berg that receives less attention than it deserves is Zemlinsky. This connection is less controversial than with Schreker, since Berg was open about his affection and regard for Zemlinsky. Berg suppressed Schreker's influence not only because he wanted to distance himself, but for fear of Schoenberg's opprobrium. More than once he was taunted by Schoenberg for maintaining contact with the composer of *Der ferne Klang;* he knew any defense of Schreker would be taken amiss.[94]

Zemlinsky presented a different problem. Schoenberg's relationship to his brother-in-law, always complicated, deteriorated after Schoenberg remarried following Mathilde's death. But Schoenberg never openly criticized Zemlinsky and always acknowledged his greatness. In Alma's circle, Zemlinsky remained a favored figure. Alma never entirely turned her back on him. Berg, Schoenberg, and Alma valued Zemlinsky's skill not only as a composer but as a conductor. That Berg thought highly of Zemlinsky's *Lyric* Symphony, a masterpiece in the manner of *Das Lied von der Erde*, is evidenced by his quoting it in the *Lyric Suite*.[95]

But this well-known homage is not the only link between Berg and Zemlinsky. In 1923 Berg and Webern went to witness the rehearsals of Zemlinsky's opera *Der Zwerg* (*The Dwarf*) before its premiere in Cologne under Otto Klemperer. Berg liked this opera, with a libretto by Georg C. M. Klaren based on Oscar Wilde's story. His initial suspicion that it would be insufficiently dramatic was allayed by the success of the premiere. He felt the music to be indescribably beautiful, even though he found its polyphony often hard to follow. For Berg, Zemlinsky's characterization of the plight of *Der Zwerg*, who had never seen himself in a mirror and never encountered his physical ugliness, was almost unbearable. The impact of the opera's overwhelming synthesis of music and emotion depressed Berg for days, perhaps because it was too naturalistic, illustrative, and close to reality. Zemlinsky pursued a conservative path in the early 1920s, one chartered by Wagner, Strauss, and Mahler. In *Der Zwerg* he used historicism in style, familiar rhetoric, and particularly tonality to amplify and translate states of being into music. With uncommon inspiration and variety, *Der Zwerg* also employed something Berg imitated in *Lulu*: recurring musical motives as markers of memory within the drama.

Berg's does not imitate Zemlinsky's musical or dramatic strategy, as he may have Schreker's.[96] Indeed, Zemlinsky inspired Berg to search for a connection in modernism between melodic gesture and the expressive—a traditional connection, audible in *Der Zwerg*, that was routinely underplayed by Schoenberg. Furthermore, is unabashedly autobiographical. This dimension of Zemlinsky's opera was not lost on Berg, a composer likewise committed to linking autobiography to art.[97] Zemlinsky, a man of extremely short stature, clearly identified with the Dwarf. The Infanta, the lead female role in Zemlinsky's opera, taunts the Dwarf by encouraging his passion for her, treating him as nothing more than a plaything, a present from the Sultan. She breaks his heart then leaves to dance at her birthday party. The Dwarf is left to die alone after confronting his physical self. With him also dies the Dwarf's one redeeming feature: his artistry as a singer and poet. In *Der Zwerg*, the female kills male creativity by turning erotic desire and romantic love into an instrument of distorted self-recognition. The cruelty rests in the female capacity to reduce the Dwarf, through his erotic desires, to nothing more than his hideous physical self. Women are unmasked as unable to transcend the sexual or encourage its resistance.

For Zemlinsky, the Infanta was Alma Mahler and he himself the Dwarf. His librettist Klaren recast Wilde's story into a thinly veiled retelling of Zemlinsky's own traumatic experience with Alma. Wilde's Infanta is twelve, an innocent before puberty. Zemlinsky's Infanta is eighteen—closer to Alma'a age when Zemlinsky knew her—no longer a girl but a young woman capable of displaying a woman's so-called natural tendency to sadism, nonchalance, and a reductive expression of female sexuality that would have been extreme even for Weininger. The Infanta reveals a heartlessness that Berg's Lulu does not possess, not even in her short career as a prostitute. The Klaren libretto also adds a second major female character to Wilde's story: Gita, the Infanta's lady in waiting. The role she plays in Zemlinsky's opera runs parallel to the role Berg assigns Countess Geschwitz in *Lulu*, not so much in terms of plot detail but in terms of its musical and dramatic prominence. Geschwitz occupies a large part of the closing scene of *Lulu*, just as Gita plays a decisive role in the closing scene of *Der Zwerg*. She, like Geschwitz, is alone in remaining capable of expressing and recognizing love.

Contemporaries and subsequent commentators have observed that Zemlinsky's opera and its libretto were influenced by Weininger's theory of the male and female. Indeed, the author of the libretto confirmed that claim, suggesting that the opera was about the "confrontation of every man with every woman," where self-doubt created by the clash between the erotic impulse and the spiritual capacity within man is complicated by his contemplation of an idealized feminine object. However, Zemlinsky's opera strips the role of the woman as the vehicle of male self-knowledge of its idealization. The desire for erotic fulfillment, the dependency on the female, leads to self-destruction and death where the male resistance is too weak, as it did in the case of Weininger himself.[98]

Zemlinsky's use of a work of literature as a protective screen with which to characterize Alma may have strengthened Berg's attraction to Wedekind. It perhaps defined his determination to offset the devastating impact of Zemlinsky's portrayal of Alma as the Infanta. Berg's intent to deepen Wedekind's sympathetic portrayal of Lulu by placing the burden of the tragedy on the men themselves, allowed Wedekind's character to serve symbolically as a redemption not only of the feminine per se (from Zemlinsky's and Wilde's caustic conceptions) but of Alma's image, particularly among the Viennese.

The role of the death of an abandoned protagonist as the traditional operatic instrument of closure in the drama connects *Lulu* with both Schreker's and Zemlinsky's operas. The main difference rests with the characterization of the feminine. If Alma was a model for Berg's Lulu, it is plausible to suggest that Berg's attraction to the *Lulu* project was motivated by the capacity to use Lulu as a counterpoint to the Infanta in *Der Zwerg*. A similar contrast applies when considering Schreker's Grete, who in the libretto is less complex than Lulu, even if Schreker's musical characterizations are varied, subtle, and affecting. Grete wavers back and forth between the innocent, loving woman and the cynical prostitute who defiantly revels in her fallen state. Her character, particularly in Act 2, suggests susceptibility to the conventional moral contrast between the loving woman and the bad prostitute. Fritz regrets his rejection of Grete the prostitute, signaling Schreker's view that the ideal of integrating the feminine into the male, the reconciliation of Weininger's archetypes in the service of either love or art, is in the end an illusion.[99] In Zemlinsky's Infanta we encounter alluring beauty with no capacity for empathy, only thoughtlessness.

But Schreker and Zemlinsky, like Berg, absorbed the central, self-destructive aspect of Weininger's problematic: that the female was dangerous to the male, the stuff of tragedy, and the unmaking of the artistic self.[100] Happiness was an illusion, as was the search for it. As Schreker wrote in 1918, "Happiness does not exist in this world. It is nowhere to be found. The intoxication of desire—it is a deceptive trick of light, a sudden immolation."[101] *Lulu,* however, offered Berg the opportunity to go beyond the limits presented by both Grete and the Infanta. The music for Lulu—from the aria and the "Freedom" music to the coda—deepen a sympathetic portrayal of the many-sided feminine character. This character, exemplified by Alma and her devotion to the posthumous reputation of Mahler, is neither heartless nor cruel, and much more than a victim, the mere object of male ambition.

At the same time, Berg's allegiance to the terms of the fin-de-siècle debate over the feminine, of which Wedekind's representation in *Lulu* is an important part, limits the power of the opera's plot. Whatever their merits, the Wedekind plays once competed with the extraordinary popularity of Strindberg, arguably the most produced playwright in the German language at the turn of the century.[102] Yet they do not retain a place in the contemporary theater comparable to *Lulu*'s place in the opera repertory.[103] The persuasive, nearly symphonic coherence and sweep of the music redeems the opera, if not the language or the ideology of the libretto.

Berg and Mahler

With *Lulu*, Berg took up a challenge implicit in Mahler's late works and Schoenberg's *Gurrelieder*: to use the massive sound resources of the concert and opera stage and create a modern work of large scale that engaged the central issues of love and nature. The encounters with Schreker and Zemlinsky may have helped him succeed not only externally, but internally in insulating himself from Schoenberg's close intervention, leaving him free, particularly after the success of *Wozzeck*, to pursue his own aesthetic agenda. No doubt Schoenberg's approval and advice remained important, but when Berg was debating whether his next opera would be based on Wedekind's Lulu plays or Gerhart Hauptmann's *Und Pippa tanzt!* Morgenstern and Adorno (despite Berg's amusement at his intensity and incomprehensibility) had greater influence on the choice than Schoenberg.[104] Berg did not respond to or exploit the timely political overtones that helped catapult *Wozzeck* into the repertory in the late 1920s.[105] Instead he decided to write an opera based on a return to an old subject, one that by the early 1930s was in danger of being overshadowed and displaced. He did not write a sequel. The music of *Lulu* may be unmistakably suggestive of the era in which it was composed, including prominent allusions to popular culture (saxophone and dance). But Berg, faced with the darkening political landscape surrounding him, retreated, returning to the social and psychological concerns of pre–World War I Vienna. The worldview surrounding Lulu as a symbol of the erotic and natural, of the feminine, and of the corruption of society was dated by the time Berg began to compose.

In the 1930s the political context shifted the terms of discourse regarding gender, the erotic, and the nature of the aesthetic, subordinating them to the overarching issue of art and politics in a world divided between the rising tide of fascism and communism. Given the Stalinist context in Soviet Russia, where Shostakovich suffered ostracism over *Lady Macbeth of Mitsensk* (1934), *Wozzeck*'s success in that country would not have been replicated with *Lulu*. Would *Lulu* have fared any better in the United States in the wake of the Depression and resurgence of a populist sensibility that culminated in Copland's shift away from modernism toward the accessible vocabulary of *Billy the Kid* (1938) and *Appalachian Spring* (1944)?[106]

With *Wozzeck*, Berg struck squarely the central issues of the post–World War I era, confronting the social and political underpinnings using Büchner's searing account of individual alienation. *Wozzeck* offered an ideal framework for the era, one in which the political and the personal became inseparable. The conceits of a rational modernity and progress were undercut by the tale of a seemingly insignificant man told with an intense, disciplined, subtle, and startlingly modernist musical voice. But with *Lulu*

Berg inadvertently courted a double isolation: rejection by fascists and communists on account of its musical modernism and, in the 1930s, a sense of irrelevancy with respect to the libretto from both the Left and the Right in the political sphere.

Berg was a slow worker by habit and character. Having failed to capitalize in a timely manner on the unexpected success of *Wozzeck*, he settled comfortably, automobile and all, into the circumscribed Austrian world in which he had grown up, his travel abroad and participation in international musical life as a celebrity notwithstanding. He confronted the unstable and often violent politics of Vienna in the late 1920s and early 1930s by deepening an interior allegiance to a vanished world. He developed nostalgia for the time before the collapse of the Habsburg Empire in which love, desire, art, and the artist took center stage over politics, where the contest over art and morality took on ideological and social significance.

A production of the completed *Lulu* in the mid-1930s might have seemed, if not dated, at least problematic in terms of the surface story and its underlying assumptions. Ironically, *Lulu*'s success was secured by the reluctance of Berg's closest associates to undertake its completion. The opera's unfinished state was an inadvertent blessing, justifying Helene's intuitive resistance to its completion. The promise of the work, first posthumously performed in 1937 in the two-act version and in the postwar era as an incomplete torso with a closing fragment tacked on, gave *Lulu* an aura and insulation against the close scrutiny to which it might have been subjected as a completed work by a living composer.

In the immediate postwar era, while Helene controlled Berg's estate, critical reception focused on his distinctive place as a modernist, though in that regard there were many skeptics.[107] But by the time a completed opera version of *Lulu* was performed in 1979, four major historical shifts had occurred that would ultimately favor the work, rendering irrelevant the misgivings of the late 1940s and early 1950s.[108] The first, which began in the mid-1970s, was the turn away from modernism among composers. The residues of Expressionism, tonality, and the sound world of Mahler were revived and young composers embraced them as attuned to the times. Modernism between 1945 and 1975 had failed precisely where Berg had succeeded, in persuading audiences of the necessary link between musical means and expressive intent.

The second shift was the rise of neoconservatism in politics, the era of Reagan and Thatcher and the erosion of the dominant terms of Cold War politics. The new conservative politics gave impetus to the revival of the ideals of individuality. They signaled a retreat from egalitarianism and the politics of social justice that had overwhelmed the 1960s. This retreat brought with it the resurgence of the narrative novel and figurative painting. In art and popular culture there emerged a renewed focus on the psyche and the private sphere rather than politics, a trend reminiscent of the fin de siècle; hence the strong revival of interest in Vienna 1900.

The third shift was the slow but genuine impact of feminist politics and the foregrounding of gender and sexuality as dimensions of political discourse in Europe and North America. The last (and most parochial) shift was an irreversible by-product of the other three: the lasting success of the Mahler revival that began in the late 1950s. It elevated Berg's beloved composer from the margins to the center of public taste, paralleling a reassessment of the history of twentieth-century music in which Shostakovich would emerge as central and Schoenberg as peripheral.[109] Likewise, the drift at the end of the twentieth century toward cultural nostalgia helped spark a revival of interest in Wagnerian music drama and the music of post-Wagnerian late Romanticism. This augured well for a revival of the operas of Zemlinsky and Schreker. Insofar as *Lulu* rather than *Wozzeck* evoked that tradition (as would the *Lyric Suite* and Violin Concerto), its prospects were more promising.[110]

Thus the completed *Lulu* made its debut in the world of the 1980s, one quite different from the one Berg experienced when writing the opera. When Berg died Mahler's music was still a matter of controversy, buffeted by the critical debates from pre–World War I Europe. After 1933, Mahler faced oblivion among conservatives owing to his Jewish origins and status as a precursor of modernist degeneracy, and among progressives as an exponent of a seemingly outdated expansive late Romanticism. By writing *Lulu*, Berg distanced himself from Schoenberg, whose own artistic and political trajectory in the 1930s can be located in *Moses und Aron*.[111] In the 1930s Alban and Helene became only closer and more dependent on Alma, who had become a reactionary figure, more likely to look backward and with sympathy for Austrofascism, if not the Nazis. In these surroundings Berg found himself intuitively closer to Schreker's, Zemlinsky's, and Mahler's aesthetic sensibilities, though not their technical and formal strategies. The hiatus Berg took to write the Violin Concerto only deepened this return to the Mahlerian so evident in the earlier Three Pieces for Orchestra.[112]

Ultimately, Berg's late music—with its intense dramatic sweep, use of fragments, sharp alternations in sonority, and thematic markers as gestures of intense feeling, loss, and nostalgia—is closest to the music of Gustav Mahler. By discovering that he could model Wedekind's Lulu after Alma Mahler, whose presence had become an important source of refuge and comfort as the conditions of the 1930s worsened and his friends fled from German-speaking Europe, Berg's engagement with the opera project deepened. Lulu provided an ideal vehicle for attempting to write the first modernist opera that explicitly evoked and emulated the Mahlerian, not only in scale and dramatic intent but in terms of the function and impact of music. By placing Alma at its center, Berg sought to pay musical homage to the composer closest to his heart and aesthetic ambition.

Berg's definition of the Mahlerian model rests on his reading of Mahler's last completed symphony, the Ninth. Writing to Helene in 1912, on the occasion of its premiere, and near the time he was working on the piano reduction of Acts 2 and 3 of *Der ferne Klang*, Berg commented on the first movement. He hears it as a premonition of death, as expressive of a resistant love of nature. Berg finds that the music alternates between repose and volcanic peaks. Death appears at the moments of the most anguished and profound expressions of the love of life. In the music Berg locates Mahler's ultimate turn to nature, remarking with pessimism on how elusive the refuge from strife into nature can be. Nonetheless, in the Ninth Berg encountered the musical expression of the "most glorious of human hearts that ever beat."[113]

The structure of the first movement of Mahler's Ninth Symphony can be compared to Berg's dramatic strategy in *Lulu*. The music evolves in large-scale scenic episodes united by thematic recurrences, fragments of memory, and self-allusions. There are extreme contrasts in sonority and interludes between dramatic events. While both the Mahler Ninth and *Lulu* are readily subject to formal analysis that reveals disciplined musical logic, it is precisely Mahler's capacity to suggest a dramatic program without too heavy a reliance on illustration, but with musical means, to which Berg responds. As in the last scene of *Lulu*, both the first movement and the entire symphony end in dissolution and disintegration.

Lulu, far more than *Wozzeck*, is a symphonic opera. With it, Berg returns to the fabric of sound similar to Schreker's and Zemlinsky's. As Webern drifted toward a more ascetic, aphoristic style, Berg indulged in his choice of pre–World War I subject matter—the construct of the feminine. His choice of a musical model, rooted in an underlying nostalgia, demanded a Mahlerian response. By editing Wedekind's plays and writing Alma into *Lulu* through music, Berg further retreated into the familiar world around him, while the recognition and notoriety he had achieved seemed increasingly bewildering and hostile.

With a bit of metaphorical license, *Lulu* could be called the Sleeping Beauty of modernism, the direct successor to the late Mahler (or the Eleventh Symphony as opera). Berg's posthumously completed masterpiece woke up after the worst of modernism's struggle for an audience was over, to become an immediate success. It had slept through more than four decades that might have received it coldly as irrelevant, regressive, and too indebted to late Romanticism. It awakened as a fully complete adult at just the right time. In this moment Berg would be seen not as the last unreconstructed Romantic,

Figure 4. Berg in front of a portrait of Mahler, in his study
in his Trauttmansdorffgasse apartment, Hietzing, c. 1935.

but as a model to be emulated: a composer who showed how new traditions of music can be expressive of the human condition not by rejecting history but by extending history into modernity. By preserving the implications of tonality, Berg paid homage not only to eighteenth-century Classicism, as Schoenberg had done, but also to musical late Romanticism. Like Mahler, Berg did not shy away from the innovative and the new—the modern. After *Wozzeck*, Berg felt confident enough to pursue the path for linking music and life defined and charted by Mahler. *Lulu* is the realization of the logic of that path. The shape the opera ultimately assumed vindicated the composer's ambition, locating Alban Berg in history not only as Mahler's successor but as a model for the musical future.

NOTES

I wish to thank in the first instance Christopher Hailey for his advice and assistance. His extraordinary knowledge of the period and its sources, his refinement and judgment as a scholar, and his generosity all deserve high praise. I also wish to thank Christopher Gibbs, whose comments and editing were invaluable, Tatjana Myoko von Prittwitz und Gaffron, Jane Smith, Irene Zedlacher, and Lynne Meloccaro.

1. See the essays collected in *The Cambridge Companion to Berg*, ed. Anthony Pople (Cambridge: Cambridge University Press, 1997); *The Berg Companion*, ed. Douglas Jarman (Boston: Northeastern University Press, 1989); and *Alban Berg: Historical and Analytical Perspectives*, ed. David Gable and Robert P. Morgan (Oxford: Clarendon Press, 1991).

2. See Oscar Thompson, "Alban Berg, Composer of *Wozzeck*, Is Dead," *Musical America* (10 January 1936): 8, 17.

3. See J. Peter Burkholder, "Berg and the Possibility of Popularity," in *Alban Berg: Historical and Analytical Perspectives*, 25–53; Erich Alban Berg and Hermann Watznauer, *Der unverbesserliche Romantiker: Alban Berg, 1885–1935* (Vienna: Österreichischer Bundesverlag, 1985), 7; and Dominik Schweiger, "Schönberg als Lehrer," in *Schüler in der Wiener Schule: Ein Programmbuch des Wiener Konzerthauses im Rahmen der Hörgänge* (Vienna: Universal Edition, 1995), 6–13.

4. The same might be said of Mahler, particularly the earlier symphonies. On Berg's ambivalence toward Strauss, see Alban Berg, *Alban Berg: Letters to His Wife*, ed. Bernard Grun (New York: St. Martin's Press, 1971), 25, 37–38, 55, 63, 72, 80, 87, 102, 219, 246, 407, 409, 422; Constantin Floros, *Alban Berg: Musik als Autobiographie* (Wiesbaden: Breitkopf & Härtel, 1992), 98–99; and Herwig Knaus and Wilhelm Sinkovicz, *Alban Berg: Zeitumstände-Lebenslinien* (St. Pölten: Residenz, 2008), 322.

5. See George Perle, "The Secret Program of the Lyric Suite," *International Alban Berg Newsletter* 5 (June): 4–12; Douglas Jarman, "Secret Programmes," in *Cambridge Companion to Berg*, 167–79, and "Alban Berg, Wilhelm Fliess, and the Secret Programme of the Violin Concerto," 181–94; Barbara Dalen, "'Freundschaft, Liebe, und Welt': The Secret Programme of the Chamber Concerto," 141–80, both in Jarman, *The Berg Companion*; Wolfgang Budday, *Alban Bergs Lyrische Suite* (Neuhausen-Stuttgart: Hänssler, 1979); and the essays in *Encrypted Messages in Alban Berg's Music*, ed. Siglind Bruhn (New York: Garland, 1998).

6. See, for example, Theodor W. Adorno, "Richard Strauss: Zum 60. Geburtstage: 11. Juni 1924," in *Gesammelte Schriften* 18 (Frankfurt am Main: Suhrkamp), 254–62; and *Essays on Music*, ed. Richard Leppert, trans. Susan H. Gillespie (Berkeley: University of California Press, 2002), 329, 329n4, 379, 380, 424–25, 648.

7. Despite its rarity, *Ariane et Barbe-Bleu* was singled out for praise by Berg, Strauss, and Korngold. See Berg, *Letters to His Wife*, 89, 89n1.

8. Controversies at the Vienna opera abound, ranging from Wagner's appearance in the repertory in the 1870s, Mahler's tenure, Weingartner's role as his successor, and the Richard Strauss–Franz Schalk years, to contested premieres, including Ernst Krenek's *Jonny spielt auf*.

9. For Berg's remarks on criticism, see "Wiener Musikkritik" (1920), 182–90; and "Warum ist Schönbergs Musik so schwer verständlich" (1924), 205–20, in Alban Berg, *Glaube, Hoffnung und Liebe: Schriften zur Musik* (Leipzig: Reclam, 1981).

10. See Theodor W. Adorno, *Alban Berg: Master of the Smallest Link*, trans. and ed. Juliane Brand and Christopher Hailey (Cambridge: Cambridge University Press, 1991); Willi Reich, *Alban Berg*, trans. Cornelius Cardew (New York: Harcourt, Brace & World, 1965); Hans Ferdinand Redlich, *Alban Berg: The Man and His Music* (New York: Abelard-Schuman, 1957);

Mosco Carner, *Alban Berg: The Man and the Work* (London: Duckworth, 1975); and Rosemary Hilmar, *Alban Berg: Leben und Wirken in Wien* (Vienna: Böhlau, 1978).

11. See, for example, David John Headlam, *The Music of Alban Berg* (New Haven: Yale University Press, 1996).

12. See Arnold Whittall, "Berg and the Twentieth Century," in *Cambridge Companion to Berg*, 247–58.

13. Berg's letters to Helene abound with references to Kraus (see Berg, *Letters to His Wife*). See also Soma Morgenstern, *Alban Berg und seine Idole: Erinnerungen und Briefe* (Lüneburg: Klampen, 1995), 88–103; and Paul Reitter, *The Anti-Journalist: Karl Kraus and Jewish Self-Fashioning in Fin-de-Siècle Europe* (Chicago: University of Chicago Press, 2008).

14. Franz Schreker, a far less "Jewish" Viennese friend and colleague, had also been fired from the Prussian Academy of the Arts. Schreker, who had only one Jewish parent, grew up as a non-Jew.

15. Armin Berg (1883–1956) was a pianist, writer, and cabaret musician who also worked in film.

16. In contrast, Webern improbably became a Nazi enthusiast long after Berg's death.

17. See Berg, *Letters to His Wife*, 370, 398–400, 413–14, 429, 429n3, 437; Hans Moldenhauer and Rosaleen Moldenhauer, *Anton von Webern* (New York: Alfred A. Knopf, 1979), 411, 451–52; and "Arnold Schoenbergs Ablehnungsbrief an Erwin Stein," in *Lulu: Texte, Materialien, Kommentare, mit einem Essay von Dietmar Holland*, ed. Attila Czampai and Dietmar Holland (Hamburg: Rowohlt, 1985), 245–47.

18. George Perle, *The Operas of Alban Berg*, vol. 1, *Wozzeck*; vol. 2, *Lulu* (Berkeley: University of California Press, 1980, 1985); and Douglas Jarman, *The Music of Alban Berg* (Berkeley: University of California Press, 1979).

19. See Soma Morgenstern, *Alban Berg und seine Idole*; and Susanne Rode, *Alban Berg und Karl Kraus: Zur geistigen Biographie des Komponisten der "Lulu,"* (Frankfurt am Main: Peter Lang, 1988). Other notable historical work dealing with Berg and his context are Christopher Hailey, "Between Instinct and Reflection: Berg and the Viennese Dichotomy," 221–34; and Martin Esslin, "Berg's Vienna," 1–12, both in Jarman, *The Berg Companion*; Andrew Barker, "Battles of the Mind: Berg and the Cultural Politics of 'Vienna 1900,'" in *Cambridge Companion to Berg*, 24–37; Margaret Notley, "Musical Culture in Vienna at the Turn of the Twentieth Century"; and Dagmar Barnouw, "*Wiener Moderne* and the Tensions of Modernism," both in *Schoenberg, Berg, and Webern: A Companion to the Second Viennese School*, ed. Bryan R. Simms (Westport, CT: Greenwood Press, 1999), 37–71, 73–127.

20. See Rode, *Alban Berg und Karl Kraus*; Knaus and Sinkovicz, *Alban Berg*, 36, 88, 115, 199; Constantin Floros, "Introduction," in *Alban Berg and Hanna Fuchs: A Story of a Love in Letters*, trans. Ernest Bernhardt-Kabisch (Bloomington: University of Indiana Press, 2001), xii, xiv.

21. See *Briefwechsel: Arnold Schönberg–Alban Berg*, vol. 1, *1906–1917*, and vol. 2, *1918–1935*, ed. Juliane Brand, Christopher Hailey, and Andreas Meyer (Mainz: Schott, 2007).

22. On tensions between Webern and Schoenberg, see Berg, *Letters to His Wife*, 235–36; Moldenhauer and Moldenhauer, *Anton von Webern*, 70–445 passim; and *Briefwechsel: Arnold Schönberg–Alban Berg* 1:68–654 passim, and 2:1–608 passim.

23. Berg's most famous extramarital affair was with Hanna Fuchs. See Floros, *Alban Berg and Hanna Fuchs*. But there were others, including the wife of the pianist Stefan Askenase. See Morgenstern, *Alban Berg und seine Idole*, 307–8.

24. See references throughout Berg, *Letters to His Wife*.

25. In the absence of DNA evidence, the identification of Helene as Franz Joseph's daughter must remain speculative. There is a firm basis for believing it, but at a minimum the rumor was widely circulated, trusted, and sufficient to have brought Berg special attention during World War I. Readers unfamiliar with the mores of the Habsburg Imperial household may not realize that the emperor—like many other eighteenth- and nineteenth-

century monarchs—was known to have serious extramarital relationships with women, since marriage was most often a matter of politics and diplomatic strategy, popular mythology notwithstanding. The emperor treated his lovers as honorably as possible and ensured that they were conveniently situated for him. In the case of Helene's mother, Franz Joseph took care that the Nahowski family lived very near the grounds of the palace in Schönbrunn.

26. Berg refuted the family's objections, point by point, in a long letter to Helene's father. See Berg, *Letters to His Wife*, 106–11.

27. Berg's "Von der Selbsterkenntnis," hereafter designated Notebooks (or Notebook in the case of an individual volume), were compiled between 1903 and 1907 and are housed in the Austrian National Library. Notebook 12 indexes all the aphorisms (from more than two hundred authors), each with Berg's assigned number, that appear in Notebooks 1–11. I want to thank my colleague Tatjana Myoko von Prittwitz und Gaffron for agreeing to collaborate with me on a project to publish a fully transcribed, complete, and annotated edition of Berg's Notebooks with commentary. They represent not only an invaluable source of biography but a mirror of the intellectual preoccupations, habits, and aspirations of Berg's generation.

28. Berg, Notebook 10:1000.

29. Consider, for example, Schoenberg's incomplete draft of the libretto *Superstition* (1901), which sustains passion through reasoning and argument, despite its surface implication of the erotic. In *A Schoenberg Reader: Documents of a Life*, ed. Joseph Auner (New Haven: Yale University Press, 2003), 23–38. On *Erwartung*, see H. H. Stuckenschmidt, *Schönberg* (Munich: Piper Schott, 1989), 112–14.

30. For Schoenberg, Mahler took on a Janus-like aspect. His public role was an inspiration, given his status as Jew and as an innovator, but his aesthetic commitments were clearly indebted to late Romanticism, the harbingers of modernism so dear to Adorno notwithstanding. See Schönberg, "Vortrag über Gustav Mahler" (1912), in *Stile herrschen, Gedanken siegen: Ausgewählte Schriften*, ed. Anna Maria Morazzoni (Mainz: Schott, 2007), 73–90; Stuckenschmidt, *Schönberg*, 101–14; and Malcolm MacDonald, *Schoenberg* (Oxford: Oxford University Press, 2008), 48–49.

31. See Berg, *Letters to His Wife*, 90, 94, 113, 132, 147, 243; Derrick Puffett, "Berg, Mahler and the Three Orchestral Pieces Op. 6," *Cambridge Companion to Berg*, 111–44; and Jarman, *The Music of Alban Berg*, 175.

32. See Berg, "Die musikalische Impotenz der 'neuen Ästhetik' Hans Pfitzners" (1920), in *Glaube, Hoffnung und Liebe*, 191–204.

33. See Arnold Schönberg, "Brahms the Progressive" (1933; rev. 1947), in Morazzoni, *Stile herrschen, Gedanken siegen: Ausgewählte Schriften*, 215–51.

34. See Berg and Watznauer, *Der unverbesserliche Romantiker*, 81; and Nick Chadwick, "From 'Freund Hein' to Herman Hesse: Hermann Watznauer and His Friendship with Alban Berg," *Music and Letters* 79: 396–418.

35. There is no reason to belabor the obvious with respect to the life and career of Sigmund Freud, whom Berg seems to have met; see Berg, *Letters to His Wife*, 335. Berg's views of psychoanalysis were ambivalent, if not hesitant, though more tempered than those of Karl Kraus. The issues that were crucial to Freud's Viennese contemporaries in Berg's circle vis-à-vis sexuality and gender were the links to creativity and the aesthetic. What most angered Kraus was that Freud had demystified and vulgarized the aesthetic imagination in a crass, deterministic fashion. See Edward Timms, *Karl Kraus: Apocalyptic Satirist*, vol. 1, *Culture and Catastrophe in Habsburg Vienna* (New Haven: Yale University Press, 1986), 174–78.

36. In terms of music, Alma's significance can be seen in her pivotal role supporting *Wozzeck* and Berg's dedication of the Violin Concerto to the memory of her daughter. The most astute observer of Alma's importance to both Alban and Helene Berg was Ernst

Krenek. See his "Alban Bergs 'Lulu,'" in *Zur Sprache gebracht: Essays über Musik* (Berlin: Langen-Müller, 1958), 241–50; and his autobiography, *Im Atem der Zeit: Erinnerungen an die Moderne* (Hamburg: Hoffmann und Campe, 1998), 364–65.

37. Christopher Hailey has suggested that Berg's attraction to Hanna Fuchs may have been intensified because she was the sister of Franz Werfel, who was intimate with Alma for years before they finally married in 1929.

38. Vain and insecure, Werfel was derided by serious writers and critics, including Kraus. The couple lost a child, quarreled frequently, and Alma, true to form, was not entirely faithful. Alma also shared Berg's misgivings about Jews. See Peter Stephan Jungk, *Franz Werfel: A Life in Prague, Vienna, and Hollywood* (New York: Grove Weidenfeld, 1990); and Morgenstern, *Alban Berg und seine Idole*, 419–22.

39. Although he idealized Alma's relationship with Gustav, Alban was keenly aware of how troubled the marriage had been. However, his sympathies, through the thick and thin of Viennese gossip, remained staunchly with Alma. See note 36.

40. Altenberg was skeptical about Berg and his marriage to Helene. See David P. Schroeder, "Alban Berg and Peter Altenberg: Intimate Art and the Aesthetics of Life," *Journal of the American Musicological Society* 46/2 (Summer 1993): 261–94; also Rode, *Alban Berg und Karl Kraus*, 18–34.

41. See Kraus, *Die Fackel* 182 (9 June 1905).

42. See Leo Treitler's analysis in "The Lulu Character and the Character of *Lulu*," in Gable and Morgan, *Alban Berg: Historical and Analytical Perspectives*, 275.

43. Frank Wedekind, *Ausgewählte Werke* (Munich: Georg Müller, 1924), 115.

44. For that matter, Berg's version of Lulu is nearer Louise Brooks's portrayal of the character in the famous silent film *Die Büchse der Pandora* (*Pandora's Box*), directed by Georg Wilhelm Pabst (Berlin, 1929).

45. It is also instructive to contrast both Wedekind's and Berg's characterizations of Lulu to Pabst's. It is probably that Berg, a film enthusiast, saw the film, which deviates considerably from Wedekind's play.

46. See Hans Jochen Irmer, *Der Theaterdichter Frank Wedekind* (Berlin: Henschel, 1975), 145, as well as Artur Kutscher, "Frank Wedekinds Lulu-Tragödie," 132–48; Frank Wedekind, "Vorwort zur Neuausgabe der 'Büchse der Pandora' (1906)," 152–58; and Karl Kraus, 'Die Büchse der Pandora,'" 158–69, all in Czampai and Holland, *Lulu: Texte, Materialien, Kommentare*.

47. Here the roman à clef parallels strike closer to home. Berg's sister Smaragda had volatile lesbian relationships with at least two lovers (and on one occasion, a clash with May Keller), which occupied a good deal of Berg's attention and concern and may have informed his conception of lesbian relationships. Berg's simplification made his Countess Geschwitz a less politically symbolic figure and more like his sister and May. See Knaus and Sinkovicz, *Alban Berg*, 399.

48. Carl Dahlhaus, "Berg und Wedekind—Zur Dramaturgie der Lulu," in *Alban Berg Studien* 2 (1981): 19.

49. Alma had serious ambitions as a musician: she was a fine pianist, studied composition with Zemlinsky, and published songs. Whereas Mahler asked Alma to jettison her ambitions in the marriage, Berg encouraged Helene, who studied voice, to consider a singing career. Ironically, it was Helene who voluntarily subordinated her admittedly less strong commitment to a vocation as a singer to her husband's future, taking on the role of muse and assistant instead. Reich, *Alban Berg*, 20–21, 34–35.

50. Curiously, Pabst's film opens with a scene in an apartment furnished with a nine-candle Hanukkah menorah in the background, suggesting Wedekind's character of the Jewish painter, Schwartz.

51. Lombroso, an Italian Jew, argued that deviancy could be inherited as depravity or inspiration. He also developed theories on phrenology and other physical markers of

character. Though widely read and admired, Lombroso's most lasting legacy is indirect: his influence on Max Nordau's influential book *Degeneration* (1893).

52. Notebook 10:1001.
53. Wedekind, "Erdgeist," in *Ausgewählte Werke*, 69.
54. Alban Berg, *Wozzeck* (opera in three acts), libretto by Georg Büchner, ed. H. E. Apostel, trans. Eric Blackall and Vida Harford (Vienna: Universal Edition, 1955), 304ff. See Perle, *The Operas of Alban Berg*, 1:99.
55. See "Der Wozzeck-Text: Büchner aus zweiter Hand," in Peter Petersen, *Alban Berg: Wozzeck* (Munich: text + kritik, 1985), 11–72, esp. 51ff.
56. See Carl Dahlhaus, "Berg und Wedekind," in Czampoi and Holland, *Lulu: Texte, Materialien, Kommentare*, 291–300.
57. Wedekind, "Die Büchse der Pandora," in *Ausgewählte Werke*, 119–219. The Elixir de Spa also appears in a scene between Alwa and Schigolch in Wedekind's *Erdgeist* (41).
58. Benedictine, first marketed in 1863, was widely available by 1873, when production reached 150,000 bottles a year. See http://www.benedictine.fr/anglais/histoire_frame.html. The first brand-name liqueur to be widely exported from France, it became so popular that the company prosecuted more than eight hundred counterfeiters. See Robert Minton, "The Secret of Succession," *Inc.*, 1 March 1982; http://www.inc.com/magazine/19820301/9043.html.
59. Alban Berg and Frank Wedekind, *Lulu Akt 1–2*, ed. Hans Erich Apostel and Friedrich Cerha (Vienna: Universal Edition, 1985), 604. See also Czampai and Holland, *Lulu: Texte, Materialien, Kommentare*, 93.
60. Berndt W. Wessling, *Alma: Gefährtin von Gustav Mahler, Oskar Kokoschka, Walter Gropius, Franz Werfel* (Düsseldorf: Claassen, 1984), 282–83.
61. Before rehearsal number 1154, *Lulu*, Act 2, sc. 2, 649.
62. Judy Lochhead, "Lulu's Feminine Performance," 237; and Whittall, "Berg and the Twentieth Century," 247, 256, both in *Cambridge Companion to Berg*.
63. See Arnold Whittall, *Musical Composition in the Twentieth Century* (Oxford: Oxford University Press, 1999), 184–200, 247, 256.
64. On Strauss and the male-female dynamic, see Leon Botstein, "The Enigmas of Richard Strauss: A Revisionist View," in *Richard Strauss and His World*, ed. Bryan Gilliam (Princeton: Princeton University Press, 1992), 3–32; and Leon Botstein, "Strauss and Twentieth-Century Modernity: A Reassessment of the Man and His Work," in *Richard Strauss und die Moderne: Bericht über das Internationale Symposium München, 21. bis 23. Juli 1999*, ed. Bernd Edelmann, Birgit Lodes, and Reinhold Schlötterer (Berlin: Henschel, 2001), 113–37.
65. Schoenberg's and, above all, Adorno's summary dismissals of the late stage works of Strauss have some parallel in Berg's relative silence on the matter, despite a residual admiration for Hofmannstahl. This prejudice, driven by a mix of envy and resentment toward Strauss and his attitude to post–World War I modernism, has blinded subsequent scholars to parallels between Berg's characterization of Lulu and Strauss's exploration of the male-female dynamic in the series of so-called marriage operas from *Rosenkavalier* to *Die Liebe der Danae*.
66. Despite Berg's admiration of Schumann's piano music and lieder, he seems not to have known Schumann's setting of the same Goethe text in *Scenes from Faust*. The evocative presence of Goethe's *Faust* in Wedekind's formal design is evident in the prologue to *Earth Spirit*, which Berg retained, and the prologue to *Pandora's Box*, which Berg chose not to use.
67. Johann Wolfgang Goethe, *Die Faust-Dichtungen*, ed. Ernst Beutler (Zurich: Artemis, 1949), 523.
68. On Berg's debt to Kraus and Altenberg, see Rode, *Alban Berg und Karl Kraus*; Knaus and Sinkovicz, *Alban Berg*, 1151; and Floros, *Alban Berg and Hanna Fuchs*, xiv.

69. See Bram Dijkstra, *Idols of Perversity: Fantasies of Feminine Evil in Fin-de-Siècle Culture* (New York: Oxford University Press, 1986), 103, 151–52, 306.

70. See Notebook 2:234.

71. See "Von Frauenverstand," Notebook 9:964.

72. "Das Ewig-Weibliche zieht uns an; Das Ewig-Weibliche zieht uns hinan; Das Ewig-Weibliche zieht uns hinab; Das Ewig-Weibliche zieht uns aus." See Notebook 1:114–17.

73. Berg appears to have used two sources and relied, in terms of sequence, on Paul Landau's 1909 adaptation. See Perle, *The Operas of Alban Berg*, 1:26–30.

74. On references to *Tristan* in *Lulu*, see Treitler, "The Lulu Character and the Character of *Lulu*," 269, 274. Berg's Notebook 5 indicates that he read Thomas Mann's 1903 novella *Tristan* closely.

75. Ironically, the portrayal of the feminine in Strauss's operas from *Der Rosenkavalier* (for which Berg had limited affinity) to *Die Liebe der Danae* owes more to a close reading of Nietzsche than anything in Mahler's oeuvre. See Charles Youmans, *Richard Strauss's Orchestral Music and the German Intellectual Tradition: The Philosophical Roots of Musical Modernism* (Bloomington: University of Indiana Press, 2005).

76. Otto Weininger, *Sex and Character* (1906; repr. New York: Howard Fertig, 2003), 92.

77. The literature on the representation of the Jewish as the feminine is immense. On this point, Weininger's suicide and Hitler's admiration for his theories speak for themselves. See Leon Botstein, *Freud und Wittgenstein* (Vienna: Picus, forthcoming).

78. See Timms, *Karl Kraus*, 1:70–80, 250–68, 350, 365; also Timms, *Karl Kraus: Apocalypic Satirist*, vol. 2, *The Post-War Crisis and the Rise of the Swastika* (New Haven: Yale University Press, 2005), 180–207.

79. In 1911 Altenberg published three poems about Helene: "H. N.," "Bekanntschaft," and "Besuch im einsamen Park," the last of which was published in his *Märchen des Lebens*. See Peter Altenberg, *Neues Altes* (Berlin: S. Fischer, 1911), 45, 87, 205; and Peter Altenberg, *Märchen des Lebens* (Berlin: S. Fischer, 1919), 223

80. Quotes from Weininger's *Sex and Character* appear in Notebooks 4 and 7; from Nietzsche in Notebooks 1, 6, and 11 (earlier entries are from *Also sprach Zarathustra*); and from Mahler himself (on tradition) in Notebook 5.

81. Floros, *Alban Berg and Hanna Fuchs*, passim.

82. The letter appears in George Perle, "'Mein geliebtes Almschi...': Briefe von Alban und Helene Berg an Alma Mahler Werfel," *Österreichische Musikerziehung* 41 (February 1988): 9–10. See also Perle, *The Operas of Alban Berg*, 2:260–61.

83. This analysis is consistent with Berg's own claim that *Lulu* was a modern equivalent of Mozart's *Don Giovanni*. There are many parallels, particularly if one takes into account Kierkegaard's idea that the Don signifies the life force and the creative impetus of the aesthetic, particularly music. Furthermore, Countess Geschwitz's final lines, in both Wedekind's play and Berg's opera, in which she muses about devoting herself to women's rights, are reminiscent of the last scene of *Don Giovanni*, in which the survivors talk blandly of future plans that suggest the shock of the sudden loss of their purpose in life. Indeed, despite the moral ambivalence of his behavior, the Don is much like Lulu, the source of life and meaning. The complexity of the Don's character and the ambivalence with which other characters (and audiences) react to him are paralleled in Lulu, particularly if she is understood through the prism of Alma. There is, however, a signal difference between *Don Giovanni* and *Lulu*. In Berg's *Lulu* the main character, as the primary musical vehicle, is given the strongest music, which is not the case in *Don Giovanni*. But similarities suggested by the inverted framing of gender, seduction, and existential meaning can be argued, especially given nineteenth-century interpretations of Mozart's opera. See Mary Hunter, *Mozart's Operas: A Companion* (New Haven: Yale University Press, 2008) and Michel Noiray, "*Don Giovanni*," in *The Cambridge Mozart Companion*, ed. Cliff Eisen and Simon P. Keefe (Cambridge: Cambridge University Press, 2006).

84. See Rode, *Alban Berg und Karl Kraus*, 59–65.

85. For Berg's thoughts on Schoenberg's theories, see the articles collected in *Glaube, Hoffnung und Liebe*.

86. Schreker was a great teacher, like Schoenberg. His pupils included Ernst Krenek. See Krenek, *Zur Sprache gebracht*, 9, 243; Theodor W. Adorno, "Schreker," in *Quasi una Fantasia* (Frankfurt am Main: Suhrkamp, 1963), 181–91; Rainer Schwob, *Klavierauszug und Klavierskizze bei Alban Berg* (Anif/Salzburg: Mueller-Speiser, 2000), 74–87; and Nick Chadwick, "Franz Schreker's Orchestral Style and Its Influence on Alban Berg," *Music Review* 35/1 (1974): 29–46.

87. On Zemlinsky, see Antony Beaumont's biography, *Zemlinsky* (Ithaca, NY: Cornell University Press, 2000).

88. *Letters to His Wife*, 348. Berg's remark stands in contrast to the draft of a letter Berg wrote to Schreker in 1928, on the occasion of Schreker's fiftieth birthday, in which Berg recalls his enthusiasm for the opera—praising the "true musical joy" he found in it—and his prediction that it would be a success. See also Alban Berg, *Handschriftliche Briefe, Briefentwürfe und Notizen aus den Beständen der Musiksammlung der Österreichischen Nationalbibliothek*, ed. Herwig Knaus, Quellenkataloge zur Musikgeschichte, vol. 29 (Wilhelmshaven: Florian Noetzel, 2004), 220.

89. To further complicate matters, Schreker had an affair with Alma Mahler shortly after Mahler's death, a fact that Berg might have known. Helene was friends with Maria Schreker, who was on *Du* terms with Alban and Helene.

90. On the influence of *Der ferne Klang*, see the comprehensive monograph by Ulrike Kienzle, *Das Trauma hinter dem Traum: Franz Schrekers Oper "Der ferne Klang" und die Wiener Moderne* (Schliengen: Argus, 1998).

91. See Christopher Hailey, *Franz Schreker, 1878–1934: A Cultural Biography* (Cambridge: Cambridge University Press, 1993), 65–66, 81–83, 91, 93, 96, 98, 100–101, 103, 178, 186.

92. For readers interested in specific examples, see Schreker, *Der ferne Klang*: Act 1, rehearsal number 25 to 4 measures after 36; 46 to 3 measures after 51; Act 2, 84 to 97, 99–100; Act 3, sc. 1, 24–29. On Schreker's effect on Berg, see Chadwick, "Franz Schreker's Orchestral Style and Its Influence on Alban Berg."

93. The Film Music can be compared to Schreker, Act 3, one after 31 to 48. Interestingly, the montage of events and complex design of Act 2 anticipate the cinematic sensibility that would become popular in the 1920s. There is also a Kurt Weill connection in *Lulu*, particularly to his 1928 *Royal Palace*.

94. Christopher Hailey has suggested that Schreker's sensuous and expansive sound world, as well as his unabashed lyricism, might have made Berg uncomfortable about his debt to the example and techniques of *Der ferne Klang*.

95. See Berg's draft letter to Zemlinsky from 1924 in which he describes his "deep, deep enthusiasm" for the *Lyric* Symphony and its "limitless beauties"; in *Handschriftliche Briefe*, 263.

96. There are further links in the self-contained world of Viennese musical life. Schreker wrote a pantomime on the Wilde story in 1908, *Der Geburtstag der Infantin*. The attraction to Wilde stems from Kraus's and Altenberg's admiration of his wit, Strauss's success with *Salome* (although the closing bars of Zemlinsky's opera are more directly reminiscent of *Elektra*), and Schreker's *Die Gezeichneten*, a libretto Schreker wrote at Zemlinsky's request.

97. Berg was not alone in his enthusiasm for locating the biographical roman à clef in opera. Christopher Hailey has suggested that Schreker's *Die Gezeichneten* contains a similar logic, including another possible evocation of Alma Mahler.

98. On the male-female dichotomy, see Beaumont, *Zemlinsky*, 301–2; Chandak Sengoopta, *Otto Weininger: Sex, Science, and Self in Imperial Vienna* (Chicago: University of Chicago Press, 2000); Nancy Harrowitz and Barbara Hyams, eds., *Jews and Gender: Responses*

to *Otto Weininger* (Philadelphia: Temple University Press, 1995); David G. Stern and Béla Szabados, eds., *Wittgenstein Reads Weininger* (Cambridge: Cambridge University Press, 2004); and Jacques Le Rider, *Der Fall Otto Weininger* (Vienna: Löcker, 1985).

99. See Kienzle, *Das Trauma hinter dem Traum*, 212–71.

100. The locus classicus for the danger of the feminine, including an obsession with *Tristan*, can be found in the writing of Artur Schnitzler, notably the novel *Der Weg ins Freie*. On Schnitzler and music, see Marc Weiner, *Arthur Schnitzler and the Crisis of Musical Culture* (Heidelberg: C. Winter, 1986).

101. Schreker to Paul Bekker, 10 July 1918, in *Der Briefwechsel zwischen Paul Bekker und Franz Schreker*, ed. Christopher Hailey (Aachen: Rimbaud, 1994), 61.

102. See Michael Meyer, *Strindberg* (Oxford: Oxford University Press, 1987), 572. On Berg and Strindberg, see Rode, *Alban Berg und Karl Kraus*, 113–19.

103. Absent the music, the narrative of Berg's and Wedekind's *Lulu* is no longer novel in light of the shift in sexual mores, severely limiting its appeal to audiences. Despite recent political conservatism, the massive exposure and commercialization of sexual behavior since the 1960s render implausible the obsession of the male characters with Lulu. The exploitation and public exposure of sexuality have dulled its novelty and the force of taboos. Nonconventional sexual behavior is commonly tolerated, and the consummation of sexual impulses with multiple partners has become a banal, albeit recurring object of fascination. The norms and perception of marriage and fidelity have undergone comparable changes that render Wedekind's and Berg's problematic regarding the erotic, love, and self-realization a distant cultural memory. Hypocrisy regarding prostitution has been considerably tempered. Although prostitution remains criminalized in many societies, its presence creates little stir except among religious groups at the margins. These considerations only strengthen the argument that *Lulu*'s success depends entirely on the ability of the music to redeem the otherwise dated dramatic content.

104. On Berg's search for an opera text to follow *Wozzeck* and the debate between the contenders—Hauptmann's *Und Pippa tanzt!* and *Lulu*—see Morgenstern, *Alban Berg und seine Idole*, 133–35; Adorno, *Alban Berg*, 120–35; and Thomas F. Ertelt, "Pippa oder Lulu?," in *Alban Bergs "Lulu" Quellenstudien und Beiträge zur Analyse* (Vienna: Universal Edition, 1993), 25–33.

105. On the popularity of *Wozzeck*, see Konrad Vogelsang, *Dokumentation zur Oper "Wozzeck" von Alban Berg* (Regensburg: Laaber, 1977); Ernst Hilmar, *Wozzeck von Alban Berg* (Vienna: Universal Edition, 1975); Rodion Schedrin's introduction to and the text in Mikhail Evgen'evich Tarakanov, *Musikal'nyi Teatr Al'bana Berga* (Moscow: Sov. Kompozitor, 1976), 5–9, 15–70; Boris Schwarz, *Music and Musical Life in Soviet Russia, 1917–1970* (London: W. W. Norton, 1972), 45, 52, 64–65, 125–26, 286, 388; and Levon Hakobian, *Music of the Soviet Age, 1917–1987* (Bloomington: University of Indiana Press, 1983), 48.

106. After all, the Zurich premiere of the two-act version took place in the protected context of Berg's untimely death and his status among some as the victim of Nazi propaganda. For Othmar Schoeck's impressions of the premiere, see Chris Walton, *Othmar Schoeck: Life and Works* (Rochester, NY: University of Rochester Press, 2009), 225–26.

107. See Whittall, "Berg and the Twentieth Century," 253–54.

108. Austrian composer Friedrich Cerha completed the orchestration for Act 3 and other passages required for continuity.

109. There are many accounts of the history of twentieth-century music. See, for example, Alex Ross, *The Rest Is Noise* (New York: Farrar, Straus and Giroux, 2007); and Leon Botstein, "Music of a Century: The Museum Culture and the Politics of Subsidy," in *The Cambridge History of Twentieth-Century Music*, ed. Nicholas Cook and Anthony Pople (Cambridge: Cambridge University Press, 2004), 40–68.

110. See Leon Botstein, "The Viennese Connection," *Partisan Review* 49/2 (1982): 262–73.

111. See Klara Moricz, *Jewish Identities: Nationalism, Racism, and Utopianism in Twentieth-Century Music* (Berkeley: University of California Press, 2008), 230–37, 313, 315, 321, 327.
112. On Berg's admiration of Mahler, see Adorno, "The Opera Wozzeck" (1929), in Adorno, *Essays on Music*, 624–25; and Robert W. Witkin, *Adorno on Music* (London: Routledge, 1998), 108–28.
113. Berg, *Letters to His Wife*, 147–48.

Index

Index to Berg's Works

Altenberg Lieder, op. 4, 92, 103, 126, 132n17, 137, 140–42, 155, 184, 291, 297n9
Chamber Concerto, 161n27, 197, 203, 207–11, 213–14, 216, 262, 279, 292, 300
Four Pieces for Clarinet and Piano, op. 5, 141
Four Songs, op. 2, 141, 297n15, 298n17
"Warm die Lüfte," 298n17
Fünf Orchesterlieder nach Ansichtskartentexten von Peter Altenberg, see *Altenberg Lieder*
Jugendlieder:
"Am Abend," 62
"Am Strande," 73, 88n145
"Augenblicke," 71
"Ballade des äußeren Lebens," 72
"Er klagt, daß der Frühling so kortz blüht," 72, 88n138
"Erster Verlust," 71
"Es wandelt was wir schauen," 63
"Eure Weisheit," 76
"Ferne Lieder," 61
"Flötenspielerin," 74, 88n153
"Fraue, du Süße," 74, 88n153
"Fromm," 72
"Furcht," 71
"Geliebte Schöne," 61
"Grabschrift," 64, 87n129
"Grenzen der Menschheit," 58
"Hier in der öden Fremde—Ach so fern von dir," 58
"Hoffnung," 74, 88n153
"Ich liebe dich," 61
"Ich und du," 72
"Ich will die Fluren meiden," 61
"Im Morgengrauen," 64, 87n129
"Im Walde," 61
"Liebe," 63, 87n129
"Lied des Schiffermädels," 59
"Der milde Herbst von anno 45," 82
"Nachtgesang," 63
"Die Näherin," 71
"O wär' mein' Lieb' jen' Röslein rot," 74
"Regen," 74, 88n153
"Reiselied," 73
"Scheidelied," 63
"Schlummerlose Nächte," 63
"Sehnsucht," 58
"Soldatenbraut," 76
"So regnet es sich langsam ein," 76
"Spaziergang," 76
"Spielleute," 58
"Spielmann, der muß reisen," 59
"Spuk," 73
"Sternenfall," 58
"Still ist's, wo die Gräber sind meiner Liebe," 62
"Süß sind mir die Schollen," 71
"Traum," 70, 87n128
"Traurigkeit," 74, 88n153
"Unter der Linde," 56–57, 85n60
"Verlassen," 74, 88n153
"Viel Träume," 61
"Vorüber," 63
"Wandert ihr Wolken," 64, 87n129
"Was zucken die braunen Geigen," 83
"Wenn Gespenster auferstehen," 62
"Winter," 73, 88n145
"Wo der Goldregen steht," 58
See also Seven Early Songs
Lulu, 9, 11, 12, 14, 21, 24, 139, 143, 144, 147, 152, 163, 171–72, 174, 182, 185–89, 193n65, 197, 217, 224, 226, 230–34, 239, 267, 282, 283, 290–92, 298n16, 299, 303–4, 310, 312–18, 326–34, 338n44, n45, 340n83, 342n103, n106
Alwa's Hymn, 233, 238, 263n17
Film Music Interlude, 198, 199, 203–5, 207, 210, 212–16, 279, 326, 341n93
Monoritmica, 207
Prologue, 198
Sextet, 198, 207
Symphonic Pieces from, 225, 233, 236–40, 242, 247–50, *252–53,* 254, 257–59, 261–62, 263n16, 264n36, 265n47, n62, 267, 275–80, 283, 299
Lyric Suite, 29, 140, 143, 161n27, 198, 201, 202, 210, 214, 216–18, 232, 262, 269, 279, 280, 300, 340, 319, 332

Night (Nocturne), 6, 15, 23, 91–132
Piano Sonata, op. 1, 12, 141, 290, 297n15, 299
Seven Early Songs, 88n145, 155–59, 211, 290
 "Im Zimmer," 73, 88n145, 158
 "Liebesode," 76, 155, 156, 158
 "Nacht," 158
 "Die Nachtigall," 73, 88n145, 158
 "Schilflied," 158
 "Sommertage," 158
 "Traumgekrönt," 158
String Quartet, op. 3, 12, 141, 297n13, 299
Three Pieces for Orchestra, op. 6, 139, 142, 197, 220n43, 297n13, 332; Praeludium, 17, 198; Reigen, 17; March, 291, 292
Violin Concerto, 12, 26, 139, 197, 202, 207, 211, 282–83, 290, 297n8, 299, 326, 332, 337n36
"Von der Selbsterkenntnis" (On self-knowledge), 6, 189, 194n74, 306, 314, 317, 321, 337n27, 340n80
Wein, Der, 26, 29, 139, 143, 198, 203, 206, 210, 211, 216, 237, 239, 264n36, 267, 278, 290
"What Is Atonality?" 271
Wozzeck, op. 7, 11, 12, 14, 15, 19, 20, 24, 28, 29, 30n15, 34, 54, 103–4, 105n18, 139, 140, 143–44, 146–51, 153–60, 193n60, 197, 202, 212, 216–18, 220n43, 224, 226, 237, 256–59, 261, 267, 271, 276, 278–80, 283, 286, 287, 292, 298n23, 299–300, 304, 305, 314, 318, 326, 330–34, 337n36
 fragments, 17, 138, 266n72

Subject Index

Académie des Beaux-Arts (Paris), 179
Adler, Guido, 196
Adorno, Theodor W., 25, 27, 181, 182, 188, 207, 217–18, 266n85, n86, 316, 330, 337n30; as Berg's student, 8, 202, 225, 272, 302; correspondence of Berg and, 163–65, 189; correspondence of Reich and, 247, 248, 261–62; dismissal of Strauss's late stage works by, 339n65; involvement with *23,* 225, 270–72
 works: *Alban Berg: Master of the Smallest Link,* 138, 144, 150, 161n20, 184–85, 272, 193n59, 210–11; "On the *Lulu* Symphony" (as "Hektor Rottweiler"), 275–80; "On Some Relationships Between Music and Painting," 172; "Remembering the Living" (as "Hektor Rottweiler"), 286–93
Ahle, Johann Rudolf, 297n8
Allgemeine Musik-Zeitung, 16
Allgemeiner Deutscher Musikverein (ADMV), 16–19, 22, 265n56, 267
Allgemeines Krankenhaus (Vienna), 60
Altenberg, Peter, 7, 9, 36, 76, 100, 132n17, 138, 168, 170, 284, 291, 297n9, 305, 306, 317, 319, 320, 322, 325, 338n40, 341n96;
 works: "Bekanntschaft," 340n79; "Besuch im einsamen Park," 340n79; "Flötenspielerin," 74, 88n153; "H. N.," 340n79; "Hoffnung," 74, 88n153; *Neues Altes,* 193; "Traurigkeit," 74, 88n153; *Wie ich es sehe,* 33
Amsterdam Mahler Festival, 16
Anbruch (Musikblätter des Anbruch), 16, 233, 272, 290
Angerer, Margit, 228
Anschluss, 225, 271, 304
Ansermet, Ernst, 237, 264n34
Antheil, George, 142
anti-Semitism, 22, 171, 224, 232, 266n77, 303
Ars Nova, 196
Art in Austria, 245
Ashby, Arved, 193n56
Askenase, Anny, 25
Askenase, Stefan, 25
Association of Viennese Music Critics, 285
atonality, 18, 19, 29, 140, 232, 245–46, 284, 298n17, 299, 300, 302
Augsburg, 227
Austria, 23, 24, 26, 267, 295, 305, 306, 331; France and, 137; Ministry of War, 96; National Library, 96, 99; Nazism and, 229, 232, 240, 244–46, 262n6, 271, 332 (*see also* Anschluss); press laws in, 294; *See also* Vienna
Austrian Composers' Union, 285
Austrofascism, 20, 332
Avenarius, Ferdinand, 100

Index

Bach, Carl Philipp Emanuel, 87n127; Minuet in C Major, 196
Bach, David Josef, 30n15
Bach, Johann Sebastian, 87n127, 135, 150, 202, 207, 235; Cantata no. 60, 283, 297n8; *Musical Offering*, 195–97
Bahr, Hermann, 26
Balla, Giacomo, 141
Ballets Russes, 297n3
Balzac, Honoré de, 104n5, 305; *Séraphita*, 9, 92, 94, 103, 107n41, 200–201
Bandel, Ernst von, 83n30
Bareis, Marie, Edle von Barnhelm (Berg's aunt), 55, 84n53
Baroque period, 3, 195, 196, 197
Bartók, Béla, 15, 137
Basel, 260
Baudelaire, Charles, 26, 290
Bavarian Broadcasting (Bayerischer Rundfunk), 23, 226–27, 230, 231
Bax, Arnold, 137
Bayer, Friedrich, 241, 245–46, 265n54; *Germany* Symphony, 246
Beardsley, Aubrey, *167*, 190n10
Beaumont, Antony, 17, 133–61
Beethoven, Ludwig van, 28, 36, 63, 64, 134, 135, 140, 150, 235, 289, 302; works: *Fidelio*, 56, 159; Last Quartets, 62; *Missa Solemnis*, 229; Ninth Symphony, 62; Piano Sonata no. 17 (*Tempest*), 93; Piano Sonata no. 29 (*Hammerklavier*), 196; String Quartet no. 11, 134; String Quartet no. 16, 195; *Wellington's Victory*, 142
Bekker, Paul, 297n14
Belgium, 17
Benjamin, Walter, 261, 266n86
Berg, Alban: adolescence of, 4, *5*, 6, 33, *39*, 40–41, 44–47, 49, 53–57, *59*, 60–61; Alma Mahler and, 308–10, *309*, 312–17, 322, 332–33; background of, 4, 6, 23, 25, 306; birth of, 4, 26, 40; Brutism and, 141–43; character of, 6–7, 24–28; childhood of, 4, 39–41; countryside retreats of, 12–13, 23 (*see also* Berghof); death of, 26, 271, *274*, 281–82, 307, 321–22; education of, 4, 33, 40, 47, 53, 55–58, 61–65, 306; extra-marital affairs of, 8–9, 24, 156, 158, 303, 305, 319; and father's death, 6, 33, 51, 54; Heinsheimer's correspondence with, 230–31, 238–39; Hietzing apartment of, 8, *10*, 11, 23; interment of, *270*, 285; involvement in new music organizations and festivals of, 14–19; Kleiber's correspondence with, 223–25, 231, 247–50, 254–57; Kraus's influence on, 319–21; literary interests of, 4, 6, 34, 92–94; Mahler's influence on, 139, 307, 320–21, 330–34; marriage of, 9, 24, 306, 322; memorial issue of *23* to, 271–96; mentors of, 6–8, 33–34, 36; modernism of, 25–26, 28, 29, 299–308, 330–31, 333; mystical interests of, 9, 11, 199–201, 269; Nazism and, 21–23, 223–27, 240–42, 258–59, 269, 303–4; politics of, 7, 19–20; portraiture and, 163–65, *166*; Regional Government Office job of, 34, 67–71, 75, 76, 82; Reich's correspondence with, 230–36; as Schoenberg's student, 14, 28, 34, 69–71, 136–37, 290, 305–8, 322; Schreker's influence on, 14–19, 138–39, 182, 184–85, 193n59, n60, 323–27, 329–30; students of, 8, 202, 225, 269, 272, 286, 302; Watznauer's correspondence with, 60–62, 64–67, 77–82; during World War I, 13–15, *95*, 96; Zemlinsky's influence on, 14–15, 139, 151–53, 161n22, 169, 310, 323–30
Berg, Armin, 286, 304, 314, 336n15
Berg, Conrad (father), 33, 37, 45, 47–50, 55, 56, 83n20, 84n51
Berg, Erich Alban, *Der unverbesserliche Romantiker: Alban Berg 1885–1935*, 34–35, 83n20
Berg, Helene (née Nahowski; wife), 35, 256, 297n13, 307, *309*, 310, 331, 336n25, 338n49, 341n89; and Alban's affairs, 9, 24, 156, 305; and Alban's death, 26, 322; Alma Mahler and, 308, 309, 314, 316, 321–22, 332, 337n36; Altenberg and, 297n9, 320, 338n40; and anti-Semitism, 22–23; correspondence of Alban and, 99, 303, 333; "Dokumentation," 4, 12; marriage of Alban and, 306, 337n26; mystical interests of, 200; widowhood of, 302, 304
Berg, Hermann (brother), 38, *39*, 55, 64–65, 84n40, n52

· 347 ·

Berg, Johanna (née Braun; mother), 37–38, *39*, 72–76
Berg, Karl (Charly; brother), 38–40, *39*, 47, 57, 66, 73, 76, 83n19, n20, 87n129
Berg, Smaragda (sister), *39*, 41, 49, 57, 62, 65, 72–74, 76, 83n24, 288, 310, 338n47
Berghof (Carinthia), 12, *13*, 33, 47–50, 55–57, 58, 60, 64, 72, 73, 76, 86n93, n108, 225, 234, 239
Bergson, Henri, 198
Berlin, 15–16, 25, 28, 179, 229, 235, 293, 323; Austrian Music Festival in, 17; Futurist exhibition in, 141; *Salome* in, 168; Schoenberg in, 15, 101, 263n13; Symphonic Pieces from *Lulu* performed in, 240, 242, 248, 249, 252, 255–57, 275; *Wozzeck* premiere in, 287, 298n23
Berlin Musikhochschule, 18
Berlin State Opera (Staatsoper), 223–25, 230, 231, 250, 257–59, 266n76, n82
Berlioz, Hector, 134, 135, 150; Requiem, 134; *Roméo et Juliette*, 134; *Symphonie fantastique*, 134
Besant, Annie, 199–201
Biber, Heinrich Ignaz Franz von, 142
Bible, 4, 14; Gospel According to St. John, 298n18
Biedermeier culture, 3
Bienefeld, Elsa, 137
Bierbaum, Otto Julius, "Lied des Schiffermädels," 59
Bischoff, Hermann, 18
Bittner, Julius, xi, 15, 171, 241, 244, 245
Black Mountain College, 271
Blaue Reiter, Der, 291, 297n17
Blavatsky, Helene, 199, 201; *The Secret Doctrine*, 200
Blei, Franz, 100; *Der Film*, 106n31
Blühmel, Friedrich, 134
Boccioni, Umberto, 141
Boehm, Theobald, 134
Böhm, Karl, 17, 223, 255, 256, 266n76
Bokot, Margit, 234, 263n20
Boosey & Hawkes, 271
Borgfeldt & Co., 83n20, 86n96
Boston, 249, 275
Botstein, Leon, xi, 9, 169, 299–343
Boulez, Pierre, 299, 329
Brahms, Johannes, 28, 64, 235, 263n23, 301, 307; Double Concerto, 134; First Symphony, 145; Piano Quintet in F minor, 145
Brand, Juliane, 193n60
Brand, Max, *Machinist Hopkins*, 18, 30n14
Braunfels, Walter, 18; *Galathea*, 30n14
Brecht, Bertolt, 25
Breslau, 267
Bridge, Frank, 137
Brilliant, Richard, 164
British Broadcasting Corporation (BBC), 266n87
British Library, xi
Broch, Hermann, 306
Brod, Max, 100; "Kinematographentheater," 106n30
Brooks, Louise, 21, 338n44
Bruckner, Anton, 286
Brussels, 141, 237, 247, 249, 250, 254, 264n32, 275
Brutism, 141–43, 155
Brutus, 11
Büchner, Georg, 14, 290, 315, 330; *Woyzeck*, 20, 297n16, 299, 314, 318
Budapest, 178
Buddhism, 199
Buffet-Auger, Denis, 134
Burgartz, Alfred, 248
Burgtheater (Vienna), 88n143
Burns, Robert, "O my Luve's like a red, red rose," 74
Busch, Adolf, 223, 255, 260
Busch, Fritz, 229
Busch, Regina, xi, 6, 91–107, 109, 132n8
Busnois, Antoine de, 196
Busoni, Ferruccio, xi, 15, 141, 145; *Doktor Faust*, 17
Busse, Carl, "Ich und du," 72

Caballé, Montserrat, 144
Cahier, Sarah, 229
Callas, Maria, 144
Capek, Karel, *W.U.R.*, 100
Carrà, Carlo, 141
Caruso, Enrico, 236
Casella, Alfredo, 18, 234, 237, 263n21
Catholicism, 3, 227, 240
Cebotari, Maria, 243, 247, 250, 254, 255, 256, 265n47
Cerha, Friedrich, 342n108
Cézanne, Paul, 8

Index

Chadwick, Nick, xi, 12, 33–90
Chaplin, Charles, 100
Charles V, Holy Roman Emperor, 11
Charles the Bold, 11
Chorverein (Vienna), 15
Clark, Edward, 261, 266n87
Classicism, 28, 133, 196, 334
Claudius, Matthias, 290, 297n16
Claus, Lillie, 248, 252, 254, 255, 257
Cold War, xi, 331
Cologne, 22, 327
Copland, Aaron, *Appalachian Spring*, 330; *Billy the Kid*, 330
Correggio, Antonio da, *Jupiter and Io*, 9, 64
Covach, John, 201, 211
Crawford, Ruth, 28, 29
Czechoslovakia, 17

Dada, 142
Dahlhaus, Carl, 313
Dalen, Brenda, 211
Debussy, Claude, xi, 15, 137, 260, 290; *La boîte à joujoux*, 157; *Cinque poèmes de Baudelaire*, 157; *Pelléas et Mélisande*, 258
Decsey, Ernst, 75
Defauw, Désiré, 18
Delius, Frederick, *Paris*, 141
Denkler, Horst, 99
Denkmäler der Tonkunst in Österreich, 196
Dent, Edward, 234, 263n21
Depression, 330
Deutsch, Friedrich, 240, 247
Deutsche Allgemeine Zeitung, 266n77, n82
Deutsche Jugendkultur, 34, 35, 82n3
Deutsche Volkstheater (Vienna), 58, 168
DeVoto, Mark, xi, 24, 269–98
Diaghilev, Serge, 297n3
Dollfuss, Engelbert, 20, 232, 240, 243, 265n53, 267
Donaueschingen Chamber Music Festival, 16
Donizetti, Gaetano, 134
Doorn (Netherlands), 230, 263n12
Dos Santos, Silvio José, 186–87
Dostoevsky, Fyodor, 92, 105n9, 109; *A Raw Youth*, 96, 97, 116
Dresden State Opera (Staatsoper), 266n76
Dufay, Guillaume, 196
Dukas, Paul, *Ariane et Barbe-Bleue*, 137–38, 301, 335n7
Dunne, J. W., *An Experiment with Time*, 201
Dunstable, John, 196

Edison, Thomas, 199
Eger, Adolf Ritter von ("Pips"), 74, 76
Eichendorff, Joseph Freiherr von, 60; "Es wandelt was wir schauen," 63
Einstein, Albert, 198
Eisenstein, Sergei, 100
Elisabeth, Empress, 42–43
Ellmann, Richard, 170
Eltern-Vereinigung zur Förderung deutscher Jugendkultur in Wien, 34, 35, 82n3
England, 17, 249; modernism in, 303; theosophy in, 201
Ernst, Otto, *Meersymphonie*, 89
Evers, Franz, 56; "Die Nachtigall," 73, 88n145, 158
Ewers, Hans Heinz, 100
Expressionism, 165, 180, 322, 326, 331

Fackel, Die, 39, 136, 225, 263n22, 269, 207n11, 303, 321; *see also* Kraus, Karl
Falke, Gustav, "Fromm," 72
Fascism, 232
Finckh, Ludwig, "Fraue, du Süße," 74, 88n153
Fischer, J. S., "Eure Weisheit," 76
Fiteberg, Gregor, 18
Flaischlen, Cäsar, "So regnet es sich langsam ein," 76
Fleischer, Siegfried, 56
Fliess, Wilhelm, 9, 200
Florence ISCM festival, 232
Fokine, Michel, 297n3
France, 17; modernism in, 303; post-Wagnerians in, 137
Francescatti, Zino, 144
Frankfurt am Main, 17, 225, 272
Frankfurt School, 272
Franklin, Peter, 179
Franz Joseph, Emperor, 73, 86n109, 88n143, 336n25
Freud, Sigmund, 9, 23, 88n148, 190n12, 303, 320, 337n35
Fuchs, Hanna, 9, 156, 158, 201, 211, 308–9, 319, 321, 338n37
Furtwängler, Wilhelm, 21–22, 248, 249, 254, 255, 258, 260, 265n64, 266n77, n82, n83, 267
Futurism, 141–43

• 349 •

Gail, Hermann, 24
Gál, Hans, 18, 171, 244
Galimir Quartet, 262n7
Garb, Tamar, 179
Gaugin, Paul, 20, 220n32
Gautrot, Pierre-Louis, 134
Gebrauchsmusik, 16
Geibel, Emanuel, "Am Abend," 62
Gemeinschaftsmusik, 16
Geneva, 249, 275
Gerigk, Herbert, 264n36
Germany, 17, 225, 226, 228, 272;
 annual music festivals in, 16–19;
 France and, 137; in World War I,
 263n12; Nazi, *see* Nazism
Gerstl, Richard, 152, 306, 310
Giannini, Dusolina, 232, 236, 243,
 265n47
Girardi, Alexander, 100
Gluck, Christoph Willibald von, 135
Glumov's Diary (film), 100
Göcking, Leopold Friedrich Günther,
 290, 298n16
Goebbels, Josef, 22, 266n77
Goering, Hermann, 230, 242, 250, 259,
 266n70
Goethe, Catharina Elisabetha ("Frau
 Aja"), 38, 82n13
Goethe, Johann Wolfgang von, 38, 60,
 76, 90n179, 82n13, 319–21; *Dichtung
 und Wahrheit*, 60; *Elective Affinities*, 61;
 "Erster Verlust," 71; *Farbenlehre*, 138;
 Faust, 317, 318, 320, 325, 339n66;
 "Grenzen der Menschheit," 58;
 Iphigenie, 61; *The Sorrows of Young
 Werther*, 58, 61; *Tasso*, 61; *Wilhelm
 Meister*, 79
Goettel, August, 86n93
Goettel, Ossi, 86n93
Gogol, Nikolai, *Marriage*, 100
Golden Book of Music, 54
Goll, Yvan, *Methusalem, or the Eternal
 Bourgeois*, 100
Goose, Benjamin, 177–78
Gothic art and architecture, 3
Götzlick, Ernestine, 41–42, 51, 83n24
Grabbe, Christian Dietrich, "Ich liebe
 dich," 61
Graener, Paul, 243, 265n48
Grazie, Delle, "Was zucken die braunen
 Geigen," 82
Green, Douglass M., ix

Greif, Martin, "Schlummerlose Nächte,"
 63
Grieg, Edvard, *Autumn* Overture, 60
Grillparzer, Franz, 61; *Hero*, 61; *The
 Jewess of Toledo*, 61
Gropius, Manon, 25, 297n7
Gropius, Walter, 297n7, 310, 314
Gropp, Helmut, 18; *George Dandin*, 30n14
Gründerzeit, 6
Gurdjieff, G. I., 199
Gurlitt, Manfred, *Wozzeck*, 20

Haas, Joseph, 18, 22
Habsburg Empire, 11, 331, 336n25
Hailey, Christopher, 3–31, 169, 193n60,
 338n37, 341n94, n97
Halévy, Jacques, *La juive*, 134
Hallstatt (Austria), 49
Hamerling, Robert, "Augenblicke," 71
Hamline University (St. Paul,
 Minnesota), 272
Handel, George Frideric, 228
Hartleben, Otto Erich, "Liebesode," 76,
 155, 156, 158
Hauer, Josef Matthias, 29
Hauptmann, Carl, "Nacht," 158
Hauptmann, Gerhart, 6; *Und Pippa
 tanzt!* 21, 25, 189, 330
Hausegger, Siegmund von, 235
Haydn, Joseph, 28, 133, 135, 160n1;
 "London" symphonies, 133; Piano
 Sonata no. 26, 196; Symphony no. 47,
 Minuet al Rovescio, 196, 198, 207;
 Violin Sonata no. 4, 196
Hebbel, Friedrich, "Spuk," 73
Heckel, Wilhelm, 134
Heger, Robert, 256, 266n76
Heine, Heinrich, 58; "Geliebte Schöne,"
 60
Heinsheimer, Hans, 226, 230–31, 233,
 236, 238–39, 264n30, n31, 267
Herlinger, Ruzena, 262n7
Hermann the Cheruscan, monument to,
 43, 83n30
Hermetic Society, 201
Herrenried, Hermann, *see* Watznauer,
 Hermann
Hertzka, Emil, 102
Hertzka, Yella, 233, 236
Hietzing, 7, 11, 23, 73, 74, 305; Berg's
 interment in, *270*, 285, 297n15; Berg's
 study at, *10*, 20

Index

Hilmar, Rosemary, 88n152
Hindemith, Paul, 20, 258, 265n64, 289, 304; *Cardillac*, 17; *Hin und Zurück*, 197; *Mathis der Maler*, 21, 266n77, n82; String Quartet, op. 16, 17
Hindenburg, Paul, 267
Hinduism, 199
Hitler, Adolf, 224, 229, 232, 240–42, 264n41, 265n55, 266n88, 267, 340n77
Hochstetter, Armin Caspar, 245
Hofer, Franz, 262n6
Hofmann, Frau, 80, 89n156, 90n179
Hofmannsthal, Hugo von, 26, 60, 85n76, 236; "Ballade des äußeren Lebens," 72; "Reiselied," 73
Hohenberg, Arthur, 254
Hohenberg, Paul, 57, 105n9; "Hier in der öden Fremde—Ach so fern von dir," 58; "Sehnsucht," 58; "Sommertage," 158
Holenia, Hans, 244
Holle, Hugo, 16, 18
Holocaust, ix
Holy Roman Empire, 3
Holz, Arno, "Er klagt, daß der Frühling so kortz blüht," 72, 88n138
Homer, 298n21
Huber, A., 242
Hülsen, Georg Graf von, 101
Humperdinck, Engelbert, 235
Hungary, 232, 267
Hutcheon, Linda, 173, 174
Hutcheon, Michael, 173, 174

Ibsen, Henrik, 6, 61, 64; *A Doll's House*, 34, 76–82; *Ghosts*, 61; *John Gabriel Borkman*, 80; *Lady Inger of Östråt*, 61; *The Master Builder*, 61; *Peer Gynt*, 318; *Rosmersholm*, 61, 74; "Spielleute," 58; *The Wild Duck*, 74
Institute for Social Research (Frankfurt am Main), 272
International Alban Berg Society, xi
International Society for Contemporary Music (ISCM), 16, 18, *19*, 224, 232, 234, 261–62, 263n21, 264n36, 265n62, 285
Ippisch, Franz, 245
Isaak, Heinrich, 197; *Choralis Constantinus*, 196
Italy, 17, 237, 239, 259, 264n32, 267; acoustics of theaters in, 134; Fascist, 232

Jalowetz, Heinrich, 8, 22, 31n24, 101, 271, 283
Janáček, Leoš, 137, 301, 302; Sinfonietta, 237
Janik, Allan, 170
Jannequin, Clément, 142
Jarman, Douglas, xi, 11, 147, 195–221, 304, 307, 316
Jarnach, Philipp, 18
Jews, 264n27, 271, 286, 309, 313, 332, 336n14, 337n30, 338n51; Berg's attitude to, 303, 338n38; Nazism and, 22–23, 223, 226–27, 229, 255, 256, 267, 304; in Vienna, 4, 6, 23, 303, 309; Weininger's conception of, 319, 340n80
Joyce, James, 201–2; *Finnegan's Wake*, 202; *Ulysses*, 201, 202, 217, 220n28
Juana, Queen, 11, 30n5
Jungwien, 26

Kabasta, Oswald, 241, 244, 249, *252*, 254, 255, 260, 266n84, 275
Kafka, Franz, 289, 306
Kahle, Eleonora, 62, 86n96
Kaiserin Elisabeth-Heim für Witwen und Waisen (Vienna), 43, 72, 83n27
Kalmus, Alfred, 239, 242
Kammerer, Paul, 200
Kandinsky, Wassily, 220n23, 298n17
Kant, Immanuel, 198
Kasack, Hermann, 220n43
Keller, Hans, 221n54
Keller, Maria (May), 310, 338n47
Kern, Stephen, 198–99
Kerr, Alfred, 100
Kick-Schmidt, Paul, 18, 29; *Tullia*, 30n14
Kienzl, Wilhelm, 245
Kiesler, Friedrich, 100
Kitzbühel (Austria), 64
Klaren, Georg C. M., 169, 327, 328
Kleiber, Erich, 17, 20, 225, 226, 230, 231, 243, *251*, 262n2, 264n32, 266n77; Nazism and, 23, 223–24, 260, 304; Symphonic Pieces from *Lulu* premiere conducted by, 233, 236, 237, 240, 247–50, *252*, 254–59, 267; and Vienna State Opera directorship, 223, 225, 247, 248, 250, 254–55, 260, 265n60, 366n83; *Wozzeck* premiere conducted by, 224
Klein, Fritz H., 147

Kleiner Musikvereinssaal (Vienna), 88n149
Klemperer, Otto, 21, 135, 233, 236–39, 247, 264n30, 327
Klimt, Gustav, 164, 303
Knodt, K. E., "Süß sind mir die Schollen," 71
Kodály, Zoltán, 137
Kokoschka, Oskar, 165, 303, 310, 314, 315; *Windbraut*, 310
Kolisch String Quartet, 226, 229–32
Kölnische Zeitung (Cologne), 18
Kon, Boleslav, 229
Kornauth, Egon, 244
Korngold, Erich Wolfgang, 171, 270, 298n20, 301; *Die tote Stadt*, 172–78, 181, 187, 192n31
Korngold, Julius, x, 7, 15, 18, 19, 29, 136, 141–42, 230, 270, 292, 298n20, 335n7
Kosinzev, Grigori, 100
Kraus, Karl, 6, 9, 20, 39, 76, 96, 136, 186, 225, 234, 263n22, 269, 284, 290–91, 297n11, 303–6, 310, 317, 319–23, 325, 337n35, 338n38, 341n96; "Den Zwiespältigen," 116, 132n3; "Mythology," 97, 113; *see also Fackel, Die*
Krauss, Clemens, 223–25, 237, 238, 247, 248, 250, 260, 267
Krenek, x, Ernst, 22, 171, 225, 230, 237, 240, 241, 244, 261, 266n88, 269, *270*, 271, 272, 277, 285–86, 294, 304, 309, 337n36, 341n86; *Jonny spielt auf,* 272, 335n8; *Karl V,* 21, 226, 228, 231, 240–41, 267; "Ravag's Message and Austria's Message," 244–46, 265nn53–56
Krishnamurti, Jiddu, 201
Kühne, Karl, 242
Kunstschau Garden Theater (Vienna), 168
Kurzmann, Rita, 262n7

Landau, Paul, 340n73
Lasner, Mark Samuels, 190n10
Laws for the Reconstitution of the Civil Service (Germany, 1933), 22
Leadbeater, C. W., 201
Lee, Sherry, x, 17, 163–94
Leech-Wilkinson, Daniel, 196
Léhar, Franz, *Giuditta*, 226, 228–31;

Land of Smiles, 229; *The Merry Widow,* 228
Lenau, Nikolaus, "Schilflied," 158
Leningrad, 19
Leonardo da Vinci, 171
Leppert, Richard, 172
Le Rider, Jacques, 164, 170, 190n12
Lessing Hochschule (Berlin), 250
Lichtenberg, Georg Christoph, 97, 116, 132n8
Liszt, Franz, 16, 150, 235
Lombroso, Cesare, 314, 338n51
London, 141, 234, 249, 261, 271, 275–77
Loos, Adolf, 6, 284, 297n10, 303, 305, 323
Lorenz, F., "Wo der Goldregen steht," 58
Lortzing, Gustav Albert, *Der Wildschütz,* 142
Lower Austrian Regional Government Office, 34, 68, 70, 71, 75, 76, 82
Ludwig, Friedrich, 196
Lukácz, Georg, 101
Lutyens, Edwin, 201
Lutyens, Mary, 201

Mach, Ernst, *Die Analyse der Empfindungen*, 26
Machaut, Guillaume de, 196
Maeterlinck, Maurice, 9
Mahler, Alma, xi, 9, 169, 237, 297n7, 308–17, *309, 311,* 327–29, 337n36, 338n39, n49, 341n97; Helene Berg and, 308, 309, 314, 321–22, 332, 337n36; and Kleiber's pursuit of Vienna State Opera directorship, 248, 255; lovers of, 308, 310, 314, 315, 323, 338n37, 341n89; Lulu modeled on, 310, 312–17, 329, 332–33
Mahler, Anna, *274,* 296
Mahler, Gustav, x, 6, 17, 64, 135, 139, 232, 235, 259, 284, 289, 305, 310, 322, 323, 325, 327, 330–34, *334,* 335n4; Alma and, 313–16, 329, 338n39, n49; concept of feminine of, 319–21; connection of Berg's operas to sound of, 259, 276, 302, 326; contrasting compositional and aesthetic impulses of, 28; death of, 26, 281–82; on Dostoevsky, 92; in Graz for *Salome* performance, 75; instrumentation princi-

· 352 ·

ples of, 277; Jewish origins of, 229, 332, 337n30; late twentieth-century revival of interest in, 303, 332; modernism and, 301, 307–8, 331, 334; Verein für musikalische Privataufführungen performances of works of, 15; Vienna Hofoper directed by, 70, 171, 300, 335n8
works: *Kindertotenlieder,* 26, 74, 88n149; *Das klagende Lied,* 155; *Des Knaben Wunderhorn,* 74, 88n149; *Das Lied von der Erde,* 14, 315, 316, 327; Symphony no. 1, 154; Symphony no. 2, 275; Symphony no. 3, 70–71; Symphony no. 5, 74; Symphony no. 6, 142, 314, 316; Symphony no. 7, 142, 160n2, 276, 280; Symphony no. 8, 287, 317; Symphony no. 9, 210, 271, 276, 280, 291, 315, 333
Malipiero, Gian Francesco, 17, 29
Mandl, Otto, 86n93
Mann, Thomas, *Buddenbrooks,* 89n166; *Tristan,* 340n74
Männergesangverein (Vienna), 63
Marc, Franz, 298n17
Marstrand, Günter, 11, 30, 30n5
Martini, Giovanni Battista, 232
Marx, Joseph, 29, 226, 230, 231, 233, 234, 236, 240, 241, 245, 265n48, 267, 295, 298n25, 304; "Japanisches Regenlied," 240, 243
Marxism, 223, 272
Massenet, Jules, *Manon,* 228
May, Karl, 34
Medlun, Mohammed, 88n144
Mell, Max, "Der milde Herbst von anno 45," 82
Melos, 16
Mendelssohn, Felix, 134, 136, 236; *Reformation* Symphony, 54
Menuhin, Yehudi, 144
Meyerbeer, Giacomo, 234
modernism, 28, 29, 300–308, 314, 327, 330–31, 333, 337n30; post-World War I, 316, 339n65; Viennese, 170–71, 190n12, 300, 301
Modern Music, 163, 190n1
Moët & Chandon, 72
Mombert, Albert, *Der Glühende,* 298n17; "Spaziergang," 76, 291
Monthly Musical Record, 232
Morgan, Robert, 199, 202, 211–13, 218

Morgan Library (New York), 35
Morgenstern, Soma, 6, 7, 22–24, 145, 271, 284, 303–5, 308, 322, 330; *Alban Berg und seine Idole,* 271
Mörike, Eduard, 60; "Soldatenbraut," 76
Moser, Hans-Joachim, 243, 265n50
Mozart, Leopold, *Musical Sleigh-ride,* 142; *Toy* Symphony, 142
Mozart, Wolfgang Amadeus, 20, 28, 133, 135, 150, 235, 246, 283; *Don Giovanni,* 340n83; *Die Entführung aus dem Serail (The Abduction from the Seraglio),* 159; *Die Zauberflöte (The Magic Flute),* 101, 173, 282
Müller, Wilhelm, 56
Munich, 227, 242
Musical America, 299
Musik, Die, 248
Musikverein (Vienna), 87n131; Musikvereinsaal, 229
Musil, Robert, 303
Mussolini, Benito, 226, 230, 232, 234, 263n15
Mussorgsky, Modest, *Pictures from an Exhibition,* 157
Mustel, Victor, 134

Nachtlicht (Viennese cabaret), 105n16
Nancy, Jean-Luc, 165
Nazism, 34, 223–26, 237, 239–42, 264n33, 267, 269, 332, 336n16, 342n106; Austria and, 23, 229, 240, 249, 262n6, 265n53, 271; Kleiber and, 23, 223, 224, 255–56, 260; musical performance restrictions of, 21–22, 230–31, 245–46, 248, 257, 259, 264n36, 266n77, 299; racial policies of, 22–23, 223, 229, 303–4, 266n77
Netherlands, 17, 196, 198
Neue Freie Presse (Vienna), 101, 141, 255–57
Neues Wiener Journal (Vienna), 236, 240, 245, 247, 248, 255–57, 295, 298n25
Newbould, Brian, 196
New German School (Neudeutsche Schule), 16
Newtonian physics, 198
New York, 249, 275
New York Times, 225, 227–29, 257–60, 265n60
Nietzsche, Friedrich, 79, 135, 199, 202, 218, 318, 319, 321
Night of the Long Knives, 264n33, 267

• 353 •

Nilsson, Birgit, 144
Nordau, Max, 339n51
Notley, Margaret, xi, 23, 223–68
Novotna, Jarmila, 229, 230
Nuremburg, 227; National Socialist Party Day Rally in, 241–42, 267

Ober St. Veit (Austria), 75, 76
Obrecht, Johannes, 196
Odyssey, 298n21
Oistrakh, David, 144
Ojetti, Ugo, 239, 243
Ostrovsky, Alexander, *Even Wise Men Err, or The Diary of a Scoundrel*, 100
Ottner, Carmen, 174
Ottoman Empire, 3
Ouspensky, Peter, 199

Pabst, Georg Wilhelm, *Pandora's Box (Die Büchse der Pandora)*, 21, 338n44, n45, n50
Pan, 239, 243
Pappenheim, Marie, 297n1
Paris, 141, 179, 299
Penderecki, Krzysztof, 142
Pendl, Emanuel, 55, 56, 73, 84n55
Perle, George, v, x, xi, 186, 203, 210, 304, 326; *The Operas of Alban Berg: "Lulu,"* xi; *The Operas of Alban Berg: "Wozzeck,"* xi
Permanent Council for the International Cooperation of Composers, 264n36
Peyser, Herbert F., 225–29, 247, 249, 256–60
Pfitzner, Hans, 6, 14, 17, 18, 290, 297n14, 307, 310; *Palestrina*, 297n14; *Die Rose vom Liebesgarten*, 297n14
Philadelphia, U.S. premiere of *Wozzeck* in, 34
Philharmonic Chorus (Vienna), 15
Pinthus, Kurt, *Kinobuch*, 100
Plečnik, Jože (Josef), 88n142
Ploderer, Rudolf, 269–70
Poe, Edgar Allan, 100; "The Raven," 109n5
Polgar, Alfred, 100, 101
Polnauer, Josef, 69, 87n125, n127
post-Romantics, 142
Prague, 138, 156, 237, 249, 264n32, 275
Pratella, Francesco Ballila, 141
Preußische Zeitung (Berlin), 242
Priestley, J. B., 201
Princeton University, 272

Proust, Marcel, 289, 290
Prussian Academy of the Arts (Berlin), 22, 23, 31n21, 224, 227, 304, 336n14
Prussian State Theaters, 263n13
Puccini, Giacomo, 75, 301, 302; *Tosca*, 171

Ravag (Vienna), 226, 230, 241, 243, 245, 266n84
Ravel, Maurice, 15, 137, 290; *Une barque sur l'océan*, 157; *Daphnis et Chloé*, 277, 297n3; *Don Quichotte à Dulcinée*, 157; *Le tombeau de Couperin*, 157
Razumovsky, Andreas, 262n2
Reagan, Ronald, 331
Realschule (Vienna), 40, 44, 46
Rebay, Ferdinand, 323
Red Vienna, 19–20
Rédi, Rudolf, 243
Redlich, Hans Ferdinand, 203
Reger, Max, 15, 16, 145
Reich, Carol, 234, 263n20
Reich, Willi, 225, 226, 230–36, 239–40, 243, 247–50, 256–57, 261–62, 263n15, 264n25, n27, n32, 265n46, 266n87, 269–72, 286, 295–96; *Alban Berg*, 271, 275, 297n14; *Arnold Schönberg oder der konservative Revolutionär*, 272
Reichenberg (Austria), 44, 47
Reichsmusikkammer (Germany), 22
Reidinger, Friedrich, 244
Renaissance, art and architecture of, 3; music of, 196
Reznicek, Emil Nikolaus von, 18; *Satuala*, 30n14
Rilke, Rainer Maria, "Liebe," 63, 87n129; "Die Näherin," 70; "Traumgekrönt," 158
Rinaldini, Joseph, 240–41, 243–45, 265n48, 267
Rintelen, Anton, 245, 265n53
Robettin, Hanna Fuchs, see Fuchs, Hanna
Rochlitzer, Ludwig, 272
Rode, Suzanne, 304–5
Rodenbach, Georges, *Bruges-la-morte*, 173, 191n31; *Le mirage*, 173, 191n31
Romans, ancient, 83n30
Romanticism, 11, 17, 196, 300; late, 316, 332–34, 337n30
Rosegger, Peter, 97, 100, 116, 306; "Love and Marriage," 132n16
Rosenthal, Angela, 179
Rosé Quartet, 152, 229

• 354 •

Index

Rossini, Gioachino, 134
Rückert, Friedrich, "Ferne Lieder," 61; "Ich will die Fluren meiden," 61
Rufer, Josef, 230, 263n13
Russell, John, 262n2
Russia, 136; modernism in, 303; Soviet, 17, 330
Russolo, Luigi, 141–42, 161n10; *L'arte dei rumori,* 141

Salzburg Festival, 16, 240, 243
Salzgeber, Baroness Marie von, 42–44, 46, 83n25
Satie, Erik, 15
Sattler, Christian Friedrich, 134
Sax, Adolphe, 134
Schalk, Franz, 335n8
Scherchen, Hermann, 135, 239, 264n36
Scherer, Georg, "Am Strande," 73, 88n145
Schering, Arnold, *Tabellen zur Musikgeschichte,* 240, 243
Scheuchl, Marie, 86n94
Schiele, Egon, 165, 303
Schiller, Friedrich, *Wallenstein,* 61
Schillings, Max von, 235; *Mona Lisa,* 171, 174
Schirach, Baldur von, 304
Schlaf, Johannes, "Im Zimmer," 73, 88n145; "Regen," 74, 88n153; "Winter," 73, 88n145
Schmid, Erich, 235, 263n23
Schmidt, Franz, x, 171, 241, 245, 304
Schnabel, Arthur, 229
Schnitzler, Arthur, 9, 26, 303; *Der Weg ins Freie,* 342n100
Schoenberg (Schönberg), Arnold, ix, x, xi, 6, 30n5, n15, 73, 87n129, 105n15, 171, 235, 246, 261, 266n87, 269, 276, 279, 284, 292, 294, 299–310, 316, 322–23, *324,* 332; Alma Mahler and, 309; *Altenberg Lieder* criticized by, 184, 291; and Balzac's *Séraphita,* 9, 92, 94, 200; Berg nominated for membership in Prussian Academy by, 31n21; Berg's studies with, 28, 34, 69–71, 136–37, 290, 306, 308, 322; in Berlin, 15, 101, 263n13; choices of color and hue of, 141; circle around, 4, 11, 17, 18, 29, 92, 104n5, 152, 220n23, 263n23, 297n14, 324; concert celebrating sixtieth birthday of, 241, 244, 265n52; correspondence of Berg and, 13–14, 99; four-hand arrangement of works of, 288; in Graz for *Salome* performance, 75; Jewish origins of, 306; on Mahler, 281, 337n30; modernism and, 301–3, 305, 307; motivic variation techniques of, 138; music society of, *see* Verein für musikalische Privataufführungen; Nazism's impact on, 22, 224, 267, 304; portraits of Berg by, 163, *166;* regional school around, 16; response of musical public to Berg versus, 143, 299, 300; Schreker and, 326–27, 341n86; self-portraits, 165, 190n9; Strindberg and, 93; summary dismissals of Strauss's late stage works by, 339n65; twelve-tone method of, 17, 140, 197, 200, 277, 302; Viennese flat of, 73, 87n130
works: Chamber Symphony, 91, 157, 291; "Composition with Twelve Tones," 195, 201; *Erwartung,* 98–99, 105n18, 277, 291, 297n1, 307, 322; *Eyn doppelt Spiegel u. Schlüssel-Kanon für vier Stimen gesetzet auf niederlandische Art,* 197; *Die glückliche Hand,* 30n14, 99, 102, 105n19, 107n41, 288, 291–92, 297n12; *Gurrelieder,* 14, 91, 137, 141, 142, 307, 323–24, 330; *Hände,* 180; *Harmonielehre,* 15, 277, 297n2; *Jakobsleiter,* 201; *Moses und Aron,* 21, 332; Orchestral Pieces, 277; *Pelleas und Melisande,* 91, 137, 211, 307; *Pierrot lunaire,* 29, 141, 197; "Problems in Teaching Art," 69; String Quartet no. 2, 161n27; *Style and Idea,* 324; *Superstition,* 337n29; Variations, 277; *Verklärte Nacht,* 265n52
Schoenberg, Mathilde (née Zemlinsky), 152, 211, 310, 327
Schönbrunnerhaus (Vienna), 36, 37, 40, 43, 45–47
Schopenhauer, Arthur, 79
Schorske, Carl E., 164, 170, 171
Schott, B., Söhne (Mainz), 16
Schratt, Katharina, 73, 88n143
Schreiber, Fritz, 244
Schreker, Franz, x, xi, 21, 25, 29, 31n18, n21, 168, 171, 193n61, 272, 301, 310, 323–27, *324,* 330, 332, 333, 341n86; Adorno on, 185, 193n60; and Berg, 14–19, 137–39, 182, 184–85, 193n59, n60, 310, 323–27, 329–30, 333, 341n88, n89, n92, n93, n94, n97; Nazism's impact on, 22, 224, 267, 336n14; orchestration approach of,

137–39; Philharmonic Chorus of, 15; regional school clustered around, 16; Schoenberg's antagonism to, 323–24, 326–27 works: *Christophorus,* 324; *Der ferne Klang,* 14, 137, 138, 142, 184, 194n66, 323, 325–27, 329, 333, 341n88, n94, 341n93; *Der Geburtstag der Infantin,* 341n96; *Die Gezeichneten,* 137, 138, 168, 172, 178–84, 325, 341n97; *Der Schatzgräber,* 325; *Der Schmied von Gent,* 21

Schreker, Maria, 341n89
Schubert, Franz, 56,135, 298n16, 305; *Die Zauberharfe,* 196
Schulz-Dornburg, Rudolf, 69
Schumann, Robert, 11, 14, 28, 150, 280; *Scenes from Faust,* 339n66; *Träumerei,* 290
Schuppanzigh, Ignaz, 134, 140
Schuschnigg, Kurt, 20
Schwarz, Hanna, 242
Schwarzspanierhaus (Vienna), 36, 43, 63
Schwarzwaldschule (Vienna), 141
Schweizerische Musikzeitung, 235
Scott, Cyril, 15
Scott, Robert Falcon, 11
Scriabin, Alexander, 15
Second Viennese School, ix, x, 17, 28, 29, 138, 196, 201, 269
Segantini, Giovanni, *Scholle,* 62
Semler, Frida, 62, 65, 66, 86n93, 96, n108; "Traum," 70, 87n128
Semler, George, 86n96
Seven Weeks' War, 83n31
Severini, Gino, 141
Shakespeare, William, 234
Shostakovich, Dmitri, 332; *Lady Macbeth of Mitsensk,* 330
Siegl, Otto, 244
Siena ISCM fesitval, 232
Sinnet, A. P., "Esoteric Buddhism," 201
Sitte, Camillo, 8
Skocic, Adalbert, 245
Smetana, Bedřich, *Dalibor,* 60
Social Democratic Party, Austrian, 30n15, 224, 267
Society of Authors, Composers, and Music Publishers, 285
Soviet Union, 17, 330
Stalinism, 330
Straus, Oscar, 314
Stefan, Paul, 100, 285; *Das Grab in Wien,* 92, 104n5

Stein, Charlotte von, 80, 90n179
Stein, Erwin, 233, 236–37, 248, 264n33, 271, 283
Steiner, Rudolf, 199, 200
Steuermann, Eduard, 262
Stiedry, Fritz, 233, 238, 239
Stieler, Karl, "Im Morgengrauen," 64, 87n129
Stoessl, Otto, 100
Stollberg, Arne, 191n31, 192n33
Stölzel, Heinrich, 134
Strauss, Emil, *Freund Hein,* 61
Strauss, Johann, 235; *Wein, Weib und Gesang,* 161
Strauss, Richard, 14, 15, 17, 18, 30n14, 137, 232, 234–36, 240, 243, 264n27, n36, 267, 300, 316, 323, 327, 335n7, n8; works: *Don Quixote,* 142; *Elektra,* 341n96; *Enoch Arden,* 234; *Feuersnot,* 75; *Die Frau ohne Schatten,* 151, 159; *Ein Heldenleben,* 236, 264n26; *Die Liebe der Danae,* 339n65, 340n75; *Der Rosenkavalier,* 234, 235, 301, 339n65, 340n75; *Salome,* 75, 134, 139, 168, 236, 341n96; *Sinfonia domestica,* 134; *Till Eulenspiegels lustige Streiche,* 142
Stravinsky, Igor, 15, 160n1, 237; *Symphony of Psalms,* 270
Strindberg, August, 6, 9, 20, 93, 104n5, 109, 116, 119, 287, 305, 317, 322, 329; *At a Higher Court,* 93; *The Burned House,* 103, 119–22; Chamber Plays, 92, 103; *Dance of Death,* 93; *A Dream Play,* 92; *Easter,* 93; *The Ghost Sonata,* 103, 118, 122–23; *Jacob Wrestles,* 92–93, 201; *Midsummer,* 93; *New Blue Book,* 102
Stuckenschmidt, Hans Heinz, 230, 263n13, 265n60
Surrealism, 143
Swedenborg, Emanuel, 104n5, 200–201, 218; *Heaven and Hell,* 201
Switzerland, 17, 271
Swoboda, Hermann, 200
Szigeti, Joseph, 144
Szymanowski, Karol, 15, 19, 137; *King Roger,* 18, 19

Talich, Václav, 237, 264n32
Tauber, Richard, 229
Tebaldi, Renata, 144
Tennyson, Alfred, Lord, "Enoch Arden," 234

Teutoburger Wald, Battle of, 83n30
Thatcher, Margaret, 331
theosophy, 199–201, 217, 218, 220n23
Thomas, Ambrose, *Hamlet*, 134
Thomas, Ludwig, 100
Thompson, Oscar, 299
Thuille, Ludwig, 16
Tiessen, Heinz, 18; *Salambo*, 30n14
Tietjen, Heinz, 230, 263n13
Toch, Ernst, 18
Todd, R. Larry, 196
Tonkünstlerverein (Vienna), 15
Toscanini, Arturo, 243, 260, 265n50
Toulmin, Stephen, 170
Trahütten (Styria), 12, 14
Trauberg, Leonid S., 100
"Turkish" percussion, 134
Twain, Mark, 135
twelve-tone technique, 17, 140, 143, 185, 197, 224, 278, 293, 302
23: Eine österreichische Musikzeitschrift, 225, 226, 233, 236, 240, 244–46, 266n88; Berg Memorial Issue, 269–98

United States, 3, 40, 142, 200, 201, 330; emigration of friends of Berg to, 271, 272; Hermann Berg in, 38, 55, 82n11; Symphonic Pieces from *Lulu* in, 236, 247, 249; visits to Berg by musicians and composers from, 28
Universal Edition (Vienna), 15, 16, 20, 21, 137, 225, 233, 239, 242, 264n31, 271

van Gogh, Vincent, 20, 220n43
Varèse, Edgard, 142
Vassar College, 272
Vaughan-Williams, Ralph, 137
Venice, 325; Festival Internazionale di Musica, 233, 237, 239, 242, 248, 264n36, 266n88, 267; ISCM festival, 232
Verdi, Giuseppe, 134, 235, 260; *Don Carlo*, 159; *Otello*, 228; *Simon Boccanegra*, 228
Verein für Kunst und Literatur (Vienna), 15
Verein für musikalische Privataufführungen (Prague), 161n22
Verein für musikalische Privataufführungen (Vienna), 15–16, 87n125, 152, 161n22, n27, 271
Vick, Graham, 193n65

Vico, Giovanni Battista, 202; *Scienzia nuova*, 199
Vienna, 3, 15, 17, 28, 52, 75–76, 168, 293, 294, 305–9, 315, 325, 330, 338n39; Berg's youth in, 40–41, 44–47, 53–55, 58, 61; concerts in, 15, 54, 152, 226, 229, 232, 241, 270, 323–24; critics in, 136; during World War II, 304; French influence on composers in, 137; Futurist exhibition in, 141; ideals of sound and style in, 135; inner city (*Innenstadt*) of, 4, 6–7, 8, 11, 25, 36, 47; Jews in, 4, 6, 23, 303, 309; Kraus's lecture on Wedekind's Lulu plays in, 186; modernism in, 170–71, 190n12, 300, 301; music publishers in, 16; old houses in, 36–37; perceptions of women in, 174, 192n35; political climate in, 223–67, 331; portrait photography in, 178; pre-World War I, social and psychological concerns of, 330; Socialist regime in, 19–20, 30n15, 224; suburban districts (*Vororte*) of, 7–9, 11 (*see also* Hietzing); theosophical interests in, 201; turbulent transition to modernity of, 164; unknown manuscripts found in Berg's apartment in, 91; *Vorstadt* of, 4, 7
Vienna, University of, 196
Vienna Court Opera (Hofoper), 70–71, 171, 335n8
Vienna Konzerthaus, 229
Vienna Landesirrenanstalt, 60
Vienna Philharmonic, 87n131, 228, 275
Vienna State Academy, 229
Vienna State Opera (Staatsoper), 223–25, 228–30, 237, 241, 247, 248, 254, 259–60
Vienna Volksoper, 137
Viennese School, 245, 246; *see also* Second Viennese School
Viertel, Berthold, 100
Vivaldi, Antonio, 135
Vogelweide, Walter von der, 57, 242
Völkische Beobachter, Der, 229, 269

Wagner, Otto, 88n142, 303
Wagner, Richard, 14, 16–18, 20, 38, 134–35, 137, 142, 234, 235, 243, 300, 301, 323, 326, 327, 332; works: *Götterdämmerung*, 288; *Lohengrin*, 259; *Die Meistersinger*, 38; *Parsifal*, 151; *Das Rheingold*, 101;

Rienzi, 228; *Der Ring des Nibelungen,* 38, 228; *Tristan und Isolde,* 38, 260, 291, 319, 322, 325, 342n100
Wagner, Robert, 244
Waldhaus (Auen), 27
Wallman, Margaret, *Last Judgment,* 228
Walser, Robert, 100, 101
Walter, Bruno, 223, 255, 260
Wangel, Hilde, 65
"Warsaw Autumn" composers, 142
Watznauer, Helene, 44
Watznauer, Hermann, 8, 12, 33–35, *59*, 84n40, 86n96, 88n148, n152, 89n156, n160; *Alban Berg,* 36–82; "Appreciation and Understanding of Art," 57; pencil portrait of Berg, *41*; *Sein Selbstmord,* 58; *Shatter: Fahrtenerlebnisse,* 34, 82n4; *Wolf und Walters Wanderfahrten,* 34, 82n4
Webern, Anton, x, xi, 9, 15, 23, 28, 99, 101, 103, 138, 143, 163, 196–98, 200, 224, 226–27, 270, 285, 287, 294, 300, 305, 307, 327, 333, 336n16; *Five Canons on Latin Texts,* 197; *Five Sacred Songs,* 197; Symphony, 197
Wedekind, Frank, 100, 143, 186, 189, 194n65, 257, 278, 312–18, 320–21, 328, 329, 342n103; *Earth Spirit (Erdgeist),* 21, 257, 291, 298n16, 310, 312, 318, 326, 330, 332, 333, 339n66; *Lautenlieder,* 297n5; *Marquis of Keith,* 297n5; *Pandora's Box (Die Büchse der Pandora),* 21, 257, 266n80, 291, 298n16, 310, 312–13, 318, 326, 330, 332, 333, 338n44, n45, n50, 339n66
Wegener, Paul, 100
Weidman, Josef, 72–73, 88n140, n143
Weidman, Julie, 72–74
Weigl, Karl, 15, 29
Weill, Kurt, xi, 20, 25; *Bürgschaft,* 21; *Royal Palace,* 341n93; *Der Zar lässt sich photographieren,* 171
Weingartner, Felix, 259–60, 335n8
Weininger, Otto, 9, 20, 63, 78, 79, 174, 180, 319–23, 325, 328, 329, 340n77; *Geschlecht und Charakter (Sex and Character),* 86n99, 169, 192n35, 319, 340n80
Weissmann, Adolf, 16
Welleba, Leopold, 245, 246
Wellesz, Egon, x, 171, *270,* 285
Werfel, Franz, 201, 308–10, *309,* 315,
322, 338n37, n37; *Spiegelmensch,* 170
Westdeutscher Beobachter (Cologne/Aachen), 23
Wetchy, Othmar, 245
Wieländer, Egon, 57–58
Wienbibliothek im Rathaus (Vienna), 34
Wiener Zeitung (Vienna), 232, 234, 248, 255–57, 262n7
Wiesbaden Music Festival, 246
Wiesengrund-Adorno, Theodor, *see* Adorno, Theodor W.
Wiesenthal, Elsa, 168
Wiesenthal, Grete, 168
Wilde, Oscar, 7, 76, 165, *167,* 168–70, 181, 190n10, 289, 318; "The Birthday of the Infanta," 168, 178, 327, 328, 341n96; *The Picture of Dorian Gray,* 168–70, 178, 189; *Salome,* 168, 190
Wilhelm, Kaiser, 230, 263n12
Wilhelm, Karl, "Sternenfall," 58
Winter, Hugo, 271, 285
Wisbacher, Franz, "Vorüber," 63
Wittgenstein, Ludwig, 303
Wolf, Hugo, 60–61, 85n80, 235, 286
Wolf, Johannes, 196
Wolter, Charlotte, 73, 88n143
Woodall, Joanna, 164, 194n65
World War I, 13–15, 100, 263n12, 307, 336n25
World War II, 271, 272, 302, 304
Wymetal, Wilhelm, 23

Yeats, W. B., 201

Zeichen und Malschule des Vereins der Künstlerinnen (Berlin), 179
Zemlinsky, Alexander, x, xi, 75, 137, 168–69, 171, 301, *324,* 338n49; and Berg, 14–15, 29, 138, 139, 151–52, 169, 310, 322, 323–30, 332, 333, 341n95; *A Florentine Tragedy,* 139; *Lyric* Symphony, 327, 341n95; String Quartet no. 2, 151–53, 161n22; *Der Zwerg (The Dwarf),* 139, 169, 171–72, 181, 327–29
Zurich, 342n106
Zweig, Arnold, 100

Notes on the Contributors

Antony Beaumont is the author of *Busoni the Composer* (1985) and *Zemlinsky* (2000) and has edited the diaries of Alma Mahler and a volume of Otto Klemperer's letters. He has completed the scores of Busoni's *Doktor Faust* and Zemlinsky's *Der König Kandaules* and orchestrated part 2 of Stefan Wolpe's ballet *The Man from Midian*. Parallel to his work on new editions of Zemlinsky, including the Cello Sonata, the Lyric Symphony, *The Dwarf*, and *A Florentine Tragedy*, he has recently turned his attention to the music of Kurt Weill and Manfred Gurlitt. As a conductor he has recorded the orchestral works of Zemlinsky with the Czech Philharmonic, and the symphonies of Weill with the Deutsche Kammerphilharmonie Bremen (Chandos Records). Other recorded repertoire, ranging from early Baroque to twentieth-century avant-garde, has been issued on Capriccio, Koch International, and Phoenix Edition.

Leon Botstein is president and Leon Levy Professor in the Arts of Bard College. He is the author of *Judentum und Modernität* (1991) and *Jefferson's Children: Education and the Promise of American Culture* (1997). He is the editor of *The Compleat Brahms* (1999) and *The Musical Quarterly*, as well as the coeditor, with Werner Hanak, of *Vienna: Jews and the City of Music, 1870–1938* (2004). The music director of the American and the Jerusalem symphony orchestras, he has recorded works by, among others, Szymanowski, Hartmann, Bruch, Dukas, Foulds, Toch, Dohnányi, Bruckner, Chausson, Richard Strauss, Mendelssohn, Popov, Shostakovich, and Liszt for Telarc, CRI, Koch, Arabesque, and New World Records. For his contributions to music he has received the Austrian Cross of Honor for Science and Art and the Award for Distinguished Service to the Arts from the American Academy of Arts and Letters.

Regina Busch has been working with the Alban Berg Gesamtausgabe in Vienna since 1986. For the Berlin project *Briefwechsel der Wiener Schule* (Correspondence of the Vienna School) she is preparing editions of the correspondence between Schoenberg and Webern, as well as between Rudolf Kolisch and Schoenberg, Webern, and Berg. Her research and publications have focused on the Vienna School (in particular Webern and his circle), its influence and compositional reception, as well as questions of performance, interpretation, and editorial practice. Additional research activity has been devoted to issues of emigration and historical and theoretical topics relating to contemporary music.

Nick Chadwick was a music specialist in the British Library, London, for nearly thirty years until his retirement in 2005. His pioneering study of Berg's early songs appeared in *Music & Letters* in 1971. Other publications include articles on Berg and Schreker (*Music Review*, 1974), Berg and the BBC (*British Library Journal*, 1985), and the correspondence between Mátyás Seiber and Theodor W. Adorno on the subject of jazz (*British Library Journal*, 1995). He has reviewed extensively, mainly for *Music & Letters*, which in 1998 published his study of Hermann Watznauer's friendship with Berg. His most recent article is an overview of the British Library's holdings of the correspondence of the music collector and bibliographer Paul Hirsch (*Brio*, Spring/Summer 2008).

Mark DeVoto, trained at Harvard and Princeton, is a composer and writer, and professor emeritus of music at Tufts University. He edited the revised fourth (1978) and fifth (1987) editions of *Harmony* by his teacher Walter Piston. He has written extensively on the music of Berg and edited the *Altenberg Lieder*, op. 4, for the complete critical edition of Alban Berg's works (1997). He is also the author of *Debussy and the Veil of Tonality: Essays on His Music* (2004).

Christopher Hailey is the director of the Franz Schreker Foundation. He has published a biography of Schreker (1993), and edited the correspondence between Paul Bekker and Schreker, as well as several scores by Schreker and Alban Berg. He is a co-editor of the correspondence between Alban Berg and Arnold Schoenberg (English, 1987; German, 2007) and a cotranslator of Theodor W. Adorno's biography of Berg (1991). From 1999–2002 he was the first visiting professor at the Wissenschaftszentrum Arnold Schönberg (Vienna) and during 2006–2007 was a member of the Institute for Advanced Study in Princeton. He has published widely on musical life in Vienna, Berlin, and émigré communities in the United States.

Douglas Jarman is emeritus professor at the Royal Northern College of Music, Manchester, and Visiting Distinguished Scholar in the Faculty of Humanities at the University of Manchester. He has written *The Music of Alban Berg* (1979), monographs on Berg's *Wozzeck* (1989) and *Lulu* (1991), as well as some thirty articles on Berg's music. In addition he has published a book on Kurt Weill (1982) and edited *The Berg Companion* (1989), as well as volumes on Henze (1999), Expressionism (1993), and *The Twentieth Century String Quartet* (2002). He has edited Berg's Violin Concerto (1996) and Chamber Concerto (2004, awarded the Deutsche Musikpreis) for the complete critical edition of Alban Berg's works.

Notes on the Contributors

Sherry D. Lee is assistant professor of music history and culture at the University of Toronto. Her research on music and culture in the nineteenth and twentieth centuries is informed by literary and critical theory, gender studies, philosophy, and aesthetics. Her essays on Wagner, Schreker, Zemlinsky, and Adorno appear in the *Journal of the American Musicological Society*, *Cambridge Opera Journal*, *Music & Letters*, and the *University of Toronto Quarterly*, and she is currently working on a book on Adorno and opera.

Margaret Notley is the author of *Lateness and Brahms: Music and Culture in the Twilight of Viennese Liberalism* (AMS Studies in Music, 2007). Her work has appeared in *Journal of the American Musicological Society*, *19th-Century Music*, *Journal of Musicology*, and a number of anthologies. For an article on late nineteenth-century adagios she received the American Musicological Society's Alfred Einstein Award in 2000. In December 2006 she became the first professor to receive the Faculty Award for Excellence in Doctoral Mentoring given by the University of North Texas Graduate Student Council.

OTHER PRINCETON UNIVERSITY PRESS VOLUMES PUBLISHED
IN CONJUNCTION WITH THE BARD MUSIC FESTIVAL

Brahms and His World
edited by Walter Frisch (1990)

Mendelssohn and His World
edited by R. Larry Todd (1991)

Richard Strauss and His World
edited by Bryan Gilliam (1992)

Dvořák and His World
edited by Michael Beckerman (1993)

Schumann and His World
edited by R. Larry Todd (1994)

Bartók and His World
edited by Peter Laki (1995)

Charles Ives and His World
edited by J. Peter Burkholder (1996)

Haydn and His World
edited by Elaine R. Sisman (1997)

Tchaikovsky and His World
edited by Leslie Kearney (1998)

Schoenberg and His World
edited by Walter Frisch (1999)

Beethoven and His World
edited by Scott Burnham and Michael P. Steinberg (2000)

Debussy and His World
edited by Jane F. Fulcher (2001)

Mahler and His World
edited by Karen Painter (2002)

Janáček and His World
edited by Michael Beckerman (2003)

Shostakovich and His World
edited by Laurel E. Fay (2004)

Aaron Copland and His World
edited by Carol J. Oja and Judith Tick (2005)

Franz Liszt and His World
edited by Christopher H. Gibbs and Dana Gooley (2006)

Edward Elgar and His World
edited by Byron Adams (2007)

Sergey Prokofiev and His World
edited by Simon Morrison (2008)

Brahms and His World
Revised Edition
edited by Walter Frisch and Kevin C. Karnes (2009)

Wagner and His World
edited by Thomas S. Grey (2009)

GPSR Authorized Representative: Easy Access System Europe - Mustamäe tee 50, 10621 Tallinn, Estonia, gpsr.requests@easproject.com

www.ingramcontent.com/pod-product-compliance
Lightning Source LLC
Chambersburg PA
CBHW050526300426
44113CB00012B/1978